# Tracing Your Dakota Roots

## A GUIDE TO GENEALOGICAL RESEARCH IN THE DAKOTAS

•

REVISED, UPDATED, EXPANDED
VERSION—EDITION No. 2

*by Jo Ann B. Winistorfer
and Cathy A. Langemo*

**Dakota Roots**
**Bismarck, North Dakota**

# Tracing Your Dakota Roots

Published by Dakota Roots, 625 44th Avenue N.W., Hazen, ND 58545.  This second edition is an expansion and update of a work entitled "Tracing Your Dakota Roots: A Guide to Genealogical Research in the Dakotas," by Jo Ann B. Winistorfer and Cathy A. Langemo. The first version was published in 1999, followed in 2001 by a reprint.

Cover design and technical assistance provided by David Luyben
Background photo of tree in North Dakota Badlands taken by David Luyben, © 2006

Cover photo provided by Jo Ann B. Winistorfer. Pictured are Faunce and Anna Slaatenhus Luyben with their two children, Virgil (father of Jo Ann Winistorfer and David Luyben) and Bernice Luyben Person. The photo was taken circa 1916.

**Library of Congress Cataloging-in-Publication Data**

Jo Ann B. Winistorfer and Cathy A. Langemo
Dakota Roots

Tracing Your Dakota Roots:
A Guide to Genealogical Research in the Dakotas
   - 2nd ed.
      p. cm.
Includes bibliographical references and index.

ISBN 0-9673808-1-2
Library of Congress Catalog Card No.  99-93349

1. genealogy  2. research  3. history  4. reference  5. self-help  6. computers
7. family and relationships

I. Winistorfer, Jo Ann B.    II. Langemo, Cathy A.    III. Title.

Edited by Jo Ann B. Winistorfer and Cathy A. Langemo

# TABLE OF CONTENTS

## A tree without a root

• To forget one's ancestors is to be a brook without a source, a tree without a root. •

—Old Chinese saying

# GENEALOGY:
## Your personal Voyage of Discovery

For the past two years, we Dakotans have focused on the Voyage of Discovery undertaken nearly 200 years ago by the Lewis and Clark Expedition. Now that the bicentennial honoring this historic event is winding down, it's your turn to take your own personal Voyage of Discovery.

Let this book be your roadmap as you travel the trail back through time to find your ancestors. In doing so, you'll discover yourself! This book was created to help you do just that—using the vast resources available to you right here in the Dakotas and elsewhere.

With all the new developments in technology, genetics and global networking , we decided it was time to furnish you, our fellow time-traveler, with an updated version of our first "Tracing Your Dakota Roots," published in 1999 and reprinted in 2001. In this, our official second edition, we've included lots of good things from the first book, adding material on Internet research, updating Websites and including information on DNA, or "genetic genealogy." You'll also find information on "geneablogy," or "blogging" your genealogy online.

We have attempted to provide you with the most recent information available. However, we know that some address changes (and especially Website information) are bound to occur. Although we have contacted top genealogy authorities (including those in our local communities) and cited reputable resources, because of our frailties as human beings, some errors will be inevitable. We apologize for them in advance and hope you will give us feedback on any items that need to be corrected, should we decide to do a future printing.

This dawning decade of a new millennium is the ideal time for looking to the future. But it's also an ideal time for looking back—reflecting on the past, thinking of our own personal history as well as the history of the Dakotas, the place that nurtured our ancestors, that sustained our roots. It's a time of awakening—as well as realizing how quickly the past is lost if we don't take the time to preserve it.

Happy trails—as you start on your own personal Voyage of Discovery!

## *Dedication*

We dedicate this book to all of our ancestors and descendants, past, present, and future.
—*Jo Ann and Cathy*

# Meet the authors

**J**o Ann B. Winistorfer has been seriously tracing her roots since 1984. Three-fourths of her roots stretch into Norway; the other fourth into the Netherlands. Retired associate editor of the North Dakota REC/RTC Magazine (now North Dakota Living), Jo Ann continues to do free-lance writing for the magazine, as well as editing projects through Astri My Astri Publishing, Waukon, Iowa.

It was while she worked at the magazine that the idea for "Tracing Your Roots" was born. In 1988-89, Jo Ann produced a 13-month series of columns on "Tracing Your Roots" in the magazine as part of the North Dakota centennial. After many requests for back issues, the magazine compiled the columns into a book, "Tracing Your Roots in North Dakota." That book sparked the idea for the book you are now holding in your hand—an update and expanded version of our first "Tracing Your Dakota Roots," published in 1999 and reprinted in 2001.

Jo Ann is an active member of the North Dakota Professional Communicators and the National Federation of Press Women and is a Certified Rural Electric Communicator. She belongs to the Bismarck-Mandan Historical and Genealogical Society and a number of Norwegian genealogy groups and bygdelags. She served as a volunteer librarian at the LDS Family History Center in Bismarck for several years and has been a presenter at numerous genealogy workshops. She also serves on the board of the Scandinavian Heritage Association in Minot and edits that group's quarterly newsletter.

Jo Ann and her husband, Nick, own a farm near Pick City, where they raise Black Angus cattle. They have three grown children, two daughters-in-law, seven grandchildren, and three great-grandchildren.

● ● ● ● ● ● ● ● ● ● ● ● ● ● ● ● ● ● ● ● ● ● ● ● ● ● ●

**C**athy A. Langemo is the owner of WritePlus Inc., a writing, editing, and research firm headquartered in Bismarck, ND. Her degrees in business administration, English, and journalism lend themselves well to the services she offers through WritePlus, including promotional materials development, resume and grant writing, magazine and newspaper articles development, book publishing, and event planning and organizing.

However, Cathy's heart is in the historical and genealogical research services she offers through WritePlus and performs for people across the country. She has also worked on her own Swedish, Scottish, and French genealogy off and on for many years. Cathy spent three summers working as a part-time reference assistant at the State Archives and Historical Research Library in the North Dakota Heritage Center, Bismarck, where she helped patrons with their research.

Cathy is a member of a number of history- and genealogy-related organizations, including the Missouri Valley Historical Society, the Bismarck/Mandan Historical and Genealogical Society, the Society for the Preservation of the Former Governors' Mansion, the Three Crowns Swedish-American Association, the Bismarck Historical Society, the Mandan Historical Society, the State Historical Society of North Dakota Foundation, The National Historical Society, the National Trust for Historic Preservation, the North Dakota Professional Communicators, and the National Federation of Press Women.

Besides her work, Cathy's life centers around her husband, Rick Knudson, pool league, music, reading, and spending time with her grandchildren. Between them, she and Rick have four grown children, one daughter-in-law, and 11 grandchildren. ●

# We sincerely thank...

Our wonderful, loving, and patient husbands, Nicholas (Nick) F. Winistorfer and Richard (Rick) C. Knudson Jr., who many times may have felt ignored, perhaps even abandoned, during the process of preparing this, our second edition of "Tracing Your Dakota Roots." We love you, and we're back—again!

David Luyben, Bismarck, ND, for his assistance in designing the cover and other graphics (including snapping the photo of the Badlands tree with its "Dakota roots" especially for our cover) and for his help on such things as scanning.

North Dakota State Archives and Historical Research Library staff members Jim Davis, Greg Wysk and Shane Molander for their review of Chapter 3.

Michael M. Miller, bibliographer, and Mary Lynn Axtman, proofreader/editor, Germans from Russia Heritage Collection, NDSU Libraries, North Dakota State University, Fargo, for their work on the Germans from Russia section of Chapter 4.

Blaine Hedberg, Naeseth chair at the Vesterheim Genealogy Center and Naeseth Library, Madison, Wis., for his review and suggestions for the material on Norwegian research and resources, found in Chapter 4.

Deb Nelson Gourley, owner of Astri My Astri Publishing, Waukon, Iowa, for her encouragement and her technical assistance on computer matters.

Family members, friends, and fellow genealogists who encouraged and supported us in this project, including several who passed away between the time our first edition was published and this second edition appears in print: Bernice Temanson, Bismarck, a former schoolteacher who, at age 86, helped us with proofreading; Shirley Jacobson, wife and genealogy research partner of Orlin Jacobson, Bismarck, who furnished research tips; and genealogist Ethel Eckroth Mandan, whose helpful suggestions appear in this book.

Last but definitely not least, those of you who are using this book. Learn, research, discover, enjoy! •

—*Jo Ann and Cathy*

## The story behind the locket

- Examine our cover closely and you'll see that the antique locket portrayed there is the same locket worn by the little girl in the picture.

Well over a century old, the locket and chain belonged to the great-grandmother of co-author Jo Ann Luyben Winistorfer. The original owner, Hilda Hanson Slaatenhus, a Norwegian immigrant to the U.S., died in 1892 following childbirth. The necklace then passed to her daughter, Anna Slaatenhus Luyben (the mother in the photo). Anna's daughter, Bernice Luyben Person, wears the necklace in the photo.

While all in the cover photo have died, the locket lives on as a treasured four-generation keepsake—a fitting memento for a book with a genealogy theme. •

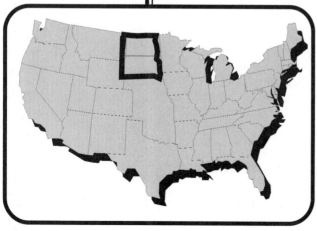

# Discovering Dakota

**H**ere in the Dakotas, Captains Meriwether Lewis and William Clark are highly revered. Their epic Voyage of Discovery, which took place two centuries ago, helped lead to the settlement of the Dakotas—land of your ancestors.

Aided by American Indians they met along the way, the party ventured into the wilderness, tracing the Missouri River to its elusive headwaters—proceeding on to discover the great golden ocean.

In a way, that's what you'll be doing, too—as you stand at the threshold of your own personal Voyage of Discovery, in search of your Dakota roots.

Before you begin your journey, take some time to read this abbreviated history of these sister states that once were joined as one territory.

Measuring the actions of your ancestors with the yardstick of history will help you better trace your family's trails and understand the ebbs and flows of their lives.

As you undertake your voyage, be sure to map your trail—and record your findings for future generations of your family.

*Captains Meriwether Lewis (left) and William Clark, leaders of the Voyage of Discovery, 1804-06.*

## Early-day explorers

**O**n 14 May 1804, captains Meriwether Lewis and William Clark and their party of 44 set out from their camp near St. Louis, Missouri, in a 55-foot keelboat and two smaller boats laden with supplies. Their mission: to explore the regions included in the Louisiana Territory, which the United States had purchased from France the year before.

Traversing the Missouri River upstream, the explorers reached present-day South Dakota on 22 Aug. 1804.

Near the mouth of the Bad River, they encountered their first Dakota residents: a band of Teton Lakotas, members of a mighty tribe whose name the future territory, and later the two states, would bear. This encounter was not a friendly one.

The corps spent the winter of 1804-05 at Fort Mandan, a log fort they constructed in the Missouri River bottomlands near present-day Washburn, North Dakota.

Fort Mandan was situated across the river and downstream from the Mandan and Hidatsa villages along the Knife River. Inhabitants of these earth lodge villages befriended expedition members.

It was here that Lewis and Clark met Sakakawea, the Shoshone Indian teen who resided with the Hidatsa. Sakakawea, married to Toussaint Charbonneau, a French trapper and fur trader, served as a guide, while her husband acted as interpreter for the expedition.

The Corps of Discovery continued on to the Oregon Coast, spending the next winter at Fort Clatsop. On their return, they again visited the Knife River Indian villages, arriving there on 12 Aug. 1806. Departing on 17 Aug., they entered South Dakota on 21 Aug. On 4 Sept., they left South Dakota for St. Louis and home.

According to Elwyn B. Robinson, author of "History of North Dakota," Lewis and Clark "spent more time in and made a fuller record of North Dakota than any other region through which they passed."

## Many footprints

The wilderness Lewis and Clark passed through had already been occupied for thousands of years. At the time of their voyage, the land was home to a variety of Indian peoples:

# Place your ancestors in a historical setting

**W**hat was happening in Dakota when your ancestors lived here? What events may have shaped their lives, influenced their decisions?

History and genealogy go hand in hand, with one often sparking interest in the other. Knowing the history of Dakota Territory, or the two Dakotas, can help you fill in the blanks of your ancestors' lives, perhaps even answer such questions as, "What prompted my ancestors to settle in South Dakota?" or "Why did Grandpa and Grandma leave their North Dakota farm in 1934 and move to California?"

As Williston genealogist Jacki Keck puts it, "Sometimes such things as reasons for moving become more apparent when one reads up on the history of one's background area. Economic changes, wars—all have an effect on whether an area is a place in which to stay."

Just as good authors place their book characters into a setting, visualizing your ancestors in the historical setting that surrounded them can help you understand their actions and reactions. When you decide someday to write a biographical sketch of your ancestor, capturing the trends and events of the times and contemplating how these happenings might have affected them can add authenticity to their stories.

Studying the history of the area of your ancestors can also suggest sources for research or can help you devise research strategies.

We hope this book will enable you to create a historical timeline of people on your pedigree chart, putting them in the context of events that occurred during their lifetimes. It will help you to view your ancestors as "real people." •

---

the earth-lodge dwelling Mandan, Hidatsa, and Arikara; the nomadic tribes of Assiniboin, Cheyenne, Chippewa, Cree, Crow, and Blackfeet —and the proud, but fierce, Lakota.

White men, too, had criss-crossed the Dakotas in the years before Lewis and Clark's expedition: men such as the French-Canadian La Verendrye, who explored the Missouri River regions in 1738, and his sons, who, on a second expedition in 1743, buried a leaden plate near Pierre, South Dakota. This plate was uncovered 170 years later.

Hunters, trappers, traders, and adventurers had all left their footprints on the land before Lewis and Clark ever set foot here.

In the years surrounding the Voyage of Discovery, a tide of white explorers, trappers, and fur traders washed across Dakota country. For the

most part, their heritage was French, and they and their Chippewa or Cree wives left behind mixed French-Indian descendants called Métis.

## From forts to settlements to statehood

When Lewis and Clark visited here, trading posts had already been planted. There was even a boom town in Dakota at the time —Pembina, in extreme northeastern North Dakota.

Taking root around a fur post, Pembina bloomed in the first quarter of the 19th century. In 1819 alone, Father Severe Dumoulin, the Pembina priest, baptized 30 of his flock of mostly Métis. Many of the citizens, loyal to the British, pulled up stakes and headed north into Canada several years after learning that, in 1818, the 49th parallel had been established as the U.S.-Canadian boundary.

The queen of posts, Fort Union, was built in 1828. It reigned for nearly 30 years at the confluence of the Lower Yellowstone and Missouri rivers in northwestern North Dakota. Like the fur trade itself, Fort Union died out in the late 1850s. Lumber from the dying fort went into the construction of nearby Fort Buford, one of a string of Army posts built to protect mail carriers and wagon trains from attacks by hostile Indians.

Dakota itself yo-yoed under the dominion of several countries (first Spain, then France, then Spain again, then France, then the U.S.) and was divided into a number of territories (Louisiana, then Missouri, then Michigan, then Wisconsin, then Iowa, then Minnesota, then Dakota) before it was separated into the two Dakotas, each of which achieved statehood on the same day— 2 Nov. 1889. •

## LOUISIANA PURCHASE:

# Not all of Dakota included

• The northeastern tip of South Dakota and some portions of North Dakota were not included in the Louisiana Purchase. The area of northeastern North Dakota whose rivers did not drain into the Mississippi River basin was considered part of Canada, a British possession. The area came under U.S. sovereignty in 1818, when the boundary between the U.S. and Canada was defined. •

# Dakota timeline ................

- **1300 A.D.:** Mandans build earth lodges along Missouri River from Grand River, SD, to Knife River in North Dakota.
- **1490s:** Spain claims America as its territory.
- **1600s:** Two Dakota/Lakota (Sioux) tribes—the Yanktonai and the Tetons—enter the Dakotas.
- **1671:** France claims area; claim reinforced when French explorer La Salle explores the Mississippi to its mouth in 1682.
- **1700s:** Arikaras (Rees) settle in central South Dakota and as far north as the Cannonball River in North Dakota. Several decades later, the Plains Chippewas (Plains Ojibways) enter the Great Plains of North Dakota and Manitoba. Cree, Crow, and Blackfeet move into buffalo country of western North Dakota.
- **1718:** New Orleans founded by French.

- **1738:** La Verendrye leads an expedition from Fort La Reine in Manitoba to a Mandan Indian village in central North Dakota.
- **1742-43:** La Verendrye's sons explore the Dakotas. They leave behind a lead marker, unearthed near Pierre, SD, 170 years later.
- **1762-63:** France defeated in French and Indian War; Treaty of Paris cedes French possessions west of Mississippi River to Spain.
- **1780:** Teton Sioux move westward to Black Hills; Yankton and Yanktonais move to James and Big Sioux valleys in Dakotas.
- **1780-1800s:** Dawn of fur trade era. South Dakota has posts as early as 1750s; first known ND trading post established near Souris River in 1781, soon abandoned.
- **Mid-1780s:** Small pox strikes, killing many Mandans and Hidatsas.

## FROM LOUISIANA PURCHASE — TO TWO DAKOTAS

- May 2, 1803: Napoleon sells Louisiana Territory (including all of South Dakota and most of North Dakota) to U.S. government.
- 1812: Northern part of Louisiana Territory formed into Territory of Missouri.
- 1818: U.S.-Canada boundary set at 49th Parallel; Red River Valley country comes under U.S. control.
- 1834: Land east of Missouri River becomes part of Michigan Territory; Wisconsin Territory in 1836; Iowa Territory in 1838; Minnesota Territory in 1849.
- 1854: Land east of Missouri River becomes part of Nebraska Territory.
- 1858: Minnesota becomes a state. Area between Minnesota's western border and Missouri River becomes a no-man's land with no territorial government.
- 1861: Dakota Territory established, consisting of present-day North and South Dakota, and most of Montana and Wyoming.
- 1863: Dakota Territory reduced to include only North and South Dakota.
- Nov. 2, 1889: Statehood. Dakota Territory divided into two states: North Dakota (39th state) and South Dakota (40th state). •

- **1794:** David Thompson, early visitor to ND Indian villages, estimates population of Mandans at 1,520, Hidatsas at 1,330.
- **1800:** Loisel builds fort on island below Pierre, SD.
- **1801:** Alexander Henry Jr. establishes trading post at Pembina, ND.
- **2 May 1803:** Napoleon sells Louisiana Territory to U.S. government.
- **14 May 1804:** Lewis and Clark expedition arrives in what is now South Dakota.
- **1804-06.** Lewis and Clark winter at Fort Mandan, near present-day Washburn, ND. Returning from the Oregon Coast, they visit the post again on 12 Aug. 1806, departing five days later for St. Louis. They enter South Dakota again on 21 Aug. 1806, exactly two years from time they first enter state.
- **1809:** Manuel Lisa, St. Louis Fur Co., establishes trading posts in Dakotas.
- **1811:** "Overland Astorians," led by Wilson Price Hunt, travel through SD enroute to Pacific Northwest.
- **1812:** Earl of Selkirk, a Scot, begins colony along Red and Assiniboine rivers near Winnipeg, extending to Grand Forks-Pembina area.
- **1818:** First school at Pembina, DT. U.S.-Canada boundary set at 49th Parallel; Red River country comes under U.S. control.
- **1820s-30s:** Hostilities with Arikaras. U.S. military retaliates, attacking and burning Grand River villages. Arikaras later join Mandans in ND.
- **In 1828,** Fort Union established.
- **1831-32:** Fort Clark trading post founded in 1831. In 1832, steamboat Yellow Stone reaches Fort Union.
- **1837:** Smallpox epidemic nearly wipes out Fort Clark-area Mandans.
- **1838-39:** Nicollet and Fremont party explores, maps eastern and central South Dakota, Missouri and James

River valleys of North Dakota to Devils Lake.
- **1840-50s:** In 1848, Fr. George Belcourt opens missions at Pembina, St. Joseph, and Turtle Mountains, ND. In 1849, Fr. Pierre DeSmet begins ministry to Teton Sioux.
- **1840s-80s:** Red River ox carts haul goods to St. Paul until near demise of buffalo.
- **1851:** Fort Laramie Treaty with Teton Sioux. Guarantees U.S. rights to build, protect roads through Indian country. First post office in Dakota Territory established at Pembina.
- **1855:** American Fur Company post, Fort Pierre (near Pierre, SD), sold to U.S. government for use as military fort. Marks end of fur-trade heyday.
- **Spring of 1857:** Sioux Falls, first town in southern DT, founded.
- **1858-70s:** Military posts established in Dakotas. In 1858, Yankton Treaty brings whites to Big Sioux and Missouri rivers. The same year, Minnesota becomes a state. In 1859, the Yanktons move to first of Sioux reservations along Missouri.
- **1860:** Minnesota Territory census shows about 2,400 white people living in Dakota, both north and south. Regular steamboat service on Missouri begins.
- **1861:** Dakota Territory established. DT's first continuous newspaper rolls off press at Yankton. Civil War begins.
- **1862:** Homestead Act becomes law. Minnesota Uprising—Sioux revolt, killing settlers and attacking military posts. Sioux defeated; 43 hanged.
- **In 1863,** DT reduced to include only North and South Dakota. DT opens for homesteading.
- **1863-65:** Gens. Sully and Sibley hunt for Minnesota Uprising participants in ND. Battles of Whitestone Hill (1863) and Badlands/ Killdeer Mountains (1864) weaken Indians' resistance.

- 1864: Sully builds Fort Rice, first Missouri River military post in northern DT.
- 1865: Many veterans take up homesteads in DT after Civil War. Drought, prairie fires, grasshoppers take toll on crops, settlers.
- 1867: Fort Totten Indian Reservation established near Devils Lake, ND.
- 1868: Laramie Treaty establishes Sioux lands west of Missouri River, SD. First homestead claim filed west of Red River in ND.
- 1868-69, Sheyenne River and Grand River agencies established on Missouri River, southern DT.
- 1868-1873: First settlement boom period accompanied by good crop years.
- 1870s: Fort Berthold Indian Reservation formed. Sioux and Chippewa cede most of present-day eastern ND. Census shows 11,000 people in southern DT. In 1872, telegraph line built from Fargo, ND, to Winnipeg, Manitoba. In 1873, *Bismarck Tribune* begins publication.
- 1874: Gold discovered in Black Hills.
- 1874-75: Drought and grasshoppers ravage Dakota crops.
- 1875: Indian uprising provoked when U.S. War Department permits white settlement on Laramie Treaty Indian lands.
- 1876: Nation celebrates its centennial. Lt. Col. George Custer and 7th Cavalry troops from Fort Abraham Lincoln (south of present-day Mandan, ND), defeated in battle at Little Big Horn, Montana Territory on 25 June 1876, by Cheyenne and Sioux, led by Chief Sitting Bull and warriors Crazy Horse and Gall.
- 1877: Black Hills opened for settlement.
- 1879-86: Settlement boom in DT—railroad expansion, population increase.
- 1881: Sitting Bull and remaining Hunkpapas from Little Big Horn battle

surrender at Fort Buford, are transferred to Standing Rock Reservation.
- 1882: Turtle Mountain Reservation established.
- 1883: DT capital moved from Yankton to Bismarck.
- 1885: First DT census taken. Immigration Office established to promote DT immigration.
- 1886-87: Drought results in exodus of Yankee and old-American stock. Cattle boom in western Dakotas ends with brutal winter.
- 1887: Standing Rock Indian Reservation opens for homesteading.
- Late 1880s: ND population 190,000; SD 340,000.

## NOV. 2, 1889:
## STATEHOOD!
Dakota Territory divided into two states: North Dakota (39th state) and South Dakota (40th state).

- 1890: Sitting Bull killed when Standing Rock Reservation Indian police attempt to arrest him.
- 1891-1910: Third settlement boom. Series of wet years and good crops.
- 1898: Dakota troops among those sent to fight Spanish-American War.
- 1898-1915: Population influx into Dakotas.
- 1906: Naturalization Act results in uniform, more detailed, applications.
- 1910-12: Bad crop years, low rainfall result in exodus from Dakotas.
- 1914-20: Good agricultural years created by World War I demand. In 1917, Dakota troops see World War I service. In 1918, Spanish flu pandemic strikes. In 1920, Dakota women vote for first time in general election.
- 1920s: Farm economy collapses, farm foreclosures and bank closings result.

# EARLY TRANSPORTATION

- 1831: First of many steamboats to ply upper reaches of Missouri River—the Yellow Stone arrives at Fort Tecumseh (post's name changed to Fort Pierre in 1832) in 1831, at Fort Union in 1832.
- 1860: Regular steamboat service on Missouri begins.
- 1860-70s: Railroads recruit workers from Europe and Scandinavia to lay track; Dakota settlement follows the rails. New towns spring up along route. In South Dakota, the Dakota Southern railroad begins service between Sioux City, IA, and Yankton, SD, in 1873.
- 1872: Westbound Northern Pacific Railroad reaches Jamestown (ND). It reaches Bismarck in 1873, Montana in 1881. Railroads promote Dakota's rich, inexpensive (or free) land overseas, hire agents and take out newspaper ads to lure settlers to Dakota. Immigrants flock to Dakota to buy land from railroads or to homestead free government land.
- 1873-85: Construction of railroads, population booming. Immigrants take free land in and beyond railroad-bed survey areas.
- 1877: Bismarck-to-Deadwood stage established.
- 1878: Mississippi Valley railroads reach eastern South Dakota, leading to further railroad development.
- 1879: Great Northern (then-St. Paul, Minneapolis and Manitoba) Railway reaches Grand Forks in 1879, reaches Montana border in 1887.
- 1879-86: Great Dakota boom—railroad expansion, population increase. Large numbers of old-stock Americans continue to come into state.
- 1880s: The first train chugs into the new town of Pierre (SD); town soon becomes a major railroad hub.
- 1886: Soo Line Railway begins construction. By 1886, land in eastern South Dakota already taken up by settlers.
- 1890: Most railroad construction in South Dakota is complete. By 1910, railroad services begin a slow decline. •

- 1924: Immigration Act limits foreign immigration.
- 1929: Stock market crashes in October; the Great Depression begins.
- 28 Dec. 1930: North Dakota capitol building burns.
- 1930s: Great Depression brings farm foreclosures, bank failures, drought, dust storms, despair. More Dakotans received federal relief than anywhere else in nation. Population declines. President Roosevelt introduces WPA, CCC, REA, etc.
- 1934: New ND skyscraper capitol completed.
- 1938: Rural electrification begins bringing electricity to Dakota rural areas.
- 1941-45: World War II;

many Dakotans in military service.
- Late 1940s-50s: World War II ends, bringing displaced persons to Dakotas. Economic and construction booms begin. North and South Dakota dams completed in mid-1950s.
- 1989: Dakotas celebrate their centennials.
- 1 Jan. 2000: World welcomes new millennium.
- 2004-06: Lewis & Clark bicentennial celebration.

———

*Information from "History of North Dakota," by Elwyn B. Robinson; "Dakota Panorama" edited by J. Leonard Jennewein and Jane Boorman; and "History of South Dakota" by Herbert S. Schell.*

# And so they came...

## A little piece of land...

And so they came, the Bohemians, the Czechs, the French, the Scandinavians, the Germans from Russia, the Yankees, the speculators, the pioneers. They came by water, by rail, by steamboat, by covered wagon. Some came seeking free land, freedom, and fortune, some to escape conditions in the Old Country.

Originally many had lived in the East—New England, Illinois, Pennsylvania, and Ohio. Soon they ventured to steppingstone states—Wisconsin, Minnesota, Iowa, and Nebraska. Their next step was Dakota Territory.

At first they came in trickles, part of a westward migration sweeping the central plains, crossing Indian hunting grounds on their way to Oregon, Utah, and the gold fields of California. The emigrants now began lapping at the east side of southeastern Dakota, along the shores of Big Sioux River.

With the pioneers came tensions between whites and Indians. In 1856, a treaty between the Teton Sioux and the U.S. government recognized the rights of whites to travel between forts Laramie and Pierre on their way to the Oregon Trail. Treaties with other Indian tribes in southern Dakota opened up vast tracts of land to settlement.

Talk of a transcontinental railroad spurred interest in settlement along the Missouri River. Steamboats and keelboats were already plying the river between trading posts in the north and markets in St. Louis.

## First town

In 1857, Sioux Falls, the first "white" town, sprang up along the falls of the Big Sioux River in southeastern South Dakota. The next year, Congress approved funding for an emigrant road from Fort Ridgeley in Minnesota to connect with the Oregon Trail. The towns of Medary and Flandreau were founded next.

The Yankton Sioux ceded land between the Big Sioux River and the Missouri in 1858, moving to a reservation. Bon Homme, Vermillion, and Yankton sprang up on these lands.

In 1861, Dakota Territory was established above the 43rd parallel; it included the two Dakotas and Montana.

All those "first towns" were abandoned during the Minnesota Uprising of 1862, when the Santee Sioux revolted, looting, burning, and killing white settlers and soldiers in Minnesota and the Dakotas. The towns were resettled once hostilities cooled.

In 1863, Dakota Territory was reduced to include present North and South Dakota. Battles broke out as Gens. Sully and Sibley scoured North Dakota for Indians believed to be Minnesota Uprising participants. Nationally, the Civil War was raging.

Shortly after the smoke cleared, the new Dakotans began washing over the land like ocean waves—many settling in and planting crops, along with their roots, deep in Dakota soil.

Many obtained land through the Homestead Act, a law giving native-born or "naturalized" citizens 160 acres of land in exchange for their living there and working the land for a number of years. Others got land via preemption or tree claims, or by buying land from previous owners, land speculators, or the railroad.

As more land opened for settlement and other land was taken, plucky pioneers settled on other, often less fertile, lands further north and west. Now they began taking land in North Dakota—first along the Red River Valley, then venturing westward.

## Migration triggers

Treaties with the Indian tribes, natural resources such as fur and coal, railroad service, and promo-

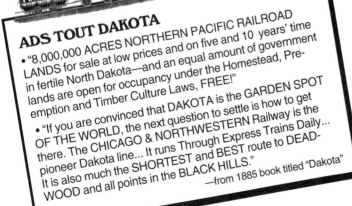

# BOOMS & BUSTS
## of Dakota settlement

Dakota settlement occurred in ebbs and flows, with boom playing tag with bust. Following are migration patterns experienced by the two states beginning in the 1850s:

- **BOOM:** Late 1850s-early 1860s—southern Dakota's first city, Sioux Falls, founded in 1857. About 2,400 white people in Dakota at time of the 1860 census.

- **BUST:** 1862—Civil War rages. Indian troubles following the Minnesota Uprising discourage settlement—despite Homestead Act, which began same year.

- **BOOM:** 1865—Civil War ends; veterans, others homestead in Dakota Territory. Railroad arrives in eastern South Dakota, recruits European settlers.

- **FIRST GREAT BOOM:** 1868-73—good crops; railroad reaches Yankton in 1873. 1870 census shows 11,776 people in southern Dakota; 2,405 in northern Dakota (most around Pembina area). North Dakota settlement begins in other areas in 1871.

- **BUST:** 1874-75—grasshoppers destroy crops two years in a row. Many settlers leave territory.

- **BOOM:** 1876-82—Settlement boom resumes. Gold discovered in Black Hills; Hills open for settlement in 1877. Old-stock Americans establish ranches in the Black Hills.

- **SECOND GREAT BOOM:** 1879-86—railroads expand, population swells. 1882 is peak year for homesteading in North Dakota, with 5,579 people filing on nearly 865,000 acres. In 1885, Office of Commissioner of Immigration opens to promote settlement.

- **BUST:** 1886-87—most land in eastern South Dakota already taken. Drought leads to exodus of Yankees and old-stock Americans from east of Missouri River. Immigrants take their place.

- **THIRD GREAT BOOM:** 1889-1910—Dakota Territory becomes two states in 1889. Immigrants keep pouring in. Series of wet years encourages settlement in dryer lands west of Missouri River. North Dakota population increases 1,000 percent from 1878 (16,000) to 1890 (191,000); 348,600 are living in South Dakota in 1890.

- **BUST:** 1910-12—Bad crop years, little rainfall, exodus of population from West River country.

- **MIXED:** 1914-30—World War I involves Dakota troops. Spanish flu strikes in 1918, killing thousands in Dakotas alone. Law passed in 1920 restricts foreign immigration; further restrictions added in 1924. Ag depression hits during 1920s; many lose farms, exit Dakotas. In 1930, South Dakota's population stands at 692,849; North Dakota's population hits 681,000.

- **BUST:** 1930-40—Great Depression results in unprecedented exodus of farmers from Dakotas to states south and west, of rural populations to urban areas.

- **BOOM:** 1940s—World War II creates demand for agricultural products. Boom in construction after war ends. Some immigration into Dakota of persons displaced by war in Europe.

- **BOOM AND BUST:** 1950s-90s—population of Dakotas declines despite building boom, discovery of oil in North Dakota, major construction projects such as dams on Missouri River, major coal development projects. Exodus of people continues into remaining decades of 20th century. Oil industry yo-yos from boom to bust to boom. Record grain prices of early '70s are followed by price plunge, farm crisis. Ag instability continues into 1980s, recurs in 1990s; leads to exodus from farms, decline of small towns, growth of urban areas. •

tions by transportation companies and by Dakota Territory itself all played a role in luring settlers to the Dakotas. For those who chose to settle here, it was a chance to make money, to be successful, to leave the old life behind, to start over.

But perhaps the biggest pull was the promise of free or cheap land, especially through the Homestead Act. Land was highly valued, especially in countries where cotters farmed land owned by others, or where land was divided into pieces too small to provide a living. For these groups, land was the determining factor in their decision to emigrate.

While these things pulled immigrants to Dakota, other factors were pushing many from their homelands: political upheavals, religious persecution, prejudice, poverty, militarism, and famine.

They came from many lands, many cultures, many religions. Some settled on homesteads surrounded by their neighbors from the Old Country. Some followed

Many early immigrants left family, friends, and their motherland, traveling for months in fragile sailing ships to plant their roots in Dakota. •

DAKOTA
·
NOT A
WILD
COUNTRY

- In 1885, the Office of Commissioner of Immigration published the book "Dakota," which promoted immigration into Dakota Territory. The book supported its claim that "Dakota is not a wild country" with excerpts like the following:

- "It has 2,500 miles of railway; more than Massachusetts, New Jersey, Georgia, Nebraska, Kentucky, or any one of 20 other old settled states.

- It has 2,000 school houses; more than Vermont, Rhode Island, Florida, or any one of 15 other states.

- It has 275 newspapers; more than any New England state, except Massachusetts, or any eastern state except New York and Pennsylvania.

- The growth of Dakota is phenomenal. In 1880, it had but 135,000 inhabitants. Now, it casts well on to 100,000 votes and has a population of 500,000." •

—"Dakota," 1885

advance scouting parties who had been sent to select land for settlement.

Others came because of letters received from relatives who had already settled in Dakota—glowing letters telling of bumper crops, the glories of land ownership, and the freedoms and blessings Dakota offered. These testimonials were some of the most compelling enticements for Dakota settlement. But there were others:

In 1885, the Office of Commissioner of Immigration was established to promote immigration into Dakota Territory.

American ship owners advertised free land and jobs in mining and industry. The railroads were especially big promoters of Dakota settlement—cashing in when settlers rode the trains to their new homesteads, shipped their harvest to market by rail, or bought railroad lands. Their advertisements appeared in newspapers across the U.S., Canada, and Europe.

## Life in a new land

Life as an immigrant to Dakota country was often harsh. The new Americans had to adapt to new customs, communicate in a new language, use new systems of exchange and marketing, even change their names to conform with traditions and laws.

Some groups didn't assimilate as readily as did others, clinging to their mother tongue and cus-

toms for generations.

Farming experience gleaned in the Old Country didn't always translate well on the unbroken Dakota prairies. Many from Europe went from a system of farm villages, complete with schools and churches, surrounded by farmland—to scattered, isolated homesteads. Schools, churches, and even neighbors were often miles away, leading to isolation and loneliness.

Pioneers often had little money to buy provisions. Their task included cultivating the soil, scratching in seed, harvesting and marketing a crop, building a home (a dugout the first year; a sod, stone, or log home several years later), planting trees, and tending animals and gardens.

These chores, combined with harsh weather, took their toll almost as much as did death by childbirth and contagious diseases, such as diphtheria, cholera, and influenza.

Pioneer churches provided solace during such times. Services were held in homes until a church could be built. Parishioners appreciated the religious freedom this country offered. Their pastors performed and recorded the major rites of their lives: christenings, communions, confirmations, marriages, and funerals.

If one's luck held, one could make a good living from the land. But when conditions turned sour, many settlers packed up their wagons and their broken dreams and headed west and south.

## Two Dakotas

By 1885, Fargo, the largest city of Dakota Territory, had a population of 12,000. Bismarck (formerly called Edwinton) had replaced Yankton as territorial capital, becoming North Dakota's capital when Dakota achieved statehood in 1889. Pierre was chosen as the capital of South Dakota.

In the years of settlement, the ebb and flow of conditions in the Dakotas —whether economics or Mother Nature's whims— determined a settler's success or failure. Cycles of drought and grasshoppers, of low farm prices, prairie fires in the summer and blizzards in the winter, led to waves of outmigration.

Some influx into Dakota occurred prior to World War I as some Europeans fled the approaching war and mandatory military service. An anti-immigration feeling swept the U.S. following the war, and immigration laws limited the number and nationalities of immigrants.

When the Great Depression struck in the 1930s, many left the two states in vast numbers. During this great Dakota exodus, letters from relatives who had moved on to the West Coast years earlier persuaded Dakotans devastated by the drought, dust, and depression to pull up their Dakota roots and replant them in areas such as California or Oregon.

Despite the depression, however, most kept their roots firmly planted in Dakota soil. •

# Genealogy: The myths and

Top: Thomas and Gys-Berta Luyben. Right: Family featured on our cover—Faunce (son of Thomas and Gys-Berta) and Anna Slaatenhus Luyben with children Virgil (front) and Bernice.

Bottom right: Hilaire "Elie" and Melanie Beaudoin pose with their two chldren, Alcide (left) and Kal, in this 1898 photo. The Beaudoins are the great-great uncle and aunt of co-author Cathy A. Langemo.

● ● ● ● ● ● ● ● ● ● ●

## RELATIVELY SPEAKING...

When you've traced your family tree back 20 generations beyond yourself, you'll be adding 1,048,576 ancestors to your pedigree chart! •

There are almost as many reasons to start collecting information on your ancestors as there are numbers of ancestors you'll unearth once you start digging! When you go back just 10 generations beyond your own, you have 1,024 ancestors waiting to be discovered. And 10 generations beyond that lurk 1,048,576 progenitors!

Of course, you probably won't find information on more than a portion of them. But it's rewarding to record as many of them as you can. One thing's for sure: You won't run out of ancestors to look for!

Tracing your roots triggers interest in the history and genealogy of areas once inhabited by your forefathers and mothers. It can lead you to visit the countries or former hometowns of your ancestors.

It helps you trace such things as physical characteristics, personality traits, and health trends.

It helps you gain a network of friends who are also interested in family history.

But perhaps most important, it adds another dimension to your life: As you learn more about your genetic past, you learn more about yourself!

While your genealogy is really about YOU, going on an ancestor scavenger hunt by yourself isn't nearly as much fun as involving other family members—your children or your spouse; your brothers and sisters, who share your genetics; your parents, whose memories of the past go back a generation beyond yours.

So grab a family member or friend, and get ready for a great adventure discovering your own personal history!

## Exploring the myths

Before you begin, let's explore a few myths and misconceptions.

• **If you see it in print, it must be true.** As Will Rogers once said, "Don't believe everything you read in the papers."

He might have added, "Or the family history book. Or the church record. Or even the family Bible."

Errors can creep into all kinds of records, since the human beings who recorded them sometimes made mistakes—from spelling errors to flawed recollections of events.

Some records are more trustworthy than others, however, as we'll discuss later. That's why you'll want to collect more than one record on each event, so you can compare records to determine the correct information.

• **If family legend says it's true, it must be true.** Think of family legends as something to build toward. But don't accept them as gospel until you have proven them through your research.

Step backward one generation at a time until you reach your legendary ancestor. Check out stories with people in other branches of your family

# the miracles

to see if they may have heard the same story. Proving such a story can be especially exciting.

• **If you want information on European ancestors, you must travel to Europe.** No way! You'll be amazed at the records you can find in your own back yard. Thanks to the telephone, the Postal Service, interlibrary loan and the Internet, you can access a lot of those records without leaving your living room.

If you do venture beyond your front door, try a trip to your nearest LDS family history center (there are eight of them in North Dakota and 14 in South Dakota; no matter where you live, there's sure to be one not far from your community). There you can access (via computer, microfilm, or microfiche) most of the records in Salt Lake City's LDS Family History Library, the world's largest genealogy repository.

Or, check out the State Archives Library located on the capitol grounds in both Dakotas. Records that are available at these centers and libraries are discussed in Chapters 2 and 3.

And if you do get to the land of your ancestors? Instead of using up valuable vacation time parked in a musty archive poring over ancient tomes, visit your ancestors' homes, find relatives who may still live in the

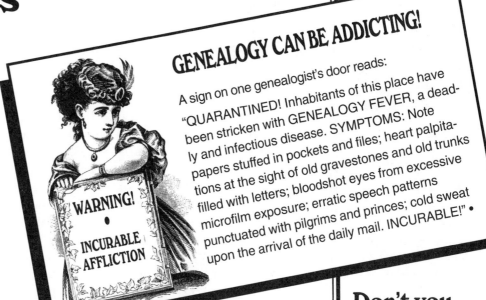

**GENEALOGY CAN BE ADDICTING!**

A sign on one genealogist's door reads:

"QUARANTINED! Inhabitants of this place have been stricken with GENEALOGY FEVER, a deadly and infectious disease. SYMPTOMS: Note papers stuffed in pockets and files; heart palpitations at the sight of old gravestones and old trunks filled with letters; bloodshot eyes from excessive microfilm exposure; erratic speech patterns punctuated with pilgrims and princes; cold sweat upon the arrival of the daily mail. INCURABLE!" •

area, take pictures of the setting, and enjoy yourself! When you get home, check in at your family history center, which most likely has records from your ancestral area.

## What about black sheep?

What if, in your quest for ancestors, you find some black sheep lurking in the ancestral fold?

Think of these forbidden fruits in your family as spice! They add flavor to your family tree. Without them, your pedigree would be pretty sterile—and pretty abnormal, since we all have them!

Instead of trying to hide them, why not flaunt them? That's what members of the Black Sheep Society of Genealogists do.

For details on this "flock" that flourishes on the Internet, turn to our high-tech chapter.

## Then there are miracles

Most of us who are involved in this fun hobby have run into miracles. Yes, miracles! Myriad are the stories—of an old book falling off a library shelf at the feet of a researcher who, upon opening it, discovers his ancestors. Of someone writing a letter overseas to uncover unknown relatives, only to find these relatives have also been searching for her branch of the family. The list goes on. So remember to believe in miracles; you just may run into them!

A word of caution before you begin your search: Genealogy can be addicting! If, knowing this, you're still ready to take a trip into your past, read on. But don't say we didn't warn you! •

## Don't you believe it!

• Be a skeptic! Don't believe everything you read in the papers—or other documents. Check out the accuracy of any handwritten or printed records containing information on your family.

• So, Grandma swears your family is descended from royalty—or that your ever-so-great-grandpa was a Revolutionary War hero. Investigate such family legends before claiming they're true—or before discarding them. Proving the validity of such legends can be exciting!

• Don't think you have to travel to the homeland of your ancestors to glean family history information. Much of that information is right here at home—thanks to LDS records and well-stocked archives. •

# Begin with yourself

## What's in a name? Often, a clue!

- No clue can pinpoint a relative or ancestor quicker than a name.

- If, when browsing through records or phone books, you discover a familiar surname, check to see whether there's a family connection. Even if you learn they're not relatives, you've learned something! •

So where do you begin your quest for ancestors?

You start with yourself and work your way backward in time, generation by generation. On rare occasions you may have to deviate from that path to check out "collateral lines" of relatives who have the same ancestors you do. When you're stuck, this detour can sometimes help you find an alternate route to your destination. But basically, YOU'RE NUMBER 1!

That means you'll collect data about yourself first, then your parents, then grandparents, and so on.

In this section, you'll learn what basic data to look for and how to record the information you find. Later in this book, you'll discover what records to search, and where to find them. But first things first!

## Three keys to the past

When you go through any records—from an old birth announcement you found stashed in a shoebox to your great-grandmother's obituary—be on the lookout for three basic clues: names, dates, and places. These three "keys" can help you unlock the door to your family's past.

These basics—names, dates, and places—can help you build a framework that you can later "flesh in" with family anecdotes and historical events that took place in their lifetimes. Armed with these basics, you have a foundation upon which to "build your ancestor."

### • NAMES provide relationship clues.

The first key to unlocking the door to your family history is names. Names can give clues to relationships.

Keep an open mind regarding name changes and spelling variations of the surnames you're researching.

In the book "Tracing Your Ancestry," author F. Wilbur Helmbold writes: "The variety of surname spellings is a pitfall that is not appreciated by beginners in genealogy research."

For a variety of reasons, our ancestors changed their names—especially when they came to America.

In order to conform to naming customs in this country, they may have Anglicized ("English-ized") their names. Or they may have changed their names to avoid confusion with others bearing the same name (too many Ole Olsons, for example). Or, a "helpful" official, recognizing that the original name was unpronounceable or contained foreign letters, may have convinced the immigrant to adopt a new name or new spelling.

Or perhaps the name is spelled wrong in a record, or other than the way you're expecting to find it. It may have been spelled phonetically (or misspelled) by a census-taker or other recorder. Our ancestors—often lacking reading, writing, and spelling skills— may not have been able to spot a spelling error in such a case.

You'll find a lot more details on researching names in Chapter 2 of this book.

But first, in order to search records for a name, you need to know a date (or time frame) and place (country, region, and/or parish) the person came from, so you know where to concentrate your search. That brings us to the next two keys.

### • DATES: Different strokes for different folks.

In the U.S., we tend to write dates in this order: month first, day second, year third. You need to be aware that in other countries (especially European countries, where many of our ancestors' data were entered into the record

---

## What's your name, sir?

- The first to adopt surnames to honor their forebears were the Chinese. The surname, however, was listed first. In the name Sun Yat-sen, for example, "Sun" is the surname.

- At one point in history, surnames were based on personality traits and physical features. Names such as Moody, Stern and Wise, and Stout, Rich and Armstrong are still in use today.

- Some names indicated a man's occupation: Taylor, Carpenter, Brewer, Mason, Cook, Tanner, Butcher, Smith, Slaughter. •

# Principles of patronymics

**W**hen we think of patronymic names (names based on the father's given name and adding a suffix denoting son or daughter), we usually think of Scandinavia. But patronymics was a common naming practice in many countries throughout Europe and the British Isles in earlier years.

The prefix "Mac-" or "Mc-" in Irish or Scottish names, for example, was followed by the given name of the father. Other patronymic prefixes included Fitz- (for "child of," as in "Fitzpatrick"), and O'- (as in "O'Brien"). Suffixes also denoted kinship, as the Ukrainian "-enko" ("son of").

In Scandinavia, patronymics were in use at the time emigration to the U.S. took place. If you have Scandinavian—and especially, Norwegian—ancestors, knowing the naming patterns used in the Old Country can help you track down your ancestors. Other Scandinavian countries used patronymics as well—but perhaps none to the extent that the Norwegians did.

Most Norwegians had three names*: their given (first) name, their patronymic name (which ended in -son or -datter), and their farm (address) name. Thus, the name "Lars Anderson Slaatenhus"

LET'S CALL HIM OLE OLSON

meant "Lars, son of Anders, from the farm Slaatenhus." His sisters' patronymic surnames would be "Andersdatter."

The patronymic name changed every generation: When Lars had sons and daughters, his children would be either "Larson" or "Larsdatter." And when they moved to another farm, their "address" name became that of their new farm in Norway. So while the name of the farm remained the same, the occupants changed their names with every move.

For a while after our Norwegian ancestors came to this country, they clung to their old naming customs, or switched from name to name (often between their patronymic and farm name).

Around 1900, a law passed in the U.S. requiring that a standard surname be chosen—one that would pass on to future generations unaltered. Some Norwegians (like Lars) adopted their farm name**, or an Anglicized spelling variation of that name, as their surname. Lars Slaatenhus gave up the name that identified him as the son of Anders, his patronymic link to the past.

Other Norwegians dropped their farm name and chose to be

known by their patronymic name. In so doing, they discarded a valuable genealogy clue: The farm name points to a specific location, from which can be gleaned the parish, from which to access church records packed with birth, christening, marriage, and death information about the family.

# Given names yield clues, too!

The patronymic system also involved strict given-name customs in which firstborn children were named after their paternal grandparents. When those names were used up, the maternal grandparents' given names were used. After that, it was the great-grandparents' turn.

There were exceptions to this rule, and not all communities followed this naming pattern as religiously as did others. But, generally, the naming patterns give a clue for determining birth order and discovering first names of ancestors.

Patronymically named Norwegian females went by their maiden names throughout their lives and were so listed in all records, making them easier to trace. •

———

*Note: Not all Norwegians used patronymic names. Those whose ancestors came from Europe and were associated with the guilds of the Middle Ages generally kept their foreign surnames. Those associated with the Danish clergy did the same.

**In some cases, the name is Anglicized, or the farm name is other than the last farm the person may have lived on in Norway.

---

books), the date is written in this order: day first, month second, year third (the style we've chosen to use in this book).

Any of you retrieving information from overseas records should be tuned in to this format, so you'll know automatically that the first digits represent the day, the second the month.

That's also the form that genealogists use to enter their date data. They record it thus: 11 May 1882. Spelling out the month avoids confusion over which system is being used.

We're also lazy. We often abbreviate the year, using only the last two digits— one reason we experienced computer problems at the turn of the millenium. Genealogists always record all four digits of the year, rather than only the last two. When doing genealogy, it doesn't take one long

## Gregorian calendar blues

At times throughout history, the calendar was adjusted to reflect actual time. One that affects genealogists exploring roots in Europe (and Colonial America) is the Gregorian calendar change.

The Julian calendar (named for Julius Caesar), in use prior to the 1580s, contained a year that was 11 minutes and 14 seconds longer than Earth's annual orbit around the sun. To resolve the problem, Pope Gregory XIII ordered astronomers to synchronize the calendar with the Earth's rotation. So 5 Oct. 1582 became 15 Oct. 1582, leaping ahead 10 days.

To further correct the old system, the Pope decreed that century years not divisible by 400 would *not* be leap years. (What about the year

## OCTOBER 1582

| 1 | 2 | 3 | 4 | 15 | 16 | 17 |
| 18 | 19 | 20 | 21 | 22 | 23 | 24 |
| 25 | 26 | 27 | 28 | 29 | 30 | 31 |

(Short month!)

2000? Well, 2000 is readily divisible by 400—which made it a leap year).

It must have been confusing enough to lose 10 days out of that first year (especially if you had a birthday during that period). To further confuse things, not everyone adapted to the new calendar system right away. Roman Catholic countries, of course, quickly adopted the new Gregorian calendar, decreed by their papal benefactor.

Many Protestant countries, however, didn't make the switch until 1700. Britain adopted the change (giving up 10 calendar days between 2 Sept. and 14 Sept.) in 1752. Russia waited until 1918—after the October Revolution of 1917 (which actually took place in November!)—to adopt the Gregorian calendar. By that time, its old calendar lagged 13 days behind the rest of the world!

In Colonial America, double dates were often used to reflect both the old style (O.S.) and Gregorian dates. Thus, George Washington, born on 11 Feb. 1732 according to the Julian calendar, had to adjust his birthday under the new system to 22 Feb. (When recording such data on your charts, don't adjust the date to our calendar; just add "O.S." to indicate an old style, Julian calendar, date.) ●

## DATE DATA

- When recording the year, always use four digits rather than two (1939, rather than '39).

- Record your data in this order: day first, month next, year last.

- Our own grandparents may not remember what date they were actually born. So back up their recollections with records.

- Establish a range of dates if the actual date is not known. ●

to get into the 1800s, the 1700s, and beyond. You can see how confusing it would be if the first two digits were missing.

Now that we've cleared up the calendar question (or probably confused you even more), what about dates our own grandpas and grandmas have given us as the days they were born? Or married? Or had children?

The rule is, always verify dates given orally with written records—remembering that our own grandparents may be mistaken about the date they were actually born! If Grandpa says he came into the world on 12 Dec. 1913, don't write that down as the official date until you've checked other records to confirm the date. You may

be surprised to learn Grandpa was wrong about his own birth date! Our ancestors weren't as concerned with dates as we are.

If you don't know an exact date, estimating the date an event may have taken place can help you in determining the range for a record search.

Be as precise as you can; record the approximate date on your chart—in pencil—as "ca. (circa) 1794" or "ca. 1865-1870."

### • PLACES: Exploring borders and boundaries.
The place your ancestors came from is one of the most valuable clues to researching them. You need to know where to look for records!

In many cases,

this involves tracing the migration patterns of your ancestors as they moved from place to place. To help you place your ancestors in the context of history, we've included a timeline and a section on settlement in our introductory section. You can also check the ethnic section for more information.

When researching and recording places, here are some things to remember:

• Be aware of border changes, caused by revolution or evolution, politics, mergers, or divisions. If your ancestors came from Alsace-Lorraine, for example, they may have listed their country of origin as either France or Germany, depending on which country controlled the province at the time they lived there.

If they settled in Dakota Territory in the mid-1800s, they were living in either North or South Dakota by the end of that decade when the territory was divided and each section achieved statehood.

Counties in both states consolidated with others, changed names, or split into two or more counties. (See the maps section in the appendix showing both early and present-day counties.)

Towns sprang up in haste. Some bloomed, while others faded and died, becoming ghost towns that are no longer listed on the map. Some of the early towns (such as Edwinton, Dakota Territory, which later became Bismarck, North Dakota) underwent name changes.

When checking maps, gazetteers and atlases for such places, it's a good idea to find a source that reflects the time period your ancestors were in an area, so you can determine in what towns and counties they had connections. (See Chapter 2 for more on maps, atlases, and gazetteers.)

Again, the three basic keys to your past are names, dates, and places.

But your family history will be much more vibrant if you include stories and anecdotes about relatives, as well.

You'll add zest to the otherwise dry facts and make your ancestors come alive as real human beings. It'll help you put flesh on the bones of your forefathers and mothers.

## PEDIGREE CHART

CHART # _____
Date compiled: _____
Name of compiler: _____
Address: _____
City: _____
State, zip: _____
Phone: _____
E-mail: _____

- B. = birth
- M. = marriage
- D. = death
- Pl. = place

PERSON 1
(SAME PERSON AS # _____ ON CHART # _____)
Name: _____
B.date: _____
Pl: _____
M.date: _____
Pl: _____
D.date: _____
Pl: _____

SPOUSE
Name: _____
B.date: _____
Pl: _____
D.date: _____
Pl: _____

2—FATHER
Name: _____
B.date: _____
Pl: _____
M.date: _____
Pl: _____
D.date: _____
Pl: _____

3—MOTHER
Name: _____
B.date: _____
Pl: _____
D.date: _____
Pl: _____

4—PATERNAL GRANDFATHER
Name: _____
B.date: _____
M.date: _____ Pl: _____
Pl: _____
D.date: _____
Pl: _____

5—PATERNAL GRANDMOTHER
Name: _____
B.date: _____
Pl: _____
D.date: _____
Pl: _____

6—MATERNAL GRANDFATHER
Name: _____
B.date: _____
M.date: _____
Pl: _____
D.date: _____
Pl: _____

7—MATERNAL GRANDMOTHER
Name: _____
B.date: _____
Pl: _____
D.date: _____
Pl: _____

8—GREAT-GRANDFATHER
Name: _____
B.date: _____
M.date: _____ Pl: _____
Pl: _____

9—GREAT-GRANDMOTHER
Name: _____
B.date: _____
D.date: _____ Pl: _____

10—GREAT-GRANDFATHER
Name: _____
B.date: _____
M.date: _____ Pl: _____
Pl: _____

11—GREAT-GRANDMOTHER
Name: _____
B.date: _____
D.date: _____ Pl: _____

12—GREAT-GRANDFATHER
Name: _____
B.date: _____
M.date: _____ Pl: _____
Pl: _____

13—GREAT-GRANDMOTHER
Name: _____
B.date: _____
D.date: _____ Pl: _____

14—GREAT-GRANDFATHER
Name: _____
B.date: _____
M.date: _____ Pl: _____
Pl: _____

15—GREAT-GRANDMOTHER
Name: _____
B.date: _____
D.date: _____ Pl: _____

# Forms that can help

Once you start to accumulate names, dates, and places, where—and how—do you record your data?

Two forms can help: pedigree charts and family group sheets. You'll use these forms to chart your progress and to point the way to future research.

Consider these forms your "worksheets." Take them with you whenever you leave your house to visit a research facility.

You'll find samples in the back of this book. You can also pick up family group sheets and pedigree charts for a nominal fee at your local LDS family history center. Or you may purchase them through a local genealogy society or a mail-order genealogy supply company (see appendix for addresses).

## • PEDIGREE CHARTS.
Your very first step is to start filling out a pedigree,

or ancestral, chart.

Begin with yourself and go as far back as you can, generation by generation, with what you know at this time. Fill in the blank lines of your personal pedigree with your family names, plus dates and places for the following vital events in their lives: birth, christening, marriage, and death/burial.

The most commonly used blank chart goes back four to six generations, but you can get charts that go back 15 generations and more. (Computer genealogy programs also enable you to print out multiple generations on one chart.)

Since this is your first chart, list yourself as person No. 1. Your father would be No. 2; your mother No. 3; your father's parents Nos. 4 and 5; your mother's parents Nos. 6 and 7, and so on.

Note that your male

# Know your locality!

- Knowing the locality of your ancestor will help you determine where to look for records!

- When recording place information, always go from smallest to largest—as in Bismarck, Burleigh County, North Dakota, USA. •

# Citing your sources

- Always record the sources from which you retrieved your information, as well as the data itself. "Knowing the source of a fact is necessary to properly evaluate its worth," according to John and Carolyn Cosgriff in their book "Climb It Right: A High-Tech Genealogy Primer."

Keeping track of your sources will enable you to recheck the source in case conflicting data is later found or should you want to doublecheck your work. •

ancestors always receive even numbers; your female ancestors, odd numbers.

Lines on the chart connect each generation, making it easy to determine relationships.

Fill out your chart as completely and accurately as you can. Use this as your work sheet for (a) adding information not listed on the chart and (b) finding more distant ancestors.

When you have filled one or more family lines on your first pedigree chart, continue the line on a second chart. Information printed on the chart will aid you in numbering each succeeding chart. It will also help you visualize what pieces of the "progenitor puzzle" are missing.

Always use maiden surnames for any females you record on your chart. It will help you link up to your maternal lines—the other half of your family tree.

• **FAMILY GROUP SHEETS.** Your next step is to fill out a family group sheet for yourself and your immediate family, using the instructions on the sheet (see Appendix, forms section) as your guide. Then, fill out similar charts for your parents, grandparents, brothers, and sisters— one for every individual family.

Fill in the blanks with the following: given name and surname, birthplace and/or christening date and place, marriage date and place, and death and/or burial date and place. Later, as you accumulate information about other family branches, you can complete group sheets for them, as well. (Or have a member of each family complete one and share with other branches.)

Typically, a family group sheet has lines for recording data

on the head of household, spouse, and children. It also allows you to enter names of the couple's parents, and to list other spouses. Many standard family group sheets don't contain enough spaces for recording all of the children in a large family. That's why we've included a second sheet (see Appendix, forms section) on which to continue information.

If there were prior or later marriages, record all information on each husband and wife grouping (including a list of children born into each marriage) on a separate group sheet.

As you learn of dates or other facts which aren't called for on the family group sheets, note them on a blank area of the sheet.

Include notes for conflicting or especially interesting information. They may provide clues for future research. Write legibly and record information as accurately as you can, taking care to enter the spelling as it is listed in various records. (If it is spelled differently in different records, note that fact somewhere on your group sheet.)

Put your name down as the recorder of the chart; include your address and phone number so someone viewing your chart later can contact you for information.

Arrange the completed sheets in logical order in file folders (see management systems, Chapter 9); use them as living documents which you take with you as you do your research. Update them as needed.

**• RESEARCH AND CORRESPONDENCE LOGS.** It's also important that you record your sources—including sources that didn't reveal the information you were looking for. Many genealogists log their research on a special form for just that reason. It helps them avoid going through the same record twice, when it has already been searched (regardless of the results).

Note, however, that sometimes a second or third look at a record can be fruitful, yielding information you may have missed the first times.

You may wish to start a research calendar for each surname you're researching, to be filed in the proper family folder (or notebook).

It's also advisable to keep a record of letters you've written to various sources for information. Such a record should contain the date you sent your request, to whom it was written, what you requested, the date you received a reply, and the results (whether positive or negative).

We've included samples of both the research calendar and a correspondence log in the appendix of this book that you can copy and use as a worksheet.

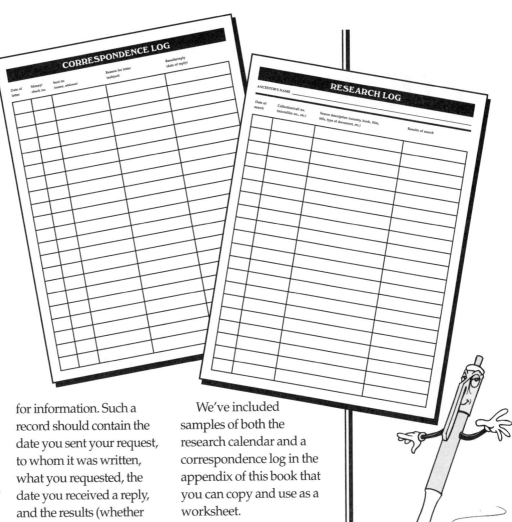

# Determining relationships

The next step to opening your genealogy gateway is to figure out how the names you've collected might be related—to you and to each other.

Records ranging from home sources to birth, marriage, and death certificates, and from newspaper clippings to Bible entries, can help you pinpoint connections between relatives. Census records are another excellent "connection" record, with parents listed first, followed by their children. Using the census, you may be able to fill out family group sheets on entire families.

Church records show connections between parents and children, with grandparents sometimes being listed, as well. Sponsors at christenings were often relatives.

If you can't figure out a family connection to a certain name, but are sure it's a relative, ask older relatives for help. Perhaps they can remember how the person fits into your family tree.

If you aren't sure whether the person is your "first cousin thrice removed" or your "third cousin," turn to the relationship chart in the Appendix, forms section. Follow the instructions on the chart to figure out just how you're related.

Once you have determined the connections, plug your collection of names into your pedigree charts and family group sheets. This will help you to better visualize the relationship and see at a glance what information you still need to collect.

Filling out group sheets with names and birth dates of family members you've already found can help you

## Charting your ancestors

• A pedigree chart forms the skeleton of your family, with you as the trunk and your ancestors as the branches.

• A family group sheet allows you to fill in the details on each family. The group sheet has three purposes: to allow you to organize data on your family, to serve as a guide for gathering further information, and to allow for easy exchange with others who are interested in the same lines. •

# Form your own FORMS!

You can devise your own customized forms for specific research.

For example, if you have Norwegian ancestors, create a form for each ancestor you are researching. At the top, leave a space for your ancestor's name. Beneath that, form columns for dates, places, and sources (such as LDS microfilm number, church parish book, bygdebok, etc.) of the following events: births, baptisms, confirmations, vaccinations (yes, the Lutheran church in Norway recorded this information!), marriage banns, marriages (leave several blanks here, as it wasn't unusual for people to lose their spouse and remarry), death, age at death, cause of death, and burial.

You could also develop customized forms for recording physical descriptions and health statistics about your ancestors—such as height, weight, color of hair and eyes, state of health while living, any known disabilities, defects or ailments, age at death, cause of death, etc. This could be a valuable tool for tracing genetic characteristics and health tendencies in your own family.

Some forms have already been customized for your convenience. For example, you can get forms for censuses ranging from 1800 to 1930 at any research sites (such as the State Archives libraries and LDS Family History Centers) and at mail-order genealogy supply houses. You'll find samples of customized census forms in the appendix of this book.

Meanwhile, think of ways to devise your own forms, based on your own specific research interests. ●

## NORWEGIAN PARISH REGISTER INFORMATION

Microfilm no. _____
Parish name: _____

Name: _____

Father's name: _____

Mother's name: _____

|  | DATE | PLACE |
|---|---|---|
| Birth | | |
| Baptism | | |
| Confirmation | | |
| Vaccinations | | |
| Marr. banns | | |
| Marriage #1 | | |
| Marriage #2 | | |
| Death | | |
| Burial | | |

## NORTH DAKOTA DEATH INDEX DATABASE

Located at the North Dakota State Archives and Historical Research Library, Bismarck; available online at https://secure.apps.state.nd.us/doh/certificates/deathCertSearch.htm

LAST NAME _____
First name _____
Alias _____
Date of birth _____
Date of death _____
Age _____ Sex _____
Resident (state, county) _____
County of death _____

## ANCESTORS' DEATH DATES/CAUSES OF DEATH

Name: _____

| | B/date: | D/date: | Age: | Cause of death: |
|---|---|---|---|---|

determine whether there might be missing persons. If, for example, there was a gap of four or five years between children on your chart, there may have been a child who died.

In our ancestors' day, the "norm" was to have children spaced about two years apart. It was not unusual for families to have many children, with a high infant mortality.

If a gap of longer than several years exists, check the death registry or church burial records to see whether the family might have lost a child at birth or in infancy or early childhood. ●

# Records: Good news and

John Henry

## Where did Grandpa sign his name?

- Ask yourself, "What records might Grandpa have been listed on during his lifetime (i.e., homestead papers, military service, occupation, school, etc.)?"

Investigate those sources for Grandpa's history information. •

So you've filled out your pedigree chart, and you've come to a halt about three generations back. You're stuck on when your great-grandfather was born and who his parents were. You've checked with relatives, and they couldn't supply any answers.

How do you fill in these and other gaps in your knowledge of your ancestors? The answer is, you need to find official records that contain bits and pieces of this information. Bit by bit, you add more evidence until you prove your ancestry.

There's both good and bad news when it comes to records. First, we'll give you the good news!

Many of these records are available right here in the Dakotas—many right in your community. Many, in fact, can be found right in your own home!

There's more good news. Thanks to technology, records are more accessible than ever. The Internet can bring many of these records right into your home. Records from all around the world are being extracted and microfilmed so they'll be available for genealogy purposes.

Interlibrary loan can deliver genealogy books, microfilms, and manuscripts right to your doorstep. Thanks to this outstanding library service,

lendable materials housed at libraries around the country can be ordered through your local library (or state library) and mailed either to your library (where you pick up your order) or directly to your home. You then return the materials when they become due.

Before we take you into specific records in this chapter, we want you to know what to expect from the records you're seeking. Where these records can be found will be covered on the pages that follow, as well as in our chapter on research facilities.

## Records realities

Before you branch out in your quest for records, you need to be aware of what rights you have to access those records.

A particular frustration for those seeking information on their family has been that the records on even immediate relatives aren't always accessible to the seeker.

And the degree of cooperation one receives at courthouses, land offices, and other places where public records are housed—and indeed, the quality of the search—varies with the person behind the counter.

The policy of each state (keeper of the vital records of its citizens) varies, as well. Some (like South Dakota) have limited pub-

lic access to such records. Others (like North Dakota) have open-records laws in place that, theoretically, enable authorized persons (such as relatives and genealogy researchers) to access the records.

"Open access," however, does not necessarily mean that you can physically search for, or view, the actual records yourself.

In cases of vital records (detailed later in this chapter), you have to fill out a request form with statistics on the relative whose record you're seeking. The staff in vital records will then search for the record based on information you provide on the form.

That means you need to do your homework before you request records. Usually, you need to supply the name of the person you're seeking and, depending on the record, many of his or her basic statistics.

At other records repositories ranging from courthouses to churches, the staff will generally perform the searches. In rare instances, you will be allowed the freedom to look through the actual records yourself. Such searches are apt to be the most productive.

Here's the really bad news: In some cases, records may be inaccessible—either because of damage by fires or floods, through careless loss of such things as cemetery ledgers or church parish books, or because officials represent-

# bad news...

ing businesses, institutions, government, organizations, or churches are purging older records to make room for more recent ones.

In other cases, records may be in poor shape—documents improperly stored and subject to deterioration, manuscripts crumbly or musty, microfilming quality poor, photos or books water- or ink-stained, pages torn or missing, documents hard to find or misfiled entirely, books lacking a proper index, etc. All of this can be frustrating for someone intent on finding his/her family history.

Despite occasional disappointments such as these, the rewards of finding your family information will be worth it!

## Arm yourself with info

As you've already learned, the key items you'll be checking for are names, dates, and places of key events in the lives of family members.

In order to search records for a name, you need to know a date (or estimated time frame) and place (location—in many cases, the parish) the person came from, so you know where to concentrate your search.

Knowing what parish Great-grandma came from, for instance, can lead to the discovery of her data and that of other generations of family members in the church records—which often served as vital records in the olden days.

A golden rule among genealogy researchers is to use courtesy when requesting records. You'll find that people in charge of handling records will be a lot

## Name quest

Can't find your ancestor's record? Ask yourself these questions:

• How would the first letter of the name be written in script? How does it look with penmanship variations? How might the name be misspelled by someone recording the name? How might the pronunciation be misinterpreted? How might the regional accent affect the position of the name in an alphabetical listing? •

---

# Primary vs. secondary records

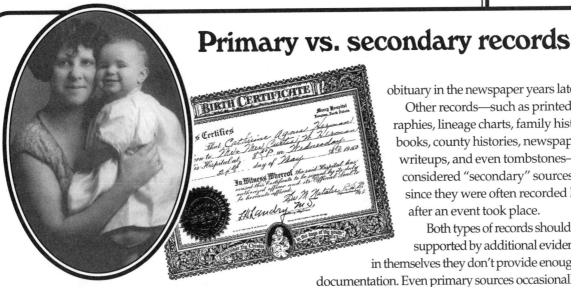

**A**s your collection of genealogy records grows, you're bound to find discrepancies and conflicting information. Which records should you trust?

Some records provide more reliable evidence than do others. These sources are known as "primary" records. Original sources—such as vital records documenting births, marriages, and deaths—are considered primary records for genealogists.

The general rule is, data recorded closest to the event is most apt to be accurate. For example, a birth certificate, recorded shortly after an ancestor was born, is more likely to contain correct birth data than is his/her

obituary in the newspaper years later.

Other records—such as printed biographies, lineage charts, family history books, county histories, newspaper writeups, and even tombstones—are considered "secondary" sources, since they were often recorded long after an event took place.

Both types of records should be supported by additional evidence, as in themselves they don't provide enough documentation. Even primary sources occasionally contain errors.

"Don't panic at the thought of a possible inaccuracy on an official document," says "Tracing Your Ancestry: A Step-by-Step Guide to Researching Your Family History" author F. Wilbur Helmbold.

"Just keep taking down all records from all sources, and these discrepancies of fact will be resolved."

It's important that you get copies of original documents and records whenever possible.

When you can't get copies at all, make sure that you write down accurately and legibly the information contained in the record. Or use a closeup camera and photograph the entry yourself. •

# One man's trash...

more cooperative if you're friendly and patient, as well as businesslike.

## Be prepared

Perhaps the most important rule of etiquette when visiting a repository to search for family data is to "be prepared." Arm yourself first with a concise list of the information you're seeking and be ready to furnish as much background information on the individual you're searching as may be required to obtain the record.

This is where your filled-out pedigree charts and family group sheets can come in handy: Take them with you when you visit the records repository, so you can refer to them for information and can see at a glance what information you need.

Most likely, however, you won't be visiting the repository in person. You'll probably do a lot of your record searching with the help of the U.S. Postal Serv-

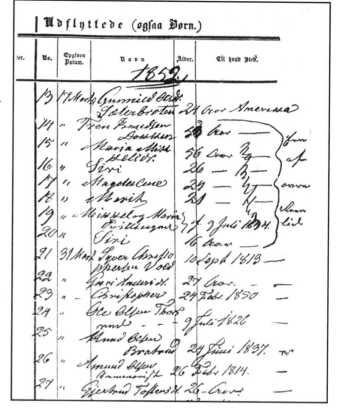

These Norwegian church records from 1852 show some common problems encountered in reading old records: The handwriting is often hard to decipher (due to both style and penmanship), and the printed material at the top is in Old German script. The heading "udflyttede" refers to the "outgoing" parishioners who were leaving the parish and heading for (in this case) America.

• • • • • • • • • • • • • • • • • • • • • • • • • •

ice. Your letter needs to make a good first impression on the person receiving it. For tips on writing to records repositories, see the sidebar on the next page.

You'll also be turning to the telephone—and possibly the Internet—for information. For ideas on reducing your phone bill, check out the sidebar on page 25.

## Name game

Don't expect your name to have retained the same spelling for many generations. The same family could have had different spellings of a name—or two brothers might have totally different surnames! Many times, beginning

researchers are not tuned in to spelling changes (or the fact names were—and still are—misspelled in records and indexes), and they may pass over their ancestors' information as a result.

In earlier times, it was not unusual to find two children in the same family with the same first name— Big Ole and Little Ole, for example. This was especially true in the patronymic naming system, where children were named for grandparents in a rigid order. (See details in Chapter 1.)

Sometimes when a child died, another child might receive the deceased child's given name.

As a general rule, the

## 'Nee' names hold clues

- When you look for names, don't just focus on your male lines or surname; always check your maternal lines, as well. You'll be missing half of your history if you don't!
- Record females on your family tree by their given (first and middle) and maiden names.
- In cases of divorce, the woman may have taken back her maiden name or the surname of her first husband. While divorce was not commonplace in earlier years, it did happen, and you need to be aware of possibilities for name changes. •

USE MAIDEN NAMES, PLEASE!

# How to send letters that get results!

Here are some rules to make sure your correspondence yields a harvest of family history data:

• Use a clean, standard-sized sheet of paper; write or print legibly, or type or use a word processor.

• Make sure your grammar and spelling are correct. (Have someone proof it if necessary.)

• Be sure you are sending your request to the proper place. Know the holdings of the specific records depository you're querying (which varies from state to state), as well as the time span of the records it holds.

• Include your name, complete address, and telephone number (or e-mail address) at the top of the letter.

• Be precise about what it is you want to receive back (i.e., birth certificate, land record, or probate packet containing your ancestor's will). Your request should be specific and easy to understand.

• Don't overwhelm with lots of requests in one letter or a request for "everything you have on John Jones." Be concise and get to the point.

• Include as much pertinent information as you can about the person whose record you're requesting, including dates and spelling variations of the name. (You may have to include, for example, an obituary on the person, if it contains crucial information that can aid in the search.)

• When a date or other specific statistic is unknown, include a range of dates (ca. 1925-1930, for example) in which the event likely took place.

• Request an alternative in the event the record cannot be located.

This might include a photocopy of the petition of administration and/or administration bond should the will you're seeking be nonexistent.

• If you know the charge for the search and photocopying work, send a check for that amount along with your query. If you're unsure of a charge, you can send an initial check and offer to send a second check if the charge is greater. If you're concerned about the possible expenses that might be involved, request a quote of the price of the search and photocopies before you give the go-ahead for the search. (Of course, never send cash!)

• Enclose a long, self-addressed, stamped envelope (with abundant postage and plenty of room for photocopies of documents).

• If sending your request overseas, check with your local post office for international reply coupons to enclose in lieu of stamps. •

---

less common the name you're seeking, the easier it is to trace. (Sorry, Don Smith and Anne Olson!) Yet information can be found on ancestors with common names, too; it just takes more reliance on the other two keys—dates and places—plus other substantiating records to pinpoint which Smith or Olson may have been your ancestor.

We heard of one case where someone claimed a certain Ole Olson (out of thousands) in his family history book—only to find out after the book was printed that he had claimed the wrong Ole!

Don't let that happen to you. Do careful research first—so you're sure you are claiming the right ancestors!

## Alphabet soup

When looking through lists of names (or any data, for that matter), you may encounter German (or Gothic) script, Old English (or Old German), Greek or Arabic or, in the case of Ukrainians and others from Russia, cyrillic writing. All can be a struggle to read, unless you've studied samples of how the letters are formed.

Records written in any of these styles or alphabets are a lot harder to read and, thus, more prone to misintrepretation—by you as you scan the records or by those who have copied the records into the alphabetical listings you're scouring.

Generally, the older the record, the harder it is to decipher—because of the old-style script and antique print fonts.

Study the characteristics of the handwritten scripts and a range of samples from the era or area you're researching. If you're studying a church book and the minister's handwriting is barely readable, photocopy multiple pages of the book and study those copies until you're more familiar with the pastor's penmanship.

Study the alphabet used by the ethnic group whose records you're seeking. For example, the Norwegian alphabet contains three extra letters: "æ" (pronounced "a" as in "cat"), "ø" ("u" as in "hurt"), and "å" (or "aa," pronounced "aw" as in "jaw"). If a surname begins with these letters, you will find it at the end of

**A good dictionary is a must when studying foreign language records.**

# Get duplicates of originals!

It's important that you get photocopies of original documents and records whenever possible. In cases where you can't get photocopies, make sure you write down—accurately and legibly—all of the information the record contains. Or bring your closeup (or digital) camera along and photograph the records yourself. •

# Tree tips

The following suggestions are courtesy of Ethel Eckroth, Mandan, long-time genealogist (now deceased):

• If you're not having luck with a line you're researching, put it on hold for a few months and concentrate on another line. When you come back to the one you were stuck on, you'll find you often have fresh ideas that can lead you to success.

• Bring your notebook with you when you research. Jot down what records you're searching and the results of your search. Otherwise, months or years later, you'll be asking yourself, "Where did I get this record?"

• Dealing with a record, letter or manuscript written in another language or script? Check around for a translator, rather than wasting time trying to decipher it yourself. If the item is in German, for example, you might try contacting the German language teacher at your local high school. •

the alphabetical listing in Norwegian records, following the "z."

What happened when a person whose name began with such letters immigrated to America—where no such letters existed?

The spelling of the name would be changed to conform to the English alphabet. The new name was likely spelled phonetically or the foreign letter dropped and written as "o," "a," or "e."

Be aware of that when searching for names in alphabetical listings—or when trying to learn how the name may have been spelled in Norwegian records.

If you're studying records dating back a century or more, you'll likely run into the use of the "leading s." In cases where a double "s" was used, our ancestors used a regular "s," preceded by a character that looked like a backward "f." This first "s" was referred to as the "leading s." You'll find this character in both script and printed materials of the time. Often, this "s" is mistaken for an "f."

# Phonics 'fun'

When searching records, go not only by the first letter, but by how the name may have sounded to the ear of a census-taker or other recorder of data—or even how it looked when written in script.

Think, "How might the name have been misinterpreted, misspelled, or misfiled?"

If the first letter is misspelled, of course, it will not be in the alphabetical position you're expecting. And since the first letter is key to any alphabetical listing, having something filed by the wrong first letter can bring your search to a screeching halt.

When researching the name "Temanson," for example, we found the scripted "T" had been mistaken for an "S." It was interpreted as "Semanson" and misfiled under "S."

If you are certain a record should exist in the location you're searching and you can't find it, ask yourself, "How would this look written in longhand? What letter(s) might it resemble and possibly be mistaken for?"

As in the example just given (Semanson versus Temanson), "S" and "T" can be confused in script. Likewise, "F" and T" in script could be mistaken for one another, as can "M," "N," and "W," or a handwritten "L" and a capital "T" or "S."

To the English-speaker's ears, our ancestors' foreign-sounding names had strange combinations of letters, not pronounced the way we would say them at all. Some examples of Norwegian letter combinations are Kj-, Kv-, Hv-, Hj-, Sj-, Skj-, and Gj-.

Sometimes our ancestors changed their names to make the pronunciation easier. For example, Sjurud ("sju" meant "seven" in Norwegian) might be changed to Syvrud ("syv" also means "seven") or Shurud (a phonetic spelling of Sjurud); the farm name Kvernum might change to Vernum or even Vernon.

If your surname was changed to Vernon, you might not recognize Kvernum as your surname when searching Norwegian records. You might, in fact, not search the "K's" at all, assuming your family surname began with "V."

Recorders of our ancestors' data must have found it tough to get used to the idea that, in German, "ei" was pronounced as a long "i," and "ie" was pronounced "ee."

Because of this, some German immigrants changed the spelling of their name to comply with the Yankee pronunciation. (Some Feists that we know of, for example, converted their spelling to "Fiest" to avoid mispronunciation.)

A few German letters sounded similar in the German dialect. They included B/P (Pence, for example, may have started off as "Bentz"), B/V (Silbernagel versus Silvernagel), G/K (Nagel versus Nickle), D/T, V/F, C/G, etc.

## Consider the accent

Along with pronunciation variations, regional accents also influenced how someone may have recorded (or filed) a name in a record.

Here's a real-life example: In one early American record, the name "Eliza" was written as it sounded to the ears of the Southern recorder: "Alahzah."

Some names changed because they were awkward to pronounce, as well as spell.

A personal example: At least one branch of the Winistorfers changed the name to "Winters."

## • Relative terms •

• You can't necessarily rely on the relationship terms you come across in wills and other old documents. Being aware of such title tribulations can help keep you from tripping over your own roots!

• When you spy the word "nephew" or "cousin" in early wills or deeds, for example, you can't assume that the terms signify the standard relationships. According to Harriet Stryker-Rodd, author of "How to Climb Your Family Tree: Genealogy for Beginners," the word "nephew" sometimes meant "grandson"; in fact, it originates from the Latin word "nepos" meaning "grandson." The term "cousin," Stryker-Rodd continues, "very often meant any blood relative." The word "in-law" could refer to stepchildren. "Sister" or "brother" did not necessarily mean a blood sibling, as these terms were applied loosely in old records.

• In "Tracing Your Ancestry: A Step-by-Step Guide to Researching Your Family History," author F. Wilbur Helmbold defines the term "my now wife" found in wills to mean a person's present wife, as opposed to anyone the will-drafter might wed following the "now wife's" death. In 17th century documents, "Mr." and "Mrs." strictly meant persons of the landed gentry, schoolmasters, ministers, and men whose official position gave them the right to use this distinguished title. "Mrs." referred to either married and unmarried women in such families. The terms "Goodman" and "Goodwife," according to Helmbold, denoted "persons of substance," but not the landed class or high-ranking officials. •

## Nicknames and initials

The three-name system is a relatively recent development. Older records may contain no middle names.

When researching first names, tune to the fact that sometimes first and middle names (or middle initials) might be switched around from the order you're

expecting to find.

"T. Scott Hanson" or "Thomas Scott Hanson," for instance, might have been listed as "Scott Thomas Hanson" on a birth certificate. Nicknames may also have been used.

In early American records, watch for abbreviations such as "Thos." for Thomas and "Geo." for George. •

## Cutting down on expenses

From the cost of stamps and photocopies, to phone calls and trips to courthouses, libraries, and the hometowns (or countries) of your ancestors; from file folders, cabinets, and storage notebooks to computer programs, how-to books, and workshops, genealogy expenses add up.

The amount you spend goes up proportionately with how deeply you dig and how much effort you

expend to collect information. To get a realistic picture of these costs, you may wish to start an account book to track your expenditures. Any costs will have to be measured against the rewards of finding family history information.

Writing letters is probably the most economical of all data-collection methods, saving you the cost of a trip to the repository holding the record you're seeking.

You can cut down on postage costs by investing in a postage scale, buying stamps in smaller denomina-

tions (so a $1.11 letter doesn't cost you three 39-cent stamps, for instance). Call the post office's toll-free number for postal rates.

Many long-distance providers have cheaper rates on weekends. This won't help you if you're calling a courthouse or library that's open weekdays. Cell phone plans, however, offer rates based on minutes used.

Before you make your call, write down your request(s) and have material close by in case you need to provide more information during your call. •

# There's no place like home

## One person's treasure...

- When searching through family records and papers, be alert for any clues that might lead you to further information. Even items that might appear insignificant at first sight may prove to be valuable for future research. •

Where do you begin your search for names, dates and places to record on your worksheets?

As Dorothy said upon winding up her visit to Oz, "There's no place like home."

For openers, go on a scavenger hunt in your own home.

Bill Linder, writing in "Discover Your Roots: How to Trace Your Family History," suggests you search the following for possible clues:

Diaries, letters, scrapbooks, backs of photos, insides of old books (for inscriptions or tucked-away items such as notes), certificates (birth, marriage, death, military, school, church, etc.), wedding books, baby books, funeral books and cards, school yearbooks, account books, business and financial papers, announcements and invitations

(birth, wedding, graduation), newspaper clippings, autograph books, and family artifacts (such as names on quilts or engraved on backs or bottoms of items).

"Squeeze all the information you can out of your home sources first," Linder writes.

"Rummage through the house for more information," says William G. Hartley in "The Everything Family Tree Book: Finding, Charting and Preserving Your Family History."

Hartley suggests places to look for records: scrapbooks, photo albums, closets, drawers, attics, basements, and garages—anyplace where items containing family history information might be lurking.

Rather than searching for these artifacts yourself, take a parent, a grandparent, or other elderly relative (such as an uncle or aunt) with you as you rummage through old trunks and boxes in the attic.

Better yet, make this a multi-generation project! Invite your children to join in this "voyage of discovery," as well; it will help stimulate their interest in family history.

Bring your tape recorder along as you rummage, suggest Christine Rose and Kay Germain Ingalls, authors of "The Complete Idiot's Guide to Genealogy." That way, you can record comments an elderly relative or children make about items uncovered

during your search.

"Record descriptions and ask questions regarding the objects," the authors recommend. "The little doll—who owned it? ...the little toy soldiers at the bottom of the trunk; they are sure to stir memories of the little boys who played with them endlessly. Who were they?"

These objects have tales to tell, according to the authors. They can also trigger memories that can lead to further genealogy information.

Keep digging, they say, and you may find old family treasures—such things as "old letters with a ribbon carefully tied around them... you open them and read in amazement. There is a letter from Great-grandpa, written in 1889..."

Take your camera with you so you can snap photos of artifacts and memorabilia you may unearth.

## Branching out

After you're done searching your own, your parents' and your grandparents' attics, contact other relatives to find out what kinds of family records they might have in their homes that might aid you in your research.

Ask whether they know of any family members who are collecting family information, or who may have documents such as birth, marriage, and death certificates; naturalization papers; deeds; etc.

Ask, too, who might

## Check those checks!

- I could have tossed my deceased pack-rat dad's old cancelled checks from the late 1930s. Instead, I went through them and found the check written by Daddy to pay for my mother's wedding ring, money paid to a hired girl who helped Mom with housework for several weeks after I, a newborn, came home from the hospital, even a check written to a farmer for goat's milk when my baby brother was allergic to cow's milk. Some of the checks reinforced items in my father's diary—complaints about having to pay for car repairs, treating himself to a new camera, buying Christmas gifts from the Sears catalog. What memories those old checks brought back!
                                                            —J.W.

# for finding family history

have old photographs of family members.

Get names, addresses, and phone numbers so you can contact these people to find out what data they may have.

Arrange for a visit and, again, take your camera with you.

If you're lucky, you may have a pack rat in your family who has kept old family mementos. Their old boxes and trunks could yield a bonanza of family history treasures.

Check to see if you can make photocopies of (or photograph) some of these items, or whether the person would be willing to part with any of it and place it in your care someday.

If relatives know you would welcome such material, they may donate it to you instead of tossing it in the junkpile or giving it to other kinfolk who have no interest in it.

When asked, your relative may say, "I don't have anything that would help." If this is their response, you may have to work to convince them of the value of the material they have tucked away.

Home sources can also include older relatives whose "living history" memories you can capture for future generations of your family. (For details on interview tactics, along with questions that bring forth meaningful answers, check out Chapter 5.)

When you've finished compiling and filing the data you dug up in your scavenger hunts, add names, dates, and places you've gleaned via your search to your pedigree and family group sheets.

Record, too, the sources of your information—whether from a newspaper clipping on your grandparents' 50th anniversary or an old family Bible.

Now you're ready to go ancestor-hunting in the many records available in the Dakotas and elsewhere. •

# Home of the clues

Check your home for the following sources. They could yield clues that will help you get to the "root" of your genealogy problem.

- Address books
- Announcements of births, marriages, graduations, etc.
- Baby books
- Bible records
- Books (with notations or items tucked inside)
- Awards, certificates, medals; plaques from occupations, organizations, military
- Checkbooks, account books, financial ledgers, bank statements, etc.
- Christmas cards, valentines, birthday cards
- Christmas card lists
- Church-related certificates (including marriage, baptism, and confirmation)
- Cookbooks, old recipes
- County history books
- Deeds, abstracts, or other land records
- Diaries and journals
- Drivers' licenses
- Engraved jewelry
- Family traditions
- Funeral cards
- Funeral memorial books
- Immigration records
- Insurance papers
- Letters
- Medical reports; letters from doctors
- Military certificates and records
- Monogrammed linens
- Newspaper clippings
- Passbook savings books
- Photographs
- Photo albums
- Postcards
- Receipts for special items
- School yearbooks, report cards, diplomas, school memorabilia
- Scrapbooks
- Social security records
- Souvenirs
- Vital records certificates (births, marriages, divorce, death)
- Wills •

# Vital records: Primary

## Vital records provide framework of a life

- "What we learn from the vital records of a person's days on this earth provides the framework for our search for other records that may illuminate his life and times and tell us who he was. The end of a life marks the beginning of our research." •

—RootsWeb's guide to tracing family trees, available via the Internet.

Four milestone events in a person's life—birth, marriage, divorce, and death—are the foundation of genealogical research.

Officially recorded soon after the event took place, these items are considered primary records, providing the strongest evidence that the event took place.

Here are the vital documents to collect and what you're likely to find there:

- **Birth certificates:** Name, date, and place of birth; parents' names (including mother's maiden name), ages, residence, and occupation
- **Marriage licenses:** Ages and places of birth of couple, names of parents
- **Divorce records:** Names of divorced couple, information dealing with custody of children, and property distribution
- **Death records:** Name, date, and place of death; age; state or country of birth; occupation; name and residence of informant; date and place of burial; cause of death; parents' names and places of birth

To reduce the chance of error, check for original vital records (rather than indexes or transcriptions), then secure photocopies of the original record.

Remember, however, that although considered primary, even vital records may contain errors.

## Different strokes

In the Dakotas and neighboring states, the state health departments hold most birth and death records, plus (depending on the state) many marriage and divorce records. For addresses of vital records repositories in North and South Dakota, see Helpful Addresses and Websites in the appendix. See also our research sites chapter.

While individual counties in the Dakotas vary as to what year they began keeping records and what records they hold, in general, the county courthouse where the event took place contains the early marriage and divorce records.

Following are resources available at the vital records departments of both Dakotas, Montana, and Minnesota. Note, however, that a search does not always yield a certificate.

- **North Dakota.** On 1 July 1893, the first law requiring registration of births and deaths in North Dakota was passed. Repealed in 1895, it was re-enacted in 1899. Until 1923, however, compliance was sporadic. After that date, registration was more complete. A few births and deaths filed with the vital records division, however, date back to 1873.

The state began collecting fetal and stillborn records in 1924. Marriage certificates start in July 1925. Earlier marriage (and all

divorce) records are kept in the courthouse of the county where the marriage or divorce took place.

Certified copies of birth and death registrations can be purchased at the State Health Department's vital records division. Cost of a birth-record search (and, if found, a subsequent certified copy) is $7. Marriage and death records cost $5 each.

- **South Dakota.** In South Dakota, county register of deeds offices are authorized to issue certificates for births (from 1921 on), marriages, divorces, and deaths that took place within their jurisdictions. A computerized index is being set up to facilitate requests.

Statewide, the South Dakota Department of Health, Data, Statistics, and Vital Records Unit has jurisdiction over all vital records. To order a certified copy of a birth, marriage, divorce, or death record, send $10 per certificate to: Vital Records, South Dakota Department of Health, 600 E. Capitol, Pierre, SD 57501-2536. (See forms section of appendix for further information.)

If you're looking for a South Dakota birth, marriage, or death record before July 1905 (the date the state vital records system officially began), check the courthouse of the county in which the original event took place. Generally, they are available from the time the county started keeping records.

Information on births that took place more than 100 years ago (1899 or

**PROVIDE BACKGROUND INFORMATION**
- When writing for vital records, provide as much background information as you can. For births, list name of person, date and place of birth, and parents' names—including father's name and mother's maiden name. For marriages or deaths, send name of person (or couple) and date and place of death or marriage.
- For all records, give the purpose of your search and identify your relationship to the person whose records you're requesting. •

# sources of information

earlier, as of this writing) can be accessed through the State Archives at Pierre. Nearly 80,000 records are currently in this searchable database. To search the site online, go to this address: www. state.sd.us/doh/vitalrec/birthrecords/index.cfm.

• **Montana.** Birth and death registration in Montana began in 1907. By about 1920, most counties were complying with the law to send information to the state office. Marriage and divorces from 1943 are also housed there.

In general, Montana researchers should check the county courthouse records in the area where their ancestors lived, before writing to the state. Those requesting birth certificates must send a photocopy of their photo ID, along with their signature and $12 per record search.

• **Nebraska.** Nebraska's Bureau of Vital Statistics began collecting birth and death records in 1904, marriage and divorce

records in 1909. Prior to those dates, records were kept in district courts. Copies of Nebraska birth certificates cost $8; marriage, divorce, and death certificates are $7 each.

• **Minnesota.** Files of Minnesota's Department of Health contain birth records from 1900 and death records since 1908 for the entire state. Older records are filed with the court administrator or county recorder in the county of the event. Copies of birth records cost $16 each; death records, $13 each. Early Minnesota death records can be accessed at the Minnesota Historical Society. The 1900-07 death records are on 62 rolls of microfilm; the 1908-16 records are being microfilmed and will be available to researchers in the near future.

• **Canada.** In Canada, each province has its own vital records office. The marriage certificates contain a lot of family history; cause of death is blacked out on the death certificates.

## Other aids

"The Handy Book for Genealogists, 11th Edition," edited by George B. Everton Sr. , lists the history of counties across the United States, telling when they began keeping their records.

The LDS Family History Center is another place to check for vital (and other) records.

A U.S. Department of Health and Human Services publication titled "Where to Write for Vital Records" (135F) is available for $4.25 from the Superintendent of Documents. Send check to: R.W. CIC-9C, P.O. Box 100, Pueblo, CO 81002-0100.

Finally, visit this Website for information: www.vitalrec.com. •

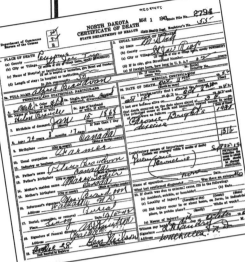

## 'Back door' searches

Can't get the vital records you need? Here are some "back doors" you can open to obtain the same data or at least narrow your search. (These resources can also help you get information you need to provide to obtain vital records.)

• Check with the county courthouse (clerk of court) to see whether county or township records exist for the families you're researching.

• Funeral homes kept death certificates. You may be able to obtain such a certificate from the mortician who handled funeral arrangements.

• Check the newspaper for a birth announcement, marriage item, or obituary.

• In North Dakota, check the computerized death, marriage, and divorce indexes. You'll find them at the State Archives and Historical Research Library, located in the State Heritage Center, Capitol Grounds, Bismarck. This may provide you with a date to aid you in searching for death records.

• Church records often parallel the basic life events of births (christenings), marriages, and deaths (funerals) and, thus, are valuable genealogy research tools. In some countries, these records are considered primary records. •

## Pioneer pastor kept diary

- A diary kept by a pioneer North Dakota pastor who made his rounds by horse and buggy could be a gold mine for genealogists with roots in Burke and Divide counties.

Valborg Zander of Bismarck inherited the detailed journal kept by her father, Adolf Buckneberg, a Lutheran pastor who served the Norwegian Synod Lutheran Church in rural Flaxton, N.D., in the early 20th century. His diary runs from 1905, when he arrived at Flaxton, through World War I and the Spanish flu epidemic, to the Dirty Thirties. It ends in 1938, the year of his death. Valborg has since translated and indexed the diary, a job that took five years. For anyone with ancestors who may have been part of this congregation, there's "an awful lot of genealogy in it," says Valborg.

If you think your family might be listed in "Dad's Book," write or call: Valborg Zander, 1822 N. Fourth St., Bismarck, ND 58501; 701-255-3438. She'll check the index. •

# Church records followed

"What church did my ancestors attend?" Knowing the answer to that question can lead you to church records.

While not considered primary records, church records can help you fill in gaps or back up data you may already have. Church affiliation is thus an important clue to your heritage.

Over the centuries, religious bodies have kept records on their members' participation in church rites and ordinances. These records can help you fill in information about entire families, especially if they were in a congregation for a number of years. This applies not only to U.S. records, but records in foreign countries, as well.

In some countries (such as Norway and Sweden), the churches were the official recordkeepers, with church books recording everything from vaccinations (Norway) to the population census (Sweden).

"Church records are generally of such potential value that you should understand how to use them," writes F. Wilbur Helmbold in "Tracing Your Ancestry: A Step-by-step Guide to Researching Your Family History."

Helmbold suggests that, in the absence of direct entries, one should "search by date, era, or names of related persons or siblings" to obtain information.

Christening entries usually contain birth dates, as well as the names of par-

ents and witnesses. (The witnesses often turn out to be relatives, by the way!) There are also (depending on the church) communion or confirmation records, including dates and names of parents. Marriage information usually includes parents' and witnesses' names, too. Death entries include death date, burial date and place, and often, the spouse's name.

There may also be entries of new families into a congregation (listing the parish they came from) or families leaving a congregation, including their intended destination. This can help you determine former or future residence.

## Locating the records

When it comes to church records, we Dakotans may have an advantage over a lot of other genealogy researchers in this country: Much of our population is either Catholic or Lutheran. Both groups kept good to excellent records on their parishioners. Not all religions placed such emphasis on keeping track of their congregations.

The Episcopal church, author Helmbold says, "kept meticulous church records," as did Quakers and Moravians.

Baptist and Methodist church books usually lack vital records information, although some pastors did enter christening and marriage dates. Membership

rolls and church minutes, however, sometimes provide family information.

See Chapter 3, research sites, for information on where to obtain Episcopal, Evangelical, Reformed, and United Church of Christ records in North and South Dakota. The Seventh Day Adventist regional headquarters is located in Pierre, SD.

The two Catholic dioceses that oversee North Dakota are located in Bismarck (which serves western North Dakota, including the Minot area) and Fargo (serving parishes in the eastern half of the state). The diocese for the entire state of South Dakota is located in Sioux Falls. (See appendix, Chapter 2 section, for addresses.)

To order microfilms of most Lutheran church parish records, contact the Archives of the Evangelical Lutheran Church in America, 321 Bonnie Lane, Elk Grove Village, IL 60007; 800-638-3522, or 773-380-2700. The Web address is www.elca.org. Included are Norwegian Lutheran Church records.

The Lutheran Church-Missouri Synod (1333 S. Kirkwood Road, St. Louis, MO 63122) has done some microfilming, too. Visit them at www.lcms.org.

The Swenson Swedish Immigration Research Center has the following Swedish-American church records on microfilm: Augustana Lutheran, Mission, Covenant, Evangelical Free, Swedish Metho-

# family through life

dist, and Swedish Baptist. The center also has available for sale microfiche records of Swedish parish books.

To contact the center, write to: Swenson Swedish Immigration Research Center, Augustana College, 639 38th St., Rock Island, IL 61201-2296; or call 309-794-7204. Or visit this Website: www.augustana.edu/administration/swenson.

Gustavus Adolphus College in St. Peter, MN, and the American Swedish Institute in Minneapolis, MN (see ethnic roots, Chapter 4), also have Swedish church records in their collections.

## Be prepared

Before you order microfilms of your ancestor's parish registers, you'll need to determine the name of the parish and the span of years covering your search (since you'll probably want to follow the family through all of the books that apply).

Keep in mind that earlier records are often harder to read because of inconsistent format and poor or old-style handwriting. Events were recorded chronologically and are not indexed.

An alternative is to go directly to the church and check the original books. To avoid copying errors, ask for a photocopy of the original record.

Unfortunately, many old rural parish records have been lost or were passed on to another parish when the old church closed its doors or merged with another.

Archives in North and South Dakota also have some parish registers on microfilm. For example, Chester Fritz Library's Department of Special Collections (North Dakota State University, Grand Forks) has a vast microfilmed collection of American Lutheran parishes in North Dakota and Min-

nesota. Many of these are older Norwegian-American parish registers.

We would be remiss at this point if we didn't mention the Church of Jesus Christ of Latter Day Saints (LDS). No church has done more for the cause of genealogy. The church has microfilmed millions of records from churches of all denominations.

To access them, visit an LDS family history center near you. (For details, see Chapter 3, research sites.)

If you don't find information on your ancestor's church listed in this book, contact the local, regional, or state diocese or synod office of the denomination your ancestors were affiliated with.

Or locate a church directory such as "The Encyclopedia of American Religions, 7th Edition" by J. Gordon Melton. This book provides addresses of more than 1,000 denominations. •

## Life events found in parish books

- Christening
- Mother's reintroduction into church following childbirth
- Marriage banns
- Marriage
- First communion
- Confirmation
- Vaccinations
- Incoming/outgoing records/transfer to another parish
- Funeral •

## Good book may hold key to family events

**B**ack in earlier years, the family Bible served as the "family records center." Special pages in the Bible provided space for listing births, marriages, and deaths of family members. It wasn't unusual to find important papers tucked between Bible pages. "You might just find citizenship papers, passports, school records, clipped obituaries and old letters," according to "Genealogy Bulletin," No. 45.

In areas (and times) where church and vital records were hard to come by, Bible entries provided similar life-event information.

That information is considered either primary (written right after the event occurred) or secondary (copied down from another record or recorded long after the event took place), depending on the following:
- **Color of ink** (different color means dates were probably recorded as they occurred; same

color throughout is considered secondary).
- **Handwriting** (if in a different handwriting, events were likely recorded as they happened, making this primary evidence; if entered by one person, they may have been copied from another record and are, thus, considered secondary). •

# Tombstones can tell tales

## 'Gone to be an angel'

- Early-day tombstones ranged from simple slabs to ornately carved monuments. The epitaphs on those early markers were equally quaint. A few come to us from the "Burleigh County Book of Remembrances":

"Gone to be an angel."

"A little flower of love that blossomed but to die."

"Budded on earth to bloom in heaven." •

Tiptoe through a cemetery, and you may find it a quiet place. Yet if you listen carefully, you may hear hushed whispers: It's the tombstones talking. Every tombstone you pass has a quiet story to tell—of the person whose grave it marks, of a life spent, of a generation passing.

Indeed, tombstones do tell tales. That is why genealogy researchers have found them to be a handy spade for unearthing family history information.

For openers, gravestone inscriptions contain two important keys to genealogy: the deceased's name, and the dates of his/her birth and death—the year, if not the month and day. In some cases, they tell relationships and offer other genealogical data. You may also find relatives of the deceased who are buried in nearby or adjoining plots.

An important book for anyone with roots in Burleigh County, ND, is the "Burleigh County Book of Remembrances." The book contains data on people buried in Burleigh County as early as 1870. The book's co-producers, Bismarckers Beth Bauman and Dorothy Jackman, and Gail Gorden of Regan, compiled information from obituaries, cemetery records, plat maps, and county and area history books.

Along with a history of each of the county's cemeteries, the book—one of the most complete compilations of its kind—provides given and last name of the deceased, birth and death dates, burial site, and names (including maiden names) and birthplaces of the deceased's parents. Thus, genealogies of entire family groups can be gleaned from this single reference book.

In the book's preface, the authors reflect, "We were surprised at the number of

unmarked graves in each cemetery."

For more information on this book, write to the publisher: Bismarck-Mandan Historical and Genealogical Society, P.O. Box 485, Bismarck, ND 58502-0485.

## Grave hunt

In pioneer days when cemeteries were first established, many of the early grave markers were made of wood, which deteriorated and disappeared over the years.

Flat stone slabs may have sunk into the sod or become buried in the grass or prairie dirt. In some cases, old graves on the borders of cemeteries succumbed to the plows of nearby farmers.

In some cases, cemeteries themselves were abandoned—or moved, when they stood in the way of development or the mighty Missouri River dams.

How can you tell the history and location of lost graves? Luckily, most cemeteries have a sexton or caretaker whose duty it is to record the burials and

## Tombstone rubbings can help you pick up hard-to-read inscriptions

In cases where tombstone inscriptions have weathered to the point where they're hard to read, try doing a "rubbing" of the marker. Bring a large role of tissue paper or white typing paper and a dark crayon or soft lead pencil. Place the paper over the inscription; rub gently over the tissue to transfer the inscription to the paper. Often, markings from older stones will show up using this method. You might also try visiting the cemetery just before sunset, when shadows cast by the chiseled letters make them more visible to view and photograph. •

# about ancestors

map the cemetery. These records should tell you where the person you're seeking is buried, whether or not you find a marker.

You'll also learn such things as the name of the person who purchased the plot and perhaps even discover relationships of persons buried there.

The condition of such books depends to a large degree on the sexton's diligence. In some cases, these books were misplaced or not kept up properly.

Cemeteries fall into five categories of ownership: public, private, family, church, and fraternal organizations. If the cemetery was church-affiliated, the sexton's book might be housed in the church. Records for county or town cemeteries may be available through the county courthouse. For private and fraternally owned cemetery information, contact the organization that maintains the cemetery.

## Cemetery search

In order to check out a cemetery, it is first necessary to know which cemetery to check! You can learn the cemetery location in several ways:

• Many genealogy groups have compiled and published indexes of cemeteries around the Dakotas. If you're exploring a North or South Dakota cemetery, check with the genealogy association closest to the

area of your search. Members of Williams County Genealogical Society (Williston, ND), for example, have compiled records on gravesites in rural Williams County.

George Barron of Jamestown, a member of the James River Genealogy Club, Carrington, has compiled a directory of North Dakota cemetery books. This listing is available through www. rootsweb.com/ ~usgenweb/nd/state/ cmscrpts/cemsurv.txt.

The North and South Dakota state archives collections may include such cemetery indexes, much of it from tombstone inscriptions.

• "Dakota Homestead," a quarterly publication of the Bismarck-Mandan Historical and Genealogical Society, has published an index of North Dakota cemeteries, arranged alphabetically by county.

The indexes contain the name of each cemetery, the date it was organized, its location (including legal description), and remarks such as the parish it belongs to or whether the cemetery was relocated.

Copies of the index for individual counties are available by writing: Cemetery Index, c/o Dakota Homestead, Bismarck-Mandan Historical and Genealogical Society (at the address listed earlier).

### Index points way to obit, death certificate

• Those with roots in North Dakota are lucky to have access to an index of deaths (plus marriages and divorces) that have taken place in the state from the early 1900s to the present. This index is accessible through computers located in the State Archives and Historical Research Library, Bismarck. One computer system uses a disk database; the other is linked directly to Vital Records and can retrieve information from that system. The index is searchable by fields such as surname (including maiden name), first name, date, and place.

• Finding your ancestor's death data on the index can be the clue you need to pinpoint statistics for securing a death certificate for your relative or checking the same library's microfilmed newspaper collection for an obituary. •

• Check the newspaper from the area and time period in which your ancestor died. Usually the obituary contained information as to the church, the funeral home handling the arrangements, and the cemetery in which the body would be interred.

• Check funeral homes in the area where your deceased ancestor lived, to learn which one might have records pertaining to his/her death.

• To determine what funeral homes operated in the area you're searching, get your hands on a funeral directory. "The National Yellow Book of Funeral Directors and Supplies" is one such directory. A local funeral director may be able to help you locate one (or offer you the old one when it is reprinted).

Once you learn the location of the cemetery, visit it in person. Viewing your ancestors' graves and exploring the grounds where they lie gives you perspective into their lives and connects you with the ages. •

## Misleading markers

• Be aware, when exploring the cemetery, that tombstones sometimes lie!

For example, the person whose name is etched on the marker may not actually be buried in that site. Perhaps a wife died and the husband purchased a grave marker assuming he would rest beside his wife after his death. Instead, he may have moved away or remarried and now has plans to be buried beside Wife No. 2.

In other cases, people may have purchased grave markers only to move to another state. When they pass away, it may be easier for the family if they are buried locally, rather than shipped back to the site of their remote cemetery plots. •

# Making sense of the census

**TRACKING FAMILIES VIA THE CENSUS**

- If you're tracking one family via the census, fill out a separate family group sheet for each decade (more if you use the state censuses). Include the data you discover on each census; list the date of the census at the top.

When you have the information filled in, compare your sheets for age differences, spellings, etc.

The census can also help you trace a family's migration patterns. •

One of the best finding aids for genealogists is the U.S. census. Depending on the year, it can help you locate family groups and their patterns of migration, revealing such things as when they were born, where their parents were born, their immigration date, and whether they were naturalized.

Here in the U.S., the first census was taken in 1790, for the purpose of determining representation. Every decade thereafter, census data have been collected by our government via a "decennial census."

The first census to actually record the names and ages of members of households was in 1850, 11 years before Dakota Territory was officially formed. Succeeding censuses elicited increasingly more detailed information.

In January 1921, a fire swept through the Commerce Department building in Washington, DC. Most of the 1890 census, housed there, was destroyed by water used to fight the fire, consuming irreplaceable genealogical data on our ancestors.

The only Dakota census data to survive the fire was that of Jefferson Township, Union County, SD. Neighboring Minnesota's Rockford Township in Wright County also came through relatively unscathed.

Some scattered records from eight other states and the District of Columbia also survived—part of the 6,000 legible entries out of nearly 63 million enumerated. Also surviving the fire were some records on Civil War Union veterans and their widows (including those for the Dakotas).

The 1900 and 1910 censuses are among the most valuable for genealogists. These censuses asked people if they were naturalized (whether they had taken out naturalization papers to become citizens), and how many years they had resided in the U.S.

Knowing the year of entry into this country can aid in finding immigration data from ship's passenger lists, emigration data from other countries, etc.

The 1880, 1900, and 1920 censuses are "Soundexed," a phonetic filing system that enables seekers to find their ancestors' data even though the name may have been spelled incorrectly, and without knowing the location—county, township, etc. (See boxed item on this page for more information on the Soundex.)

Less than half of the states included in the 1910 census have been Soundexed; North and South Dakota 1910 censuses are not Soundexed.

The box on page 36 details what information can be gleaned from the 1850-1930 censuses, as well as the 1885 Dakota Territory census.

The 1930 census is the most recent census to be released as of this writing (privacy protects the records for 72 years). The 1940 census will be available in 2012. (You can, however, request information on your family from the Bureau of the Census for more recent years.)

## State censuses

The earliest Dakota census information can be found on the 1836 Iowa territorial census schedule. The Minnesota Territory censuses of 1850 and 1857 included statistics on the Pembina settlement in northeastern North Dakota, as well as South Dakota settlement. In 1860, 1870, and 1880, Dakota Territory censuses were taken.

In 1885, Dakota Territory was among five states/

---

### SOUNDEX can help you search the census

- Some censuses (including the 1880, 1900, 1910,* 1920 and 1930** censuses) are on Soundex, a phonetic indexing system that allows genealogists to find names of ancestors despite spelling errors and without having to know a specific locality. The head of household's surname was given a four-digit code using the name's first letter plus numbers representing sounds of the three succeeding consonants. Vowels and the letters H, W, and Y were ignored (unless they were the first letter); double consonant sounds (including the first letter) were coded only once. Zeros were inserted in names with fewer than three consonant sounds after the initial letter.

Be aware that names with prefixes, such as De, Le, Van or Von, may be listed either with or without the prefix on the Soundex. Names with side-by-side letters with the same soundex number should be treated as one letter. Examples: CKS in "Jackson" = drop the K and S. PF in "Pfeifle" = drop the F.

- Consonant codes:
1—B, P, F, V
2—C, S, K, G, J, Q, X, Z
3—D, T
4—L
5—M, N
6—R

* Some states (including the Dakotas) do not have a Soundexed 1910 census.
** Only 12 Southern states have their 1930 census Soundexed.

---

territories that chose to take a statewide census. Census records for 17 North Dakota counties (Allred, Bowman, Buford, Dunn, McIntosh, McKenzie, Mercer, Mountrail, Oliver, Renville, Stanton, Towner, Villard, Wallace, Ward, Wells, and Wynn) and 20 South Dakota counties ( Beadle, Butte, Charles Mix, Edmunds, Fall River, Faulk, Hand, Hanson, Hutchinson, Hyde, Lake, Lincoln, Marshall, McPherson, Moody, Roberts, Sanborn, Spink, Stanley, and Turner) survived. This census is invaluable for picking up data on pioneer Dakota ancestors. It also included a veteran's census.

Six South Dakota counties (Beadle, Brule, Pratt [now Jones], Presho [now Lyman], Campbell, and Charles Mix) are included on the 1895 South Dakota census—the first to be taken after Dakota Territory was divided into the two Dakotas. The originals, done on ledgers, are now available on microfilm at the South Dakota State Historical Society.

In North Dakota, statewide censuses were taken in 1905, 1915, and 1925.

The 1905, 1915, 1925, 1935, and 1945 South Dakota state censuses were done on 3-by-5-inch cards—more than 3 1/2 million of them! They have been indexed by the LDS Family History Center in Pierre, SD, and are currently awaiting microfilming by the South Dakota State Archives library.

The project will be a boon to researchers. Knowing just one person's name in a family enables one to search the index for the entire family.

The 1905 South Dakota census is especially valuable for genealogists because it includes a description of the land, the length of time the person was in the state, and the time of entry into the United States (if born elsewhere).

A book called "State Census Records" lists census records, state by state, for all years in which a state census was conducted. Written by Ann S. Lainhard, the book tells where each state's census can be found and what you can learn from the records.

Another helpful book is the "U.S. and Special Census Catalog," published by Ancestry Inc.

## How to do a census search

Before you visit an archive, do your homework! Make a list of heads of households you hope to find. (Be aware of varying surname spellings.) Also jot down estimated dates of their lifespans, and the probable place of residence.

The lifespan and locality information will suggest a starting point for your search. Locating the county of residence of the person you're searching is important, as censuses were filed by state and county, and then by town or township.

Check to see if an index (or Soundex) exists for the censuses you plan to search. Determine what microfilm you need to order based on the index.

As a general rule, start with the latest available census containing your family information and work your way back, one decade at a time. Some years you may be able to pick up a family every five years, by combining the U.S. and state censuses.

When you find the family you're looking for on a census, look for others who may have lived in the same household—such as a widowed grandparent or an unmarried sister who

## Where to find census records

- Dakota Territory censuses and related U.S. censuses for North and South Dakota are available in both states' archives.

- The National Archives and Records Administration in Washington, DC, has microfilms of every states' censuses; these are available via interlibrary loan.

- Major university libraries such as Chester Fritz at the University of North Dakota in Grand Forks and Concordia College, Moorhead, MN, contain federal and state census microfilms.

- Census records (including Indian censuses) are available through your local LDS family history center. •

## Get census information, forms online

- For a downloadable pdf file of a book containing information and forms for all the U.S. censuses (including the 1930 census),visit the following Website: heritagequestonline. com/prod/genealogy/ images/censusbook/ Section5.pdf •

# What you'll learn from the censuses

| | 1850 | 1860 | 1870 | 1880 | 1885* | 1900 | 1910 | 1920 | 1930 |
|---|---|---|---|---|---|---|---|---|---|
| Name and age | Yes | Yes | Yes | Yes | Yes | Yes | Yes | Yes | Yes |
| Name of street, house number | No | No | No | Yes | Yes | Yes | Yes | Yes | Yes |
| Relationship to head of family | No | No | No | Yes | Yes | Yes | Yes | Yes | Yes |
| Month of birth (if born within the year) | No | No | Yes | Yes | Yes | Yes | Yes | Yes | No |
| Sex, race, birthplace, occupation | Yes | Yes | Yes | Yes | Yes | Yes | Yes | Yes | Yes |
| Whether naturalized (or papers taken out) | No | No | No | No | No | Yes | Yes | Yes | Yes |
| Number of years in U.S. (or year of immigration) | No | No | No | No | No | Yes | Yes | Yes | Yes |
| Value of personal estate | No | Yes | Yes | No | No | No | No | No | No |
| Value of real estate | Yes | Yes | Yes | No | No | No | No | No | Yes |
| Whether home/farm free of mortgage | No | No | No | No | No | Yes | Yes | Yes | Yes |
| Marital status | No | No | No | Yes | Yes | Yes | Yes | Yes | Yes |
| Whether married within the year | Yes | Yes | Yes | Yes | Yes | No | No | No | No |
| Month of marriage, if married within the year | No | No | Yes | No | No | No | No | No | No |
| Whether temporarily or permanently disabled | No | No | No | Yes | Yes | No | No | No | No |
| Whether suffering from acute or chronic disease | No | No | No | No | No | No | No | No | No |
| Whether crippled, maimed or deformed | No | No | No | Yes | Yes | No | No | No | No |
| Time unemployed during census year | No | No | No | Yes | Yes | No | No | No | No |
| Whether deaf, dumb, blind or insane | Yes | Yes | Yes | Yes | Yes | No | Yes | No | No |
| Whether a pauper | Yes | Yes | No | No | No | No | No | No | No |
| Whether a prisoner or homeless child | No | No | No | No | No | No | No | No | No |
| Whether a convict | Yes | Yes | No | No | No | No | No | No | No |
| Whether able to speak English | No | No | No | No | No | Yes | Yes | Yes | Yes |
| Whether able to read/write; if attended school within the year | Yes | Yes | Yes | Yes | Yes | Yes | Yes | Yes | Yes |
| Birthplaces of father, mother | No | No | No | Yes | Yes | Yes | Yes | Yes | Yes |
| Whether father or mother of foreign birth | No | No | Yes | Yes | Yes | Yes | Yes | Yes | Yes |
| Number of living children, if a mother | No | No | No | No | No | Yes | Yes | No | No |
| Whether soldier, sailor, marine during Civil War (U.S. or Conf.), or widow of such person | No | No | No | No | No | Yes | Yes | No | No |
| Number of years in present marriage | No | No | No | No | No | Yes | Yes | No | No |
| Number of children born | No | No | No | No | No | Yes | Yes | No | No |
| Mother tongue | No | No | No | No | No | Yes | Yes | No | No |
| Age at first marriage | No | No | No | No | No | No | Yes | Yes | Yes |
| Type of industry worked in | No | No | No | No | No | No | No | No | Yes |
| Whether a veteran, and if so, which war | No | No | No | No | No | No | No | No | Yes |
| Whether owner of a radio set | No | No | No | No | No | No | No | No | Yes |

*Surviving 1885 Dakota Territory census includes 17 North Dakota and 20 South Dakota counties

## Indian censuses

- Separate censuses counted Indians living on Dakota reservations.

For more on Indian censuses and other records covering American Indians, turn to our ethnic roots chapter. •

lived with the family. Note, too, the names and ages of the children. Some older siblings may already be working and, thus, not living at home when the census-taker visited.

The census can provide clues to help you determine when a family member may have died (for example, Grandpa is listed on the 1900, but not the 1910, census; did he die during that period?), or when adult children left home.

Once you have "found" your family's information, photocopy the census page (or pages). Include the enumeration district and page number(s).

If you do not have access to a copier, use forms that are customized for each census year, and hand-copy the information into the appropriate spaces. Make sure your writing is legible and that you are copying information accurately.

When you have completed one census search, look for the same family in earlier censuses, watching for such things as name spelling variations, number of family members, births of children, occupations, etc. In the case of an immigrant ancestor, check out the naturalization date (if contained in the census you're searching) and the date the person entered the U.S. to get a time frame in which to search for passenger lists and other immigration information.

Keep in mind, though, that census records are secondary records and, thus, more apt to contain errors. You're bound to find discrepancies from one census account to another.

The handwritten census data is sometimes hard to decipher. In other cases, microfilming quality may be poor. Census-takers may have misunderstood, or misspelled, names. Not all information given by the informants was totally accurate, either—due to faulty memories or even false data given on purpose!

But, in general, the census is a superior tool for finding family groups and their migration patterns. •

# Where there's a will...

The courthouses in the communities our ancestors came from hold many of the records of their lives and deaths.

When Dakotans first began keeping records, it was the courthouses that were the keepers of those vital records: births, marriages, divorces, and deaths. The Departments of Health of both states now hold the birth, marriage, and death records. But earlier marriage records—and divorce records—can usually be found at the courthouse where the event took place.

## The scoop on probate

Among the more interesting genealogy documents found at the courthouse are wills (or probate records).

When our ancestors died, their personal property and real estate were usually disposed of through legal processes. The wills they left behind—and/or legal documents involving settlement of their estates—can yield valuable genealogical clues, as well as information on the type and value of goods and property the deceased person owned and how it was divided.

Like the census, estate records can help you identify and compile early family groups. They are often one of the few ways to identify married daughters in early American families.

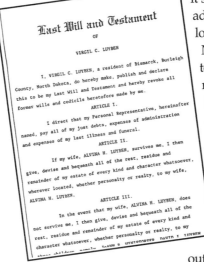

These estate records were produced by the civil courts and usually housed in the courthouse nearest the deceased's last place of residence. While each state may have slightly different procedures, in North Dakota these records are kept in the office of the district court; in South Dakota, they are in the county clerk of court offices.

Write the probate court (in care of the county courthouse) to request photocopies of these records. Give as much detail as you can about your ancestor—including the full name, residence, and date and place of death.

Be sure to ask for copies of the probate packet, rather than just the will itself. This way you will receive a copy of the will, the person's death date, family members' names, relationships and current residences, and a listing of the person's property and its value.

Remember, there will be a charge for copying, and

it's polite to send a self-addressed, stamped envelope with your request.

Note that you may have to look for probate records in each county (or state) where your ancestor owned property, as each locality's courthouse may have records. Note, too, that only a few probate records are indexed.

Even if your ancestor died without leaving a will (intestate), his/her estate was still handled through legal channels, which meant official records were drawn up and, thus, may be on file at a courthouse near his/her former home. These documents can be just as valuable as wills when it comes to revealing family history information.

Much of the early probate material—from the New England states, for example—has been published and can be found in many research libraries or in genealogical journals.

Many of these early records and indexes are also available from the LDS Family History Library in Salt Lake City, UT. Microfilms of these records can be ordered via North and South Dakota's family history centers. (For locations, see the LDS section in Chapter 3.)

Often, these documents will list entire families and other relatives—which can help you locate more branches of your family tree. •

## Other records

The courthouse shelters a number of valuable genealogical documents. Here are a few:

- Early marriage records
- Divorce records
- Guardianship papers
- Immigration and citizenship papers
- Name changes
- Orphan's court records
- Lawsuits
- Contesting of wills
- Criminal trials

Minor court cases are listed in chronological order in a civil docket.

In cases where our relatives may have had a scrape with the law, this information appears on the criminal docket. Records of lawsuits and court cases (including criminal cases) are also housed at the county courthouse. If the case was more complex, it might have been handled in circuit, district, superior, or supreme court.

Note that information may also be contained in the court minutes, as well as case files. •

# Land records help trace

## Bounty-ful land

- If your Dakota ancestor fought in the Civil War, he may have received land in lieu of wages. About 450,000 bounty-land claims are on file at the National Archives. The number of acres was based on rank and ranged from 100 to 1,100 acres. Applications provided name, age, residence, military branch in which he served, and term of service. If a widow or other heirs made the claim, their names, ages, and places of residence were given. •

When our ancestors settled in the Dakotas or elsewhere, they left a paper trail—of abstracts, deeds, and records pertaining to the lands they claimed. Luckily, many of these records are accessible, thanks to our chief "warehouse," the National Archives and Records Administration (NARA) in Washington, DC, as well as other regional and local repositories.

Those who took up land in the Dakotas either purchased it from the railroads, land speculators, or the federal government—or settled on free land offered via the Pre-emption, Homestead, and Timber Culture acts. Others—mostly Civil War veterans—staked claims on free bounty lands offered in lieu of wages.

### Land division system determined in 1785

| 6 | 5 | 4 | 3 | 2 | 1 |
| 7 | 8 | 9 | 10 | 11 | 12 |
| 18 | 17 | 16 | 15 | 14 | 13 |
| 19 | 20 | 21 | 22 | 23 | 24 |
| 30 | 29 | 28 | 27 | 26 | 25 |
| 31 | 32 | 33 | 34 | 35 | 36 |

•The Land Ordinance of 1785 set up a system of 6-mile-square townships, divided into 36 sections. A 160-acre homestead was actually one-quarter of a section, or 1/4 square mile. Legal description of the land includes range, township number, and section number. (Example: Township 151, Range 139, Section 7, Southwest 1/4.) •

## Home on the range...

The Pre-emption Act of 1841-1891 allowed settlers to claim 160 acres of public land for $1.25 per acre, for which subsequent claims

would be "pre-empted." Proof records establishing these claims included the number of people in the household and their relationship, plus a description of improvements made to the property.

## Homestead Act becomes law

On 20 May 1862, the initial Homestead Act passed, going into effect 1 Jan. 1863. This law allowed settlers to claim up to 160 acres of public lands free (for a small filing fee), if they met certain requirements.

Basically, applicants had to be citizens, live on the land for three years, and improve it by clearing land, planting trees and crops, and erecting homes and buildings.

Since the Dakotas were public lands and not settled until after the Homestead Act was passed, many of our ancestors homesteaded.

The official papers homesteaders had to fill out often provide good clues to help

their descendants discover their roots. Through these papers one can learn:
—Name, age, place of birth
—Date land was first settled
—Number and relationship of family members
—Description of home and property

The official documents were in several parts:

- The land entry papers consisted of the original application. This was sent to the General Land Office (GLO, which later became the Bureau of Land Management in Washington, DC) by the local land office where our ancestors filed.

- Once the claim was "proved" and the homesteader had met all requirements, the final proof certificate was filled out.

- If the final proof papers were approved, the patent was issued to the applicant and recorded in the local county deed book. The patent conveyed full title and ownership to the homesteader.

If the applicant was naturalized (or had declared

# families' settlement

his/her intention to become a citizen), the naturalization papers be- came part of the homestead files (see "Records documented our ancestors' ship passages," page 42, for more on naturalization).

## Acreage boost

On 19 Feb. 1909, the number of acres one could claim under the Homestead Act was boosted to 320 in some states, including North Dakota, where 160 acres was deemed too small to support a family. South Dakota became eligible for 360-acre homesteads in 1915. In 1916 the Stockraising Homestead Act increased grazing acreage.

More than half of the homestead applicants did not meet the conditions and were denied homesteads, yet their papers contain the same valuable genealogical information.

## How, where to access records

When you order the homestead papers, be sure to ask for the homestead packet, as this will yield all related papers, including naturalization papers.

Homestead files are housed in the NARA. To request the homestead files of your ancestor(s), ask for NATF-Form 84, National Archives Order for Copies of Land Entry Files. Send

## Public land states

• Both North and South Dakota are among the 30 public land states for which land grants were issued. Land records on these lands include credit, cash, and donation entries; military bounty land; homestead entries; and private land claims. •

# Wanted: Legal description of land

**B**efore you can ask for homestead papers, you need to know the legal land description and, if available, the patent number. Here are several ways to get that information:

• If you have any old deeds, or if the property is still in your family's possession, you may already have this data. If so, jot those numbers down carefully, then write (or go in person) to the register of deeds office in the county where your ancestor's homestead was located, giving them the legal description and your ancestor's name. Check for land transactions regarding that property.

If you don't know the legal description, check the tract index at the register of deeds' office. The office should be able to supply you with the legal description, the homestead application number, and the final certificate number.

Request two photocopies of these papers. Keep the first copy for your files; send the second to the NARA along with your request for the homestead packet.

Or, send the following information extracted from the patent: patent number, legal land description, name of the state and filing location (town and

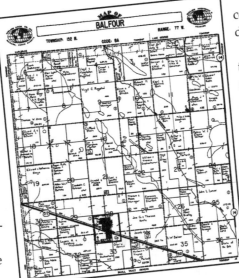

county), patentee name, and date of issue.

• Check a historical atlas containing the original township plat maps. Most register of deeds offices have such books for their own county; if not, historical atlases of most of the state's counties are available at the North and South Dakota state archives. Be aware, though, that not every county had plat books printed.

• Old county or area histories often contain historic plat maps with names of pioneers printed across the land they owned. Legal descriptions can often be gleaned from these books.

• If your ancestor was the first to settle the land, you'll find homestead documentation along with a legal description of the land recorded in the tract books. The North Dakota State Archives and Historical Research Library has microfilmed the tract books originally held by the Bureau of Land Management (formerly called the General Land Office).

These records provide the legal land description, category (homestead, tree claim, etc.), acreage, price or rate per acre, name of purchasers, case file number, and name of person who was issued the patent. •

# MAPPING YOUR FAMILY HISTORY:
## Use maps, atlases to 'locate' your ancestors

Whenever possible, check maps of the locale and times in which your relatives lived. Studying those maps can help you determine possible sites and sources of records. In fact, learning the name of the place where your ancestors lived is the key to being able to access the records.

Compare older maps with present-day maps to check for border changes, county consolidations, and once-booming towns that are now ghost towns.

Check out a county or area history book from your ancestor's old neighborhood. Look for the plat map for your family's township. Notice whether the map shows your family's plot of land. See if you can determine the legal description from this.

### USE MAPS TO:

• Trace migration patterns of your ancestors.

• Examine the topography to see what geographic features may have influenced your ancestors' livelihoods and lifestyles (for example, mountain ranges that may have limited their travel or bodies of water that may have divided them from neighboring communities, provided navigation, or furnished fish for food).

• Check out nearby towns to see what connections your ancestors may have with other relatives, proximity to town of marriage partner, etc.

### ASK YOURSELF:

• What town did my ancestor live in or near?

• Was it near the border of a county? (If so, that could impact where your relative's records might be kept, and where she/he married, attended school, etc.)

• Has the county name or shape changed while or since my ancestors lived there?

• What was the county seat that may have held the family's records?

• What town/city did the family trade in? Where did they attend church? School?

• Does the map show a railroad track nearby? What impact did the railroad have on my family's moving to or away from a community?

• Did the family emigrate via railroad? Market crops by railroad? Help build the railroad?

### GETTING CLOSE

• Close-up maps are especially valuable and can give you an in-depth perspective of your family's community.

• If you know the county where your ancestor settled, check atlases and plat books; plat maps may reveal the land description and lead you to a homestead record.

• Both North and South Dakota's state archives have collections of early atlases and county plat books, with maps showing land ownership by township. Some have been micro-filmed.

• Also check state historical societies, county histories, and old atlases for historical maps.

---

request for the complete homestead packet to: Textual Reference Branch— Land (NWDTI), National Archives and Records Administration, 7th and Pennsylvania Ave. N.W., Washington, DC 20408; 202-501-5395.

## Check regional archives, too

The Denver Branch of the National Archives (see address in appendix) holds the records of the Bureau of Land Management. This includes tract books and abstract books that were held at local land offices.

More information can be found in the land entry case files of the NARA.

## Good deeds!

When land changed hands, the transaction was

---

## Who owned the land first? Grandpappy or the railroad?

Even though your forebears may have been first to settle on a particular plot of land, they may not be listed in the tract books as the original owners—if the railroad owned the land first!

"The railroad owned lots of land [in both North and South Dakota], and not necessarily just the land adjacent to the tracks," says Jim Davis, head of reference services at the North Dakota State Archives and Historical Research Library.

"If the land was owned by the railroad first and your ancestor bought it later," he says, "you won't find your ancestor listed in the tract books as a homesteader." •

WHO WAS HERE

FIRST?

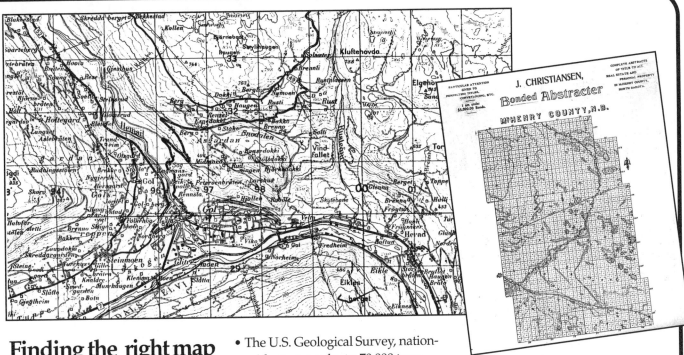

# Finding the right map

Following are leading U.S. map sellers (for contact information, see address section in appendix):

- Rand McNally Map Store

- Magellan Geographix's "The Map Store." Sells maps, atlases, historic and specialty maps

- DeLorme's "The Map Store," source for maps, atlases; recently printed gazetteers of both Dakotas

- The U.S. Geological Survey, nation-wide map products; 70,000 topo-graphic maps, available in a variety of scales

- The Gold Bug: Historic maps of many countries around the world (including a 1915 railroad map of North Dakota, and 1885, 1900, and 1920 maps of North and South Dakota). Write for a list of available maps and prices

- Map Machine Atlas (National Geographic Society); provides maps, flags and facts on all countries and states: www. nationalgeographic. com/ngs/maps/atlas/index.html

For maps of foreign countries, see the ethnic roots section. •

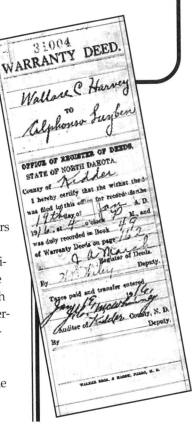

officially recorded in the county courthouse. The deed recording the land transaction can contain family history information.

Another land record—the abstract—traces the ownership of property (and names of owners) from the original sale to the present.

For those with roots in Colonial America, before such things as census records, deeds are often the best genealogical source.

Many of these early deeds have been micro-filmed by the Church of Jesus Christ of Latter Day Saints' (LDS) Family History Library in Salt Lake City, UT. Films can be accessed via microfilm or computer, through that church's family history centers.

In the Dakotas, deeds are housed at the county register of deeds office in the county where they were filed and are available upon written request. They're filed by legal description, rather than surname.

## Helpful guides

The North Dakota State Archives and Historical Research Library has some helpful information sheets that deal with land laws and records of land ownership and settlement. Compiled by the State Historical Society of North Dakota, these papers are available by writing: State Archives and Historical Research Library, State Historical Society of North Dakota, North Dakota Heritage Center, 612 E. Boulevard Ave., Bismarck, ND 58505-0830. The information is also available on the archive's Website: www. nd.gov/hist. •

# Records documented our

## Passport to Old World

- Sometimes our ancestors returned to their homeland for a visit or to relocate there. If so, they would have filled out an application for a passport.

A copy of this document can be retrieved via the Correspondence Branch, Passport Service, Department of State, Washington, DC 20524.

To ease the search, furnish your ancestor's name, place, and approximate date of application. •

We can only imagine what the trip to this country by our immigrant Dakota ancestors must have been like: crossing the ocean in a sailing ship or steamship, leaving homeland and beloved family members behind, a lengthy and perhaps perilous sea voyage, glimpsing the New World for the first time, eventually to "land" in the Dakotas.

Not every Dakotan, of course, had that traditional immigrant experience. Some were native to this land; some came later, perhaps even by plane.

Those who did travel in ships, who passed through major U.S. or Canadian ports, left records of their passage—in port registers in the country of their departure, in passenger rosters on the ships they boarded, or in arrival records at the ports where they docked. Finding these records can be the bridge linking the New World to the Old.

The ships, too, had histories that have been preserved by major maritime museums. When you know the name of the ship, it is possible to secure a history and photograph of the vessel that carried your ancestors to their new home.

## Passenger arrivals

Ship passenger arrival records to this country began as early as the 1530s. Major U.S. ports—New York, Boston, Philadelphia, Baltimore, and New Orleans— began keeping these lists on a regular basis around 1820. Records for Galveston and Mobile began later in the 19th century. Seattle and San Francisco records date back to the late 19th century.

The National Archives and the LDS Family History Library have microfilms of passenger arrival records primarily from 1819 to 1940. National Archives films are available on interlibrary loan.

These rosters include names of passengers, ages, sex, place of origin, and destination. Also included are names of those who were born or died aboard ship.

Indexes are available for many of these passenger lists, a boon to researchers.

To order "Immigration and Passenger Arrivals: A Select Catalog of National Archives Microfilms" (1820-1954), send $2 and your request to: National Archives Trust Fund, Dept. 510, P.O. Box 100793, Atlanta, GA 30384.

If your ancestor came through a Canadian port, write to the Library and Archives Canada, 395 Wellington St., Ottawa, Ontario, Canada K1A0N4.

Information is also available in book form:
- "American Passenger Arrival Records" by Michael Tepper.
- "They Came in Ships" by John P. Colleta.
- "Württemburg Emigration Index" (includes Germans leaving Russia).
- "The Source: A Guidebook of American Genealogy" by Arlene Eakle and Johni Cerny (contains passenger list information on other European ports).
- "Morton Allan Directory of European Passenger Steam Ship Arrivals" (lists vessels arriving at major U.S. ports).

## Passenger departures

On the other side of the world, records were also kept at the European ports from which our ancestors departed. Some emigration lists exist for these ports.

If your ancestor boarded a ship at Stockholm, Copenhagen, Oslo or Hamburg, for example, you may be able to pick up

# ancestors' ship passages

their information (including names of those booking passage, former home, name of ship, destination, etc.) on these records.

The LDS has an index of Hamburg passenger lists from 1850-1934. These records are divided into direct (no stopovers) and indirect (stopping at a European or British port before coming to the U.S.).

Unfortunately, most of the lists for the port of Bremen were destroyed during World War II, and British Isles lists are not compre-

hensive. (The LDS library has microfilmed one Bremen card file for 1904-14, arranged by country.)

Check at an LDS family history center near you for a list of what immigration/emigration records are available on microfilm.

If you think your Norwegian (or Swedish) ancestors may have boarded a ship at the port of Oslo (formerly Kristiania) for their trip to America, check the "emigrant protokoller," a register of departing passengers. This

chronological list beginning circa 1869 gives detailed information on the passengers and may offer the farm name and parish, a clue for future research. This multi-roll microfilm resource is available through the LDS family history centers.

The following Websites can also help:
- Cyndi's List: www.Cyndis List. com/ships.htm.
- Olive Tree Genealogy: www.rootsweb.com/ ~ote. •

## When your ship comes in...

- Once you learn the name of the ship that carried your ancestors to this country, write to the Steamship Historical Society, Langsdale Library, University of Baltimore, 1420 Maryland Ave., Baltimore, MD 21201-5779. Send them the name of your ship and the date of arrival in a U.S. port and ask whether they might have your ship's picture and history in their vast archives.•

# Naturalization

Perhaps the biggest clue to the name of the ship, the date and port of arrival of our immigrant ancestors comes from the naturalization papers—especially if they were dated after 27 Sept. 1906.

Before an immigrant could become a citizen, he/she was required to fill out naturalization papers. The "first papers" were called the declaration of intention. These papers were filed in the county courthouse.

The "second papers," or the petition papers (or "naturalization records") included affidavits declaring that the applicant had met the residency and other requirements. This paper was filed about three to five years after the first papers were filed.

Following this, the applicant received a certificate of naturalization indicating that citizenship had been granted.

Naturalization laws began in 1790. Before 1906, the law required only the head of each household to be naturalized; family members automatically became citizens at the same time. Women and children weren't required to file separately until the late 1920s (although some did anyway).

Prior to 27 Sept. 1906, forms weren't standardized and asked for little information other than name and country of origin. Thus they are usually not as helpful to genealogists as are the later forms.

After that date, applicants were asked to give their birth date and place, physical description, name of ship,

date and port of entry, and marital status. The petition called for information on spouse and children, as well.

Locally, these papers can be found at the courthouse or the state archives. The National Archives has the Immigration and Naturalization Service records of naturalizations since 1906.

North Dakota's naturalization papers are housed at the State Archives and Historical Research Library in Bismarck. All are indexed by surname and county.

In South Dakota, naturalization records for all but two counties—Brule and Campbell—are available to researchers at the State Archives in Pierre. Many of these records have been indexed.

Be aware that not everyone who immigrated to this country was naturalized, which means you will not find a record for everyone. •

# Archives preserve history

## Census can lead to military records

- Don't know if Great-grandpa fought in a war? Check the census! In the 1840 and 1890 censuses, military data was collected. The portion of the 1890 census that survived the fire (see census records section) includes Union veteran and pensioner statistics. The 1900, 1910, 1920 and 1930 censuses contained categories for military personnel. •

If you have a relative (or ancestor) who served in the military during one of this country's wars, chances are his/her information could add depth and details to your collection of family history.

There are two basic types of military records: service records (for volunteer and enlisted personnel) and veterans' benefits records (including pensions and bounty lands).

American military records range from our country's earliest colonial conflicts to data on those currently serving in the military. In addition, states kept records on some who served during periods of peace—such as militia and National Guard members.

Most military records are housed in the National Archives and Records Administration (NARA) in Washington, DC. Many have been indexed and some have been micro-filmed, with films available on interlibrary loan. These records not only add a his-

torical perspective on the ancestors they cover, but they also provide valuable genealogical information.

Especially valuable for genealogy purposes are the pension applications from veterans and their widows, since the applicant was required to list detailed personal and family information to establish eligibility for pension funds.

## Two military records sites

Military records are housed nationally in two related archives:

- **Before 1917:** Records on most of those who fought in our country's early wars—including the Revolutionary and Civil Wars—are housed in the NARA. When writing for early military service records, use NATF Form 26. Use NATF Form 86 to request Civil War service records. To request Civil War pension records, use Form 85.
- **After 1917:** Military records for all veterans who served after 1917 are housed in St. Louis, MO. Requests for military data after that date should be sent on "Standard Form 180—Request Pertaining to Military Personnel Records." To request this form, write to:
  National Personnel
  Records Center
  (NPRC), General
  Services Administration, 9700 Page Blvd., St. Louis, MO 63132.

Because of privacy laws which restrict public access to information recorded less than 75 years ago, you'll need to enclose a letter of permission from the veteran or next-of-kin. Family members, however, can access these records if the person is deceased.

## What you'll find at NARA

To learn what military records you'll find at the archives, write for a free pamphlet, "Military Service Records in the National Archives of the United States, Leaflet No. 7." The address is: Publication Sales Branch, General Services Administration, Washington, D.C. 20408.

The book "Guide to Genealogical Research in the National Archives" is an excellent source for finding out what records —military and otherwise —are housed in our country's number one historical warehouse. If you don't find this book in your local library, you can order it via interlibrary loan. It's published by the NARA. (Be sure to ask for the latest revision.)

The NARA has also produced its own military records information publication entitled "Military Service Records: A Select Catalog of National Archives Microfilm Publications."

For further information, visit the following NARA Website: www.archives.

## DAKOTA MILITARY RECORDS

- Pensioners on the Roll as of 1 Jan. 1883 (living in Dakota Territory). Park Genealogical Books, 1996
- Minnesota in the Civil and Indian War, 1861-1865 (Sibley and Sully campaigns),St. Paul Pioneer Press, 1890-1893, 2 vols.
- Register of North Dakota Veterans; Vietnam Conflict, 1964-1973: ND Adjutant General, Bismarck, 1981
- Register of North Dakota Veterans, World War II, 1941-1945, and Korean Conflict, 1950-1953. ND Adjutant General, Bismarck, 1968
- Roster of the men and women who served in the Army or Naval Services (including the Marine Corps) of the United States or its Allies from the State of North Dakota in the World War, 1917-1918. North Dakota Adjutant General, Bismarck, 1931 •

# of those who served

gov/genealogy.

• To learn about military records for World War II housed in the National Archives, read "Guide to Records Relating to U.S. Military Participation in World War II," compiled by Timothy P. Mulligan. This 170-page book (#200119) sells for $20 and is available through the NARA at the following Website: www. archives.gov/publications

## OUR COUNTRY'S WARS

| WAR | DATE |
| --- | --- |
| Colonial Wars | 1607-1763 |
| Pontiac's Rebellion | 1763-1765 |
| Revolutionary War | 1775-1783 |
| Indian Wars | 1790-1811 |
| War of 1812 | 1812-1815 |
| Mexican War | 1846-1848 |
| Civil War | 1861-1865 |
| Spanish-American War | 1898 |
| Philippine Insurrection | 1899-1902 |
| World War I | 1914-1918* |
| World War II | 1939-1945* |

| | |
| --- | --- |
| Korean Conflict | 1950-1953 |
| Vietnam Conflict | 1965-1973 |
| Desert Storm (Kuwait) | 1991 |
| Afghanistan/Iraq | 2004- |

To determine whether your ancestor may have been affected by or fought in any of these conflicts, determine his/her birth date, and whether he/she was born in the 50-year period preceding any war.
—www.rootsweb.com; "Twigs & Branches," Bureau Co. Gen. Soc. Newsletter, 1992

*The U.S. entered World War 1 in 1917; World War II in 1941.*

## Revolutionary War records

The Daughters of the American Revolution, or DAR, has published name indexes of many Revolutionary War patriots. Many Dakota libraries have this three-volume set (called the "DAR Patriot Index").

This publication provides data on men and women who aided the patriots' cause between 1774 and 1783. Pension information for soldiers and/or widows is also listed.

If you find your ancestor's name on these indexes, you may request (for a fee) information by writing: Treasurer General, National Society of the DAR, 1776 D St. N.W., Washington, DC 20006.

## Civil War records

In addition to the excellent records at the National Archives, a recently completed "Civil War Soldiers and Sailors Project" database lists information on

3.5 million Union and Confederate soldiers. A joint project of the National Park Service, the Federation of Genealogical Societies, and the Genealogical Society of Utah, the database is available on CD at each of the Civil War National Battlefield parks, the National Archives, and the Family History Library and branch centers around the country.

For more information, contact the Federation of Genealogical Societies Business Office, Civil War Project, P.O. Box 830220, Richardson, TX 75083-0220. Or visit this Website: www.civilwar-data.com.

A government publication, "Civil War at a Glance," features chronologies, narratives and maps illustrating and describing major Civil War battle campaigns. To order, send your check for $2 to: Superintendent of Documents, R.W., CIC-9C, P.O. Box 100, Pueblo, CO 81002-0100. Or visit this Website: www. pueblo.gsa.gov.

## Military miscellanea

At many Dakota libraries, you'll find books listing the names, ranks, serial numbers, tours of duties, and, in some cases, brief narratives on residents of our state who served their country during both world wars.

• For veteran burial information, write to: Cemetery Service, National Cemetery System, Dept. of Veterans Affairs, 810 Vermont Ave., Washington, DC 20422.

• An excellent guide to general and Revolutionary War records is "U.S. Military Records: A Guide to Federal and State Sources, Colonial America to the Present." Written by James C. Neagles, this book gives descriptions and samples of records and information on finding them.

Note: See Chapter 3, research sites, for more information on the holdings of the NARA. •

## Check LDS military indexes

• The LDS Family History Library in Salt Lake City has a collection of more than 25,000 microfilms of the National Archives' U.S. military records. Check with a family history center near you (see locations in next chapter under LDS Records section).

While at the center, check the Family History Catalog under National Archives Microfilm Publications and United States–Military Records [War]. Wars are arranged chronologically.

The Family History Library has also microfilmed military records held by states, such as militia, national guard, and volunteer regiments. •

GET YOUR RECORDS HERE!

## Lots of alternate records

Check out these sources for possible records on your ancestor:

- Social Security Administration records

- Social Security death index

- Employment records

- Union records

- Political records

- School records

- Alumni publications

- Records from clubs and fraternal organizations

- Hospital, clinic, nursing home, institutional and other medical records

- Social histories from state mental institutions •

# Miscellaneous records

In addition to the major records we've already covered in this chapter, there are hundreds of other less familiar records that can help you trace your roots. In this section, we discuss several miscellaneous records that can help.

## SSA, hooray!

If you have an ancestor who died after 1935 (the year the Social Security program began), odds are good that person was required to fill out Form SS-5, an application for a Social Security card and eventual benefits.

This application, filed with the Social Security Administration in Washington, DC, helps pinpoint where the individual was living and employed at the time he/she filled out the form. It also gives personal and family information ranging from the applicants' birth date and place to parents' names (including maiden name of mother), birth dates, and places.

These records can be accessed by using Form SSA-711 (optional), available from your nearest Social Security office, filling it out and mailing it, along with a copy of your deceased ancestor's death certificate and a copy and search fee ($27 to $29 per record), to: Social Security Administration, OEO FOIA Workgroup, P.O. Box 33022, Baltimore, Maryland 21290-3022.

Be sure to request a photocopy of the original microfilmed record.

Researchers have another important resource in the Social Security death index, accessible at LDS family history centers around the world. As of December 2005, this database (also available via the LDS Website—www. family-search.org) contained about 76 million names of deceased persons whose deaths were reported to the Social Security Administration. The information lists the following: name, Social Security number, state where number was issued, month and year of death, and residence at time of death.

Finding the death date and place for anyone listed on this database can lead to an obituary, which can lead to a precise death date and yield data needed to obtain a death certificate.

## Big business

The firm where your ancestor worked can often be a resource for family history. Depending on the firm, you may be able to access employee records for your ancestor.

Some companies were particularly thorough about keeping records on those they employed and have opened up their earlier records to the public. One such company was the Northern Pacific Railroad. Union records can also provide genealogy

data. The applications filled out by those seeking work were especially valuable, since they contained personal information.

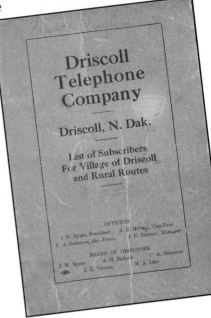

Driscoll Telephone Company

Driscoll, N. Dak.

List of Subscribers For Village of Driscoll and Rural Routes

OFFICERS
J. W. Byers, President    A. H. Meland, Vice-Pres.
C. A. Swanson, Sec.-Treas.    J. E. Tierney, Manager

BOARD OF DIRECTORS
J. W. Byers    A. H. Meland    C. A. Swanson
J. E. Tierney    M. A. Lien

## Check the directory!

If you have an unusual surname, it may behoove you to search phone books or Internet directory databases for your surname. You can then call (or write letters or send e-mail to) those with the same name to see whether and how you might be related.

Some Dakota libraries have collections of phone books from major cities around the country. Old city directories can also help you establish the residence or even the occupation of an ancestor.

You might try addressing a letter to "occupants" of houses where your relatives once lived.

Genealogy researcher Orlin Jacobson of Bis-

# School days!

In the Dakotas, any-one of school age was listed in the school census, taken yearly. These files are located in the county superintendent of school's offices. These legal-sized documents list the name of the child, age, and names of parents or legal guardian. And don't forget school annuals, newsletters, or alumni publications, either, usually located in the school or in the local library or historical society headquarters. •

marck says, "I wrote a letter to the occupant of the household and asked them when these people lived there. If you know the address, just address the letter to 'occupant.'"

You can then ask the party to check with others, who may have lived in the neighborhood when your relative lived there, to see if they remember him/her.

## Famous–or infamous–relatives!

It's not all that rare for someone to have relatives who were famous—or infamous.

"Be aware of books on such people. Who knows, your relative could be written up in *Time-Life Books*," says Jacobson.

You don't have to have noted (or notorious) ancestors, however, to find them in already published family history books.

"People should be aware of other genealogies," Jacobson says. "You can work into families who have already done a genealogy."

He found his own great-grandfather this way, through a book he found at the University of Wisconsin library.

"He had actually written the book!" he says.

So check libraries—especially ethnic libraries, which often collect histories on particular nationalities (depending on the emphasis of their collections)—for such books.

Conversely, if your ancestor (or relative) was in a penal institution of some sort, you may be able to access the records.

## Voters, taxes

The county auditor's office keeps such records as voter registration and tax records. If the records are old, they may have been sent to the state archives. •

# FIRST AID!

More than ever, records of ancestors are being sought by descendants who want to examine their medical histories for possible clues to hereditary diseases. Some who are looking for these records may not be doing their genealogies at all; they may be searching for clues that could determine their course of treatment.

As a bonus, medical records can yield important genealogical information about your family members.

Hospitals, clinics, and institutions such as sanitariums or nursing homes are sources for these records.

If your ancestor spent time in a state mental hospital, a social history would have been obtained from the patient. Check for social records from the institution that provided treatment.

Death certificates are often another way to determine cause of death—an important medical clue. Unfortunately, the earlier certificates were not always filled out completely or accurately—especially if the person died at home and was not under the care of a physician. •

# Finding family in cases of

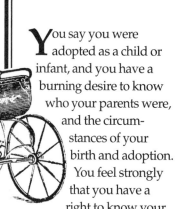

## Non-ID data

- Generally, when a child is adopted, the adoptive parents are given "non-identifying background information." This information, provided by a social services or adoption agency, may include such things as ages of family members (including grandparents and others), family deaths (for example, a grandparent's death date), medical information, the region in which the birth parents were living, occupations, military service, etc.

  If you can't get this information from your adoptive parents, you may be able to secure it from the agency that handled your adoption. •

You say you were adopted as a child or infant, and you have a burning desire to know who your parents were, and the circumstances of your birth and adoption. You feel strongly that you have a right to know your own personal history—your original name and your medical, genetic, and ethnic backgrounds.

There are some realities you must deal with before you pursue your search.

- First, your natural parents may not want to be found.
- Second, the information you're seeking may be shielded by people and facilities whose duty it is to protect the privacy of the birth parents.
- Third, your adoptive parents may not approve of your search—they may discourage you from exploring your past and may even withhold information.
- Fourth, in some states, access to sealed adoption records is granted only if there is a compelling medical reason that justifies opening the records.

These "reality checks" do not mean you won't eventually gain access to your history. They're our way of pointing out that, unlike accessing most information, you may have to use diplomacy and finesse to glean access to the truth you're seeking.

The National Adoption Information Clearinghouse (NAIC) Website features information on finding birth relatives. Under a subtitle "Some Things to Think About" there's this note: "If you decide to conduct a search for a birth relative, you are sure to experience many different emotions. Fear, guilt, anger, anxiety, and exhilaration all may play a part."

Despite the emotional roller coaster, the NAIC site (naic.acf.hhs.gov) states that "most searchers say that knowing as much as possible about their birth relatives provides a feeling of closure and satisfaction that cannot be duplicated."

And, indeed, we've all heard the stories of happy reunions between birth parents and children.

If you feel a strong pull to find your birth parents and you're determined to go through with your search, the following may help you in your quest:

- Write down everything you currently know about your birth, birth parents, placement, and adoption. Also list things you don't yet know, but hope to find out. As you accumulate information, log its receipt.
- Get all information you can from your adoptive parents. Ask what they know about your birth parents, your birth city and hospital, your name, circumstances of your adoption, the agency and/or court that handled the adoption, and whether you were adopted as an infant or placed in foster care first. Ask whether they received any written "non-identifying" information or documents. If information was in written form, ask for a copy.
- Collect documents such as the following: an amended birth certificate (via state registrar), a petition to adopt (county clerk), the final decree (also from the county clerk), your hospital birth records, and any "non-identifying" data. Write for any documents you don't have.
- Check to see what the laws and policies are regarding access to adoption records in the state where you were born/adopted. To find out, contact a social services organization in that state or search for this information on the Internet.

## Beginning your search

A personal visit to places that may hold your records is usually best (although you may also send a written request or have someone else represent you in requesting records).

If you can't go in person to do your search, see whether relatives living near the area of your birth

---

**PLACES TO CONTACT IN NORTH & SOUTH DAKOTA**

- N.D. Dept. of Human Services, Post Adoption Unit, State Capitol, Dept. 325, Bismarck, ND 58505-0250; 701-328-4805 • www.nd.gov/humanservices/services/childfamily/adoption
- S.D. Dept. of Social Service, Post Adoption Unit, 700 Governor's Drive, Pierre, SD 57501; 605-773-3227 • www.dss.sd.gov.

# adoption

might be willing to perform the search on your behalf. Or contact a genealogy group for the name of someone who might be willing to help you find your birth parents (or birth child). Or hire a professional research firm to aid you.

• Go to the adoption agency. If you don't know the name of the agency, check with the adoption division of your state or county social services department for help. They can also give you information on adoption information disclosure laws in your state.

When you confront the person behind the desk at a facility that holds your records, be polite, not demanding. Tell him/her you wish to know your history, your background. (If there's a specific medical reason for needing the records, you're more apt to gain access to them.)

You can generally get answers to the following questions: age of parents when child was born, state of their health, education level, occupation, and physical features. Ask for any "non-identifying information" documentation the agency may have.

Ask whether you might have access to your adoption records. If not stored at that facility, ask if he/she can obtain them for you.

If there was no agency involved in the adoption, find out whether the state department of social services holds the records. If so,

locate the lawyer who handled the adoption case. Ask for copies of documents the lawyer may have that pertain to your adoption.

• Visit the hospital where you were born and ask for records of your birth.

• Go to the clerk of court's office at the courthouse that handled your adoption and ask to see the civil docket. Check for a surname change transaction entered in the books at around the time you were adopted. You may be able to learn your original surname this way or glean the surname of an adopted child.

• If, after visiting the adoption agency, birth hospital, and the state adoption bureau, you don't get information, your next step may be to file a "Waiver of Confidentiality" at the hospital of your birth, adoption agency, and/or state adoption bureau.

Depending on laws in the state of your birth and adoption, the institution, upon the signing of such a waiver by the adoptee and the birth parent/parents, may release information.

•Register with a "mutual consent registry," usually operated by the state or by private citizens. Both North and South Dakota have such a registry. This will let anyone going through the registry know that you are seeking your parent (or child) and could lead to a match with another seeker.

• Many states (including North Dakota but not

South Dakota) and provinces allow intermediaries, or search-and-consent systems, to operate. In such cases, adoptees or birth parents authorize the state, an agency official, or a trained confidential intermediary (CI) to search for and locate the child or parent. This person would have access to files from the court and/or agency and could use that information to locate and contact the missing party.

If the located birth parent then desires to meet the child who is seeking him/her, the court authorizes the CI to give the name and address of the birth parent to the person who initiated the search. The same holds true for a parent conducting a search for a birth child.

• Contact a support group that believes in a birth child's right to know his/her history (and a parent's right to information on a child given in adoption). There are many such groups out there, including ALMA (the Adoptee Liberty Movement Association), the pioneer organization in fighting for the rights of adoptees. Visit www.almasociety.org for more information.

• In cases where you are legally entitled to records access but agencies are refusing to hand over the information, consider hiring an attorney to retrieve the records for you. •

# Printed sources: Reading

## Know where to look when searching old papers

- A sad reality when dealing with older newspapers: You may have to wade through an entire early-day newspaper to find notices on such things as births, marriages, wedding anniversaries, and deaths of your ancestors.

These items might be buried anywhere in the paper, rather than confined to a certain page.

Usually, in fact, the front pages were "canned" national news pages. Toward the back were one or two pages with local news tidbits, ads, etc. •

It may be true, as humorist Will Rogers once said, that you can't believe everything you read in the newspapers. But newspapers are a good place for the genealogist to go ancestor hunting.

Think about it: Today, our own families' life events—births, marriages, court appearances, real estate transfers, school and employment news, military service, probate and other legal notices, engagements, weddings, milestone anniversaries, and deaths—make the local newspaper.

So it was in pioneer days in North and South Dakota, in Minnesota and Montana—or wherever our ancestors resided.

The newspapers you'll want to search, then, are the local ones—the ones closest to the home of the ancestor or family whose information you're seeking. You'll also want to search papers published within the time frame in which your family was in a certain community.

Sometimes your search will carry you into neighboring communities' newspapers, looking for news of your ancestors.

Many of these older newspapers have been preserved in historical archives in the states in which they were originally printed.

## Newspaper collections

The North Dakota State Archives and Historical Research Library has a vast collection of North Dakota newspapers, available on microfilm.

The South Dakota State Archives in Pierre, SD, has now microfilmed nearly 1,400 of the state's newspapers.

The goal of both states' newspaper projects is to preserve as many newspapers as possible, to gain access to and microfilm the "lost" newspapers (publications with no known copies existing), and to make these newspapers accessible to researchers.

The oldest newspaper in the North Dakota State Archives' collection is the oldest publication in either of the Dakotas—*The Frontier Scout,* published in 1864 at Fort Rice military post, south of present-day Mandan, ND.

19th-century issues of *The Bismarck Tribune,* North Dakota's oldest continuous newspaper, can also be found there.

Most of the newspapers in the library, however, begin in 1905, when a law was passed to preserve two copies of any legal publication, including newspapers.

The good news is, "Many years ago there were 350 newspapers operating at one time in North Dakota," according to Jim Davis, head of reference services at the North Dakota State Archives. "In some areas, every small town had a newspaper."

## Obituaries can yield a

Of all the items we may find about an ancestor in the local paper, it's the obituary that usually yields the most family history information.

The obituary (especially the more recent ones) may give you the person's birth date and place (which may lead you overseas, in cases of a pioneer ancestor), marriage details, names of children and grandchildren, and, often, a photo of the deceased, where the person worked, organizations he/she belonged to, accomplishments, where the person died, what funeral home handled the arrangements, and what cemetery contains the body.

By giving you the parents' names, the obituary can help you get back a generation.

If you're lucky enough to find a detailed obituary, you may even be able to fill in entire family group sheets, based on the information you glean from the obituary.

Be aware, though, that some of the early "news nubs"

# between the lines

The bad news is, in both the North and South Dakota State Archives, some early issues are incomplete, as not all issues could be located. In addition, quality on some earlier microfilming was poor.

## Where's the paper?

The staff of both State Archives libraries will search for obituaries (and other items) in state newspapers in their collection.

In order to search, "We need the person's name, the date of death, and the name of the newspaper," says Davis. "If you don't know the name of the paper, at least give us the county and location."

The North Dakota archives has a two-volume Newspaper Inventory, which lists North Dakota newspapers by county, names of the papers, what dates they were published, and tells what copies are in the library's collection.

The South Dakota State Archives has a database catalog listing the name of the paper, place it was published, name of publisher, and frequency of publication. These catalog records are available for searching on the South Dakota State Library Network (SDLN), an electronic catalog found at many libraries. Microfilms are also available through interlibrary loan, or one can purchase them.

Some foreign language newspapers were also published in North Dakota earlier in the 20th century. The State Archives libraries have copies of some of these early newspapers.

Check with specific ethnic organizations to see what foreign-language newspapers may have pertained to their group.

## Newspaper office may have copies

If you don't find a newspaper at the state historical library, you can also check with the newspaper office itself to see whether their collections might

## Interlibrary loan: Try it, you'll like it!

- Printed sources are usually available on interlibrary loan through your local library.

To order, furnish complete information about the book so the librarian can search the library's computer database to see whether the book is available for loan.

If it is, the book (or in some cases, microfilm) will be mailed to your library, where you can then pick it up and research it either in your home or using the library facilities (and microfilm viewer). •

# wealth of genealogical data

were incomplete and didn't contain much information, including maiden names (or even first names of women).

The following 1904 death notice from a Racine, MN, newspaper is an example:

*"Mrs. Olson died at her home near Racine Friday night. She was one of the earliest settlers in this section. The funeral services were held Monday at the Lutheran Church."*

According to the "Burleigh County Book of Remembrances," a listing of burials in Burleigh County, N.D., "Early newspapers carried very few obituaries, preferring the sensational and well-known to the mundane, and telling burial places was not important (a fault that was repeated frequently in subsequent years)."

Even with such a sketchy obituary as the one in our example, however, one can still pick up clues for further research: the death date (necessary to seek out a death certificate, the fact she was a pioneer (and thus may have been featured in an early history of the area), the church (and denomination) that conducted her funeral service (so one can seek church records on her life and death).

Keep in mind, however, that obituaries are secondary records, as the history of the person's life was furnished to the newspaper long after the events (birth, marriage, etc.) took place. •

**OBITUARIES**
▼
**Oswald 'Punch' Beaudoin**

WALHALLA, N.D. — Oswald "Punch" Beaudoin, 67, St. Paul, formerly of Walhalla, died Thursday, Feb. 6, 1992, in a St. Paul hospital.

Oswald "Punch" Beaudoin was born Sept. 2, 1924, in Grand Forks, the son of Arthur and Agnes Beaudoin. He worked as a farm laborer in LeRoy, N.D., and served in the U.S. Navy in World War II. In 1950, he moved to St. Paul, where he worked as a welder until retiring.

Survivors are his brothers, Duane, Mariposa, Calif., and Larry, Milaca, Minn.; sisters, Lucille (Mrs. Donald) Braget, and LaFern (Mrs. Clifford) McFarland, both of Elk Grove, Calif.; Geraldine (Mrs. Curtis) Herman, Minot, Elaine (Mrs. Dalton) Gendron, Walhalla, Ramona (Mrs. Floyd) Stone, Drayton, N.D., Patricia (Mrs. Ray) Rossenborg, Byron, Wyo., and Faith (Mrs. Dave) Rahier, Carson, Calif., and several nieces and nephews.

He was preceded in death by his sister, Judith Beaudoin.

■ **Memorial Mass:** 10 a.m. Tuesday, St. Boniface Catholic Church, Walhalla. Arrangements are with Nelson Funeral Home, Walhalla.

## Newspaper Project

- Both North and South Dakota are participants in the U.S. Newspaper Project, whose objective is to catalog all newspaper holdings of all states onto an international Online Computer Library Center (OCLC) database. Information on newspaper holdings are accessible to researchers at more than 10,000 libraries worldwide.

- The State Historical Society of North Dakota has microfilmed 3.3 million pages of papers ranging from the *Wyndmere Missile* to the *Gladstone Rustler,* a cowboy publication. For information on North Dakota papers, log onto www.nd.gov/hist/newshome.htm

- South Dakota has cataloged 1,000 titles and includes articles dating back to 1859, 30 years before statehood. Information on South Dakota newspapers can be viewed at: www. sdhistory.org/arc/arc_ nwsp.

- For detailed information on the project, check this Website: www.loc.gov/preserv/newspaperbrochure. html, or visit: www.neh. gov/projects/usnp. html.

- Another online source for U.S. newspapers is: www. newsarchives.com. •

include the editions you're hoping to research. Historical and/or genealogical societies operating in the area where a newspaper is (or was) printed may also know whether newspapers are available for the dates you specify.

## Other states' newspapers

If your ancestors came from a location outside the Dakotas and you want to find out whether there was a newspaper published in that vicinity, contact that state's historical library. The address of each state's library is listed in "The Handy Book for Genealogists, "edited by George B. Everton Sr. This book has

been reprinted throughout the years, so check for the latest edition.

The book "The Source: A Guidebook of American Genealogy," edited by Arlene Eakle and Johni Cerni, contains a state-by-state bibliography of union lists and directories that contain names and publishing dates of newspapers.

Newspaper directories can help, too: The "Ayers Directory of Publications," for example, lists papers that were printed in each community, along with their issue dates. Many libraries in the Dakotas carry this directory. You can also check union lists for newspapers published in this country. North Dakota's newspapers are

listed in "Union List of North Dakota Newspapers, 1864-1976," by Carol Koehmstedt Kolar.

In addition, a special nationwide project—the United States Newspaper Project—gives genealogists access to microfilms of nearly every newspaper in the country, dating back to 1690, via interlibrary loan. The North Dakota State Archives and Historical Research Library and South Dakota State Historical Society and Archives are part of this project.

If you have access to the Internet, check out the following Web addresses for information on both states' historical society collections: w.ww. nd.gov.us/hist or www. sdhistory.org/arc/arc_gene.htm •

# County and area histories

● ● ● ● ● ● ● ● ● ● ● ● ● ● ● ● ● ● ● ● ● ● ● ● ● ● ● ● ● ● ● ● ● ● ● ●

When towns celebrated their 50th birthday parties or their diamond jubilees or a county paid tribute to the bicentennial (1976) or the Dakota centennials (1989), they often went a step beyond a special newspaper commemorating the event. They would publish an area history book—often hard-bound and peppered with photos and stories of area pioneers and their descendants.

What's especially rewarding for those of us seeking family history is that, while some of the books contained only facts about the region, some contained a lot of biographies.

If a family lived in the area since pioneer times, there was apt to be a special write-up on the earliest members of a community, including people living on farms in the area. In many instances those writeups reveal such valuable genealogical data as the town or farm where the person lived in the Old

Country; birth, marriage, and death dates; immigration dates; and the woman's maiden name.

The North Dakota and the South Dakota State Archives have limited collections of such books. While there is no group index to all the names contained in these books, many of the books themselves

# Look for celebration-edition newspapers, area histories

**D**uring special historical events, such as when the town celebrated its 50th birthday or other anniversaries of note, special editions of newspapers often appeared. Many of these "celebration" editions contain stories of pioneers and historic items that can help genealogists who have early roots in a community. Thus, it behooves you to know when your community might have celebrated its jubilee or centennial. Other historic issues were often printed in conjunction with such events as the nation's bicentennial, or the state's 50th, 75th, and 100th birthdays. Also check the library of the area you're researching for county and community history books printed to commemorate such events. •

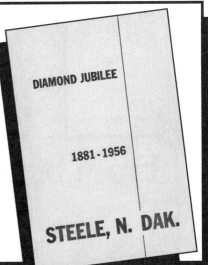

DIAMOND JUBILEE

1881-1956

STEELE, N. DAK.

contain an index listing names of people portrayed between their covers.

Books housed at the State Archives libraries are not loaned out. You need to visit the archives in person and study them on site to access these books.

But don't wring your hands in despair; the State Libraries, located near the archives in both Dakotas, have a large collection of area history books. These books on communities and counties—as well as similar books from other states— are available on interlibrary loan via your local library.

Also check the local libraries in the areas you're searching (whether in the Dakotas or elsewhere) to see what community histories they have in their collections. These books are also candidates for interlibrary loan (see sidebar).

"The Handy Book for Genealogists," mentioned earlier, tells you which counties (in every state) have published area histories. Another excellent reference book, "A Bibliography of American County Histories," compiled by P.

William Filby, lists titles and publishing dates of most every county history book published in the United States prior to the bibliography's publishing date.

## More than one book!

In many cases, area history books were published a number of times during the lifespan of a county or community. According to "A Bibliography of American County Histories," Grand Forks County, North Dakota, for example, has four such books, the first one published in 1900, the second in 1921, a third in 1964, and one in 1977-78 . If you know your ancestor was among the first to settle in an area, check the area history book with the earliest possible publishing date. But check them all, just in case!

Keep in mind that, as towns celebrated their centennials, the turn of the century, and the new millennium, they may have commemorated those events by publishing a history book.

Look for a rash of such books in 1976, 1989, and 2000. These books, of course, won't be included in indexes or bibliographies published before these dates. Check the library of the community you're researching to find out what books may have been published more recently.

Another good way to get an update on what area histories may have been published is to visit an LDS family history center (see Chapter 3 for Dakota locations and resources of these centers). Check the family history library catalog (FHLC) under the location category (of whichever state your ancestor came from) to find out whether an area history book for the county or community you're researching might be available via microfilm (as well as on computer) from the Salt Lake LDS Family History Library. As a bonus, you'll also learn what other resources are available for the same area. To rent the microfilms, order them at the center. About a week later, the film should be in and ready for viewing.

While you're there, check the LDS Family Registry, a listing of thousands of names, addresses and phone numbers of those (like yourself) who are seeking or compiling family history information. Hunt for your family surnames in this registry.

When your research extends beyond the U.S. and Canada borders, remember that other countries also published such community histories. •

# From biographies to genealogies

**F**ollowing are other sources of compiled records that may contain information on your family:

- **Genealogy and family history books.** Lots of families have already published their histories. Such books are often housed in state historical libraries, as well as local libraries. You should check to see whether such a book exists for your family. Also check with ethnic organizations to see what family histories may have been published containing their family information. The North Dakota State Archives facility has an extensive card catalog containing names of families who have published a family history book. If a book has an index, names most commonly appearing in the index are listed in the library's card catalog.

- **Biographies and oral histories.** Check the state archives of both North and South Dakota for special biographical collections. The North Dakota State Archives is the repository for interviews conducted during the Depression years by the Works Progress Administration (WPA). In addition, the Mother's Biographies (unpublished interviews of women living in North Dakota prior to 1900), and the archive's oral history collection should also be checked to see whether a relative may have been among those interviewed.

- **Pioneer histories.** Early history books containing numerous biographies of prominent North Dakota pioneers (such as "Andreas' Atlas," published in 1884 during Dakota Territory days, which includes North and South Dakota biographies;

"Compendium of History and Biography," 1900; and three "History of North Dakota" books, authored by Hennessey (1910), Lounsberry (reprinted in 1917), and Crawford (1930). The North Dakota State Library in Bismarck also has some of these early histories, which can be checked out or ordered via interlibrary loan.

- **Manuscripts, diaries, letters, scrapbooks.** The university libraries in both Dakotas have collections of manuscripts, written records, letters, diaries and scrapbooks, along with many family and county histories.

- **Church, business histories:** Groups such as churches or businesses sometimes printed histories, as well, to mark anniversaries or milestones. Check with organizations or libraries in the communities of your ancestors to learn whether such a book may exist for your areas.

- **Directories.** Business directories from the communities (and era) of your family can yield

much data, including occupations of family members. Also check for pioneer phone directories to see whether your ancestors are included there or whether others in the area might bear the same surname and possibly be relatives.

- **Other resources.** For other collections or resources not listed here, contact a historical or genealogical society near your search area for information. Also check out your nearest LDS family history center's FHLC for resources pertaining to particular areas or communities, including biographies, genealogies and histories.•

# Research sites: Keepers

This basket contains my PEDIGREE!

## Genealogy motto: Be prepared!

• When you visit any research facility seeking information on your roots, be sure to bring your basic family history information with you. This includes filled-out pedigree charts and family group sheets for the people whose records you are hoping to access. Ask the person on duty to aid you in locating the resources that can lead you to discovering your roots. •

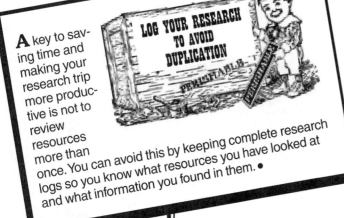

Above: Jim Davis, head of reference services, checks a microfilm reader-printer at the North Dakota State Archives and Historical Research Library, Heritage Center, Bismarck. Left: "Tracing Your Roots" co-authors Jo Ann Winistorfer (standing) and Cathy Langemo examine maps at the Archives Library. Above left: Cathy Langemo checks the computerized death index at the Archives.

O ne of the first steps before embarking on a successful genealogical research trip is organizing your research information—what you have, what you know, and what you need. This step will help you determine your purpose and goals for the trip. That way you will get the most done in the amount of time you have at each location. Research takes time, so allow enough to do the trip justice.

You might consider setting up a special travel binder by location, with copies of family group sheets, timelines, pedigree charts, and other assorted records

for that research location. This will avoid the chance of misplacing or damaging original documents or other information. Though you may want to take all of your information along on the trip, you could take just the one special binder into a research facility.

Also, consider taking along a tape recorder and camera—both still and video—and extra film and flash batteries in case you meet some long-lost relatives, visit cemeteries where ancestors are buried, or see the ancestral home of your great-grandparents.

If you are researching more than one branch of your family at one site, it is particularly important to be organized. Concentrate on just one ancestral line at a time while at that facility. If that's not possible, keep a

handy reference list of all of the surnames you are researching.

A very important part of your preparation will be determining the appropriate research sites at which to find the information you are seeking and contacting the sites or checking their Websites on the Internet. Here are a few things to consider:

• Check on hours and days of operation, as well as upcoming holidays.

• Ask about restrictions at each site and what materials you can take into the site. Follow the site's rules without exception.

• Get a list of the resources available at each site and find out whether you need an appointment to use any of the resources.

• Let staff know before your trip what kinds of information you want to research in case any is stored off-site and needs

A key to saving time and making your research trip more productive is not to review resources more than once. You can avoid this by keeping complete research logs so you know what resources you have looked at and what information you found in them. •

LOG YOUR RESEARCH TO AVOID DUPLICATION

# of Dakota records

to be retrieved ahead of time, or in case any require special permission.

• Ask if you can make copies of materials and if you need change for coin-operated equipment.

• Ask what resources are available by correspondence or through interlibrary loan in case you run out of time during your visit.

• Ask if the research site has a Website you can review before your visit. Perhaps the Website can answer all of your questions without taking a staff member's time.

Once you have information on each of the research sites, make a "wish list" to prioritize the sites you want to visit and what resources you want to review at each site. Also, contact the local tourism offices or Chambers of Commerce for maps of the areas for finding research sites, churches, and cemeteries, as well as general tourist spots in the area.

Once you reach the research site, remember to treat the librarians and archivists with kindness. They will be invaluable to you in your research.

Be polite, patient and courteous—you will get much better service. The research staff, often underpaid and over-worked, can make your research trip a success or a very bad memory.

## Top U.S. research sites

According to a "Genealogy Bulletin" article, the top six genealogical resource sites nationally are:

• The Family History Library, Salt Lake City, UT
• The National Archives and Records Administration (NARA) in Washington, DC
• The American Antiquarian Society Library, Worcester, MA
• The Allen County Public Library, Fort Wayne, IN
• The Library of Congress, Washington, DC
• Daughters of the American Revolution (DAR) Library, Washington, DC.

In addition, there are many regional sites that are well-known and extensively used by genealogists in their research.

A large number of sites also exist at the state and local levels. Usually, these state and local facilities

## These archives are 'keepers'!

The two official keepers of North and South Dakota records and their contact addresses are as follows:

• South Dakota State Archives, 900 Governors Drive, Pierre, SD 57501-2217; 605-773-3804. E-mail: archief@state.sd.us. Website: www. sdhistory.org/arc/ archives.htm

• North Dakota State Archives and Historical Research Library, 612 E. Boulevard Ave., Bismarck, ND 58505-0830; 701-328-2091. E-mail: archives@state.nd. us. Website: www. state.nd.us/hist/sal. htm •

## Do's & don't's

### OF VISITING A RESEARCH FACILITY

In order to preserve their historical materials, most research facilities require that visitors complete a registration form and review the rules for the facility. Some do's and don't's include:

**DO:**
• Handle materials with care.
• Maintain the order of materials in folders or boxes.
• Have only one box open at a time; remove only one folder at a time.
• Use only pencils for taking notes, to protect the research materials.
• Use personal computers, laptop computers, cameras, and dictating equipment only if they will not disturb other researchers. Make arrangements with a staff member.
• Put your personal belongings in a locker, which is free of charge.
• Ask questions if you have them, to make your research trip as successful as possible.

**DO NOT:**
• Bend or fold documents.
• Photocopy fragile materials without permission.
• Mark materials or erase existing marks.
• Make changes on archival or reference materials.
• Take notes on top of archival materials.
• Apply paper clips, fasteners, tape, or "post-it" notes on materials.
• Reshelve materials.
• Eat, drink, use tobacco products or chew gum in the research room.
• Remove materials from the research area.
• Allow unsupervised children in the research room.
• Touch surfaces of photos with fingers.
• Wait until too late in the research day to request materials or copies. •

# Which is which?

What is the difference between a library and a state archives?

- The public library's collection of books and periodicals will depend on the demand of the local patrons, the funding for collections development, space constraints, and the knowledge and support of staff.

- Some of the larger libraries may have most of the census microfilms for all the states, as well as a substantial collection of books and materials of local and regional interest. Small libraries may have only microfilm for their state and surrounding areas.

- A state archives provides more resources than a public library. Typically, the state archives maintains the original documents for all counties in that state. Many records, such as estate papers, service and/or pension records, land records, tax records, all types of court records, and a wealth of other records, may be stored at a state archives. •

are more beneficial to the genealogist because they are closer to the area where his/her ancestors lived. These sites would have more information about the local history of the ethnic groups and migrations in that particular area and perhaps hold more historical documents, both primary and secondary sources.

State or local sites may include regional or state archives and public genealogical society and university libraries. Checking Directory Assistance, city directories, and the Internet can provide you with addresses and telephone numbers for research facilities in the areas of interest to you.

For contact information on sites listed in this chapter, turn to the bibliography and the address list in the Appendix.

## North Dakota research sites

- The State Historical Society of North Dakota's State Archives and Historical Research Library is an important starting point for genealogical research in the Dakotas.

Located in the North Dakota Heritage Center on the Capitol grounds, Bismarck, the archives and library maintain extensive genealogical, historical, and manuscript collections, as well as:
- Naturalization records
- Census records
- Newspapers
- Town/county histories
- Land information, such as county atlases and

land tract books
- The Historical Data Project (WPA) biographies
- Oral history project biographies (audiotaped interviews done in the 1970s)
- The Necrology of North Dakota project resulting in six scrapbooks and obituaries from 1920-26
- The Photo Archives with over 100,000 black and white images from 1865 to the present
- The Pioneer Mothers Project, organized by the North Dakota General Federation of Women's Clubs during the 1930s (files contain family histories, biographies, obituaries, and lineage charts).

Two finding aids are particularly useful at the library—the "Guide to Manuscripts" and the "Guide to the North Dakota State Archives," both compiled by David P. Gray.

Although the archives and library materials generally cannot be used outside the research facility, most North Dakota newspapers, state censuses, naturalizations, and early atlases are on microfilm and available through interlibrary loan. The loan fee within North Dakota is $1 per roll, while microfilm going outside the state is $2 per roll.

Very limited research is done by the library staff. Research requests, with as

much information as possible, must be in writing, with each containing no more than three items to search. Each census, naturalization, or newspaper search is $5, plus the charge for photocopies or copies from microfilm, and postage. A list of area researchers is also available upon request.

The library is open Monday through Friday from 8 a.m. to 4:30 p.m. CT, as well as the second Saturday of each month. For more information on hours and on naturalization records, the 1885 census, and the newspaper databases, see the Website at www.state.nd.us/host.

- Another strategic North Dakota research site is the Elwyn B. Robinson Department of Special Collections at the Chester Fritz Library, University of North Dakota, Grand Forks.

The Department of Special Collections contains a family history/genealogy room with a variety of resources emphasizing the Dakotas and northwestern Minnesota.

Materials include censuses, land tract books, American Lutheran Church records, and naturalization records for the Red River Valley counties. Researchers will also find materials on the three major ethnic groups that settled in the Dakotas and Minnesota—the Scandinavians; the Canadians of English, Irish and Scottish descent; and the Germans fromRussia.

More than 1,000 Norwegian local history books or

# Dakota repositories house vital records

The North Dakota Department of Health's Division of Vital Records, located in the State Capitol, Bismarck, will be an important stop for researchers. The Vital Records office is responsible for the registration and certification of all vital events occurring within North Dakota, including births, deaths, marriages, and divorces.

Copies of the certificates are available if you have sufficient information for a certificate search. Minimum information requirements for death certificates are name of person and date and place of death. If you do not have that basic information, you can acquire it through the computerized death index at the State Archives and Historical Research Library. For birth certificates, more information than the above is desirable, such as parents' names, including the mother's maiden name.

Birth records exist from 1870 to present, while death records are available from 1881 to present. However, birth and death records prior to the early 1900s need to be researched at the county level. In 1923, records were required to be centralized at the Vital Records office in Bismarck, but many events were registered at the state level before then.

Marriage records exist at the Vital Records office from July 1925 and can be researched through a computerized marriage index at the library. The original records are maintained on the county level and start earlier than 1925.

A computerized divorce index begins in July 1949, but no certificates are issued by the Vital Records office. Copies can be requested from the county clerk of court's office where the event occurred.

Copies of birth certificates are $7 each, and marriage and death certificates are $5 each.

The Data, Statistics and Vital Records office, a division of the South Dakota Department of Health, has maintained the state's vital records (birth, marriage, divorce, and death records) since July 1905. Prior to that, records were kept at the county level.

The Department of Health is in the process of transferring birth records to its computer system, making it easier for researchers and others to get certified copies of birth records for anyone born in South Dakota since 1981 at any of that state's county register of deeds offices.

Unofficial birth records over 100 years old are available on the Department of Health's Website (see Chapter 3 bibliography). This effort, when completed, will make about 80,000 records available for genealogical research free of charge.

Marriage, divorce, and death records can also be ordered via the Website.

Copies of vital records are available at $10 per search by writing to the Department of Health—Data, Statistics and Vital Records. Payment must accompany the request, whether it be check, cash, or money order through the mail or a credit card order through the office's Website.

Some early records may also be found in the register of deeds office in the county where the event occurred. A list of county offices is included in the address section of the appendix. •

"bygdeboks" are particularly valuable, and a guide to them is available.

The family history room also has church, county, and city anniversary books; histories of North Dakota; city directories for Grand Forks and Fargo; telephone directories; published family histories and genealogies; and various bibliographies. A guide to the resources is available to assist researchers.

The Department of Special Collections is open Monday, Tuesday, and Thursday from 8 a..m. to 5 p.m. CT, on Wednesday from 8 a.m. to 9 p.m. CT, and on Friday from 8 a.m. to 4:30 p.m. CT.

• The Germans from Russia Heritage Society's research library, in Bismarck, emphasizes Germans from Russia information. The society maintains extensive records, published works, maps, passenger lists, obituary files, cemetery listings, bibliographies, family histories, and other materials on this ethnic group. Hours for the library are Monday through Friday from 8 a.m. to 5 p.m. CT.

• The North Dakota Institute for Regional Studies, North Dakota State University libraries, Fargo, is a favorite stop for many genealogical researchers. There you can find one of the major genealogical collections in North Dakota, including an extensive collection of Germans from Russia materials.

Researchers are also encouraged to review the institute's extensive pho-

## Churches kept tabs on members

- Church archives hold records of their parishioners—past and present. This is a valuable resource for researchers. Refer also to our section on church records in Chapter 2 for information on the archives and what you'll find there. •

tograph collections with invaluable historical images, census records, naturalization records, church histories, pioneer biography files, North Dakota biography index, pioneer mothers' project records, North Dakota newspapers, land tract books, published family histories, and other materials and databases.

During the academic year, the institute is open Monday through Friday, 8 a.m. to 4:30 p.m. CT (and 8 a.m. to 8 p.m. on Wednesdays); summer hours are 7:30 a.m. to 4 p.m. CT. Check their Website for more information: www.lib.ndsu. nodak.edu/ndirs.

- The North Dakota State Library, on the Capitol grounds in Bismarck, holds source material and coordinates libraries statewide. Though the library's resources are limited for genealogical research, it does have county histories and other similar materials that can

be used through interlibrary loan.

- Historical and genealogical societies in North Dakota offer materials and various published information to assist genealogical researchers. They include the Bismarck-Mandan Historical and Genealogical Society, Bismarck; the Mouse River Loop Genealogical Society, Minot; the James River Genealogical Society, Carrington; the Red River Valley Genealogical Society, Fargo; and the North Dakota State Genealogical Society, Bismarck; and others.

These organizations offer many finding aids, family histories, community and county histories, and other resources to aid researchers.

## South Dakota research sites

- South Dakota's Cultural Heritage Center in Pierre houses the State Historical Society, the

State Museum and the State Archives.

The State Archives portion of the center is open Monday through Friday and the first Saturday of each month from 9 a.m. to 4:30 p.m. CT and is closed Sundays and on all state holidays.

The public may use the archives and library collections; limited assistance is provided by staff and several volunteers. Finding aids and online catalogs are available. A list of local genealogists who do research for a fee is also available upon request.

Researchers are allowed to retrieve microfilm personally and return the rolls to an assigned spot when finished. There is no charge for using materials in the research room, which holds about 20 researchers and is equipped with microfilm readers/ printers and some audiovisual equipment.

Check on the latest fees for photocopies, photographic prints and other services shortly before your visit to the archives.

The genealogy resources of the archives, which began in 1891 with the creation of the South Dakota State Historical Society, is a comprehensive collection of state, federal, and private records documenting the state's history. It continues to grow through the efforts of the State Historical Society, state government agencies, genealogical societies, and private individuals.

State government records available at the

## Ellis Island center documents U.S. immigration story

**A** major national genealogical research site is located on Ellis Island in New York. Since the American Family Immigration History Center opened at the Ellis Island Immigration Museum in 2001, many new and exciting things have become available for researchers with ancestral connections to Ellis Island. The center's main focus is a computerized database providing researchers with automated access to more than 22 million passenger records, about 60 percent of all U.S. immigration records. The work of digitizing the Ellis Island records, completed in 2000, began in 1993 as a volunteer cooperative effort of the National Park Service, the U.S. Department of the Interior, and the Church of Jesus Christ of Latter-day Saints. Five computer kiosks throughout the museum enable visitors to view multimedia presentations highlighting the research activities available at the center. •

archives include population censuses from 1895 through 1945 (only 1895 is available on microfilm through interlibrary loan), school censuses, naturalization records, probates, penitentiary prisoner files, atlases, maps, and veteran bonus files.

Federal government records include population censuses from 1860 through 1930 and the 1885 special territorial census (available on microfilm through interlibrary loan), homestead land tract books, military post returns during the 1800s, Bureau of Indian Affairs records and censuses, and WPA cemetery survey files.

Other resources include over 1,000 newspaper titles on microfilm and available through interlibrary loan, as well as photographs, town and county histories, court records, the Pioneer Daughters collection, and assorted manuscripts.

Indexing of the naturalization records is under way, with all but two counties available online. The archives is also acquiring Bureau of Indian Affairs microfilm pertaining to South Dakota reservations from the National Archives and Records Administration (NARA) .

The library contains about 26,000 volumes relating to South Dakota and the northern Great Plains, such as town, county, and church histories; city and business directories; and family histories.

A significant collection of early New England genealogy is housed in the library for those with ancestors from that area of the country. A South Dakota authors' file and a "notable South Dakotans" biographical file are also maintained. The surname reference file was created for researchers to find others working on the same family lines.

Once the patron has reviewed the research room rules, he/she can settle into a comfortable chair at a nice wooden table while deciding what resources to delve into.

• The Alexander Mitchell Library in Aberdeen contains a very good genealogical collection, as well as railroad employee records.

• Augustana College's Mikkelsen Library in Sioux Falls holds the church archives of the Episcopal Church in South Dakota. Visitors can review the "Guide to the Archives of the Episcopal Church in South Dakota" by Alan Schwartz, or visit www.inst.augie.edu/library/services/service.html.

The fall and spring semester hours at the library run on Sunday from noon to 11 p.m. CT, on Monday through Thursday from 8 a.m. to 11 p.m. CT, on Friday from 8 a.m. to 6 p.m. CT, and on Saturday from 10 a.m. to 5 p.m. CT.

• Another genealogical research site in South Dakota is the Center for Western Studies, also at Augustana College. The center includes information on both Dakotas, as well as northwestern Iowa, and is especially noted for its collections on South Dakota's American Indians, its Scandinavian pioneers, and the archival church records for the Evangelical, Reformed, and United Church of Christ churches throughout North and South Dakota.

• The archival records for both North and South Dakota Methodist churches are housed at the Dakotas Conference offices in Mitchell. You can reach the office at www.umc.org/churchlibrary.

• The Sioux Valley Genealogical Society in Sioux Falls maintains a library that has a good microfilm collection of cemetery and old church records, information on South Dakota history and family records, surname files with obituaries, and other vital records.

The library is free and open to the public. It is open Monday through Saturday from 1 to 5 p.m. CT. The society can be reached at Old Courthouse Museum, 200 W. Sixth St., Sioux Falls, SD 57104-6001.

• The South Dakota Genealogical Society, with offices in Pierre, can be very helpful in advising on where to find certain records, whom to contact, and other intricacies of genealogical research in South Dakota.

The society is a statewide organization of genealogists in South Dakota and across the U.S. The Alexander Mitchell Library, Aberdeen, houses

State libraries of North and South Dakota are excellent places to look for county histories, biographies, and general histories of both states.

Don't forget interlibrary loan! If you live in a rural area away from a local library, you can access books through interlibrary loan from your state library. Addresses are:

• North Dakota State Library, 604 E. Boulevard Ave-Dept. 250, Bismarck, ND 58505-0800; 701-328-4657, Fax 701-328-2040

• South Dakota State Library, 800 Governors Drive, Pierre, SD 57501-2294; 605-773-3131 or 800-423-6665 •

# More research sites

(ALL CENTRAL TIME)

- Bonanzaville, U.S.A., 1351 W. Main Ave., Interstate 94, Exit 343, West Fargo, ND 58078; 701-282-2822. —May: Mon.-Fri. 9 a.m.-5 p.m. —June–Sept.: Six days a week, 10 a.m.-5 p.m.; Sun., noon-5 p.m. —Oct.–Dec.: Mon.-Fri., noon-5 p.m.

- Concordia College, Carl B. Ylvisaker Library, 901 St., Eighth St., Moorhead, MN 56562; 218-299-4640. Mon.-Thurs. 7:45 a.m.-midnight; Fri. 7:45 a.m.-7 p.m.; Sat., 10 a.m.-7 p.m.; Sun., noon-midnight. August: 7:45 a.m.-5 p.m.

- North Dakota State University Libraries, NDSU Station, 1201 Albrecht Blvd., P.O. Box 5599, Fargo, ND 58105-5599; 701-231-8876. Mon.-Thurs., 7:30 a.m.- midnight; Fri., 7:30 a.m.-5 p.m.; Sun., 1 p.m.-midnight. Summers and breaks, hours slightly different.

- Red River Valley Genealogical Society and Library, 112 N. University Drive, Suite L-116, Manchester Building, Fargo, ND 58106-9284; 701-239-4129. Tues., Wed. and Sat., 11 a.m.-3 p.m.

- West Fargo Historical Center, 109 Third St. E., West Fargo, ND 58078 (in West Fargo Public Library); 701-433-5460. Opens at 10 a.m. every day except Sun. Closes at: Mon.-Wed., 9 p.m.; Tues.-Thurs., 8 p.m.; Fri.-6 p.m.; Sat., 5 p.m. •

many of its collections.
- The South Dakota National Guard Museum in Pierre is the repository for historical information on the Guard. The museum is open Monday through Friday from 9 a.m. to 4 p.m. CT.
- The South Dakota State Library, a division of the South Dakota Department of Education and Cultural Affairs, maintains research and reference resources on South Dakota. Located in Pierre, the library is open Monday through Friday from 8 a.m. to 5 p.m. CT.
- The I.D. Weeks Library at the University of South Dakota, Vermillion, holds archival and historical collections on South Dakota, along with manuscripts, government documents, business and church records, ethnic information, and more. Monday through Thursday, library hours are 7:45 a.m. to midnight; Friday, 7:45 to 10 p.m.; Saturday, 10 a.m. to 5 p.m.; Sunday, 1 p.m. to midnight.

## Sites around the country

- The American Historical Society of Germans from Russia, in Lincoln, NE, maintains a library of family histories that can be accessed through interlibrary loan at your local library. The histories are set up alphabetically by family name, by author/title, and in order as they are on the library shelves.
- The DAR Library, founded in 1896, contains some of the most valuable research material in the U.S. Its collection of

genealogical and historical publications is used by staff genealogists for verifying National Society of the Daughters of the American Revolution (DAR) application papers. And with many of its resources online at www.dar.org/library, you can do much of your research from home.

Located at 1776 D St. N.W., Washington, DC 20006, the library is one of the country's premier genealogical research centers and has been ranked by *Heritage Quest* as the third most important national institution because of its unique sources. Hours are 8:30 a.m. to 4 p.m. weekdays; 9 a.m. to 5 p.m. Saturday.

- The Library of Congress has many of its historical collections available on the Internet through the American Memory Website and its National Digital Library Program. Totaling more than one million items, the library's unique materials have been collected and preserved since its founding in 1800. Visit this Website for more information: lcweb.loc.gov

- The National Archives and Records Administration (NARA) is another source for genealogical information outside of the Dakotas. The NARA stores and oversees millions of valuable records from the three branches of the federal government. These records may relate to anyone who ever had dealings with the federal government, including census schedules; Indian, Black,

District of Columbia, and military service records; public land records, including homestead files; naturalization records before 27 Sept. 1906; passenger arrival lists; birth, marriage and death records for events that occurred at U.S. Army facilities; passport applications; personnel records for federal government civilian employees; military pension application files; district court records, both civil and criminal; and bounty land warranties.

These records may contain a little or a lot of information, and searches may be very time-consuming because many of the records do not have surname indexes. The key you need to know is how the person you are researching came into contact with the federal government.

An excellent resource from the NARA is "Getting Started: Beginning Your Genealogical Research in the National Archives." The book discusses the various records that NARA maintains and how to use them.

Another resource is ARC, the Archival Research Catalog (formerly called NARA Archival Information Locator, or NAIL), an interactive database indexing part of NARA's holdings. Offering more sophisticated search capabilities than NAIL, ARC can be used to search hundreds of thousands of descriptions for key words or topics and to retrieve digital copies of textual documents, photographs,

# Abbeys, monasteries preserve history

Monasteries and abbeys can be important genealogical resources because many of them maintain excellent archives and libraries for their region or state.

Assumption Abbey near Richardton is just one example in North Dakota. With more than 95,000 accessions dating back to the 1500s, there is an extensive card file and materials on southwestern North Dakota. You can get more information about the abbey and its collections through its Website at: www.assumption-abbey.com/AbbeyTour/Library/ Library.html.

South Dakota is also home to several monasteries and abbeys with excellent archives and libraries. With its first monks coming to what is now South Dakota in the 1870s to work with the Indians, the Blue Cloud Abbey in Marvin, SD, maintains considerable information on the Indians of South Dakota. For more information, you can visit the abbey's Website at: www.bluecloud.org

In Watertown, SD, the Mother of God Monastery offers archival records on their Benedictine order and on their work in South Dakota. To learn more about the monastery, check out its Website at: www. watertownbenedictines.org •

---

maps, and recordings.

If enough identifying information is provided, the NARA will do record searches. However, staff members are unable to pursue extensive searches.

The agency has 17 Regional Records Services Facilities throughout the U.S. where individuals can do research.

• Denver is the NARA branch for the Rocky Mountain Region, including North and South Dakota, and is located in Building 48 of the Denver Federal Center, at W. Sixth Ave. and Kipling St.

The Denver branch is open to the public weekdays from 7:30 a.m. to 3:45 p.m. MT, remaining open on Thursday evenings until 7 MT. It is also open the first and third Saturdays of each month from 8:30 a.m. to 4:45 p.m.

The Denver branch's historical holdings, dating from 1860, consist mainly of local court records; U.S. censuses; military service records, pensions, and bounty and warrant applications; IRS assessment lists; an extensive collection of American Indian censuses; and various passenger arrival lists.

Researchers should schedule visits in advance. If using original records, they will receive a researcher ID card. Records may be photocopied unless their condition prohibits it. The facility has a self-service microfilm reader room where no appointment is necessary. Paper copies can be made from microfilm.

• NARA's Central Plains branch in Kansas City, MO, opens its research room from 8 a.m. to 4 p.m. CT, Monday through Friday. It is also open on the third Saturday of each month from 9 a.m. to 4 p.m. CT. Though the Central Plains branch covers Kansas, Missouri, Iowa, and Nebraska, it has records relating to North Dakota.

• When you are in the Washington, DC, area, plan some research at the National Genealogical Society's library. Write for information on its holdings at 3108 Columbia Pike Suite. 300, Arlington, VA 22224-4304. You can call NGS at 703-525-0050 or 800-473-0060, or check out this Website: www. ngsgenealogy.org

• If your genealogical research has led you to New England, check out the oldest and largest genealogical society in the U.S., the New England Historic Genealogical Society. The society allows access to its extensive genealogical collections of over 200,000 volumes of family histories, vital records, town histories, and other published works. The circulating book collection contains more than 30,000 volumes, available via interlibrary loan, for a fee.

The research center is staffed by knowledgeable genealogists who can assist you. Hours are Tuesday, Thursday, Friday and Saturday, 9 a.m. to 5 p.m. ET; and Wednesday, 9 a.m. to 9 p.m. The library is closed Sunday, Monday and holidays.

Or check out www. newenglandancestors.org •

## Military records

• The U.S. Army's Military History Institute at Carlisle Barracks, PA, houses one of the nation's finest collections of research material on World War II, as well as materials on the Spanish American War, World War I and Korea. You can contact the institute by telephone at 717-245-3971 or visit: www. carlisle.army.mil for details.

• If you have an ancestor who was in the Confederate military during the U.S. Civil War, you might want to contact the Confederate Research Center at P.O. Box 619, Hillsboro, TX 76645.•

- Here are some tips for anyone planning a trip to the world's number one genealogy records repository—the LDS Family History Library in Salt Lake City:

- Before you go, do your homework: Decide which section(s) you wish to visit (i.e., Scandinavian, colonial, Germany), as well as the resources you plan to research while you're there. Jot down the library's hours, and be sure to bring money along for making copies, etc.

- Allow plenty of time for research, as it's a big place with lots of wonderful records. •

# LDS records: Available at family history centers

You don't have to travel to Europe, or even to Minnesota or Montana, to get answers to many questions that pertain to ancestors in other states, countries, or continents—thanks to a handful of mini-genealogy centers based in the Dakotas and elsewhere.

They're linked to the largest collection of genealogical information in the world—the holdings of the LDS Family History Library in Salt Lake City.

"LDS" stands for the Church of Jesus Christ of Latter Day Saints (Mormon church). The LDS Church's emphasis on genealogy is based on the belief that the family is eternal and that identifying ancestors (and performing ordinance work, including proxy baptisms), helps unite families in the afterlife and extends the family relationship for all eternity.

To help its members glean their ancestors' genealogical data , the church has microfilmed records and extracted names of people and families, their vital statistics, and documents attesting to their place and space in history, from more than 110 countries around the world.

Copies of original records include vital statistics, census, church, land, pro-bate, and other records of value to genealogists. Also available are compilations of information found in original records, such as biographies, genealogies, and family and area histories. Nearly 2.3 million rolls of microfilmed records are stored in vaults tunneled into Granite Mountain near Salt Lake City.

The library, located in the city's center, contains copies (mostly on microfilm) of records housed in these vaults. You don't have to be Mormon to use—and benefit from—these vast resources. Salt Lake City is a Mecca to genealogists; information on people of all races and reli-

## What you'll find at the LDS family history centers

The family history centers are prime places to search for pre-1900 records. Resources include the following:

- The Family History Library Catalog (FHLC) is an index to hundreds of thousands of microfilms and microfiche housed in the main library in Salt Lake City (most of which may be ordered through the centers). Remarkably, this entire catalog, filed by locality, all fits onto one compact disk! Look here to find out what resources—from church records to area histories —are available for the community you're searching.
- The Ancestral File, a FamilySearch computer file consisting of genealogies of families from around the world, contains millions of names and is linked to pedigrees showing ancestors and descendants.
- The Family Registry helps patrons locate others who are researching the same names.
- The Social Security Death Index is a computer file listing millions of names of people who died in the U.S. since 1962.
- The Accelerated Indexing System (AIS) lists names taken from the U.S. censuses; it is available on microfiche at the centers.

- The International Genealogical Index (IGI) is an index of around 600 million names from 110 countries, with more being added daily. It includes dates and places of births, christenings, and marriages. (The IGI does not include burials or deaths.)

The IGI can be viewed via compact disk on a center's computer and is also available on microfiche. Most of this data has been extracted from original records created by governments or churches from the 1500s to the early 1900s.

Other major indexes are also available via computers at the centers. •

# LDS centers in the Dakotas

Following are North and South Dakota family history centers, their locations and hours (all times Central Time unless otherwise noted).

## • NOTE •
Before you travel a long distance to visit an LDS family history center, call first to confirm hours in case of schedule changes or church holidays. •

## NORTH DAKOTA

**Bismarck**
1500 Country West Road
Bismarck, ND 58503
701-223-6384
Hours: T & Th–6 to 9 p.m.; W–9 a.m. to 3 p.m., 6 to 9 p.m.; S–9 a.m. to 3 p.m.

**Dickinson**
1200 N. Alder Road
Dickinson, ND 58601
701-227-0267
Hours: T–5 to 8 p.m., W–9 a.m. to noon (MT)

**Fargo**
2501 17th Ave. S.W.
Fargo, ND 58102
701-232-4003
Hours: W–9 a.m. to 1 p.m., 6:30 to 8:30 p.m.; Th–9 a.m. to 1 p.m.; S–9 a.m. to noon

**Grand Forks**
2814 Cherry Street
Grand Forks, ND 58201
701-746-6126
Hours: T & Th–5-9 p.m.

**Jamestown**
2237 S.E. 2nd St.
Jamestown, ND 58401

701-237-9505
Hours: M–1 to 9 p.m.; T, Th & F–by appt.; S–10 a.m. to 2 p.m.

**Minot**
2025 Ninth St. N.W.
Minot, ND 58701
701-838-3149
Hours: T–10 to 11:30 a.m., 7 to 8:30 p.m.; W–7 to 8:30 p.m.; Th–10 a.m. to 1 p.m.; S–10-to 11:30 a.m.

**Wahpeton**
505 Richland St. W.
Wahpeton, ND 58075
701-642-2463
Hours: Th–1 to 7:30 p.m.

**Williston**
1805 26th St. W.
Williston, ND 58801
701-572-3502
Hours: W–10 a.m. to 4 p.m., 6 to 9 p.m.; F–11 a.m. to 5 p.m.

## SOUTH DAKOTA

**Aberdeen**
1115 24th Ave. N.E.
Aberdeen, SD 57401
605-225-0601

Hours: W & Th–6:30-9:30 p.m. ; S–noon to 5 p.m.

**Belle Fourche**
1105 Todd St.
Belle Fourche, SD 57717
605-892-3700
Hours: W–7 to 10 p.m.

**Brookings**
200 22nd Ave.
Brookings, SD 57006
605-692-7533
Hours: T–9:30 a.m. to noon; W–5:30 to 8:30 p.m.; S–9 a.m. to noon

**Gettysburg**
530 S. Mannston St.
Gettysburg, SD 57442
605-765-9270
Hours: by appt.

**Hot Springs**
2133 Albany St.
Hot Springs, SD 57747
605-745-6119
Hours: W–9 a.m. to 4 p.m.; F– 10 a.m. to 5 p.m.

**Huron**
1450 Frank St. S.E.
Huron, SD 57350
605-352-6849

Hours: T & Th–10 a.m. to 6 p.m.; S–1 to 6 p.m.

**Madison**
927 N. Lee Ave.
Madison, SD 57042
605-256-6335
Hours: W & Th–7-10 p.m.; other times by appt.

**Pierre**
506 N. Jefferson
Pierre, SD 57501
605-224-9117
Hours: T–1 to 5 p.m.; W–1 to 9 p.m.; Th & F-7 to 9 p.m.; S–10 a.m. to 2 p.m.

**Rapid City**
2822 Canyon Lake Drive
Rapid City, SD 57701
605-343-8656
Hours: T–9 a.m. to 8:30 p.m.; W–1 to 8:30 p.m.; Th–9 a.m. to 5 p.m.; F–1 to 5 p.m.; S–9 a.m. to 1 p.m.

**Rosebud**
Highway 7, West St.
Rosebud, SD 57570
605-747-2128

Hours: M, W, Th & F–9 a.m. to 4 p.m.; T–2 to 5 p.m.; S–9 a.m. to 1 p.m.

**Sioux Falls**
3900 S. Fairhall Ave.
Sioux Falls, SD 57101
605-361-1070
Hours: T & Th–9 a.m. to 3 p.m., 6:30 to 9:30 p.m.; F–1 to 4 p.m.; S–9 a.m. to 3 p.m.

**Vermillion**
20 Michelsen Ave.
Vermillion, SD 57069
605-624-7139
Hours: W–6 to 9 p.m.; S–10 a.m. to 2 p.m.

**Watertown**
1200 19th St. N.E.
Watertown, SD 57201
605-882-2299
Hours: Th–7 to 9 p.m.

**Yankton**
23rd and Douglas
Yankton, SD 57078
605-665-0901
Hours: W–7 to 9 p.m.; S–1 to 3 p.m. •

---

gions is filed there and accessible to anyone.

There are original church records; birth, marriage, and death records; lists containing names (and points of departure and arrival) of passengers who sailed on emigrant ships; early newspapers; and out-of-print reference works, such as maps, gazetteers, and atlases.

And there are census and military service records; wills and court documents; immigration and land records—to name just a few.

You don't have to travel to the Salt Lake Family History Library to access these records—thanks to more than 4,000 family history centers located in 88 coun-

tries. A number of these centers are sprinkled around the Dakotas, as well (see box above for listing of North and South Dakota centers).

Each center has its own hours. They're closed on Sundays (except to members) and during holidays and special church festivities. So it's best to phone ahead to check on hours if you plan to visit a center.

## Library with few books

When you first visit a center near you, you may be expecting to see thousands of books lining the shelves. While there are some reference books, most of the cen-

ters' resources are on microfiche or microfilm.

Microfiche and microfilm viewers are part of the furniture at the centers. These and other records are available on user-friendly disks, which can be accessed via a computer set up at each center.

The centers are staffed by volunteers. Most are doing family research on their own lines and are eager to help you learn more about yours.

Many of the items at the centers are indexes or catalogs (on microfiche or compact computer disks) that tell you what microfilm (or in some cases, microfiche) you can order to get more information.

# Goin' fiche-in'

- LDS family history centers typically have a permanent microfiche collection of the most-used genealogy reference materials, ranging from gazetteers and atlases to books and documents. Before you order film or fiche, check to see what resources the center already has on hand. •

## Be a copycat!

- Basic hardware in most family history centers includes microfilm and microfiche viewers, a computer set up to access the International Genealogical Index (IGI) and the Family History Library Catalog (FHLC), a printer, a microfilm/microfiche copier, and a photocopy machine. Ask the volunteer on duty if you have questions about using the equipment. Remember to make copies of any pertinent information you find. •

## Ordering films, fiche

When you find your ancestors or community listed on any of a center's indexes, you put in your order at the center for microfilms of the original records from which the information was extracted. Your order will arrive in a week or two.

Many times, you don't have to order a film or fiche, as the centers have a large permanent collection on hand. This includes microfilms of the 100-most-used genealogy books, as well as gazetteers and atlases for many localities worldwide, and special microfiche collections dealing with many genealogical subjects.

Renting a microfilm costs you $5.50 for a 30-day loan, $5.50 to renew for 60 more days, and $5.50 more for additional time. In some cases, the center may choose to hold your film as part of its permanent collection, depending on its value to patrons.

When your microfilm comes in, you'll be notified. It can then be read on the readers housed at the center; it cannot be removed from the center, but you can view the film during center hours.

While not all the films you order will lead you down the path to discovering another ancestor, many do contain information that can help you add twigs—perhaps even branches—to your family tree.

Should you find data on film or fiche that you'd like to take with you, ask for photocopies (for a small fee) or copy them yourself via a special viewer-copier, also available at each center. Or transfer data from the center's computer files to your own CD !

While the centers all have the same basic resources, they also house special materials geared toward researchers in their region. The Bismarck center, for example, contains 110 films (indexed) containing American Indian census records and other data, and lots of Norwegian parish records, all on microfilm. It also subscribes to Ancestry.com as a free resource to patrons.

Other resources at the centers include in-house reference books, as well as blank genealogy forms: pedigree charts, family group sheets, and research calendars.

## Guided tour

Among the LDS Family History Library's many helpful tools are genealogy Research Guides, available for every state and most countries worldwide.

Check for these inexpensive guides at your local LDS family history center, or look for them on the following Website: www. familysearch.org •

## Find LDS Family History Library sources on-line!

A major development for genealogists is the availability of LDS Family History Library records on line, free of charge. This site—www.familysearch. org—first went online in the spring of 1999; today, it is one of the most-visited Websites.

The site contains links to one billion names, some dating back to the 1500s. Names and other data are being added continuously. Information found on the site includes "how to get started" (a genealogy primer), a listing of family history centers around the world, and standardized genealogy forms (pedigree charts, family group sheets, and research logs).

Categories you can click on for more details include censuses and lists, court and legal records, ethnic and religious group resources, family databases and personal narratives, key genealogical sites, emigration and immigration resources, passenger lists, military records, places around the world, institutions and businesses keeping records, research support and finding aids, heraldic and nobility records, genealogy vendors, family names and organizations, and vital records.

The site is also a marketplace for genealogical materials —especially, compact disks. These include a "SourceGuide" (containing more than 150 resource guides), a Personal Ancestral File companion (that prints quality charts and reports), and a Vital Records Index to North American records.

Crowning the list is the LDS church's genealogy software program—the Personal Ancestral File (PAF). This popular (and relatively inexpensive) program is used by genealogists worldwide. For more on this and other genealogy programs, refer to Chapter 6, high-tech genealogy. •

## They came from many places

- Dakota settlers came from many lands around the globe. Some were native to this land, with roots going back generations before the arrival of the settlers. We salute all groups for the major contributions they made to the Dakotas we know today.

- The sequence and number of pages devoted to each group were based (with some exceptions) on the number of emigrants from each group/related group, the resources available for each group, and the technical, space and time limitations we had to work with. No slight is intended to any group omitted here or those for whom we did not find much information.

- On the following pages, we list major ethnic and cultural groups with roots in the Dakotas, their settlement patterns, and genealogical research materials available for each group.

- We thank all the original historians and researchers who made this information available. We have merely compiled it into one book for your convenience. We hope the material we're presenting here will pique your interest in history and help you discover your Dakota roots. •

# British Isles peoples

English-speaking emigrants from the British Isles left an early and lasting impression on Dakota settlement. Many had already lived for generations in either the U.S. or Canada, so were familiar with the politics and the rules. Their names live on in Dakota towns and streets, and in their systems of government.

### BRITISH, OLD-STOCK AMERICANS, CANADIANS

Much of North and South Dakota's early leadership came from people whose ancestors had planted their roots in eastern and/or central United States a generation or so earlier, pulling up stakes to settle in—and civilize—the Dakotas. These old-stock Americans and Canadians, often of British Isles descent (but also from other European nations), brought with them their laws, their language, their educational systems, their systems of government.

Many became prominent educators, lawyers, business leaders, bankers, politicians, and statesmen.

Some came as land speculators, buying land and selling it later for a profit. When the Dakota boom turned to bust, many moved on to seek their fortunes elsewhere.

Perhaps their most lasting settlement was in the West River country of both North and South Dakota. Around 1874-80, Yankees and their descendants began moving into the western Dakotas from the New England and middle Atlantic states by way of Ohio, Iowa, and Minnesota. Some came up from Texas to claim Dakota lands. Many of their great-grandchildren continue to inhabit these lands today.

The British had much influence on the Dakotas during the fur-trade era, when British traders competed with the French, Spanish, and, eventually, the Americans for Native American customers.

The Scottish were, in fact, among North Dakota's earliest explorers and settlers. In 1811, Thomas Douglas, Earl of Selkirk, established a colony at the juncture of the Pembina and Red rivers in northeastern North Dakota.

In the early 1820s, several years after the Canada-U.S. border changed to the 49th parallel, Pembina residents with British connections pulled up stakes and moved north to what was then British America.

In North Dakota today, Bottineau is perhaps the most Scottish community.

Like their English and Scottish counterparts, the Scotch-Irish (Scottish people from Protestant sections of Ireland) and the "true" Irish were part of the tide of early Dakota inhabitants. Like the English and Scotch, some were Yankees; others came down from Canada.

The potato famine of the 1840s brought a flood of desperate, starving Irish emigrants to the shores of America. Some of this group eventually migrated to the Dakotas.

In 1859, they settled in and near Jefferson, SD. In 1915, there were 26,643 Irish living in South Dakota, many in compact settlements.

North Dakota counties with the largest percentages of people with ancestors from the British Isles and Canada include Pembina and Cavalier. •

| NATIONALITIES IN NORTH DAKOTA, 1980 | | |
|---|---|---|
| | Single ancestry | Multiple ancestry |
| English | 14,419 | 38,021 |
| Scottish | 2,465 | 16,954 |
| Irish | 12,752 | 51,795 |
| Canadian | 3,744 | 244 |
| **TOTAL** | **33,380** | **107,014** |
| Norwegian | 97,515 | 86,750 |
| German | 170,007 | 136,739 |

Based on information from "Plains Folk: North Dakota's Ethnic History"

# RESEARCH TIPS & SOURCES
## CANADIANS

• The **Library and Archives Canada** holds records documenting Canadian history from the 18th century to the present. Included are records of former military and public service employees, wartime sailing lists, and Royal Canadian Air Force records. Many are indexed and/or on a database. Primary holdings include census, military, immigration, and naturalization records. Many records are in both English and French, although most descriptions are in English. For information, contact: Library and Archives Canada, 395 Wellington St., Ottawa, Ontario, Canada K1A 0N4; 866-578-7777 toll-free. Or visit this Website: www.collectionscanada.ca.

Primary genealogical records for Canada include the census; soldiers of World War I's Canadian expeditionary force; records of "home children," children sent to Canada from Great Britain during the child emigration movement (1869 -1930s); dominion land grants; and Canadian newspapers and directories.

For information on accessing Canadian vital records, check with the Library and Archives Canada. Or check the **Family History Library Catalog** at your local LDS family history center for indexes and microfilms of earlier births, marriages, and deaths, as well as Canadian cemetery records. Births, marriages, and deaths after 1902, 1917, and 1927 respectively are available to direct relatives by contacting the registrar general of the appropriate province.

• Contact the **Provincial Archives** in the province where your ancestors resided (see bibliography).

• The **Canadian Genealogy Centre, inGeneas,** is busy building databases that include passenger list records for immigrants arriving at Canadian ports between 1748 and 1873. Recently added to the database were 11,507 passenger records for more than 50 ships from England, Ireland, and Norway, arriving at the port of Quebec City from early July to early October 1872. To find these and any other records that are currently on the database, go to www.ingeneas.com/ingeneas/index.html and do a search.

• **Canadian censuses** conducted in 1851/52, 1861, 1871, 1881, 1891, 1901 and 1911 are available to researchers. Later Canadian censuses are protected by privacy laws for 92 years, making the 1911 census the latest accessible as of this writing (2006). Earlier regional censuses can also provide genealogical information.

• If you don't find **church records** at the national or provincial archives, contact the diocese or synod to learn where the records are held. Also check the Family History Library Catalog to see what indexes or church records exist for your search locality.

## ENGLISH/WELSH

• As with any overseas research, do your homework in the U.S. and/or Canada first, starting with yourself and working back in time, generation by generation, and record by record, to the place your ancestor came from in Great Britain. Until then, your research will involve U.S. and Canadian records.

• The **Newberry Library in Chicago** (www.newberry.org) is a good place to start. This library holds many records for English genealogy and local history outside the British Isles. The library also contains a collection of English genealogies linked to the nobility or gentry. Also check the LDS family history center's Family History Library Card Catalog CD for emigration/immigration records, Canadian records, and early American records.

• A basic book that will introduce you to the records and resources available for British Isles research is Angus Baxter's **"In Search of Your British and Irish Roots."**

• **"The Parliamentary Gazetteer of England and Wales"** (4 volumes, 1843) can help you locate communities and parishes of English ancestors.

• Major genealogical sources for those who have made the leap back in time to England include parish registers, wills, and census records (every 10 years starting in 1801, except for 1941). Of particular value are the **"Census Returns of Great Britain, 1841,"** available on microfilm through the LDS family history centers. Reels cover England, Wales, the Channel Islands, and the Isle of Man. Other censuses of Great Britain are also available through the LDS centers. Parish records have also been microfilmed.

• Check the **International Genealogical Index (IGI)** at an LDS family history center for extractions of births and marriages for England and Wales. Also check the LDS Family History Library Catalog (FHLC) CD for other records available on Great Britain. Or visit the LDS Website (see Chapter 3 for details).

• Copies of civil registration certificates (1 July 1837 to present) are available by writing the **General Register Office,** St. Catherine's House, 10 Kingsway, London, England WC2B 6JP.

## IRISH

• An understanding of administrative jurisdictions in Ireland is helpful in locating Irish records. Today, the country is divided into four administrative districts: Ulster, Munster, Leinster, and Connacht. **"The Alphabetical Index to the Townlands and Towns of Ireland"** by Alexander Thom (on microfilm and microfiche from the LDS Family History Library and its centers) can help you find old Irish place names.

• Most early Irish census records are fragmented; others burned. The 1901 census is the earliest complete enumeration available; microfilms can be ordered from family history centers.

• Catholicism and the Church of Ireland were the principal religions; other groups included Huguenots, Presbyterians (mainly the Scotch-Irish), Baptists, and Quakers. Most parish registers date back to around 1770. Natural vital records registration began in 1864; many have been microfilmed.

• The **Irish Genealogical Society International,** P.O. Box 16585, St. Paul, MN 55116-6585, may be able to help you find your Irish roots. The Website address is www.rootsweb.com/~irish.

• A book by Edward MacLysaght entitled **"Irish Families, Their Names, Arms and Origins"** gives insight into the history of Irish names and families.

## SCOTTISH

• Before 1855, Scotland's vital records were maintained by the church. Many were destroyed by war or lost through poor record-keeping. The official church of Scotland changed (beginning in 1550) from Catholic to Presbyterian to Episcopalian to Quaker, back to Episcopalian and, in 1695, back to Presbyterian.

• Civil registration began in 1855. Indexes from 1855-1955 and vital records from 1855-75, 1881, and 1891 have been microfilmed by the **Family History Library** in Salt Lake City, UT, which means you can access them through a family history center. The old parochial registers (1558-present) , census sheets (from 1841-91), tax rollssasines (title transfers), and deeds registers are on microfilm.

• **"In Search of Scottish Ancestry"** by Gerald Hamilton-Edwards (Phillimore and Company, London, 1972) offers insight into records available and places to look.

## SCOTCH-IRISH

• The Scotch-Irish were descendants of Presbyterian Scots, cleared out of Scotland by the English government and placed in northern Ireland in the early 1600s. Many emigrated to America and British America (Canada) from 1718 on.

Refer to Great Britain and Irish research information listed on this page for availability of Scotch-Irish records. •

## Different strokes for different 'volk'!

According to the book "Plains Folk: North Dakota's Ethnic History," the German colonists in Russia settled in districts (each containing a number of villages) according to church affiliation. The primary religion of each settlement is as follows:

• The primary Catholic regions were Crimea, Liebental, Prischib, Kutschurgan, Beresan, Bessarabia, and Mariupol.

• Evangelical (Lutheran) settlements included Liebental, Crimea, Prischib, Gluckstal, Beresan, Bessarabia, Caucasus, and Mariupol.

• The Mennonites and Hutterites settled in Chortitza, Molotschna, and Mariupol.

• Members of the Reformed religion resided in Gluckstal and Beresan.

• Some Separatists moved on to the remote South Caucasus. •

# Germans from Russia

The epic migrations of the Germans from Russia began in the 18th century, when German-speaking peoples accepted the invitation from a Russian czarina to settle in her country. Over the next two centuries, thousands of people living in and near present-day Germany moved to the Volga and Black Sea regions of Russia. Broken promises led to another mass migration—this time across the ocean to North and South America.

## VOLGA AND BLACK SEA GERMANS

In 1763, Czarina Catherine II (the Great) of Russia issued a manifesto that, more than a century later, would have a profound impact on Dakota settlement.

The manifesto invited people from other European nations to settle in Russia. It was Catherine's hope that this influx of new blood and new ideas would spark her country's agricultural and economic development. Her manifesto promised prospective immigrants free land, religious freedom, self-government, and exemption from military service.

Accepting Catherine's invitation, thousands of German-speaking peoples from Western and Eastern Europe migrated to the steppes of Russia.

The first wave of colonists to respond to Catherine's invitation arrived in Russia in 1763, settling on both sides of the Volga River south of Saratov, north of the Caspian Sea (in what is now Ukraine).

These **Volga German** colonists settled in agricultural villages, farming the surrounding lands. Though they became Russian citizens, they retained their German culture, traditions, and language.

Another plea for colonization came from Catherine's grandson, Czar Alexander I, who ruled Russia from 1801 to 1825. His manifesto invited skilled, successful German farmers and craftsmen to serve as role models in occupations ranging from agriculture to industry. Emigrants from this group settled primarily in the northern Black Sea region (now Ukraine). **Black Sea Germans** had begun migrating to this region as early as 1781, but came in large numbers after 1804 following Alexander's manifesto.

Successive waves of immigration, coupled with a high birth rate, soon exploded the German-Russian population. When village resources and lands could no longer support the growing number of people, daughter colonies were formed, including some in the Caucasus region.

According to the book "Dakota Panorama," edited by J. Leonard Jennewein and Jane Boorman, the Volga German population increased from 23,019 in 1768 to 668,896 by 1914. By 1859, there were 153 German colonies in the Black Sea region, totaling 106,123 people. This increased to 526,795 by 1914. Altogether, there was a total of more than a million German people in the two Russian areas by 1914.

Generally, these people prospered on the fertile steppe lands they settled. But dark shadows soon appeared on the horizon. In 1866, the Russians began an assimilation policy that took away some of the German-Russians' privileges. Compulsory military training went into effect in 1871. German control of local government was abolished in 1876, and Russian was declared the official language in the 1890s. These factors, plus poor crops between 1884 and 1897 and "America letters" from relatives who had already emigrated, prompted the Germans to leave Russia in large numbers.

The exodus to America began in 1872, and continued to World War I (1914).

The railroads, under construction when the Germans from Russia first came to Dakota but completed by the first decade of the 20th century,

## Mapping your history

- Maps of the Germans from Russia colonies (11-by-17-inch color laminated maps of the German villages of South Russia, including those of the Black Sea, Bessarabia, Dobruscha and Volga Germans) are available at the Germans from Russia Heritage Collection Website:www.lib. ndsu.nodak.edu/ grhc/order/maps.html. Or write to: Germans from Russia Heritage Collection, NDSU Library, P.O. Box 5599, Fargo, ND 58105-5599.

- Cyndi's List is another source for maps: http://www.cyndislist. com/germruss.htm

- Refer to the Chapter 2 section on land records for other sources of maps. •

influenced their settlement patterns.

The Volga group settled in an area between eastern Montana, Colorado, and the Pacific Coast. Some moved into Butte and Perkins counties in western South Dakota.

The Black Sea Germans settled mainly in North and South Dakota. Other prime areas of Black Sea German settlement included Nebraska, Kansas, Washington, California, and Canada (particularly, Saskatchewan and Alberta). Many also settled in Brazil and Argentina.

In North Dakota, the Black Sea Germans settlements formed a pyramid. Referred to as the "German-Russian triangle," the pyramid's base stretched from Dickey to Hettinger counties in the south, peaking in McHenry and Pierce counties. This triangle has one of the largest concentrations of Black Sea Germans in the world.

## 'New Odessa'

The hub city for Germans from Russia settlers coming into Dakota Territory was Yankton, dubbed "New Odessa" by many. From this springboard community, the new immigrants launched out into neighboring counties, then to what is now northern South Dakota, and (beginning in 1884) into McIntosh County of North Dakota. Often, the names of their new communities reflected those of their hometowns in Russia. Those who couldn't find suitable land moved east to Michigan, Illinois, and Wisconsin, and south to Nebraska.

## Many religions

Most Protestant Germans from Russia were Evangelical (Lutheran). Others were Baptists, Stundists, Congregationalists, Reformeds, Mennonites, and Hutterites. The Baptists flourished around Eureka, SD (originally named Petersburg after a Russian city), during the last decades of the 19th century.

Strict pacifists, the Mennonites—opposed to military service—performed civil service instead. When their military exemption privileges were revoked in Russia, whole villages migrated to America, set-

tling in Kansas, the Dakotas, Nebraska, and Minnesota.

The first group of Mennonites from the Crimea arrived in Yankton, Dakota Territory, in 1873.

Another group of pacifist Protestant German-Russians—the Hutterites —arrived in Yankton between 1874 and 1879. Half settled on individual farms (many becoming Hutterite Mennonites), the others eventually setting up communal colonies in eastern South and North Dakota, as well as Montana, Washington, and Canada. Today, there are 54 colonies located in eastern South Dakota and six in eastern North Dakota.

Catholic Black Sea Germans began immigrating into Dakota Territory in 1875, coming first to Yankton, then branching out to Ipswich and Aberdeen.

Most of southern Dakota land was already settled by the mid-1880s. So newly arrived Germans from Russia went farther north, by wagon and ox cart. Others went to St . Paul, traveling to central Dakota Territory by rail and embarking at either Aberdeen, Ipswich or Eureka —major

Germans from Russia settlement areas.

In 1884, Black Sea German settlers flocked to northern South Dakota. The first German-Russians to seek homesteads in south-central North Dakota came in the latter part of 1884, taking up claims near present-day Zeeland, ND (in McIntosh County).

The same year, the **Dobrudja Germans** (from present-day Rumania) began coming down from Winnipeg, settling around Sheridan, Wells, and McLean counties in North Dakota. Many of these were Baptists and Seventh Day Adventists.

Another group coming down from Manitoba (Gretna) was the **Volhynian Germans** of northwestern Ukraine, who

## RESEARCH TIPS & SOURCES
### GERMANS FROM RUSSIA

Germans from Russia belong to a number of organizations that promote the history and culture of their group. (Note: Many of the resources found in this list can also be applied to German and related research; see also Russia research tips and sources.)

• **The Germans from Russia Heritage Society** (GRHS), 1125 West Turnpike Ave., Bismarck, ND 58501 (701-223-6167; Website: www.grhs.org). GRHS is an international resource for those with Germans from Russia roots. This excellent research facility's collection includes thousands of pedigree charts containing more than 300,000 German surnames; obituaries; passenger lists; family, church, and county histories; newspaper microfilms; and birth and death records. GRHS has extensive genealogical resources on the Bessarabian, Black Sea, Dobrudja, and Crimean Germans.

• **The American Historical Society of Germans from Russia** (AHSGR), 631 D Street, Lincoln, NE 68502 (402-474-3363; Website: www.ahsgr.org). AHSGR has extensive genealogical resources on the Volga Germans, as well as Bessarabian and Black Sea Germans.

Both of the above organizations have ongoing village research projects, which gather and record information on the history and peoples of specific German-Russian ancestral villages. For information on these organizations and/or the village research projects, see contact information in the bibliography and address sections.

• **Glueckstal Colonies Research Association** (GCRA), 611 Esplande, Redondo Beach, CA 90277 (310-540-1872; Website: www.glueckstal.org) researches family histories of the German colonists living in the Black Sea colonies of Bergdorf, Glueckstal, Kassel, and Neudorf, and their daughter colonies. GCRA has published the hardcover book, "The Glueckstalers of New Russia and North America: A Bicentennial Collection of History, Genealogy and Folklore" (2004), 800 pages, two CD-ROMs and an award-winning documentary, "Heaven Is Our Homeland: The Glueckstalers of New Russia and North America."

• **"Plains Folk: North Dakota's Ethnic History,"** edited by William Sherman and Playford Thorson, is a must-read for anyone with ancestors in North Dakota, including those with Germans from Russia roots. This thorough, well-documented book details North Dakota immigration history, listing ethnic groups, origins, areas of settlement, and religious affiliations.

• A user-friendly resource for anyone researching their ancestry is **"Handbook for Researching Family Roots,"** which emphasizes German-Russian heritage. Compiled and written by Diane J. Wandler, this book ranges from basic research information to specifics for regions of Russia, including maps and current record names.

• Considered the "Bible" of Germans from Russia research is Dr. Karl Stumpp's **"The Emigration from Germany to Russia in the Years 1763-1862."** This important book provides dates and names on 20,000 German-Russian families. In some cases, it can help make the connection between these colonists and their ancestral homelands. A section on "Handbook for Researching Family Roots" gives guidance for research.

• More and more these days, Russia and Ukraine are opening up their records to genealogists, including parish records that cover Germans from Russia colonies. Check the **Family History Library catalog** at your local LDS Family History Center to find out what records are available for the village/parish of your ancestors.

• The hardcover book, **"Extended Relationships of the Kulm,** Leipzig and Tarutino Communities in Bessarabia, Russia" by Arthur E. Flegel (2005), includes thousands of family names as well as a history of Bessarabia and of the villages of Kulm, Leipzig, and Tarutino. Book available at: www.libndsu.nodak.edu/grhc.

• **"Researcher's Guide to McPherson County, South Dakota, Cemeteries,"** researched by Selma Job Lapp and Keenan L. Stoecker, edited and compiled by Duane E. Stabler (2005), summarizes information for over 100 family plots, grave sites, and cemeteries. McPherson County was a key destination for many immigrants from South Russia. Website: www.lib.ndsu.nodak.edu/grhc/order/nd_sd/mcpherson.html.

• Some special collections in the Dakotas focus on Germans from Russia records. One outstanding repository is the **Germans from Russia Heritage Collection** (GRHC), NDSU Libraries, Fargo, ND 58105-5599 ( 701-231-8416; Website: www.lib.ndsu.nodak. edu/grhc). GRHC is one of the major German-Russian resources in North America and the world. The mission of the Germans from Russia Heritage Collection is to collect, document, preserve, exhibit, translate, publish, promote, and make accessible resources on the culture, history, folklore, textiles, clothing, and foodways of the Germans from Russia, particularly Bessarabian Germans, Black Sea Germans, Crimean Germans, Dobrudja Germans, Volhynian Germans, and their descendants in North Dakota and the Northern Plains. A comprehensive annotated bibliography, "Researching the Germans from Russia," was compiled in 1987 by Michael M. Miller, Germans from Russia bibliographer. Since then, many new records and resources have been added, in part through Journey to the Homeland trips Miller and others have made to Ukraine, Russia, and former German villages. GRHC's Dakota Memories Oral History Project focuses on interviews with older Germans from Russia in the Dakotas and Saskatchewan.

Books on specialized Germans from Russia research are also available through the Germans from Russia Heritage Collection. Valuable resources for family historians and genealogists include: "Homeland Book of the Bessarabian Germans" by the late Pastor Albert Kern (translated to English); "Prairie Churches of Bon Homme County, Dakota Territory" by Maxine Schuurmans Kinsley; "Fond 53: Grossliebental, Odessa State Archives"; and "Fond 252: Odessa Office of Foreign Settlers in Southern Russia (1806, 1814-1834, 1843, 1850) Guide."

• **The State Historical Society of North Dakota,** Bismarck (www.state.nd.us/hist); Special Collections, Chester Fritz Library, University of North Dakota, Grand Forks (www.library.und.edu/Collections/spk.html); Institute for Regional Studies, North Dakota State University Libraries, Fargo (www.lib.ndsu.nodak.edu/ndirs); and the South Dakota Historical Society, Pierre (www.sdhistory.org) collect county and community histories, church histories, county atlases, historic photographs, and literary works. Included are microfilms of German-Russian language newspapers published in North Dakota and South Dakota homesteading days.

• **The Institute for Regional Studies** at NDSU has the extensive North Dakota Biography Index, the best place to begin a search for information about North Dakotans, including Germans from Russia, both living and deceased. The North Dakota Biography Index contains over 185,000 biographical sketches found in more than 660 publications. Further information is at the NDBI Website: www.lib.ndsu.nodak.edu/ndirs/bio&genealogy/ndbioindex.html. •

(Note: See address section in back of book for more Websites and addresses pertaining to Germans from Russia research.)

homesteaded in Cavalier and Pembina counties of northeastern North Dakota.

Richland, Cavalier, and Pembina counties became home to many **Galician Germans.** Originating in Poland, the **Mariupol German-Russians** emigrated from the Mariupol colonies of South Russia to Stutsman County, ND.

By the time the migration ceased, 300,000 Germans from Russia had left their homeland to live in the U.S. and Canada. The relatives and friends they left behind in Russia would soon face political changes, revolution, famine, starvation, war, forced migration and dispersion, slavery—and for many, death.

The Great Depression took a toll on Dakota Germans from Russia, as it did Americans everywhere.

Those who couldn't eke a living from the land during the Dirty Thirties left it to join relatives already living in states west and south.

Most stuck it out, however, and today many of their descendants continue to live in the German-Russian triangle. Proud of their heritage, many are now seeking to know the story of the Great Migration of their ancestors. •

## Dakota Germans read the paper!

- At one time, 29 German-language newspapers made the rounds to German-Russian readers in North and South Dakota.

- The most widely read German-Russian newspaper was the *Dakota Freie Presse*, founded in Yankton, SD, in 1874 and published by Richard Sallet, author of a groundbreaking book, "Russian-German Settlements in the United States." Eventually, the paper was edited in Bismarck, ND. In 1913, there were 12,000 subscribers. The paper ceased publication in 1954.

- Like the *Dakota Freie Presse, Der Staatsangeiger* was widely read. The paper began in Rugby, ND, in 1906 and was moved to Bismarck in 1912.

- *The Nord-Dakota Herold* (published from 1907-54) was printed in Dickinson. Its audience consisted primarily of Catholic Black Sea Germans. •

# Other Germanic peoples

**Many German-speaking people who settled in the Dakotas in the 19th and 20th centuries did not come by way of Russia. Some came directly from Germany, others from lands bordering on or ruled by the German empire. Many had their own languages and customs. Following is their history.**

S ince colonial times, a combination of factors ranging from the push of poor harvests, political oppression, and compulsory military service to the pull of free land led Germans to emigrate to this country. Only the British Isles contributed more to the U.S. population.

In all, 5 million Germans emigrated to the United States in the 19th century. They crossed the ocean in ships, then trekked overland—by covered wagon and/or by train—to reach Dakota. They came from lands that bordered on or were a part of Germany, depending on the political boundary at the time of their emigration: Bavaria, Austria-Hungary, Prussia, Czechoslovakia, Bohemia, Schlesvig-Holstein in Denmark, and Alsace-Lorraine in France. Altogether, they made up a large portion of the total population of the

Dakotas, spreading out widely across the two states—some settling in compact groups.

Most came as single or several families rather than in large contingents. Many came from eastern states, such as Wisconsin and Illinois; others came directly from the Old Country.

## GERMANS FROM GERMANY

Wisconsin was a hub for **Reichsdeutsch Germans** (Germans from Germany). Many second- and third-generation Germans from that area eventually made their way to Codington and Brown counties, SD. Others came directly from Europe.

Germans began settling in northern Dakota Territory in the 1870s—in single and family groups or in

colonies. The first group of German Lutherans settled in Traill County, others in Walsh County. Most came from Iowa, Minnesota, Wisconsin, and Michigan; others, directly from Germany, settled in south-central Pembina County about 1880. German Lutherans also settled in Cavalier County and the area around Devils Lake.

German Catholics, some from Michigan, moved into Grand Forks County in 1882. A large group of Reichsdeutsch settled in Richland County, moving there from Wisconsin, Iowa, and Minnesota. Germans soon spread across the state. A strong German colony sprang up in McIntosh County, ND, which would also be settled by Germans from Russia. Many German church records are preserved through the Missouri Synod Lutheran Church.

# BANAT GERMAN-HUNGARIANS ALSO COLONIZED FOREIGN LANDS

**A** German ethnic group with a history that parallels that of the Germans from Russia is the **Banat German-Hungarians** (also known as the "Donauschwaben" (Danube Swabians). In 1763, they were invited by Empress Maria Theresa of Austria-Hungary to colonize the Banat region of her country (today part of western Rumania and northeastern Yugoslavia in Eastern Europe). Additional settlements continued under the reign of succeeding monarchs. These people were predominantly Roman Catholic. Descendants of these colonists began settling on the Dakota plains in the late 1880s and continuing into the early 1900s, primarily in southwestern North Dakota in Stark, Hettinger, Dunn, and Morton counties. A hub for this group's history can be found at Lefor, ND. Parish records are located in the century-old St. Elizabeth's Church in Lefor. The book "Family History Research for North Dakota Pioneers from the Banat," by David Dreyer (1999), can guide anyone looking for ancestors with Banat connections. •

## Finding Palatine ancestors

• An excellent Website for anyone seeking Palatine genealogy is www.hankjones.com. A professional genealogist, Henry Z. "Hank" Jones Jr. has written several books on emigrants from this area of Germany. •

## BOHEMIANS, CZECHS, HUNGARIANS AND POLES

The first colonies of Bohemians (part of western Czechoslovakia) entered southern Dakota in 1869. Coming from Chicago (a Bohemian and Czech hub), they took land in Knox and Bon Homme counties, then migrated westward into Charles Mix, Douglas, Brule, and Bennett counties, and on land opened on the Rosebud Reservation. They were predominantly Roman Catholic.

Some Czechs (particularly the Moravians) entered the U.S. via southern ports, then made their way upriver, settling west of Yankton in 1869-71. Many left the state during the droughts of the 1890s.

In North Dakota, ethnic German emigrants from northeast Bohemia (Sudetenland) settled in Cass (1880s) and Griggs (later 1880s) counties. Another group of Bohemian Germans settled in western North Dakota.

The Burgenland Germans (German-Hungarians) emigrated from western Hungary (today part of Austria) to southeastern North Dakota in the 1880s-90s. Nearly all were Roman Catholic. The first emigrants settled in Barnes County, near Fingal. Others settled in Morton and Wells counties.

In 1885, Poles (primarily Catholic) took up land around Grenville and Lesterville, SD. North Dakota Polish settlers moved into Walsh and Grand Forks counties, establishing towns named Warsaw and Poland. •

## RESEARCH TIPS & SOURCES
### ETHNIC GERMANS AND OTHERS

• The **Family History Library Catalog** (LDS family history centers) should be checked to determine resources (including parish records) available in the locality of your ancestor.

• The book **"Finding Your German Ancestors,"** by Dr. Ronald M. Smelser, outlines German archives holdings that are especially valuable for anyone researching German roots. They include: church records (parish registers), civil registers, guild records, emigration/immigration records (including the Hamburg and Württemburg lists, both available through LDS family history centers), census records, and gazetteers (especially the **Meyers Orts- und Verkehrs-Lexikon des Deutschen Reiches,** which can help you find old place names of the German Empire).

• The *German Genealogical Digest,* a quarterly publication, contains valuable information for German research. Publications on everything from German church, military, and guild records to using the Meyers gazetteer are also available from this source. For information, write them at P.O. Box 112054, Salt Lake City, UT 84147 (www.german-digest.com). Back issues are available.

• Check out the many German resources available at **Park Genealogical Books,** P.O. Box 130968, Roseville, MN 55113-0968 ;

Website: www. parkbooks.com. Ask for their catalog. German Empire maps are also available here.

• **Church records for Hungary (Magyarorszag)** can be accessed through the LDS family history centers. Other LDS resources: A 19th-century gazetteer of the Kingdom of Hungary— "Magyarorszag Helysegnevtara Ket Kotethen," by Janos Dvorzsak, and maps of the old counties of Hungary. A road atlas called "Magyarorszag Autoatlasza" shows roads, towns, and villages.

• The **Newberry Library** in Chicago holds many records of Czech/Bohemian research. Contact the library at 60 W. Walton St., Chicago, IL 60610-3305; 312-255-3512 (www.newberry.org). Collections include "Genealogical Research for Czech and Slovak Americans" by Olga K. Miller; and "Czechoslovakia: A Handbook of Czechoslovak Genealogical Research" by Daniel M. Schlyter.

• Check the holdings of the **CzechoSlovak Genealogical Society,** P.O. Box 16225, St. Paul, MN 55116-0225 (www.cgsi.org).

• People with roots in Poland can contact the **Polish Genealogical Society,** 984 N. Milwaukee Ave., Chicago, IL 60622-4199; Web address: www.pgsa.org.

Also check out the resources available through **FEEFHS (Federation of East European Family History Societies)** , P.O. Box 510898, Salt Lake City, UT 84151-0898 (www.feefhs.org). •

# Other Europeans

**N**on-Germanic nations of Western Europe also left their mark in the Dakotas—some contributing to the early history of both states.

## FRENCH

**T**he French played an important role in the early history of the Dakotas. Many active French fur traders, hunters, trappers, and explorers married Indian women and entrenched themselves in the area. Their Métis descendants bear names reflecting this French heritage. And so do many places in the Dakotas—among them, Belle Fourche and Pierre in South Dakota, Rolette and Bottineau in North Dakota.

In South Dakota, Union and Spink counties continue to have significant French populations.

In North Dakota, the northeast and north-central areas drew French settlers whose descendants still reside in this region.

## DUTCH

A large group of Frieslanders from the Netherlands moved into Illinois, Michigan, Wisconsin, and other eastern states between 1866 and 1873. From there, they moved to Iowa, then South Dakota. Later, others came directly to Iowa. And later still, they came directly to the Dakotas from the Old

## Oriental flavor

- During settlement days, a few Chinese made the Dakotas their home. The Chinese, along with the Itallians and others, were key in building the railroads that traverse both states. In South Dakota, the Chinese were essential in the mining industry. Early entrepreneurs, the Chinese opened laundries and restaurants. Chinese-run oriental restaurants continue to entice Dakota diners. •

---

## RESEARCH TIPS & SOURCES
### FRENCH

• Many French who settled in the United States came through Canada. If this is the case with your ancestors, explore U.S. and Canadian sources before jumping into French research.

The book **"French and French-Canadian Family Research"** by J. Konrad; Summit Publications (available through Ye Olde Genealogie Shoppe, P.O. Box 39128, Indianapolis, IN 46239), offers information about French immigration, as well as French history and maps. Once you know the name of your emigrant French ancestor and his or her place of residence in France, there are a number of resources to check. Special indexes exist for those with roots in Alsace or Lorraine (old names were Bas-Rhin and Haut Rhin), areas that bounced back and forth between French and German control. Particularly valuable is the **"Alsace Index"** of 25,000 names of people who emigrated from the area between 1817 and 1866. Many of these people came to the U.S. Included in the index are names, birthplaces (or residences), and destination. Another index contains names of 350,000 people who left in 1871 or later.

Write to the **French Embassy Press and Information Service,** 4101 Reservoir Road N.W., Washington, DC 20007, for a list of genealogy societies and archives in France. For titles on books relating to French research, write to **Genealogical Publishing Co.,** 1001 N. Calvert St., Baltimore, MD 21202 (www.onegreatfamily.com).

The **French National Archives'** address is: Archives Nationale de France, 60 rue des Francs-Bourgeois, F-3000, Paris, France.

The **LDS Family History Library** has a large collection of microfilmed French records, including many civil and church registers. (See also Canada research tips and sources.)

### DUTCH (HOLLANDERS, NETHERLANDERS)

• Primary records for Netherlands research include civil registrations (which began in 1811), population registration or census records (1850-1920), church records (1545-1811), and immigration, military, colonization, and emigration records. Holder of most of these records is the **Centraal Bureau voor Genealogie (Central Bureau for Genealogy),** P.O. Box 11755, 2502, The Hague. Also check the LDS family history center catalog to see what microfilms they have available for the location of your ancestors.

• The **Herrick Library,** 300 River Ave., Holland, MI 49423 (www. herrickdl.org, is a leading repository for Netherlands genealogy information. The collection includes early church and census records of Dutch emigrants—especially Protestant Dutch. Included in the Herrick Library collection are 600-plus Dutch genealogy books. A map shows Dutch settlements across the U.S.

• A book titled **"Netherlanders in America"** was written by a Dutch visitor in 1924 who did an extensive study of Dutch emigrants. It contains 57,000 names of people who left the Netherlands from 1847-80. Also check the book **"Dutch Households in U.S. population censuses 1850, 1860, 1870"** by R.P. Swierenga.

### BELGIANS

• Many records for Belgium have been microfilmed by the LDS Family History Center in Salt Lake City. These include civil registration and church records (mostly Roman Catholic) covering most of the country. The **National (Royal) Archives in Brussels** is located in Brabant, one of nine provinces.

The book **"Ancestral Research in Belgium"** by Erica Hartman Nederhand will give you guidance.

Visit this Website for more information on Belgian resources: belgium.rootsweb.com.

### ITALIANS

• Thorough records of births, marriages, and deaths (often with multi-generational information) can aid people in finding their Italian roots. These records began in the early to mid-1800s.

• Try this Website for Italian genealogy resources: members. aol.com/geneaita.

### GREEKS

• Registers of the Greek Orthodox Church (which begin in 1707) are a primary source for Greek research. Check out this Website for genealogy resources: www.greekgenealogy.com. •

---

## Africans, Indians, Asians part of Dakota's history

• African-Americans have been residents of the Dakotas since fur-trading days. A few homesteaded here; others worked the ranches of the western Dakotas or the Bonanza farms of eastern North Dakota. Perhaps our most famous black citizen is Era Bell Thompson, editor of *Ebony* magazine, who was raised near Driscoll, ND.

• Today, African-American veterinarians, professors, teachers, nurses, students, and athletes continue to live in and make their contributions to North and South Dakota.

• Professionals from India, Pakistan, Japan, and Southeast Asia (including Filipinos, Vietnamese and others) have also made their homes in the Dakotas. •

Country. These "Hollanders" settled in Lincoln, Union, Turner, Bon Homme, Grant, Douglas, and Charles Mix (SD) counties. By 1900, Dutch settlements had been established in much of southeastern South Dakota. Additional Dutch settlements sprang up in Hamlin, Deuel, Brookings, Minnehaha, and Campbell counties.

In North Dakota, the oldest and earliest (circa 1884-85) settlement of Hollanders was in southern Emmons County, near the towns of Hull, Westfield, Zeeland, and Hague. Other Dutch eventually settled in Burleigh, Barnes, Griggs, Stark, Hettinger, and Grant counties.

The Holland-Dakota Land Company brought a large contingent of Dutch families into the Belfield area of Stark County in 1910 as part of a cooperative farming venture. By 1920, most had left the area, some returning to Holland.

## OTHERS

Small groups of Belgians settled in Pembina County in North Dakota.

Some Italians who settled in the Dakotas were part of the crews building and maintaining railroad lines.

Railroad work gangs also included people from Greece. By 1910, Greek-born residents could be found in nearly every county of North Dakota—but especially in Ward, Rolette, and Ramsey counties. Some eventually homesteaded in the state.

A few Swiss emigrants were among the thousands from Western European countries to find new homes in the Dakotas and, thus, leave their footprints etched on the Dakota landscape. •

# Other groups

**S**ettlers from non-Germanic nations also chose the Dakotas as their destination. They came from Central and Eastern Europe, the Near East, and Ukraine, transplanting their roots in Dakota soil.

## UKRAINIANS

**U**krainians were among the thousands of homesteaders flocking into the Dakotas in the late 1800-early 1900 era. In the 1930s, North Dakotans with a Ukrainian connection numbered around 5,000 (compared to 114,000 in Manitoba).

While sharing the same language, the Dakota Ukrainians actually came from two distinct cultural and religious groups: The Western (Zapadni) Ukrainians (also called "Ruthenians" for an area in Upper Hungary where some of them originated) were Ukrainian (Byzantine Rite) Catholics. They came from the Austria-Hungarian province of Bukovina. The Eastern (Kievan) Ukrainians were Russian Orthodox or Evangelical Protestants. The areas they lived in were under Russian control.

The first Western Ukrainian families into North Dakota (circa 1896) came from Canada. Principal areas of settlement were Dunn, Billings, and Stark counties, concentrated around the Fairfield-Belfield-Dickinson area. Western Ukrainians also established homes in Oliver, Mercer (near Mannhaven), Burleigh (at Wilton), and Pembina counties.

During the Great Depression, many Ukrainians moved to the West Coast. The Ukrainian Cultural Institute was organized in Dickinson, ND, to preserve Ukrainian history and cultural traditions.

Eastern Ukrainians came to America largely to avoid religious persecution in Russia. They settled principally in McHenry, McLean, Ward, and Sheridan counties. One of the towns they settled bears the name of the region many had come from in Russia: Kiev (Kief). Religions associated with the Eastern Ukrainians included Stundist, Mennonite, Baptist, and Seventh-Day Adventist. Another group of Eastern Ukrainians, affiliated with the Russian Orthodox church, moved into Dunn, McKenzie, and

# RESEARCH TIPS & SOURCES
## UKRAINIAN

• In the 1800s, the Ukraine was divided into Crown Colonies of Austria (Galacia, Bukowina, or Subcarpathia) and Gubernias (equivalent of U.S. states). After World War II, Ukraine was made up of oblasts and raions (also spelled "rayons"). Presently, there are 26 oblasts, with a number of raions in each.

• To find your ancestral home, check the **"Columbia Lippencott Gazetteer of the World"** or an atlas for your ancestors' area.

• The principal archives are located in Kiev (Kyiv, eastern Ukraine) and Lviv (western Ukraine). Addresses are:

—**State Committee on Archives of Ukraine** (Holovne Arkhivne Upravlinnia), Prof. Dr. Henradii Boriak, Director General, 03110, m. Kyiv vul. Solomianska 24, Ukraina (lemko.org/genealogy/oblasts. html).

—**Central State Historical Archives** in Lviv, Ukraine: Ukraina 290008, Lviv-8, pl. Soborna, 3-a, Tsentrainyl derzhavnyi istorychnyi arkhiv Ukraony, Lviv (TsDIA-L). Director: Orest Iaroslavoych Matsiuk. Deputy director: Diana Pelc.

• An excellent resource for Ukrainian roots is the following Website: infoukes.com. This site will lead you to information on oblasts and archives, as well as the famine of 1932-33.

• Ukrainians with connections to the Seventh-Day Adventist Church can check with the regional headquarters in Pierre, SD, for church records. (See address in bibliography.)

• The **Ukrainian Cultural Institute**, Dickinson, ND, collects history and cultural information on the western Ukrainians who settled in North Dakota. (See bibliography for address.)

• Contact the **Ukrainian Genealogical and Historical Society of Canada** (located in Cochrane, Alberta) for more information on Ukrainians who settled in the U.S. and Canada.

## RUSSIAN

• Contact the **Embassy of the U.S.** in Moscow, c/o Department of State, Washington, D.C. 20521.

• If looking for pre-revolutionary genealogical records, check the **revision lists** (poll tax census) and **parish registers** (or parish transcripts). The revision lists begin in 1719. Other revisions took place in 1743, 1761-67 (first one to include females), 1778-87, 1794-1808, 1811-12, 1815-25, 1833-35, 1850-52, and 1857-59. The only universal census during the era of the czars was taken in 1897.

• Primary religions in Russia were Russian Orthodox, Roman Catholic, Evangelical (Lutheran), and Jewish. Parish registers for the Russian Orthodox church began in 1722, following a decree by Peter the Great. Recording of christenings, marriages, and deaths began two years later.

• The **Genealogical Society of Utah** has filmed many of these records in the following areas: Armenia, Belarus, Estonia, Georgia, Lithuania, Moldava, Russia, and Ukraine. A major microfilming project included the St. Petersburg Lutheran church records.

• For more information on Russian genealogical sources, check this Website: feeths.org/fri/ru/rusgens.html.

## JEWISH

• Those seeking Jewish roots should check the **JewishGen®, Inc.** site—the primary Internet source connecting researchers of Jewish genealogy worldwide. Features include a discussion group, links to records, and several databases, including one with over a half million names. Access the site at: www.jewishgen.org.

• Archives/genealogical societies focusing on Jewish people include: **American Jewish Archives,** 3101 Clifton Ave., Cincinnati, OH 45220; **Jewish Genealogical Society,** 300 E. 71st St., Apt. 5R, New York, NY 10021; and **Jewish Genealogical Society of Canada,** P.O. Box 446 Station 'A', Willowdale, Ontario, Canada M2N 5TI.

• The book **"Plains Folk: North Dakota's Ethnic Heritage"** contains information on Jewish settlements in North Dakota,.

## SYRIAN-LEBANESE

• **"Ethnic Heritage in North Dakota"** and "**Plains Folk: North Dakota's Ethnic Heritage"** both contain sections on Syrian (Lebanese) settlement in North Dakota.

• The book **"Prairie Peddlers: The Syrian-Lebanese in North Dakota"** (2002) provides fascinating facts about this ethnic group.

• Find more facts in **"Syrians in America"** by Philip K. Hitti." •

---

Williams counties. Some Kief-Max families soon migrated to these areas.

Second and third waves of Ukrainian emigration occurred after both world wars, with several hundred displaced persons settling in the Dakotas from 1948-51. Many later moved to California, Nebraska, and Canada.

## SYRIAN-LEBANESE

Over 350 Syrians (Lebanese) filed for homesteads in early-day North Dakota. Their former home was in the Ottoman Empire.

Thus, the place of origin for 662 Syrian immigrants on the 1910 census appears as "Turkey." Their ethnic roots, however, were Arabic.

North Dakota Christian Arabic colonies were formed in Pierce, Sheridan, Walsh, and Williams (the largest settlement) counties.

Muslim Syrians settled in Mountrail and Foster counties. A mixture of Christian and Islamic farmers chose homesteads in Rolette County.

## JEWISH

Jewish families from Western and Eastern Europe were among early settlers in North Dakota. Many moved to the state's larger cities, where they established synagogues and became merchants and community leaders. Others settled in rural areas in Burleigh, Logan-McIntosh, Ramsey, Nelson, Grand Forks, Slope, Bowman, and Grant counties. Many eventually left the state, leaving their traces on tombstones in silent country cemeteries. •

## Spanish Dakotans

• Spanish-speaking people left their mark on early Dakota history. Spain ruled the territory from 1762 to 1800; Manuel Lisa established fur posts here in the early decades of the 1800s. From 1930 on, migrant workers with Mexican or Hispanic backgrounds have worked the farms and fields of North Dakota and Minnesota. A few settled permanently in the Red River Valley area. •

# Scandinavian settlement

## Hub of heritage

- A heritage center in Minot, ND, preserves the culture and history of all five Scandinavian groups that settled in the Dakotas. The Scandinavian Heritage Association visitor's center is located in Scandinavian Heritage Park in Minot's heart. For information, contact SHA, 1020 South Broadway, P.O. Box 862, Minot, ND 58702-0862; 701-852-9161; www.scandinavianheritage.org. •

Together, the Scandinavians (Norwegians, Swedes, Danes, Icelanders, and Finns) make up a sizable portion of the population of both North and South Dakota. On the following pages, we present their settlement history, along with research tips and resources for each group. We begin this section with the Norwegians, the largest Scandinavian group to settle in the Dakotas.

## NORWEGIANS

The first colony of Norwegian emigrants bound for America left Norway aboard the sloop "Restauration" in 1825. After 14 weeks at sea on a vessel that was only 54 feet long and barely seaworthy, the 54 passengers made it to the port of New York.

The voyage had been organized by Cleng Peerson, known today as "the father of Norwegian emigration."Once the "Sloopers" set foot on American soil, Peerson led them (most of them Quakers) to the Kendall settlement on Lake Ontario in New York, a spot he had selected prior to their arrival.

During his lifetime, Peerson founded several colonies—including Fox River in Illinois. He spent his final years in Texas.

Word of these ventures spread to Norway, and soon Norwegians were packing their trunks and preparing to leave the Old Country for a new life in America.

The first trickles of Norwegian immigration, which started in the 1830s, would soon become a flood, emptying out many Norwegian valleys of some of their most promising citizens.

According to the book "A History of the Norwegian Settlements" by Hjalmar Rued Holand (translation published in 2006 by Astri My Astri Publishing), between the years 1866 and 1915, nearly 700,000 Norwegians came to the United States.

## 'Bygdeboker'

Regional histories called bygdeboks (technically, "bygdeboker") are available for many districts (or "bygd") of Norway. Though the quality varies (and not all communities had them), many are good-to-excellent reference tools for those researching their family roots. These books provide a genealogy of Norwegian farms, some stretching back to the 1500s or even earlier in some communities. All known owners of these farms are listed, along with vital statistics on family members. (See also patronymic names, Chapter 1.)

The key to researching these books is knowing the area your ancestor came from. Once you determine that, check to see whether that community has published a bygdebok.

The Elwyn B. Robinson Department of Special Collections at the Chester Fritz Library, University of North Dakota, Grand Forks, houses a collection of over 1,000 bygdeboks. This library does not lend its materials, which means that, if you visit the library, you'll likely find the book on its shelves. A free "Guide to Norwegian Bygdeboker" is available upon request by phone (701-777-4625) or through the Special Collections Web

site at www.und.nodak.edu/dept/library/Collections/Famhist/bygdebok.html.

Some libraries do lend out their bygdeboks—which means you can order them through interlibrary loan. The books, written in Norwegian but not hard to follow, generally come in multi-volume sets.•

**BOKA OM GOL**

**GARDS- OG ÆTTE- SOGE**

Halvor Arneson Golberg f omkr. 1660 d 1705 g m Barbo Håvelsdtr. Haukstad d før 1724.
Born:
1. Endre Halvorson Haukstad f omkr. 1688 d 1764 g m Liv Fingarsdtr. Brekke.
2. Birgit Halvorsdtr. f omkr. 1690 d 1746 g m Ivar Steinson Steingarden.
3. Sunneiv Halvorsdtr. Spildrebråten f omkr. 1692 d 1748, ug., hadde vore trulova med Arne Johanneson Rust–Hognuset.
4. Dordei Halvorsdtr. f omkr. 1693 d 1751 g m Vilhelm Fingarson Brekke, attg 1738 m e.m. Endre Pålson Golberg–Vermåker.
5. Jøran Halvorsdtr. f 1695, var ug. i 1724, men i 1736 var ho g m ein Ola Fauske. – Det er Fauske i Hemsedal, men der er det ingen Ola som høver i dette tidsrommet. Og det er Fauske i V. Slidre. Det næraste ein har kome der er ein Ola Eirikson Øye (seinare Hamarsnes), som vart g 1736 m ei Jøran Halvorsdtr. Fossei (ingen Halvor på Fossei i høveleg tidsrom som kunne vera far til denne Jøran). Dei døypte same året dottera Sebber, og Jøran døydde alt i 1739, 42 år.
6. Berte (Birgit) Halvorsdtr. f 1697 d 1698.
7. Berte (Birgit) Halvorsdtr. f 1699 skft. 1735 g m Reiar Knutson Elbjøro–søre Lykkja (Reiargarden).
8. Håvel Halvorson Rudningen (Rudningsbakkadn) f 1701 d 1747 g 1727 m Margit Gautesdtr. Kjednbal.
9. Margit Halvorsdtr. d 1732, 36 år, ug. (ho er ikkje reg. dpt., men ho er ført slik i skifte 1724 at ho var yngst av døtrene).

Barbo Håvelsdtr. vart attg før 1720 m e.m. Fingar Olson Brekke.

## Viking farmers

The new Scandinavian Americans, arriving in the 1830s and '40s, took land first in Illinois, then Wisconsin. They were usually the first to settle the land, slaving to turn the wilderness into productive farms.

In choosing their homesites, they sought wooded land near rivers or streams. The first Norwegians to settle in Minnesota began coming in the early 1850s. It wasn't until most of the woodland was taken that they spread out onto the prairies of Iowa (1850s and '60s), eastern South Dakota (1859), and eastern North Dakota (1870).

Factors prompting Norwegians to come to America included overcrowding in their homeland, free land promised by the Homestead Act (1862), and "America letters" from relatives already in the U.S., touting conditions in the new land.

The tide of immigration was interrupted by the Civil War (1861-65) and by the Minnesota Sioux Uprising (1862). Yet, once things calmed down, the settlers again poured in. Illinois, Wisconsin, Iowa, Nebraska, and Minnesota served as "springboard states," where many immigrants settled for a time, then pushed farther west, including into the Dakotas.

The first Norwegians to arrive in South Dakota came up from Nebraska in 1858, settling in Clay County around Vermillion. Others took land in Hutchinson and Turner counties to the north and west. The Canton area of

Lincoln County was first settled around 1868. By 1870, more than a thousand Norwegians were living in Clay County. By the end of the century, there were 10,745 Norwegians in eastern South Dakota.

In North Dakota, settlement began in 1870; by 1880, Red River Valley land was all taken up. New arrivals from Norway now flocked to northern and western North Dakota. So plentiful were they in the area north and west of the Missouri River that the region was known as the "Norwegian Sea."

The Norwegians spread across both states, sparse only in the German-Russian triangle areas of south-central North Dakota. A few pockets of people from the same valleys in Norway settled near each other: Hallings settled around Kindred and Northwood. The Cooperstown area became home to many from Stavanger. •

## Log on to BYGDE-LAGS!

• The Norwegian-American Bygdelagenes Fellesraad is the national headquarters for 32 affiliated organizations called bygdelags. It's also the place to contact for information on these associations of emigrant descendants from particular areas of Norway who now live in North America. These groups meet annually, usually in the Upper Midwest. They're an excellent means of gleaning genealogy information via the lag's resources and from other lag members who have roots in the same area. Most lags put out a publication in which members can place queries.

For more information on the bygdelag that focuses on your research area, visit this Website: www.fellesraad.com. Or write for a brochure listing all the bygdelags and their addresses. You can contact the organization through its president, Marilyn D. Somdahl, 10129 Goodrich Circle, Minneapolis, MN 55437; 952-831-4409. •

## SWEDES

The great Swedish migration began about 1840, when the farms of Sweden could no longer support the increasing population.

Like the Norwegians, the Swedes also had their "father of immigration": Gustav Unonius, who emigrated in 1841 and founded the first Swedish settlement in Wisconsin.

The earlier Swedes emigrated in groups. But after 1860, large numbers of individual Swedes migrated. When they arrived,

most South Dakota land had been taken by earlier immigrants, so Swedes settled wherever they could find land, in scattered, isolated patterns.

After the Civil War, Swedes settled in Wisconsin, Minnesota, Iowa, Nebraska, and the Dakotas. Of these states, Minnesota drew the largest number; North Dakota and Nebraska tied for second place.

The Swedes settled in South Dakota in the late 1860s and '70s, in Union, Clay, and Minnehaha counties. In 1870, there

were 380 Swedes in Dakota Territory, compared to 1,179 Norwegians.

In the 1880s, settlements were made in Grant, Rob-

# NORWEGIAN
# RESEARCH TIPS & SOURCES

• A key to Norwegian genealogy is learning the full name of one's Norwegian ancestor (see **patronymic naming system** information in Chapter 1). This name can provide clues as to your ancestor's place of origin. Most Norwegian names consisted of three parts: the given name (Knud), the patronymic name (Olsen, meaning "Ole's son"), and the farm name (Storlien, meaning "from a farm called Storlien"). The second name (the patronymic) tells you the first name of the father; the **farm name** can offer a clue to the place (farm) your ancestor lived on in Norway. This can help you determine a parish, which can lead you to church records.

• Check home sources. If you don't know the farm name, check your home (or ask relatives) for any old papers or Bibles containing this name; look at deeds, wills, abstracts, or similar records where the name may have been recorded; check old **Norwegian-American Lutheran parish records** in the community and time period matching your ancestor's residence there. Ask older relatives whether they remember (or have documents indicating) a farm name, or community in Norway your mutual ancestor came from.

• **Church records** on both sides of the ocean are primary resources for anyone with roots in both Norway and the Lutheran church (for information on where to find U.S. church records, see church records section in Chapter 2 and research sites, Chapter 3). On the U.S. side of the ocean, the records from the earliest church your ancestor attended after immigrating may yield the farm name. Some of these old records may also reveal the location of the farm. That can narrow your search for the parish that holds your family's information.

On the other side of the ocean, the Lutheran Church was the official state church of Norway, keeping records of everything from vital records (births/christenings, marriages, and deaths/funerals) to vaccinations. Once you find the parish of your ancestor, the **Norwegian parish books** are the first records to research. These records are accessible via microfilm, ordered from an LDS family history center (see research sites, Chapter 3, for more on records and resources that can be viewed at the centers). Check the LDS Family History Catalog CD for the name of the district in Norway your ancestors came from, then order the film that covers the time frame and parish of your ancestors. (Note that Norwegian-American parish records are not available through the LDS family history centers; only records from parishes in Norway have been extracted.)

If you have a farm name but still don't know its location in Norway, go to your nearest LDS family history center and order a microfilm of old **Norwegian post offices** (the Bismarck Family History Center has this microfilm on permanent loan). This resource lists names of all the farms in Norway and the areas where each is located. If the farm name is an unusual one, it may be found in only a few communities. Use the process of elimination to narrow your search down to the right location.

• Another resource containing Norwegian farm names and locations is Oluf Rygh's 19-volume **"Norske Gaardnavne" (Norse Farm Names).** These books can be found at the **Elwyn B. Robinson Department of Special Collections in the Chester Fritz Library,** Grand Forks. Listed are names of 45,000 Norwegian farms in Norway in 1886. A database of this important genealogy resource is available via the Internet, covering all volumes. The information can be accessed at this Website: www.dokpro.uio.no/rygh_ng/rygh_felt.html. The Chester Fritz Library also has one of the largest collections of bygdeboks in the U.S.

• A fascinating Website with information on genealogy and Medieval Norway is: www.the-orb.net/essays/text02.html. This site includes an excellent bibliography of resources.

• The book **"Normaendene i Amerika" ("Norsemen in America"),** a two-volume guide by Martin Ulvestad, lists complete names (often including farm names) of immigrants who settled in America prior to 1900, along with their original community in Norway. Names are listed alphabetically according to the place of origin, along with the name and place of settlement in America. The North Dakota State Archives and Historical Research Library has this book in its collection, as do other research sites such as Chester Fritz' special collections department. It is accessible on the Internet at the following site: freepages.genealogy.rootsweb.com/~maggiebakke/ulvestad.html. The text of the original book is in Norwegian; the Website is an English translation.

• The biggest and best-known Norwegian fraternal organization is **Sons of Norway,** headquartered in Minneapolis, MN. This organization promotes Norse culture and traditions through its many chapters in North America. Its publication, *The Viking,* features "The Lost Branch," a query column for those seeking Norse connections. For more information, visit the Sons of Norway Website: www.sofn.com/home/index.jsp. While there, request a pamphlet titled "Some Basic Genealogy Information" and a flyer with information on records held by the Norwegian Emigration Center in Stavanger, Norway. Check, too, for large-scale maps of Norway.

• Visit digitalarkivet.uib.no/sab/howto.html **(Norway's National Archives site)** for an online genealogy guide called "How to Trace Your Ancestors in Norway." Revised in 2001, the guide gives dozens of Web addresses and links for Norwegian and Norwegian-American genealogical sources.

• If your ancestors departed from a Norwegian port in 1867 or later, you can check the **"emigrantprotokoller,"** essentially, police passport records for the emigrants. These records are especially useful, as they often include the immigrant's last residence in Norway, ship of departure, and destination in America. The available Norwegian emigration records have been transcribed and indexed and are are available at digitalarkivet.uib.no/cgi-win/WebFront.exe?slag=vis&tekst=meldingar&spraak=e.

• Another excellent resource for Norwegian researchers is the **Vesterheim Genealogical Center and Naeseth Library,** 415 W. Main St., Madison, WI 53703; 608-255-2224. Its collection includes Norwegian and Norwegian-American church records; Norwegian and Norwegian-American census records, emigration records, Norwegian bygdeboker and many ship passenger lists. Research queries can be placed in the organization's newsletter, *Norwegian Tracks.* Maps of Norway—the Statens Kartverk M711 series of maps, which feature nearly 800 detailed topographic farm maps, at a scale of 1:50,000—are also available through Vesterheim.

• The **Norwegian-American Historical Association (NAHA),** St. Olaf College, Northfield, MN 55057, has compiled over 150,000 obituaries of Norwegian-Americans who died between 1915-1980.

• A resource for anyone interested in Norwegian emigration is **"History of the Norwegian Settlements"** (source for material on pgs. 78-79). This translation of a 1908 book, originally written in Norwegian, is based on pioneer interviews by author Hjalmar Rued Holand. For details, contact: genesis@westriv.com.

• The **Norwegian American homepage** can be found at www.lawzone.com/half-nor/nor-am.htm. Another site for you to explore is: museum.snett.no/emigrantmuseum/gensocie.htm, the Norwegian Emigrant Museum.

• And don't forget **Cyndi's List:** www.cyndislist.com/norway.htm. It's one of the best places to find links to genealogy resources. •

erts, Marshall, Day, and Brown counties. In the 1900-10 era, Swedes settled in Dewey, Stanley, Harding, and Lawrence counties west of the Missouri River in South Dakota. There were 22,872 Swedes in South Dakota in 1915 (compared to 56,731 Norwegians and 12,898 Danes).

In North Dakota, Swedes settled alongside Norwegians in scattered settlements across the state. In 1910, Cass County in the Red River Valley had the largest concentration, at 1,190. Pockets of Swedish settlement sprang up in Burleigh, McLean, and Burke counties of North Dakota. According to the 1910 census, northern Burleigh County had 102 Swedish households. Other Swedes settled near Kulm in LaMoure County.

While Swedes were originally Augustana Synod Lutherans, many became Methodists, Baptists, or Episcopalians. •

## SWEDES HERE FIRST!

The Swedes (and Finlanders from the Finn forests of western Sweden) were among the earliest settlers in America, landing on the shores of Delaware in 1638. The area they settled became known as "New Sweden." •

# SWEDISH RESEARCH TIPS & SOURCES

• Researching in Sweden by Americans with Swedish roots must begin on this side of the ocean, with U.S. records. The key items to know are the original name of the forefather (before leaving Sweden, the way it appears in Swedish records), birth date and place, name of the parish, the "län" or district where the parish is located, and date of departure from Sweden. To retrieve this information, check first with relatives to see whether they might know (or have documents containing) this information; then check documents in church records, libraries, or archives.

• In Sweden, the **Lutheran Church** was the official recorder of vital statistics for the nation. Since the late 1600s, the church has kept registers of Swedish births/christenings, confirmations, marriages, deaths/burials, and parish removals and entries. Especially valuable for genealogists are the **"husförhörslängder," household examination rolls** taken when the clergyman made parish visitations. This register served as a census for the country. Its name was changed to "församlingsböcker" in 1895. The "landsarkiv" or "stadsarkiv" holds records that are more than a century old. The older parish records are stored there. Only parishes in Dalarna landskap (about 40 in number) have been allowed to keep their old records. In all, there are more than 2,000 parishes in Sweden.

• When our Swedish ancestors were about to leave their homeland, they were issued a **"flyttningsbevis,"** a document granting them permission to leave. This paper listed family members' names and birth dates; vaccination, confirmation, and literacy information; their marriage date; the parish they belonged to; their destination, and the date of their departure. This "moving permit" was issued by the church. This valuable genealogy document, which Swedish families carried with them to America, can be a steppingstone to gaining access to Swedish church records.

• The **American Swedish Institute (ASI)** historic house/museum houses books, papers, and photographs focusing on the Swedish-American newspaper "Svenska Amerikanska Posten" and Swedish history, immigration (especially to Minnesota), and culture. A book entitled **"Tracing Your Swedish Ancestry"** is available from the institute's "Bokhandel" bookstore. To order, contact: Bokhandel, 2600 Park Ave., Minneapolis, MN 55407; 612-871-4907; or visit the online store at www.americanswedishinst.org.

Or, try the following Website and you can view the entire book, free, online: genealogy.about.com/library/authors/ucolsson1c.htm.

• For public records, newspapers, directories, and other historical sources for Minnesota (including books on Swedish immigrants), consult the **Minnesota Historical Society:** www.mnhs. org.

• Researchers whose ancestors settled in states other than Minnesota or were members of non-Lutheran Swedish-American churches, may find the resources of the **Swenson Swedish Immigration Research Center** helpful. Check this Web address: www. augustana.edu/swenson.

Also check out the following Websites:

—**Swedish Genealogy Group** (of the Minnesota Genealogy Society): www.mtn.org/ mgs/branches/swedish.html.

—**Riksarkivet (Swedish Archives, or SVAR),** P.O. Box 125 41, SE-102 29 Stockholm, Sweden 4687376474. Website: www.ra.se or www.svar.ra.se.

The sources listed below may also help you find your roots:

• **"Cradled in Sweden: a practical help to genealogical research in Swedish records"** by Carl-Erik Johansson, a Swedish research guide listing parishes and other resources

• **"Vägatlas över Sverige"** (Lantmäteriet ), largest scale map book for Sweden; shows parish boundaries and farms

• **"Finding your Forefathers: Some hints for Americans of Swedish origin,"** published by the Royal Ministry for Foreign Affairs, Stockholm

• **"Beginner's Guide to Swedish Genealogical Research"** and **"Genealogical Guidebook & Atlas of Sweden,"** by Finn Thomsen

• **"Swedish Exodus"** by Lars Ljungmark; chronicles migration from Sweden to America in the late 1800s-early 1900s

• Vilhelm Moberg's four-volume **"The Emigrant" books** follow the lives of Swedish emigrants who settle in southeast Minnesota

• **Anderson Butik,** Lindsborg, KS, is a leading mail-order supplier of Swedish gifts, food, and books. Ask for catalogs of Swedish imports and hard-to-find book titles on Scandinavian subjects. This is a major source for close-up topographical maps of Sweden.

• Check out the many resources (including Swedish information) available at **Park Genealogical Books,** Dept. WWW, P.O. Box 130968, Roseville, MN 55113-0968 ; Website: www. parkbooks.com.

• The **Swedish Council of America** (2600 Park Ave., Minneapolis, MN 55407 (612-871-0593), national center for over 200 Swedish-American organizations in the U.S., Canada and Sweden. North Dakota groups include: Three Crowns Swedish-American Association, Bismarck; Lake Region Swedish Heritage Society, Devils Lake; Swedish Cultural Heritage Society of the Red River Valley, Fargo; Svenska Vänner, Jamestown; and Swedish Heritage Society of North Dakota, Minot. South Dakota's lone chapter is Dalesburg Scandinavian Association, Vermillion.

• Visit the **American west: European emigration Website** for an excellent depiction of Swedish emigration: www.americanwest. com/swedemigr/pages/emigra.htm.

• The **Federation of Swedish Genealogical Societies'** Website address is: www.genealogi.se/roots. •

# Norsk Høstfest

- Minot, ND, is home to the Norsk Høstfest, an internationally acclaimed Scandinavian festival that takes place each October. For information, contact P.O. Box 1347, Minot, ND 58702-1347; 701-852-2368; www.hostfest.com. •

## DANES

The Danes were the third-largest Scandinavian group to plant their roots in the Dakotas.

A number of young men left Denmark to escape compulsory military training in the German army (which had taken over Schlesvig-Holstein, the southernmost Danish province). Most Danes came to the Dakotas by way of the steppingstone states of Wisconsin, Minnesota, and Iowa.

In 1864, the first Danes took land in Turner County, SD. Others soon settled in Yankton, Clay, and Turner counties. By 1890, Danes had spread out into 55 South Dakota counties. One of the largest concentrations of Danes in the U.S. was in Danville, Spring Valley, and Swan Lake townships in Turner County, SD. Nearly as large was the settlement in Kingsbury County, SD.

According to "Dakota Panorama," in 1928, Danes comprised about one-sixth of the Scandinavians who settled in South Dakota. Many Danes were Lutheran; others became Methodists, Baptists, Adventists, Presbyterians, and Unitarians. A group of more than 2,500 Danish Mormons came to the U.S. around 1850.

The oldest North Dakota Danish community began in Hill Township, Cass County, in 1878. The book "History of the Danish Settlement in Hill Township, Cass County, ND," published in 1906, documents this settlement. Danes who settled there came principally from Jutland and Schlesvig.

The 1910 North Dakota census shows Danes at 2.1 percent of the state's population. The largest concentration of Danes in North Dakota can be found in the north-central counties of Burke, Renville, and Ward. Hub cities are Kenmare, Norma, and Flaxton. While a few were in the area as early as 1889, most came in the next decade, settling initially at Kenmare and spreading out from there. A windmill in the Kenmare city park, built by a Danish pioneer, stands as a monument to these early Danish settlers.

Other Danes settled in western Grand Forks, southern Steele, Divide, and McLean counties. •

## DANISH
### RESEARCH TIPS & SOURCES

- **Lutheran Church parish records** (the state church) are your primary source once you make the leap to Denmark. Records in the state archives include military and land records, wills, and emigration documents. Do the legwork first to learn the parish of your ancestors, as well as the name they went by in Denmark (see also information for Swedish and Norwegian ethnic groups).
- Check the **Family History Library Catalog CD** (under the locality category) at an LDS family history center near you to see what records are available in the areas your ancestors once frequented.
- The **Danish Immigrant Museum's Family History & Genealogy Center** houses records ranging from immigration to Danish Brotherhood and Sisterhood membership rolls. Especially interesting is the museum's online exhibit called "Across Oceans, Across Time." It can be viewed at the museum's Website: www.danishmuseum.org/DanishCulture/DanishCulture101.html. The museum's address and phone number: 4210 Main Street, Elk Horn, Iowa 51531-0249; 712-764-7008.
- The **Danish Emigration Archives** (P.O. Box 1731, 9100, Aalborg, Denmark), has nformation on emigration from Denmark to America from 1869-1940. It includes Danes, Germans, and others who left from Copenhagen. Website: fwww.emiarch.dk. •

# Icelandic census fact

- Did you know...the 1703 Icelandic census is likely the first in the world to list the population of a whole nation, including name, age, and status of every person. •

## ICELANDERS

The latter half of the 19th century was a period of natural and economic hardships in Iceland, ranging from volcanic eruptions to severe winters, poor crops and loss of livestock. Large numbers of Icelanders, unable to sustain themselves or their families, left Iceland in search of a better life. By 1914, around one-fifth of all Icelanders had left for the New World.

They settled in highly concentrated colonies in North Dakota and Manitoba. The North Dakota Icelandic communities are the largest such settlements in the U.S. Primary areas of settlement were western Pembina County, Mc-Henry County (along the Mouse River near Upham —a daughter colony of the Pembina County group), and Milton in Cavalier County (part of the Pembina County settlement). In 1910, there were 2,784 Icelanders living in North Dakota.

Iceland is noted for its volcanoes and earthquakes. It's also noted for its emphasis on genealogy, some of which traces back to the ninth century when the island nation was first settled by Norwegians. Sagas written by Icelandic poets in the next centuries preserved the history of both Norway and Iceland.

The Pembina-area Icelanders also have well-documented roots, thanks to two area histories published in 1906 and 1953: "The Icelandic Settlement of Pembina County" and "Modern Sagas: The Story of the Icelanders in North America."

Many of the earliest pioneers came from Manitoba, settling near Cavalier, Mountain, and Gardar.

While most Icelanders were Lutheran, a few early settlers became Unitarians.

Many Mouse River Icelanders lost their land in the mid-1930s to the Clark Salyer National Wildlife Refuge. Those displaced moved to the West Coast or to the Red River Valley. •

# Finn facts

• Unlike their Nordic-speaking Scandinavian neighbors, the Finns speak Finno-Ugric. The language is most closely related to Estonian, and a distant cousin of Hungarian, Sámi, and several languages spoken in European Russia and Siberia.

• From the late 1300s until 1523, Finland was part of the Kalmar Union, which united Sweden, Denmark, Norway, Iceland, and Finland as a single kingdom. •

# FINLANDERS

You could tell a Finn settlement by its characteristic saunas (or steambath houses). These wooden structures were often the first buildings to be erected by sauna-loving Finlanders. Another trademark was the Finn Hall, a building that housed everything from political rallies and co-op meetings to community and athletic events.

The first Finns to settle in America were part of a group from Sweden who landed in Delaware in 1638. But it wasn't until the mid-19th century that a mass migration took place, with Finns settling in the Upper Midwest. More than 300,000 Finns emigrated to America before World War II.

Before their arrival in the Dakotas, many Finns worked the mines of upper Michigan and the iron range country of northeastern Minnesota. In South Dakota, they settled chiefly in Hamlin and Brown counties, and Lawrence/Butte counties in the Black Hills, where they put their mining experience to work in the area's gold mines.

The first North Dakota Finns arrived in the mid-1880s, settling near Ellendale in eastern Dickey County. Eventually, they settled in six more areas: in Nelson, Ramsey, and Walsh counties (1886); Logan (early 1890s); Towner (1896); Emmons (1899); Burleigh (1900); and Mountrail counties (1903). By far the largest concentration of Finns settled in Towner County.

Most North Dakota Finns were from northern Finland. Their faith was primarily Lutheran. Several books published by the Finns themselves preserve the history of their settlements (see bibliography).

In recent years, Finns have taken steps to preserve their unique history and celebrate their heritage by holding an annual Finn-fest USA. •

# American Indian roots

**I**n this last section of our ethnic roots chapter, we pay tribute to those who were here first—the American Indians. Their roots stretch back to the last Ice Age or beyond, when a bridge between Asia and America enabled their pre-historic ancestors to cross from one world to another. Or perhaps, as their legends say, they have always been here. Over the eons, many tribes have called Dakota home. Here are the ones we know about.

## A nation named 'Sioux'

- The word "Sioux" is said to be derived from a Chippewa word meaning "lesser enemy." The name the Sioux gave themselves was "Dakota," the suffix "-kota" signifying "friend" or "ally."

- Three linguistic and cultural divisions developed as a result of tribal migration: Dakota (Santee), Nakota (Middle Dakota or Yankton), and Lakota (Teton). The Lakota form the largest group in the Dakotas.

- The Dakotas were made up of seven tribes: the Wahpetons, Sissetons, Mdewakantons, Wahpekutes (Santees), Yanktons, Yanktonais, and Tetons. The Tetons consisted of four subgroups: the Oglala, Brule, Hunkpapa, and Minneconjou.

- Many Dakota Indians had ancestors who were once members of the Seven Council Fires or Sioux Nation. These tribes included the Lakota, Dakota, Yankton, and Yanktonai. •

They came from the forested regions of the East and from the plains of the south: the Mandans, Arikaras, and the Hidatsas who built their earth lodges and cultivated their gardens along the Missouri River in central Dakota; the nomadic bands of Dakota/Lakota, also known as Sioux; the eastern and Black Hills Cheyennes; the Plains Chippewas (Ojibways), and the Assiniboin, entering the Great Plains of North Dakota and Manitoba; the Cree, the Crow, and the Blackfeet, moving into the buffalo country of western North Dakota.

## 1300-1800

The Mandans are believed to be the first to settle in the Dakotas, beginning in the 1300s. In time, other tribes arrived, pushed westward by white expansion or perhaps drawn here by the abundance of their chief food source, the buffalo.

The Sioux entered the Dakotas in the 1600s; the once-nomadic Hidatsa moved into central North Dakota around the same time, settling alongside the Mandans. Their cousins the Crows—and the Cree and the Blackfeet—came around the same era. The Arikara (who would later settle near the Mandans in central North Dakota) entered southern Dakota in the 1700s; the Chippewa moved into northeastern North Dakota sometime in the mid-1700s.

Around 1790, the Teton Sioux began moving westward to the Black Hills. Around this same time, the fur trade era was beginning, with the French, British, and Spanish competing for Indian trade.

While the fur trading posts enabled the Indians to exchange pelts and pemmican for trade goods, there was a deadly downside: diseases, such as smallpox, were introduced to the tribes by the whites. In 1781, a smallpox epidemic killed many Mandans and Hidatsas.

## 19th century

In 1801, Alexander Henry Jr. established a trading post at Pembina (ND). Pembina soon became a bustling community made up largely of mixed-blood Euro-American/Indian Métis (meh-tee').

When Lewis and Clark arrived in north-central Dakota in 1804, the Mandan and Hidatsa Knife River villages were already well established. It was there that the two explorers met Sakakawea, the teen-age Indian girl who helped guide them on the remainder of their Voyage of Discovery.

Fort Union, queen of trading posts, was established at the confluence of the Lower Yellowstone and Missouri rivers in northwestern Dakota in 1829. Fort Clark trading post (near Stanton, ND) was founded in 1831. In 1837, another smallpox epidemic, carried upriver by steamboat, nearly wiped out the Fort Clark Mandans.

In the mid-1840s, caravans of Red River ox carts began hauling buffalo hides and other trade goods from Pembina to St. Paul, Minnesota Territory. These twice-a-year treks by the Métis continued until the near demise of the buffalo some 40 years later.

## Treaties and reservations

The 1850s saw a large influx of whites—including missionaries—into Indian country. Two major treaties between the Teton Sioux and the U.S. government went into effect during this decade: The 1851 Fort Laramie Treaty guaranteed U.S. rights to build

# run deep in Dakota

and protect roads through Indian country. Another treaty was signed at Fort Pierre (SD) in 1856, giving whites the right to travel the Oregon Trail between forts Laramie and Pierre.

In 1857, the Santee Sioux ceded their lands east of the Big Sioux River in South Dakota and moved to a reservation.

The Yankton Treaty of 1858 opened up lands between the Big Sioux and Missouri rivers for white settlement. In 1859, the Yanktons moved to the first of the Sioux reservations along the Missouri.

## Prairie conflict

A government action profoundly impacting the Dakota tribes was the Homestead Act, signed into law in 1862. The act would soon bring many thousands of white settlers into Indian country.

In 1862, a band of Santee Sioux in Minnesota revolted, resulting in the "Minnesota Uprising," which spread into the Dakotas. Stirred into action, the U.S. Army erected a string of military posts in the Dakotas. From 1863 to 1865, forces led by Gens. Alfred Sully and Henry Sibley combed northern Dakota looking for uprising participants. The battles that followed (Whitestone Hill, 1863, and Badlands/Killdeer Mountains, 1864) killed many hundreds of Indians.

In 1867, the Devils Lake Sioux (Fort Totten) Indian Reservation was established near Devils Lake (ND). A year later, the Sioux ceded their lands west of the Missouri River.

Fort Berthold Indian Reservation was formed in 1870 in west-central North Dakota, home to the three affiliated tribes of Mandans, Arikaras, and Hidatsas.

## New way of life

Discovery of gold in the Black Hills in 1874 brought a rush of prospectors and settlers to Indian lands, provoking hostilities between Indians and whites.

The climax came on 25 June 1876. On that fateful day, Lt. Col. George Armstrong Custer and his 7th Cavalry troops (stationed at Fort Abraham Lincoln in northern Dakota), sent to punish the "hostiles" who remained off the reservations, discovered a huge Indian encampment along the Little Big Horn River in eastern Montana. During the ensuing battle, Custer and all 280 of his men died.

This "victory" for the Indians led to a series of military clashes in the years that followed, culminating in a tragic encounter at Wounded Knee Creek in South Dakota in 1890.

In 1882, the Turtle Mountain Indian Reservation was established near present-day Belcourt, ND.

On Nov. 2, 1889, Dakota Territory became the two separate states of North and South Dakota.

The next decades would see a massive influx of non-Indian people into the Dakotas and reductions in the sizes of reservations as a series of land cessions opened them to settlement.

American Indians of today have a renewed pride in their heritage. Their traditions live on in colorful powwows held across the country, including many in North and South Dakota. Their artistic and cultural contributions continue to enrich the Dakotas.

And many are now seeking to discover their Indian ancestry. •

## What's in a name?

- In the 18th and 19th centuries, many Cherokees adopted European surnames. Others translated their names into the English equivalent word, such as Walker, Wolf, Pigeon, or Smoke.

- Most tribes used compound names such as Standing Bear, Yellow Hammer, or Two Shields. Most (but not all) Cherokee names referred to a single animal, insect, plant, or environmental object.

- Many names were first anglicized by the census-takers. The spelling depended on how the enumerator interpreted the spelling, based on the pronunciation. Regional dialects also played a role in how these names sounded to the census-taker's ears.•

## INDIAN RESERVATIONS IN THE DAKOTAS

### SOUTH DAKOTA RESERVATIONS (east of Missouri River):
- Lake Traverse ( Sisseton) Agency (Wahpeton-Sisseton Sioux); extends into extreme southeastern North Dakota
- Crow Creek Agency (Santee Sioux)
- Yankton Agency/Greenwood Agency (Yankton Sioux)
- Flandreau Agency (Santee Sioux)

### SOUTH DAKOTA RESERVATIONS (along or west of Missouri River):
- Pine Ridge Agency (Oglala Lakota, Brule Sioux)
- Rosebud Agency (Teton Sioux)
- Lower Brule Agency (Brule Sioux)
- Cheyenne River Agency (Minneconjou, Sans Arc, Blackfeet, Two Kettle)
- Standing Rock Agency (Yanktonai, Blackfeet, Teton Sioux)

### NORTH DAKOTA RESERVATIONS
- Standing Rock (Sioux)
- Devils Lake (Spirit Lake) Sioux/Fort Totten (Wahpeton-Sisseton, Yanktonai)
- Fort Berthold (Hidatsa, Arikara, Mandan)
- Turtle Mountain (Chippewa, Métis) •
*(See also Lake Traverse Agency, SD)*

# AMERICAN INDIAN
# RESEARCH TIPS & SOURCES

• The first step in tracing your Native American roots is to determine what tribe(s) your ancestor belonged to. A resource you can check is "**The Indian Tribes of North America**" by John R. Swanson (published by Smithsonian Institute Press). Next, study the tribe's history and its location during your ancestor's lifetime.

• When you've determined names of family members living around 1900, you're ready to check out the **National Archives and Records Administration (NARA).** The Denver branch has records of the Wind River (WY) Agency dating from 1873-1952, including letters, files, photos, censuses, and land records. Kansas City has most of the records pertaining to Indians in North and South Dakota. For a detailed account of these holdings, refer to the book "**The Archives: A Guide to the National Archives Field Branches**" by Loretto Dennis Szucs and Sandra Hargreaves Luebking (published by Ancestry Inc. in 1988). A more specific resource is the "**Guide to Records in the National Archives of the United States Relating to American Indians** " by Edward E. Hill (Washington, DC). Also check "**American Indians: A Select Catalog of National Archives Microfilm Publications**" for a list of records available on microfilm for the tribe and time period of your ancestor. Or you can check the catalog out online by visiting this Website: www.archives.gov/publications/microfilm/amerindians/indians.html.

• The NARA and/or its branch offices contain **Bureau of Indian Affairs (BIA) records,** including accounting records, reports, land records (allotment, leasing/sale and determination of heirs), correspondence, and some school records. (See Chapter 3, research sites, for more on NARA holdings.) If your ancestors left the tribe or if records burned, you may not find your family listed.

• Check the **Indian census rolls** listing statistics on members of your ancestor's tribe. These censuses, taken annually starting in 1885, contain name (English and/or Indian), age/birthdate, sex, and relationship to head of family. In 1930 and beyond, they listed marital status and percent of Indian blood. A "Select Catalog" lists contents of 692 rolls of film. Some pre-1885 annuity rolls, agents' records, and earlier censuses are also available. Also check the 1900 U.S. federal census Soundex index for your ancestor's name.

• During the Great Depression, **Indian Civilian Conservation Corps (CCC)** camps were established on the reservations. These records are available through the NARA or its branches. NARA and branch offices also contain records of American Indians who served in the U.S. Armed Forces. (See Chapter 2, military records.)

• If your ancestors were Cherokee, check the "**Dawes rolls**" of the Five Civilized Tribes. More than 100,000 people were registered during 1898-1907 to establish their eligibility for land allotments. Also check the Henderson Roll (1835), the Old Settlers Roll (1851 and 1896), and the Drennen Payment Roll (1851).

• The South Dakota State Archives in Pierre has many (and plans to eventually have all) BIA microfilms from the NARA pertaining to the South Dakota Indian reservations. These Indian censuses are available through interlibrary loan.

• The North Dakota State Archives and Historical Research Library has microfilms of the original **Standing Rock Indian census.** This census covers the years 1876-1939. The originals are housed at the National Archives/Central Plains Region in Kansas City. Other Indian reservation census records available at the state archives are Fort Totten, Turtle Mountain, and Fort Berthold.

• Major public and university libraries in the Dakotas are also storehouses of information on Native American history, culture, and records. (See Chapter 3 on research sites.)

• The LDS family history centers' **Family History Library Catalog (FHLC)** should be checked for Indian records.

• Since missionaries were often active among Indians, **church records** may contain information on Indian ancestors.

• An organization that seeks North American Indian family information is the **Métis Genealogical Society** (East 1658 Central, Spokane, WA 99208). Membership entitles you to the newsletter, which contains data on North Dakota, as well as other tribes.

• **Pembina State Museum** (Exit 215 off Interstate 29, 805 Highway 59, P.O. Box 456, Pembina, ND, 58271-0456; 701-825-6840) salutes the area's history, including the Métis .

• The **Brenorsome Historical Society** (contact person Louis Garcia, Box 232, Tokio, ND 58379) has much information on Devils Lake Indian history, with emphasis on the genealogy of Devils Lake Sioux tribal members.

• The **Turtle Mountain Indian Historical Society** (P.O. Box 257, Belcourt, ND 58316-0257) preserves and makes available for research the written documents and artifacts of the people of the Turtle Mountain Band of Chippewa (Ojibway) Indians.

• Those with Turtle Mountain Chippewa roots should find the book "**Collections of the State Historical Society,**" Volume 5, edited by O.G. Libby, a good read. Located in the North Dakota State Archives and Historical Research Library, this very old volume contains the genealogy of Victor and Joseph Renville and gives information on 19th-century Chippewa-Métis families.

• **Boarding-school records** for Indian children attending BIA-operated schools are another source. (Note that many Indian children were sent to boarding schools far from their native reservations. Check with the reservation your tribe is affiliated with to determine name of boarding school.) **Religious schools** also operated on many reservations. Check for the denomination operating the school and determine the church archives address.

• In the 1870s, missionary monks established **Blue Cloud Abbey** near what is now Marvin, SD, opening missions and schools on four reservations: Immaculate Conception School on Crow Creek Reservation, St. Michael on Fort Totten Reservation, St. Paul on Yankton Reservation, and St. Ann on the Turtle Mountain Reservation. A fifth school—St. Bernard's on Standing Rock—was later turned over to monks from Conception, MO. In recent years, Blue Cloud Abbey turned over the missions and schools to the Tribes for their administration. The abbey has since formed a culture center for the West River Lakota. For information, contact the **American Indian Culture Research Center, Blue Cloud Abbey,** P.O. Box 98, Marvin, SD 57251-0098; phone 605-398-9200. Check out their Website: www.bluecloud.org/dakota.html.

• **Native American colleges** contain records and information on their students and their history and culture. Names, addresses, and phone numbers of Dakota-based Native American colleges can be found in the bibliography for this chapter.

• **Augustana College** in Sioux Falls, SD, is noted for its collections on Native Americans (see also Chapter 3, research sites).

• Check out the following excellent Native American genealogy Website: hometown.aol.com/bbbenge/front. html. This site contains Lakota history and genealogy, the Sisseton-Wahpeton Sioux tribe home page, maps, and other Native American links.

• An exceptional reference for anyone with North Dakota Indian roots is "**North Dakota's Indian Heritage**" by Mary Jane Schneider. Especially valuable are sections on state reservations, detailing churches and schools that operated there. Also included is information on treaties and land cessions affecting North Dakota tribes. •

**88 • Oral interviews can reap
harvest of family data**

- **What is oral tradition?**
- **Be thankful for technology**
- **Preparation is the key**
- **Time is running out**
- **Decide on an objective**
- **Know your subject**
- **Preserve interview for posterity**
- **Put subject at ease**
- **After the interview**

# Oral interviews can reap

## Family folk-lore

The Africans and American Indians have long been noted for their oral traditions. In both groups, special individuals are assigned the honored function of listening to the group's oral history—centuries worth of family stories—and then remembering it and relaying it to the next generations. But what about the rest of us?

## What is oral tradition?

Oral tradition is the passing on and recording of stories and history from past generations to current and future generations.

In the past, oral history was gathered mostly by historical societies or public libraries, but families have become active participants in the practice themselves to complement the written histories they've compiled. They want a record, whether written, audio or video, of their parents' and grandparents' times in their own words.

## Be thankful for technology

We are fortunate today to have the technology to record not only voices, but also faces and facial expressions, through video. Years from now, we will be able to see and hear our ancestors as they tell about their lives and their families.

Oral history helps to flesh out the facts and figures you may have already gathered from military, church, and vital records or from land deeds and obituaries.

A record of a family's stories and experiences will bring those facts and figures to life. It will give you a better understanding of your parents and grandparents and other ancestors—how they lived, where they lived, and the people they lived with.

Older people have a wonderful aptitude for telling their life stories, and it's unlikely any of them will refuse to share with you. They have a desire to connect with the generations that will survive them, creating a link between past and future.

Telling the stories also serves as a way for them to "sum up" their lives—to bring them full circle. Don't deny your elder relatives that opportunity.

And don't get so busy writing everyone else's oral history that you forget about writing your own. Do it for your children and their children. You have much to tell, just

as your ancestors do or did. And then, ask your parents about their childhoods, schooling, teen years and early married life.

## Preparation is the key

Interviewing is an art, not a science. And though you may not be Barbara Walters or Tom Brokaw (a native of South Dakota, by the way), you can learn to conduct a successful, productive oral interview.

Basically, an interview is a conversation, though structured and a record kept of it. It can be just simply sitting down with Great-uncle John or with Nana Jones and asking basic questions about their lives.

Once you've set up an interview time with your Grandma Larson or Aunt Jane, then what? Prepare for the interview by developing a list of questions—one or two may be all it takes to get one person rambling for hours, but then you might need pages of questions to get someone else to talk about her/his life. And it may not be because there are no interesting stories or some deep, dark family secrets. It may simply be that the person is not comfortable talking about the past or perhaps talking about herself or himself at all.

In the process, it is important to not intrude into someone's private territory and to not pull old family skeletons out of the

### The gift of family history

What do you do with your tapes and transcripts of the interview you've conducted with a beloved relative? First, give copies to the person you interviewed. Next, consider reproducing them and giving them as gifts to others who would also value these family memories (with the interviewee's permission, of course). You couldn't give a more thoughtful gift than this. As time goes by, this gift will become an even more treasured family legacy. Capture the memories now, then share them with others. (See Chapter 10 for ideas on how to incorporate interview information into a family history book.) •

# harvest of family data

closet—skeletons that might cause harm, embarrassment or even worse. Though you may have a serious curiosity about some of those skeletons, resist pulling too hard to get that information right now. Perhaps it will come out later from that person or from another family member.

Though family histories need to be truthful to be valuable to future generations, some chapters are best left unwritten.

## Time is running out

Since much of your family's history may exist only in the memories of older family members, interviewing those people immediately is key to compiling a complete history. Otherwise, the memories die with the people who hold them, and they are lost forever.

Plan some interview sessions today. Explain thoroughly to the person you are contacting what the interview process will involve, about the recording equipment you will be using, and what kinds of information you are looking for.

Resist directing the interview too closely to your list of questions unless the interviewee has totally strayed from the subject. Once the person starts talking, just let her or him talk—you'll get the best information that way.

Interviews can sometimes go off on tangents and, though interesting, may not be the type of information you want to gather. On the other hand, however, those tangents may lead to some valuable information you will be pleased to have later.

## Decide on objective of interview

Interviewees can also offer interesting tidbits of information about others, alive or dead, as well as about themselves.

Though it may be tempting to schedule interview sessions at a family reunion, it is not recommended.

Distractions can interfere with conducting a productive interview, but scheduling private interview sessions a day or two before or after the reunion may work well for all involved.

If you want to collect facts and figures at

## Dakota Memories interview project

- Dakota Memories, an oral history project co-sponsored by the Germans from Russia Heritage Collection, NDSU Libraries, Fargo, ND, is collecting memories from folks with Germans from Russia heritage. The project involves interviews with older citizens who lived in such communities as Linton, Strasburg, Lehr and Rugby. Future sessions will involve video interviews in Saskatchewan. For further information, contact www.lib.ndsu.nodak. edu/grhc/history_ culture/oral/interviews/ project.htm. •

## Interview tips & tricks

Here are some helpful interviewing tips:

- Before the interview, prepare a list of questions to help you get the kind of information you are searching for.
- Even if you use a tape recorder or camcorder, still take written notes. There's always the chance the machine won't work properly. Ask permission to record the interview and explain the equipment to the interviewee before starting the interview.
- Choose an interview location that is quiet and away from distractions, including the telephone, children, neighbors, traffic, etc.
- Avoid interviewing more than one person at a time. Also avoid having other people in the room during the interview. That can be distracting and possibly inhibiting to the interviewee.
- If the interviewee pauses to recall a past event or decide how to say something, don't jump in to fill the silence. You could miss out on some really valuable information.
- Be sure to ask for the correct spelling of names and places.
- Ask open-ended questions rather than those that can be answered with "yes" or "no."
- Though the interviewee cannot remember an exact date, help her or him narrow down the timeframe or at least record the event being remembered. You may be able to determine the date later. •

References: www.reuniontips.com; www.familytreemaker.com

# 'GRANDMA, TELL ME 'BOUT THE GOOD

You can approach oral interviews in a variety of ways, and the questions you ask will be determined by what kinds of information you want to gain from the interview. Here are just a few ideas to consider:

## CHILDHOOD

**If you want to know about events and experiences in each phase of a person's life, ask questions about his/her childhood, such as:**

- What is your earliest memory? How many siblings did you have and where did you fit into the group?
- Who were your playmates? Did you have pets? What were their names?
- What do you remember about your home?
- What family traditions do you remember?
- Who was your favorite teacher? What are some of your school memories?
- How did you spend your summer vacations?

## TEEN YEARS

**Ask about the person's teen years with the following questions:**

- What kinds of parties did you attend?
- When did you start dating? Who was your first love?
- What was your first car?
- What extracurricular activities did you participate in?
- What goals did you have for the future? What did you want to be after high school?
- Did you have a job as a teen-ager?
- What was your curfew/punishment for breaking it?

## ADULTHOOD

**Questions about a person's adulthood might be:**

- What college did you attend? What was your major?
- What was your first job as an adult?
- When and where did you get married?

- What activities and organizations were you involved in?
- What church, if any, did you attend?
- How did you feel when your children were born?
- What is your favorite memory from adulthood?
- What would you consider your most important lifetime achievement?

**Another approach might be to ask questions related to events outside the person's own family by looking at them or events of the decades during which the person lived. Questions for this approach might be:**

## PRE-DEPRESSION ERA

**Questions for the first three decades of the 20th century might be:**

- Did anyone in your family have the Spanish flu that swept the nation in 1918-19?
- Did you experience the Roaring '20s? What was it like?
- Did you or a family member lose money in the Stock Market Crash of 1929?
- Where did you live during the 1920s? Did you have electricity and indoor plumbing?
- How did your family celebrate birthdays, holidays and other special events?
- Did your grandparents or any other relative live with you? Who, and for how long?

## DIRTY '30s ERA

**Questions for the 1930s might be:**

- How did the Depression affect you and your family? Was your family on public assistance? Did you have to move because of losing your farm/home? Did you or any family members work for the WPA or CCC?
- When did your family get electricity? What was the first electrical appliance the family purchased?

# Words of wisdom

- "When a knowledgeable old person dies, a whole library disappears." •

–African proverb

an upcoming family reunion, let people know ahead of time about your goal. Ask people to bring old family Bibles, journals, wills, letters, birth and death certificates, old photos, and other items. Set up a display area at the reunion where you and other researchers can view each others' information.

Perhaps someone can line up a portable photocopier to make it easy for everyone to take information home with them.

The interview approach and the kind of information you want to gather will depend on what you already know. One approach is searching for facts and figures for pedi-

gree charts and family group sheets. This does not require in-depth interviewing and may work well at family reunions.

Another approach is when you want to collect oral history–which requires talking directly, one on one, with a person, often for hours at a time. You need to decide which type of

# OLD DAYS...'

## THE WAR YEARS

**The 1940s could be covered by questions such as:**

- Did anyone in your family serve during World War II?
- Did any family members assist in the war effort by working in the munitions or plane factories or in the shipyards?
- What was the worst part of rationing?
- How did you feel about the U.S. dropping atomic bombs on Japan?
- Did you know any Japanese, Germans or Italians who were interred during the war?
- What was the most valued appliance in your home during the 1940s?

A quick review of history will give you ideas for more questions about the decades during which the person you are interviewing lived.

## FEELINGS/OPINIONS

**A way to get more information about a person's feelings, emotions and opinions might be by asking questions like the following:**

- What characteristics of your parents and grandparents have you retained?
- What is your best-remembered feeling when your children were born?
- Did you like school? Did you struggle or excel in school? Who was your favorite teacher?

- What did you think of Elvis Presley, the Beatles and the Rolling Stones?
- Who was your favorite musician and athlete?
- What American and world events most affected your life? Why?
- Did you ever have a friend or family member betray you? How did you feel about that?
- When you first fell in love, how did you feel?
- When did you know who you wanted to marry and spend the rest of your life with?
- How did you deal with your spouse's death?
- How was life different after World War II? Did you like it more or less than before the war?
- What was your first experience with discrimination and prejudice? How did you feel about it?
- Where were you when you heard about President Kennedy's assassination? What was your reaction?

Audiotaping and videotaping the interview are great ideas. Check out the discussion on things to consider in taping an interview, featured elsewhere in this chapter. Above all, don't delay, as you could lose valuable family history if you wait too long. ●

interview you want to do and work from there.

## Know your subject

For a truly productive interview, you need to know as much as possible about your topic or interviewee.

Also, having a specific

objective(s) is important. Unless you have a clear objective(s), you won't know if you accomplished what you wanted to.

Bring notes with you on what you want to cover, including family group sheets and documents, photographs, letters, and other items that will trigger the interviewee's memo-

ries. These tools will help the interview move more smoothly and lead to a more productive interview.

Your choice of place and time is important. Choose a quiet place where there will be few distractions.

Turn off the telephone ringer or set the answering machine to take all calls. Make sure the location is

## Seek out the stories

- Now is the time to interview people about their memories of your family from earlier years, before death and illness take away this link to the past.

- Try using "memory triggers" during your interview. Start talking about family heirlooms, or about the delicious dinners Great-grandma used to make. That will get the conversation started and get the person's mind focused on heritage and the past. Then you can ask more detailed questions about these items, or about traditions and events from that era.

- Ask elderly relatives for their memories. And don't forget old neighbors or family friends. They, too, may have stories about your family. If some of those old friends are now in a nursing home, pay them a visit. They'll enjoy the visit, and you may reap memories—and some new friends! •

someplace where the interviewee is comfortable.

Depending on the interviewee's age and health conditions, don't try to overdo the session. Schedule the interview for the amount of time the interviewee thinks will be comfortable or watch closely to see if the person is tiring or becoming confused.

Providing the interviewee with a list of questions before the meeting may be helpful to get the person thinking about some of the topics and about memories that go with them.

You can structure your interview questions by: topics; decades; life passages (i.e., childhood, teen years, adulthood, etc.); major personal, local or world events during the person's lifetime; family traditions; or names, dates and places.

Find ideas for specific questions in a number of resources listed in the Family Reunion Bibliography, such as: the Family Tree Maker Website at: www. familytreemaker. com; "Family Reunion Handbook" by Barbara Brown and Tom Ninkovich; or "Unpuzzling Your Past" by Emily Anne Croom.

## Put subject at ease

Spend a few minutes at the beginning of the interview just visiting and "breaking the ice."

Whether you know the interviewee well or not, this technique works. However, when the

interviewee seems ready, make it clear that the interview is starting by adjusting in your chair, opening your notebook and starting the recorder.

Though you have come prepared with a list of questions, don't miss the opportunity to ask follow-up questions to information the interviewee has volunteered.

Be flexible and able to vary from the prepared questions. Try to verify dates and places mentioned and who was involved. Ask more questions if you're not sure whom the interviewee is talking about. You may not have the opportunity to verify that information later.

Building rapport with the interviewee is one of the keys to a successful interview. Let the person know you can be trusted with confidential information.

Be polite at all times, both with your questions, your manner and facial expressions and your comments to the interviewee's information.

Pay attention to whether or not the interviewee is getting tired or confused. Use that observation to determine when to end the interview. Ask about calling later to verify information or to tie up loose ends.

## Preserve interview for posterity

Recording the interview on audiotape or videotape will make for wonderful material for future generations, but those proc-

esses are not foolproof.

Take notes, also, just in case and as if the recorder were not there. However, make sure to tell the interviewee you are taping the session and explain the equipment to her or him.

It is best to not have anyone else in the interview session. Even though the person sits silently and listens, it can interfere with the flow of the interview for a variety of reasons. For instance, the interviewee may not be comfortable talking about certain subjects with the other person present. Or the third person may not be able to resist asking a question or expanding on comments.

## After the interview

It is recommended to transcribe the interview notes verbatim, even if the grammar is not proper or the information is not in chronological order. Verbatim text may someday be valuable to you or other researchers.

If it is impossible to interview someone in person, try a telephone interview or a video conference. If all else fails, consider sending the person a list of questions and ask her or him to write out the answers for you.

Most of all, don't let the questions go unasked and your ancestors' stories go untold. Record them now for future generations. •

# High-tech genealogy

## 'Netting' your genealogy

Here's just some of the information you'll find on the Web without ever leaving your home computer:

- Census records
- Military records
- Obituaries
- Church records
- Newspapers
- Family associations
- Social Security death index and other SSA records
- State and local libraries, archives, and genealogical and historical societies
- International databases
- Cemetery indexes •

Can you do genealogy without a computer? Of course you can. However, as in many other areas of our lives these days, computers have become very important and, in many cases, essential. The same could be said for genealogy.

With more affordable computer technology and increased Internet activity, the world of genealogy has changed considerably. You can see it in the indexes for various records, in the rapidly increasing number of genealogy-related Websites, and in the myriad selection of software for developing your own genealogy.

And, since genealogical research is such a paper generator, computers have made it easier for genealogists to duplicate information digitally, rather than with paper.

Being able to do genealogical research via com-puter can also save time and money on long-distance phone calls, postage, and travel.

This chapter features discussion on using computers in four facets of your research:

- Computer software for tracking the information you are gathering;
- Doing research on wonderful new Websites;
- Connecting with various branches of your family through genealogy-related Websites, and
- Communicating via e-mail, message bulletin boards, mailing lists and listserves.

## First, a little history...

ARPANET was the beginning of the Internet. That was 1969. In the 1980s, it was replaced by two separate and new net-works—a military network and a network of scientific and academic computers funded by the National Science Foundation.

Today, the Internet is a massive grouping of millions of computers, linked together on a network. A business or system that provides Internet service is called an **Internet Service Provider (ISP).** Your ISP talks to other ISPs everywhere so that you can get information from around the world.

**Browsers** are software programs that enable you to view sites and documents and to navigate on the World Wide Web. Examples of browsers include Netscape Navigator, Microsoft's Internet Explorer, Mosaic, Macweb, Lotus Notes, and Netcruiser.

A **Website address** is called a Uniform Resource Locator (URL), which is a unique address for a Web page.

## NEWSGROUP NEWS

Subscribing to genealogical newsgroups, such as Usenet/Netnews, connects you to people with similar interests. A newsgroup is similar to a mailing list, but uses e-mail to send a message that many subscribers can read. The eight major categories include:

- **Comp** – computer science-related topics
- **Humanities** – philosophy and classics
- **Misc** – miscellaneous items
- **News** – topics about Usenet itself
- **Rec** – recreational hobbies and interests
- **Sci** – science topics not related to computers
- **Soc** – social interaction and hobbies; most genealogy topics fall in this category
- **Talk** – general conversation

Topics under the Soc category include surnames, computer genealogy and methods, medieval genealogy, and many others. Topics dealing with specific countries and ethnic groups enable you to narrow your focus to the area you're researching.

Some useful newsgroup addresses might include alt.genealogy, fido.eur.genealogy, soc.genealogy.computing, soc.genealogy.marketplace, soc.genealogy.misc, and soc.genealogy.surnames.global.

Keep in mind that information gathered there is secondary, not primary, and should be checked for accuracy.

Other networking methods include message boards, mailing lists, surname sites, and personal Web pages. •

# Genealogy programs help you compile, sort, edit data

• If you have investigated genealogy software at all, you have probably seen advertisements or displays for **Family Tree Maker, Version 11.** It is one of the top-ranked genealogy software products. From MyFamily.com, Family Tree Maker is closely aligned with www.genealogy.com. It is easy to use, especially for publishing genealogy information online. In addition, it can be controlled and displayed in a variety of formats.

• **Legacy Family Tree** by Millennia is often the No. 1 pick for genealogy software today. It is powerful, but easy and enjoyable to use. Legacy's **Version 6.0** is loaded with features that amaze both beginners and experts.

• **Ancestral Quest, Version 11,** is also one of the top genealogy software programs. Easy to use and one of the most versatile Windows genealogy programs on the market, Ancestral Quest offers three main input screens: pedigree, family, and name list.

• **Personal Ancestral File (PAF)** is designed by the Church of Jesus Christ of Latter-Day Saints (LDS). In **Version 5.2,** it is a reliable genealogy software package, designed for ease of input, import, and export.

• Serious and professional genealogists often look to **The Master Genealogist** software. **Version 6** offers greater depth and flexibility, along with great organizational strengths.

• **Version 3** of **RootsMagic** is probably the easiest to use of all the genealogy software programs. Also one of the most powerful, it is used by professional and beginning genealogists.

• **Family Tree Legends' Version 5.0** is powerful and sophisticated. It is designed to make it easy to collect, display and organize information, whether notes, medical facts, photo, or other pieces of information.

• **Version 6.2** of **Brother's Keeper** will help you organize your family history information and let you print a variety of charts and reports. It also works with many versions of Windows.

• **Genbox Family History** is a complete genealogy software. Now in **Version 3.6.5,** it manages genealogy information and produces great charts and reports.

• **Family Historian, Version 3,** works well in comparing and merging two family files. The user has considerable control over the appearance and content of the charts and reports.

• **DoroTree** is a software program designed for Jewish genealogists. Its **Version 2.1** offers Holocaust information, date conversion, bilingual reports, and Jewish lineage entries.

• **Cumberland Family Tree** automatically links names as they are entered. You can add up to 250 events per person, as well as scanned photos and documents, sources, stories, and more. **Version 3.1** allows you to index your family history book.

• **WinFamily's Version 6.02** offers a main screen for entering personal data and a "family" icon that links to the page for registering family connections.

• **GEDitCOM** is a customized genealogy software for Macintosh. Its **Version 3.72** allows you to design your own genealogy user interface and provides a powerful, user-friendly interface to all features of the GEDCOM standard.

• **Reunion** is also a genealogy software program for Macintosh. Rated as one of the best, it helps you document, store, and display information in an elegant, graphic format. **Version 8** makes it easy to publish information and share it.

• **LifeLines** is a genealogy software program that helps with your genealogical research. Now in **Version 3.0.50,** it has a powerful scripting language and the ability to easily import and export information in the GEDCOM format.

• **Heredis 7.2** has no limits to data entry and is equipped with powerful tools for the professional genealogist. It is available in Mac and Windows.

• **Famtree** is easy to use. Its **Version 4.42** offers an on-screen form for each person and can link people into family groups with a few clicks of the mouse. •

# High-tech doesn't mean low standards

Standards for use of technology in genealogical research (paraphrased from National Genealogical Society recommendations):

- Learn the capabilities and limits of your equipment and software and use them appropriately.
- Refuse to let computer software automatically enhance your work.
- Treat compiled information from online sources or digital databases like that from other published sources.
- Accept digital images or enhancements of original records as satisfactory substitutes for originals only when there is reasonable assurance that the image was accurately reproduced.
- Cite sources for data obtained online or from digital media with the same care appropriate for sources on paper and other traditional media, and enter data into a digital database only when its source is clear.

- Always cite the sources for information or data posted online or sent to others, naming the author of a digital file as its immediate source, while crediting original sources cited within the file.
- Preserve the integrity of your databases by evaluating the reliability of downloaded data before adding it into your files.
- Provide a description of any changes in data whenever it is shared with others.
- Personally verify or correct information, or note it as unverified, before passing it on to others. Keep in mind that not all information found on the Internet is accurate.
- Treat people online as courteously and civilly as you would treat them face to face.
- Accept that technology has not changed the principles of genealogical research, only the procedures. •

## Join a 'CIG'

- Computer users with similar interests often band together in computer interest groups (CIGs). They learn from each other— about computers or particular genealogy software programs or share advice and ideas on pursuing their research.

Each year, the January-March issue of *Genealogical Computing* usually includes a CIG directory. •

The Internet is important for genealogy purposes because it keeps families connected (via e-mail). Website research is also a way to learn more about your family and ancestors.

Though there are many benefits from Internet use, there are some dangers, and one is viruses that come through e-mails and Websites. It is crucial that you have an anti-virus program, such as Symantec's Norton AntiVirus or McAfee's ViruScan, on your computer to catch those viruses before they infect your computer.

## Researching on the Web

Many more people than you might realize have gotten into doing their genealogical research on the Internet and the World Wide Web. The old and young, blue collar and white collar, those with eighth-grade educations and those with doctorates—they are all grabbing onto the excitement of communicating and researching through the Web.

Before we go further, though, let's clarify the difference between the Internet and the World Wide Web (definitions are adapted from "Genealogy Online for Dummies"):

- **The Internet** is a system of computer networks joined together by high-speed data lines called "backbones." Basically, it is the telephone cables used to transmit information on the Web.
- **The World Wide Web** (most often referred to as the Web or www.) is a system for viewing and using multimedia documents over the Internet.

Web documents are created in Hypertext Markup Language (HTML) and are read by Web browsers, such as Netscape Navigator or Internet Explorer.

Now let's talk about the advantages to genealogists of using the Internet and the Web.

A genealogist's Web use might be in a number of areas. She/he may just sign up for e-mail to communicate with family, friends, and other genealogists and to exchange information, advice, and encouragement. The convenience of using e-mail, rather than the endless chore of trying to reach busy people by telephone, cannot be underestimated.

Being able to prepare and send your message at any time of the day or night and any day of the week is a tremendous convenience. In addition, it is easier for others to be in touch with you on their own schedules, rather than on yours.

But once you're hooked up to the Internet and using e-mail effectively for communicating, why stop there? Why not investigate the Web? Read the how-to books suggested in this chapter and in the index.

Now that you know something, what's next?

Dive right in. Investigate some of the major search engines and look for a subject you're particularly interested in and want to know more about.

**Search engines,** you ask? Those are programs that can search either a large index of information generated by "robots" or a particular Website. They are a bit more sophisticated than directories.

A **"robot"** (also called a "spider") is simply a program that travels all over the Internet collecting information about sites and resources it comes across.

Some major search engines include:
• altavista.com
• askjeeves.com
• dogpile.com
• excite.com
• google.com
• hotbot.com
• infoseek.com
• metacrawler.com
• vivisimo.com
• yahoo.com

Judge Websites on their benefit to you. Consider their timeliness, usefulness, and organization.

## Web addresses of interest

Most anything you read these days probably includes a Web address or two. The extension on a Website address helps identify the type of business or organization that owns the Web address, such as:
• **.com** - commercial, such as companies and businesses
• **.edu** - educational organizations and institutions
• **.gov** - governmental agencies and entities
• **.mil** - U.S. military
• **.net** - network
• **.org** - nonprofit organizations

To get a list of genealogy Websites, just type in the word "genealogy" on a search engine. You'll be shocked at how many entries you get—for all different ethnic groups and all sorts of locations and records around the world.

This chapter includes a number of Websites that we are sure you will find quite useful. Also, see the list of Helpful Addresses for Chapter 3, appendix.

## From internet to intuition!

• Ever get the feeling that an unseen hand has aided you in finding branches of your family? Genealogists often tell tales of strange coincidences leading to their discovery of family information. To read some of their stories, visit this Website: genealogytoday.com/family/stories/serendipity.html

• Noted genealogy researcher and lecturer Henry Z. Jones Jr. is so sold on serendipity's role in ancestor hunting that he's written a book about it called "Psychic Roots: Serendipity & Intuition in Genealogy." For information, contact: www.hankjones.com/psychic.htm. •

## Let's talk tech terms!

Here are some terms that you might find helpful to know as you delve into computers and the Internet:

• **Browser** – software programs that allow users to navigate the World Wide Web, like Internet Explorer, Netscape Navigator, etc.

• **Directory** – an Internet tool that is created entirely by human editors who look at the Web pages and assign them to logical or appropriate categories.

• **Filters** – software that allows you to specify the action you want the mail program to take when a message matches certain conditions.

• **FTP** (File Transfer Protocol) – a way of getting files from one computer to another through the Internet.

• **Home page** – the first page of a Website, like a title page in a book.

• **HTML** (Hypertext Markup Language) – the language that turns a text document into a www.-browsable one.

• **Internet bulletin boards** – an Internet service where messages can be posted and that can go out to the whole world.

• **ISP** (Internet Service Provider) – like Qwest, Midcontinent Communications, Yahoo, AOL, etc.

• **Link** – a pointer or Web address you can click on in one Website to get to another Website.

• **Mailing list** – a facility on the Internet that uses e-mail to distribute a single message to all subscribers. There are literally thousands of genealogy-related mailing lists on the Internet.

• **Message board** – a place on the Internet where people sharing the same interests can post electronic messages. People then visit the message board to see posted messages.

• **TCP/IP** (Transmission Control Protocol/ Internet Protocol) – the standard communication format for the Internet – the standard way to connect to other computers.

• **URL** (Uniform Resource Locator) – the web address. •

## Got 'net nerves'? Read a how-to book!

- You say you don't have a clue how to surf the 'net? Well, don't let that stop you—there are many tutorial-type materials available in book-stores, through book clubs, at libraries, and on the Web just waiting for you to peruse.

- One of those resources is "The Internet for Dummies" by John R. Levine, Carol Baroudi, and Margaret Levine Young. Another is "Internet and World Wide Web Simplified," from maranGraphics. Both are good tools for getting started.

- For genealogy specifically, check out "Genealogy Online for Dummies" by Matthew L. Helm and April Leigh Helm. This book will provide some excellent assistance in learning about the Internet and using the Web. •

# Researching online

With the development of the Web, genealogists can now do much of their research online from their homes. Huge amounts of information and records are added to the Web every day. And much of that information is useful to genealogists.

Many library card catalogs are now online so you can learn what is available at a particular library before you visit it. Some research libraries allow lending of their resources and have indexes online so people can see what is available and determine what they want to order through interlibrary loan.

You can visit government and other Websites that contain records important to your research, such as the Bureau of Land Management's land records for those who received homestead land.

Many censuses and naturalization records are now online in various states, including North and South Dakota. Though they are valuable resources, genealogists should keep in mind that they are probably tran-scribed records and that all information should be verified with other documents and sources.

Some sites for census and naturalization information include www.census-online.com/links/index.html, www.vitalrec.com/index.html, www.genealogysitefinder.com, www.archives.gov/genealogy, and www.glorecords. blm.gov.

The Geographic Names Information System (www.geonames.usgs.gov) and the U.S. Census Bureau's Gazetteer (www.census.gov/cgi-bin/gazetteer) are both sources

## Hats off for these super sites!

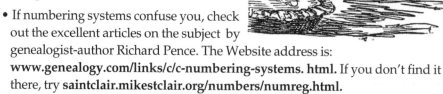

Check the following helpful sites and publications for genealogy-related information:

- Internet Family Finder at Genealogy.com is the place to go for a search engine featuring a 325 million-name index from 3 million genealogy-related Websites. To begin your search, visit: **www. genealogy.com/genealogy/ifftop.html.**

- If numbering systems confuse you, check out the excellent articles on the subject by genealogist-author Richard Pence. The Website address is: **www.genealogy.com/links/c/c-numbering-systems. html.** If you don't find it there, try **saintclair.mikestclair.org/numbers/numreg.html.**

- Check out Eastman's Genealogy Index. You'll find it at **www.ancestry.com/home/times. htm.**

- The Genealogy Today newsletter can be found at **www.enoch.com/genealogy/ newslet.htm.**

- One of the best sites on the Web for novice genealogists is **firstct.com,** where you can choose from all sorts of genealogy categories and links.

- **Ezine.rootsweb.com** keeps you up to date on the Rootsweb site, genealogy news and success stories.

- The Dear Myrtle newsletter at **members.aol.com/dearmyrtle** is a daily collection of tips and online courses, etc.

- **Filemine.com** or **itprodownloads.com** offers a vast collection of software for genealogists. •

for census information and search options.

Another site for transcribed census records is www.census-online.com/links/index.html. Another would be www.mapquest.com. The www.usgenweb.org and www.worldgenweb.org are both excellent resources for genealogy information in specific counties and states throughout the U.S. and in countries around the world.

For more helpful Web addresses, see Chapters 2 and 3, and the Helpful Addresses in the appendix.

## Library that never closes

Sometimes referred to by genealogists as "the library that never closes," the Internet offers a number of Websites for new genealogists.

Beginners can use them to learn the ropes of genealogy. They will help you get started in your family research by offering ideas and research information.

Just a few are:
• ancestry.com
• ce.byu.edu/is, with free family history tutorials
• genealogicalstudies.com, the National Institute for Genealogical Studies
• genealogy.com
• genealogytoolbox.com
• globalgenealogy.com
• heritagequest.com/gen101, a Genealogy 101 course
• ngsgenealogy.org
• rootsweb.com/~newbie, a site for newcomers to genealogy

## Software aids genealogists

Computers can aid you in developing and printing address lists for contacting family members, in searching for information others have asked for, and for indexing and organizing your records and files.

They also can make it possible to create charts and printouts, enabling you to see more clearly where you are in your research and allowing you to show off your work in a more presentable fashion.

If you go shopping, you will probably find a dozen or so software programs for recording the names, dates, and places you have discovered in your research. Some are less expensive than others; some, simpler to use than others; and some, more compatible with other genealogy software programs and, in particular, with the LDS program.

We aren't recommending one or the other in this chapter, but we will simply review several of them and their capabilities and features (see page 95). The order in which they are discussed does not indicate any preference on our part.

You could use just word-processing or basic database software for genealogy purposes. However, with the large selection of genealogy software, it is not really necessary to design your own programs, charts, and group sheets.

Virtually all of the

genealogy software packages can handle scanned photographs and other graphics and, at a glance, can produce professional-looking charts that quickly show what areas need more research and information.

Contact information for most of the items mentioned in this chapter can be found in the Bibliography or in the Helpful Addresses appendices for Chapter 6.

## Genealogy Websites

There are so many wonderful genealogy Websites available these days that it is hard to know which to point out in this chapter. However, a few of the larger ones come to mind.

Online for nearly 10 years, Ancestry.com's Website in Salt Lake City, Utah (www.ancestry.com), is one of the world's largest online genealogy libraries. Ancestry.com itself is about 15 years old and publishes books, magazines, and other materials related to genealogy.

To search its databases, you must become a mem-

## Just for starters

Following is a list of genealogy-related Web links for beginners, compiled from the MSNBC Website at www.msnbc.com/news/254376.asp# general. Next time you go online, check out these sites:

• Blank Family Tree provides a basic, blank pedigree chart on which you can enter your family data. To access it, visit: users.erols.com/emcrcc/Family_Record.htm.

• Rootsweb:Kids is a site that gets the younger generation involved in genealogy. Here's the address: www.rootsweb.com/~usgwkidz.

• "A Beginner's Guide to Family History Research" can be accessed at this address: biz.ipa.net/arkresearch/guide.html. •

## Baa, baa, black sheep!

• Got a black sheep in the family? Flaunt it! That's what members of the International Black Sheep Society of Genealogists (IBSSG) do. Anyone with a dastardly ancestor or family member of ill repute "within 1 degree of consanguinity of their direct lines" is eligible for membership. Check out this Website for details on joining the "flock": www.homepages.rootsweb.com/~blksheep. •

# Time-Passages a prime site

- A Website that's particularly interesting for the Dakotas is www.time-passages.com. The site has been recommended by The History Channel. Called a "Genealogy of the Dakotas," it contains all sorts of records for the two states.

Creator Don Smith, Horace, ND, says the site's mission is to preserve the history and cultural heritage of the Dakotas. Smith also offers research services for those who might want extra help. •

ber, which is a fairly painless process. Nearly every day, a new database is added to the site, making it more and more valuable.

The Ancestry World Tree, accessed through the Ancestry.com site, is the largest, free, online database of family files available. Also, the site is a spot to sign up for *Ancestry Daily News,* a newsletter providing a "daily dose of genealogy."

The newsletter offers some great ideas on where to find records, advice on how to proceed with research, and information on other topics. You can subscribe simply by providing your e-mail address. There is a lot more; check out the site soon.

We also recommend the Heritage Quest Website at www.heritagequest.com. HQ's vision is to produce easy-to-use genealogical materials that are "convenient and readily available," and the company's site is another step toward that vision.

Features of the site,

which went online in April 1998, include free online query submittal, the opportunity to browse and submit genealogy-related URLs, and secure shopping for beginners.

Also, check out the www.heritageconsulting.com site. Developed by Heritage Consulting and Services, Salt Lake City, it offers professional consultation and research for a number of European countries.

With so many fast-growing Websites available today, one stands out for genealogists worldwide—www.rootsweb.com—the Internet's oldest and largest genealogical research site, born in 1983.

RootsWeb has two primary missions: (1) to make large volumes of data available to the online genealogical community at minimal cost, and (2) to provide support services to online genealogical activities, such as USENET newsgroup moderation, mailing list maintenance, surname list generation, etc. The site hosts the

largest and most comprehensive collection of genealogical Websites and mailing lists for its users.

The www.usgenweb.org site is divided into individual state and county projects. Each Website is responsible for identifying genealogical resources available on the Web for that particular county. The main site provides links to all state pages and, in turn, to existing county pages.

The National Archives and Records Administration's Website, www.archives.gov/genealogy, provides information on genealogical resources and publications at NARA. More information on what types of records are available there can be found in Chapter 3.

Genealogists can find some real treasures on the Library of Congress Website—www.lcweb.loc.gov/rr/genealogy, including catalogs for libraries (mostly academic) all over the U.S.

Another useful site to check out is www.gendex.com/gendex. If you want

## Use Internet directories to search for relatives

- Using online directories to find people on the Web can help you find long-lost (or hitherto undiscovered) relatives—and save money, too! On www.search.com, for example, you'll find a link to phone numbers and e-mail addresses, as well as yellow pages.

- Clicking on "phone numbers" brings up a screen in which you enter data about the person you're seeking (name, address, city, state, etc.). The search engine then goes to work to find a matching name in its directory. If a match is found, the name, address and phone number pop up on your screen. You can also

view a city map showing the location.

- Another Website that has city directory information from more than 700 American cities is www.kinquest.com/genealogy/resources/citydir.html.

- Save time and money by checking the Internet for the number you're seeking, rather than going through your phone company's information service. Note that many times your telephone company is your Internet Service Provider (ISP), enabling many South and North Dakotans to have local access to the Internet and save on long-distance charges. •

# Finding family on the Web through surname search sites

Many Websites today can help you find living family members. One such site is **www.online-genealogy. com**. It offers FamilySearch Internet Genealogy Service, with a variety of resources available.

• Genconnect.com has a global surname search feature for finding queries for specific surnames posted in connection with certain counties, states, or countries. Check it out at **www.genconnect.com.**

• The Seeker.com site allows for placing your own message saying you are looking for relatives. On that site, you can also find out if they are already looking for you, as a section of the site allows you to see if anyone is researching your name. It is at **www.genconnect.com**

• RootsWeb.com can help you find those people who are researching the surnames you are on the RootsWeb Surname List (RSL). It is a list of nearly 1.2 million surnames submitted by more than 75,000 genealogists, and it grows daily. You can learn more about this option at **www.rsl.rootsweb.com/cgi-bin/ rslsql.cgi.**

• In Common Threads, a searchable database, you can find others researching the same names you are. The site was developed as a free resource to help genealogists discover each other, and you simply enter the information you have on an ancestor, hoping others will see it and realize it is the same line they are researching. You can find the site at **www.gensource. com/common.**

• Free genealogy queries can be posted on **www. lineages.com/queries.** Since 1983, the site has traced more than 100,000 family lines for its clients.

• Genealogy's Most Wanted may be the site where you find the surnames and information you are searching for. Designed to put researchers in touch with each other through e-mail or postal addresses, you can place information on the site asking for assistance. Check it out at **www.citynet.net/mostwanted.**

• Another interesting site is Irene's Genealogy Post

Forum at **www.thecore.com/~hand/genealogy/post.** You can post the surnames you are looking for on the forum so other genealogists can contact you to exchange information. Or check what is already on the site—it might be just what you're looking for.

• Internet FamilyFinder (**www. familytreemaker.com/iffintro. html**) makes locating family quick and easy.

• The Social Security Death Index is an excellent resource for locating family. Though the person you are researching has died, you may be able to get information on living relatives from the person's file, at **www.ssa.gov.**

• A bit of a twist to posting surnames is posting the fact that you are preparing or have already published a family history covering certain surnames. This will make others aware of the work you are doing and may avoid duplication in research. The Website to check is **www. gengateway.com/listings.html.**

• Mailing lists can prove valuable in locating living family members. Join mailing lists for the surname lists for the surnames you are researching and see. Check out the mailing lists discussion on **www.rootsweb. com/~jfuller/gen_mail.html.**

• Some surname search sites mentioned in "Genealogy Online for Dummies" (2nd edition) include **www.hamrick.com/names,** a surname distribution site; **www.genealogytoolbox.com,** which lists sites with a variety of links to genealogical resources on the Internet; Guild of One-name Studies (**www.one-name.org/top.htm),** an online organization of registered sites that focus on one particular surname (6,000 surnames); Surname Web (Surname Genealogical Web Project) **(www.surnameweb.org),** where you can view articles and use surname research links; **www.soc.genealogy.surnames; www. familyhistory.com;** the Genealogy Exchange and Surname Registry at **www.GenExchange.com; www.isleuth.com; surnames.com; gentree.com;** and **www.genforum.genealogy.com.** •

## SUPER SURNAME SITES

- www.citynet.net/mostwanted
- www. familyhistory.com
- www.familytreemaker.com
- www.genconnect.com
- www. genealogytoolbox.com
- www.GenExchange.com
- www.genforum.genealogy.com
- www. gengateway.com
- www.gensource. com
- www.gentree.com
- www. hamrick.com
- www.isleuth.com
- www.lineages.com
- www.one-name. org
- www.online-genealogy.com
- www.rootsweb.com
- www.rsl.rootsweb.com
- www. soc.genealogy.surnames
- www.ssa.gov.
- www.surnames.com
- www.surnameweb. org
- www.thecore.com

## 'Dak-links'

- Some historical and genealogical societies in the Dakotas have Websites listing records useful in learning more about your ancestors. To access their home pages, simply go into a search engine and search by society name for the one you are interested in.

- You'll find a list of all genealogical and historical organizations in the Dakotas through each state's Historical Society Website (www.state.nd.us /hist or www.state.sdhistory.org). •

to find out what genealogy sites are available on the Web, check out www.genealogy.com /links, a directory of over 50,000 genealogy-related Websites.

## LDS puts records online

One of the most exciting advances in genealogical research is the addition of records on the LDS Website (www.familysearch.org).

The site, receiving up to 7 million hits per day since it went on line in April 1999, contains links to millions of names of people, some who lived as long

ago as 1500. Access to the site's data is free.

The Genealogy Mall (www.genmall.com) is possibly the only genealogy mall on the Internet. It provides information on research materials, software, publishing, researchers, and advertising space. It reaches thousands of genealogists daily.

Everton initially published "Roots Cellars" in *Genealogical Helper,* but now has the data available directly to genealogists through computer. Although not a free service, the Everton site (www.everton.com) contains a lot of information and point-

ers to other resources. Everton also produces books, CD-ROMs, and a Website which contains links to queries, online classes, blank charts, and much more.

Information in Social Security records can be very useful to genealogists. Information and numerous forms are available on the SSA Website (www.ssa.gov).

Cyndi Howells' Website (www.cyndislist.com) is a guide to the most powerful research tools since personal computers became common in our homes. The site makes genealogical research possible on a large scale right

## Geneablogy: 'Blogging' your family history

Until recently, researchers logged their findings in a notebook, filled out a research log, or tagged their notes onto their paper pedigree chart. Those who were more tech-savvy may have ventured onto the World Wide Web to create a family Website.

Taking that a step further, many genealogists have begun logging their research, as well as their roots, on something called a "weblog."

You, too, can become a blogger! A weblog or "blog" or "geneablog" enables you not only to keep your research notes on your computer, but also allows others to view your work in progress on your Web pages. Visitors to your blog site can then learn from your methods and may be able to furnish you with answers to your ancestral puzzles. What's more, often the sleuthing you do to find your roots is just as fascinating as the discoveries you make during the research process.

To view a model genealogical blog site, visit **www.brandi.org/geneablogy,** set up by Ralph Brandi in 2000.

Watch for the following features on his site:
- Entries listed in reverse chronological order (typical of blog entries)
- Many links to digitized images of sources (thus, an image of, say, the actual hand-written church record containing his ancestor's christening or marriage information) can be viewed on this site!
- An archives of each month's activities, indexed and accessible from any other month's entries.

Should you decide to create your own genealogy weblog, look for a genealogy program designed especially for establishing blog sites. Or check out the services offered by Blogger (**www.blogger.com,** a free blogger host site that assists you in setting up a blog site).

Once you post your research on your very own geneablogy site, you can decide whether you prefer to keep your blog's URL private, allow access to family members only, or open your site to genealogists around the world.

To check out the blog sites of others, visit this Web address: **search.blogger.com.** On it you'll find sites ranging from journals of amateur genealogists to broad-based sites with information on the latest resources for tracing your roots. •

**NETIQUETTE:**
**Minding your**
**'NET**
**manners**
**STICK NO BILLS**

**B**ecoming a member of the online genealogy community has many privileges, but it also carries with it some duties. Communicating effectively and politely on the Internet can be achieved by following some simple guidelines:

- Don't send anything on the Internet that you would not want posted at work or in a public place.
- Don't violate copyright laws by exchanging large parts of published works through e-mail.
- If you receive a "heated" message, try to ignore it or wait a few days to respond.

- Make sure that, when responding to a message sent to a group of people, you are responding to just the sender, unless you want to respond to the entire group.
- Using all uppercase letters in an e-mail is as if you are shouting at the receiver.
- If you're joking, use a smiley face or some other graphic to show you are joking. Otherwise, the receiver may think you are serious. You can create these "emoticons" through combinations of keys. Try a colon, a dash and a right or left parenthesis, for example. •

from home. The www. genealogylinks.net site has grown in just nine years to over 40,000 links—from passenger lists to church records to censuses for the U.S. and many European countries.

The site is easy to use because links to other sites are indexed by country and, from there, by type of link (i.e., cemetery transcription, census, military, or ship's passenger list).

Another source for locating professional genealogy researchers and genealogy services is www.genealogyPro.com.

## ISPs offer online help

Many of the major search engines offer genealogy services. America Online has a Genealogy Forum with three sections: an Ancestral Digs conference room, a Software area, and a Message area.

CompuServe offers a Genealogy Forum that hosts thousands of genealogists from all over the world every day. In addition, more than 10,000 genealogy-related files are available on CompuServe.

Prodigy has an online genealogy advice column and also lists a number of genealogy topics on its Bulletin Board.

## Websites for the Dakotas

A number of interesting and helpful sites specific to the Dakotas exist on the Web. We will discuss just a few of those within this chapter, but look for many more Web addresses in the Chapter 6 Helpful Addresses in the appendix.

A key Website for those doing research in the Dakotas is the USGEN-WEB Project. Developed by a group of volunteers, the project provides indi-

vidual Websites with genealogical information for every county and state in the U.S. The project is committed to allowing free access for everyone.

Begun in Kentucky in early 1996, the Websites for this project are set up under the RootsWeb.com domain name. The databases are indexed and cross-linked so that a researcher can find an ancestor even if that individual was located in more than one county within a state.

Sites have been developed for North and South Dakota, and each one shows the counties within the state that have been developed and those that have been adopted by a coordinator.

Databases and other resources are listed on the first screen of each site for the visitor's information. The address for the South Dakota site is www.

## Names from old Bibles go online

- The Bible Archives is a database of names collected from old family Bibles. The purpose of the project is to make the information available to researchers.

For more information, go to www.geocities. com/Heartland/Fields/ 2403. •

# 10-step plan for online research

A 10-step guideline for Internet research can be found at: genealogy.about.com/od/basics/a/internet.htm. Check it out! •

rootsweb.com/~sdgenweb and for North Dakota, www.rootsweb.com/~ndgenweb.

New information and databases added to these sites are reported in the *RootsWeb Review*, published regularly by the company. Other useful RootsWeb.com associated sites include:
• www.rootsweb.com/roots-1/USA/nd.html
• www.genconnect.rootsweb.com/indx/ND.html
• searches.rootsweb.com

Another worthwhile site to visit for North and South Dakota information is Park Genealogical Books. The company's Website at www/parkbooks.com features all sorts of materials about Minnesota, Wisconsin, North and South Dakota, and the surrounding area.

The site also lists general forms and other materials for the genealogist's use. Also, check out the Time Passages Website (see page 100) and information on how to find Web addresses for North and South Dakota-related genealogical societies.

Of course, there are also the research sites and their Web addresses that were mentioned in Chapter 3. Check those out for more information. •

# More family connectors

Joining newsgroups and chat groups can be very beneficial for genealogists. Others in the group may have some leads on family members or some advice on how to proceed with the research. And still others may be willing to create an electronic family newsletter. The newsletter idea makes keeping in touch with family easy and less expensive.

There are also the sites where people can advertise their genealogy-related home pages. In some cases, that home page is specific to the surnames the person posting to the page is researching. Others visiting the site may come across the same surnames they are researching and be able to make contact through the home page.

**MyFamily.com,** a division of Ancestry.com, offers a new kind of family reunion. It specifically targets families by providing them with their own free, secure Websites. Nothing can compare to a family reunion, but this option runs a close second. You can also check out a site called **Yourfamily.com**.

**Kindredkonnections.com** has links to searchable databases and various other genealogy-related topics.

**The olivetreegenealogy.com** site offers more than 1,700 pages of free genealogy to help you find your brick-wall ancestors.

The International Genealogical Index (IGI), found

in **www.familysearch.org,** contains 285 million names of deceased persons worldwide dating from the early 1500s to the early 1900s.

**DistantCousin.com** is an online archive of genealogy records and images of historical documents from various sources, such as newspaper obituaries, city directories, census records, ship lists, school yearbooks, military records, and more. The site includes more than 6 million records from over 1,500 online sources. **Cousinconnect.com** is a similar site.

Check out **www.genealogyportal.com**, which will enable you to search the full text of several Websites at one time, the Federation of Family History Societies **(ffhs.org.uk)**, and the Federation of Genealogical Societies **(fgs.org)**.

Another way to connect with family is through Virtual Family Records Vault, a collection of newspapers from throughout the U.S. **(www.vfamily.com/news.htm).** The online newspaper indexes through **www.lcweb.loc.gov/rr/news** may also prove helpful.

Other online newspaper collections include **www.ida.net/users/dhanco/news.htm, www.historybuff.com,** and **www.historicnewspaper.com.**

If your ancestors were members of a particular religious group or fraternal organization, search online records for those organizations. A Google search **(www.google.com)** should provide sites for them. •

**JOIN A GENEALOGY CLUB TODAY!**

## Enjoy the benefits

- Join a local and/or state genealogical society.
- Share advice, ideas, and information with other members.
- Gain the most from membership by being active, helping, and sharing.●

**3 Crowns American-Swedish Club Membership Card**
Name Cathy Langemo
Address 205 E Arbor 105-a
City Bismarck Zip 58504
Signature
Issue Date Dea 04 Member Since
Expiration Date: Dea. 05

**American Swedish Institute**
Individual 30610
Cathy Langemo
205 E Arbor Ave #108-G
Bismarck, ND 58504-5717
Expires 7/31/2005
*Membership Card*

**SONS OF NORWAY**
**OFFICIAL MEMBERSHIP CARD**
JO ANN B MINISTORFER
MEMBER SINCE: 1990
MEMBER NO 9328462
LODGE 4-107 SVERDRUP
EXPIRY DATE: 1/31/2000
1455 West Lake Street, Minneapolis, Minnesota 55408
(612) 827-3611/Fax # (612) 827-0658
http://www.sofn.com

Need help with your genealogical research? Don't know where to go next with your ancestral hunt? How about trying other genealogists for advice.

## Benefits of joining a genealogical society

Even though you may not typically be a "joiner," you might reconsider for the success of your genealogical research. Your research could be moved forward quickly through networking with other genealogists—sharing ideas, resources, success stories and solutions to "up-against-the-brick-wall" research problems.

Networking and tapping into the resources and knowledge of other genealogists can help you solve research problems more easily and quickly than working in isolation could ever accomplish.

Genealogical organizations come in all forms and sizes, with a variety of missions. They may range from a society with a dozen or so members interested only in gathering information for a local history book—to one with countrywide coverage, like the Federation of Genealogical Societies (FGS).

Founded in 1976, the FGS has three major purposes: serving the needs of its member societies, providing products and services needed by member societies, and marshaling the resources of its member organizations. FGS publishes the "Forum" and sponsors a national conference each year for genealogists at all experience levels.

Another group with nationwide membership is the National Genealogical Society, an organization for all genealogists and family historians.

And then there are the in-between ones, like state genealogical societies with maybe 20 member societies and a handful of individuals. These groups attempt to coordinate the efforts and information of all the genealogical societies in a state to better assist and inform individual genealogists statewide. They also help reduce any duplication in research or indexing projects that may be in the discussion stages, bringing coordination and cooperation among the groups.

If you are a serious genealogist, you are probably already a member of one or more genealogical societies. You likely belong to your local society, even though you may not have ancestry in the area.

You may carry a membership in the statewide society, as well as an ethnic group, such as the Sons of Norway, the Germans from Russia Heritage Society, or others.

Other possibilities are the geographic and the family or surname-based societies, as well as cyber-societies (that exist on the Internet, which we discuss later in this chapter).

## Historical and genealogical societies in the Dakotas

North and South Dakota have their fair share of historical and genealogical societies. In fact, South Dakota alone has 45 historical and 14 genealogical societies organized to share information, sponsor workshops, and cooperate in joint genealogical projects, such as indexing cemeteries or microfilming newspapers.

North Dakota has about 74 historical and at least six genealogical societies. In addition, both states have State Genealogical Societies.

## Patriotic or hereditary societies

Some societies are based only on lineage and gaining proof of descent, thus qualifying a person for membership. These patriotic or hereditary societies may vary consider-

# genealogists pays off

ably in purpose and mission.

One well-known example of a hereditary society is the Daughters of the American Revolution (DAR), which has a large membership and provides support to an outstanding library.

Other examples include the Jersey Blues (members of military units of Colonial America), the National Society of Colonial Dames of America, and the Society for the Descendants of the Colonial Clergy.

A complete listing of hereditary societies and their purposes may be found in the Hereditary Register of the United States of America.

## Genealogical scholarship

Genealogy began centuries ago to legitimize succession to the throne. The passing of real estate to survivors and the privileges of the aristocracy were mostly based on genealogical information. Since those times, genealogical research has been pursued by people at all economic levels and in all walks of life.

Often, a milestone event, such as a town or state centennial or the bicentennial of the country, prompts increased activity in genealogical research.

Such was the case with the transition to the 21st century and the new millennium. Many people became interested in preserving theirs and others' memories of the 1900s.

Genealogists should develop a broad knowledge of local history to help understand the reasons their ancestors moved where they did and when they did.

Genealogical information can be used for many purposes, including by attorneys settling family estates, by biographers working on a book about someone, by geneticists searching for hereditary information from pedigrees, and by historians to show family relationships and the broader implications of historical events.

A professional genealogist must be knowledgeable of the research sources, aware of the events and migration of previous genera-

tions, able to analyze a research problem and solutions to it, have the detective's nose to follow a lead, and obviously have the perseverance necessary to keep working on a research problem.

The field of genealogy has become a respected occupation, and courses have been developed to educate those interested in genealogical scholarship. Just a few of the programs include the National Institute on Genealogical Research in Washington, DC; Samford University's Institute of Genealogy and Historical Research in Birmingham, AL; and Brigham Young University in Provo, UT.

Some are one-time courses, while others offer two-year programs; their history departments also offer individual courses for genealogical research.

And, of course, don't forget

## Think 'local'!

- Considering joining a genealogical society or heritage organization? "Think local." Join the one(s) that is apt to have the most information on your ancestors—the one closest to the area where she/he lived.

- Many groups have a genealogist who answers queries and helps people with research. Make a connection with this person by letter, e-mail or phone; she/he may be able to answer your research questions.

- Many genealogical organizations have periodicals with special query columns. Try running a query in the publication. This has worked for lots of folks! •

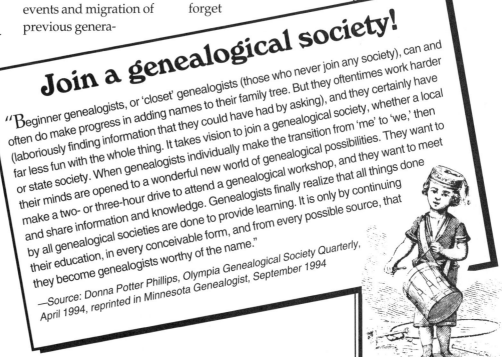

## Join a genealogical society!

"Beginner genealogists, or 'closet' genealogists (those who never join any society), can and often do make progress in adding names to their family tree. But they oftentimes work harder (laboriously finding information that they could have had by asking), and they certainly have far less fun with the whole thing. It takes vision to join a genealogical society, whether a local or state society. When genealogists individually make the transition from 'me' to 'we,' then their minds are opened to a wonderful new world of genealogical possibilities. They want to make a two- or three-hour drive to attend a genealogical workshop, and they want to meet and share information and knowledge. Genealogists finally realize that all things done by all genealogical societies are done to provide learning. It is only by continuing their education, in every conceivable form, and from every possible source, that they become genealogists worthy of the name."

—Source: Donna Potter Phillips, Olympia Genealogical Society Quarterly, April 1994, reprinted in Minnesota Genealogist, September 1994

# PUZZLED? Consider hiring a researcher!

Though you may be extremely interested in researching your ancestry, there may be reasons why it is not possible for you to do all or any of the research yourself.

For one example, you may not live in the area where your ancestors did. Or you may not have the time available to do research during the operating hours at area research facilities. Or you may not have the vacation time or money to take a research trip to another state or country.

In those cases, you may need to hire a research facility staff member or a person in the area to do the research for you.

Many research facilities have a list of local people interested in doing research for others. Some of these researchers will do the work at no cost, but typically they charge a fee for each record search or a per-hour fee.

Some professional researchers may limit their services to researching select records at select locations. Others may offer broader services that might include travel and even extend to publishing family histories. If a person is listed on the research facility's list, you can probably trust him/her to do a thorough and knowledgeable check of resources within the time frame and price range agreed upon up front.

However, if you require a greater level of comfort in the arrangement, you can develop a more official agreement form with the specifics included and have the researcher sign it. You can also ask for references and a resume.

In any case, we suggest being specific with the researcher about how much money you are willing to spend and what research expenses will be reimbursable. Also be specific about the type of information you most want to find out about your ancestors.

Stay in contact on a regular basis with the researcher so you know the status of the project, how much time has been spent on it, and how much has been incurred for expenses.

If any of the researchers on the list are certified genealogists, they would be the likeliest contacts. However, other local researchers may be just as knowledgeable and come a little less expensively than a certified genealogist.

Those are all choices you will need to make after reviewing the researcher list. Your other option is to pay facility staff members to do the research. This is fairly inexpensive, but may take a longer time to get the information.

Most research facilities receive large numbers of requests each day, and that, along with being short staffed, makes for a longer time before you will receive the information you are seeking.

If you subscribe to various historical and genealogical publications, you may also see ads placed by people willing to do research for hire. This is just one more option to pursue in hiring a researcher. •

# Giving back

• Part of being an avid genealogist is "giving back" in some measure what one has received by way of the rich blessing of family history. That may mean volunteering with a cemetery-recording project, sharing one's discoveries with others, or helping those who are researching areas one is familiar with. Writing this book was our effort to "give back." •

—The authors

the workshops sponsored by your local or regional genealogical societies. Conferences and workshops can be of tremendous benefit to you and to your ancestral research. They can provide you with information on getting organized, on where to search out information, and on keeping you motivated to continue the journey. They are perfect networking opportunities—where you can meet other researchers and share advice, insight, and encouragement.

Two excellent Websites featuring information on conferences and workshops (as well as other valuable family history information) are:

• globalgenealogy. com
• genealogy.com (Family Tree Maker's Website)

The Association of Professional Genealogists (APG), formed in 1979 by 19 genealogists as a non-profit, educational corporation, promotes the standards and ethics in the genealogical field. Membership is open to any person or institution supporting the objectives and the APG code of ethics.

APG publishes a quarterly journal ideal for those interested in professionalism and sponsors lectures and presentations. You can contact the association at APG, P.O. Box 350998, Westminster, CO 80035-0998. Or you can send an e-mail to: apg-admin@ genealogy.org.

North and South Dakota fall into APG's Region 2 (the Midwest).

The National Genealogical Society offers private home study with the "American Genealogy: A Basic Course." You can also learn from the work of other genealogists by reading case studies in quality genealogical journals, such as "The NGS Quarterly," the "New England Historical and Genealogical Register," and "The American Genealogist."

# Genealogical Internet sites

Though computer genealogy was covered extensively in Chapter 6, it would be glaringly absent here were it not mentioned as a networking tool.

Internet news, chat groups, and blogs (called "geneablogy" when related to genealogy; see Chapter 6 for more details) can be excellent resources for genealogical information—whether they be general or specific to the surnames you are researching.

These groups are comprised of individuals with similar interests, making participation a wise investment of time.

Newsgroups are much like mailing lists because you e-mail a message that others in the group can read. Your message is basically stored on a news server, where it is copied to other news servers.

When you want to read a message on the newsgroup, you simply use a news reader program that connects you to a news server. You need to check,

however, how your Internet service provider receives a news feed, and then set up your newsreader to pick up the feed.

To be safe, spend some time monitoring various newsgroups before posting a message on any of them. Reviewing the group's charter will tell you what is appropriate to post to the group.

If you can't find the charter, review what types of messages are posted to learn what is appropriate. Each group has someone who serves as monitor and manager.

Chat rooms, on the other hand, are Internet sites where you can log in and be involved in real-time conversations. Some chat rooms are comprised of individuals with a specific interest, such as genealogy. Sometimes sessions are pre-arranged so you can plan to meet certain people in the

room at a certain time.

For information on genealogy-related chat rooms, check www.genealogy. org/~jkatcmi/genealogy-irc/welcome.html.

The page tells what's available, lists frequently asked questions, and gives instructions for downloading the chat software and joining chat channels.

Many genealogical Websites also offer list services—mailing lists of people with similar interests, those researching the same surnames, those researching the same areas of the United States or other countries, and others. Through these lists, you could very well discover

## Attention, veterans!

- Here's a way for you to share your wartime experiences and leave a legacy at the same time. The nationwide Veterans Oral History Project honors our nation's war veterans, and those who supported them at home, through recorded interviews and other documents chronicling their wartime experiences. The project, initiated by Congress via the Library of Congress, seeks information from veterans across the country. For more information, North Dakotans can check out the following Website: www. state.nd.us/hist/ veterans. South Dakotans can access information at www.loc. gov/vets/partners/ sdakota.html. •

## Make the right connections!

Here's a list of some of the networking connections that will benefit you:

- Join a genealogical society (not just the ones in your area, but ones in areas where ancestors on your research list once resided. At home, get the word out that you're willing to help out. When you're in the town of your ancestors, learn who the nearby genealogical society's genealogist is and establish a friendly connection.
- Join an ethnic-related group that has genealogy as its primary mission. The Germans from Russia Heritage Society and the Norwegian bygdelags (see information on each in Chapter 4) are prime examples. Get to know people who had ancestors living in the same Old Country communities where yours lived. You may be surprised to learn you have blood connections, as well as networking connections.
- Network with family members. A great time to do this is during family reunions—a natural time to talk about family. Make sure the connection is also made between generations and that young people in your family are involved and welcomed.
- Make connections with historians in your ancestor's hometown, or visit with relatives and old-timers in that community. Ask them for information about your ancestor.
- Volunteer to help out at your local LDS family history center or at an archives or library near you. It's a great way to learn what resources are available and how to access them. You'll also meet lots of nice folks who have the same passion for genealogy you do, and together, you can explore ideas. •

# Genealogical researchers' certification program

The Board for Certification of Genealogists (BCG), established in 1964 and located in Washington, DC, views genealogy as a profession or hobby that requires training and advanced skills. It not only sets the standards; it co-sponsors two institutes each year—the Institute of Genealogy and Historical Research at Samford University, and the National Institute on Genealogical Research at the National Archives. Individuals certified by the BCG must pledge to:

- Strive for the highest level of truth and accuracy in all phases of work;
- Act honorably toward other genealogists and toward the field as a whole;
- Adhere to the Board for Certification of Genealogist's Standards of Conduct; and, if doing research for others, act in a client's best interests; and
- Protect the client's privacy.

In addition, the organization's goals include protecting the public, the consumer (client or colleague), and the profession itself.

As of October 2005, the certification process has been changed, as follows:

- Three research categories—Certified Genealogical Records Specialist, Certified Lineage Specialist and Certified Genealogist—have been consolidated into one category, that of **Certified Genealogist** (CG). A CG is qualified to do broadly based genealogical projects, find evidence, assemble proof, and compile a coherent historical account of the identities and relationships of descendants of a particular ancestor.

In addition, the board established two new teaching categories, as follows:

- A **Certified Genealogical Lecturer** (CGL) is qualified to deliver oral presentations that address genealogical subjects (sources, methods and standards).
- A **Certified Genealogical Instructor** (CGI) is authorized to present lessons showing students how to begin and/or continue their own genealogical studies.

For more information, check out the following Website: www.bcgcertification.org •

## Questions to ask researchers

Here are questions to ask when hiring a professional researcher:

- Is he/she certified or accredited? If so, by what organization?
- How many years' experience does he/she have in researching?
- What professional genealogical organizations does he/she belong to?
- What is his/her experience in the area where you need help?
- How does he/she charge for services? What payment methods are acceptable?
- When will the research results be available?

*—From "Genealogy Online for Dummies"*

other family members or obtain information relevant to your ancestry.

Genealogy blogging is the latest twist in high-tech family history. For information, check the archives of "Genealogical Computing" for an article called "Easy as Falling Into a Log" (www.ancestry.com/learn/library/article)

## Genealogical publications

One of the benefits in most genealogical and historical societies is the organization's newsletter. Whether published monthly, quarterly, or at other intervals, these publications could be worth every cent of the member-

ship dues paid to the organization.

Some newsletters include queries that individuals have sent to the organization. They are worth reviewing because you may come across a surname you recognize from your research. Other newsletters publish pedigree charts submitted by members. You never know when you might find a mutual relative on one of them or at least a common surname.

The National Genealogical Society publishes a scholarly publication, the "Quarterly," that includes book reviews and articles useful to researchers.

"The American Genealogist" contains articles on

creative ways to use data from original records.

You can check the "Genealogical Periodical Annual Index" for other publications to assist in your research. Look for those specific to the ethnic groups or church affiliations of ancestors you are seeking.

Speaking of "specific," "Family Tree Magazine" features a bonus State Research Guide section in each issue. To see what states have already been covered, visit www.familytreemagazine.com/state guides. As of this writing (May 2006), the Dakotas have yet to be featured. •

## 112 · Stumped? Here are some research suggestions

- **Birth date quest**
- **Where did family live?**
- **Finding Uncle Charlie**
- **Crossing the ocean**
- **How do I find my birth parents?**
- **What about Orphan Train children?**
- **Talk to the moon!**
- **What if you reach a dead end?**
- **Hiring a professional researcher**
- **Genetic genealogy**
- **Genealogy dos 'n' don'ts**
- **Records search guide**

# Stumped? Here are some

## Scraping the bottom of the barrel?

• When all else fails, try the phone book!

In 1985, when we wanted to make a "Dutch connection," we asked someone who was traveling to the Netherlands to check an Amsterdam phone book for our surname. I then wrote a letter to the person whose address he found, asking if there might be a family connection. Six weeks later, a letter came back: "You will be happy to know we have just finished publishing a family history book. Your grandfather is on page..." This led to a visit by our Dutch relatives to North Dakota, and a dream trip to the Netherlands the next year for my brother and me, to visit the homeland of our grandfather!

These days, you could easily make such a connection via the Internet! • —J.W.

Some of you reading this chapter may have experienced various times in your research when you came to a brick wall that seemed impassable. When that happened, it was hard to know how to get beyond that wall—whether it be going over, under or around it.

This chapter is included to give readers ideas on how to knock down that brick wall that seemed so formidable and how to move forward with their research. We will share stories from many friends and fellow genealogists— "war stories" of how they "knocked down brick walls" in their personal or other research projects.

Our goal is to give you some ideas you might use in your own situation when your research comes to a standstill. Some solutions may seem logical after reading them, while others may require a serious effort toward thinking "outside the box." Either way, we hope they will help.

## Birth date quest

How do you find a person's birth date when you can't find a birth record?

There are quite a number of resources for gleaning birth dates besides the birth certificate or record itself. You can:

• Try locating the death information on a person. That will likely list his/her birth date.

• Check the person's drivers license.

• See if you already have the birth date listed in military records or in land or homestead records.

• You might also check the family Bible or church records. If you already know where the family lived and what denomination they belonged to, half of your work is done. Even if the parish records don't list births, they will certainly list baptisms, which typically (in many religions) occur soon after the birth of a child. The baptism entry may include the birth date.

• The cemetery tombstone may yield the birth date.

• If you have the marriage license or certificate, or the church record of the marriage, check whether the birth dates and/or ages for the bride and groom are listed.

• Census records are an obvious solution for finding a birth date (or at least the approximate birth date, depending on which census you are working with).

• If you know where the person was employed, you might gain access to his/her personnel record, which may contain the birth date.

• If it's someone who received Social Security payments or was registered with the Social Security Administration, try his/her Social Security record.

• If there are family members or close friends

still alive from the person's era, they may know the answer to your dilemma. In fact, visiting with elderly relatives can provide you with a wealth of information for your family history. That information may come in bits and pieces over the course of many visits, but be patient—it will be worth the wait.

## Where did the family live?

What can you do if you know the family was in a particular state, but you don't know exactly where in that state?

• If you have access to a computerized death index, such as those available in the Dakotas, you could check the surname that way. Even if this step does not yield you the specific person you are searching for, it might help you at least see where in the state that surname seems to occur most often.

• If you don't find the person on the death index and the surname seems to be spread out all over the state, then what? If you know first names of other generations of that family, you might do a search for those first names, along with the surname. First names tend to occur over and over from generation to generation.

• If the above step proves successful, you now have at least a smaller part of the state in which to continue your search. From

# research suggestions

here you can go to census records, land records, cemetery indexes, town and county histories, and other resources.

## Finding Uncle Charlie

What if you simply can't find any information on an ancestor—perhaps one who was estranged from the rest of the family or who left the area and hasn't been heard from since?

Again, try the Social Security death index if the person would have lived during that time frame.

• Search family records for any correspondence from or reference to the person and a hint as to where the person was during various times. You might be able to trace his/her steps from place to place and, if a movement pattern develops, you might be able to guess where the person might have gone next.

• You could check the Soundex index to the census for all the states where the person might have located, based on some of the above information.

• If you have any idea what the person's occupation was, you might check union rolls, railroad employee records, teacher certifications or other records, depending on the occupation.

• If you have any idea at all where the person might have been, check city directories for the area. That's a

**COULD THIS BE OUR LOST BRANCH?**

long shot, we realize, since the person may have lived in a rural area that did not have directories. But sometimes long shots pay off!

• Of course, then there are atlases showing land ownership.

## Where is Grandpa's homeland?

If you know the person came to the Dakotas from another country and you know the country and even the city but can't seem to locate it on a current map, what can you do?

• Many research libraries have old atlases for countries worldwide. Try checking one near you, keeping in mind that you need to look at an atlas from the time frame your ancestor lived in that country.

• Once you find a map or atlas of the country, if you have trouble finding the town or city, consider

how else the place name might be spelled. Perhaps the spelling you have from various records is a phonetic version of the actual spelling.

## What about dead ends?

What if you have searched and searched for information on an ancestor, with no results or successes?

• Double-check that the first name you are searching for is correct. Perhaps the name you have always heard for the person is a nickname or his/her middle name. Most important records would likely be in the person's official or leagal name, so check those.

• Try variations on the spelling of the surname. You would be surprised how many different ways a name can be spelled. Try saying the name aloud with the pronunciation that your

## Leaving something behind

• When Bismarck researchers Orlin and Shirley Jacobson were on a genealogy road trip a few years ago, they visited a cemetery where they found a tombstone bearing Shirley's ancestors' surname. It was close to Memorial Day—a good day, Shirley adds, to find possible relatives who may be visiting the cemetery.

When no one showed up to visit this particular grave, Shirley tied a note around the tombstone. It read: "If you have information on this family, let us know." She added her address.

The note netted another kinship connection for Shirley, after a man who visited the site found her note and contacted her.

"Leave something behind, like a note," Shirley says. "Maybe someone will come along and find it." •

# 'Crossing the ocean' on the genealogy express

The real stumper for many who are searching their Dakota roots is getting the evidence needed to begin researching in the country of their immigrant ancestor. How do you find the information you need to make that giant step?

As we've already mentioned, you need to do your research in the U.S. and/or Canada first. The documentation you'll need likely exists on this side of the ocean. You may even find it in your own home—or a library (or family history center) near you, or in the community of the family you're researching.

Let's just say you've gotten as far back as your great-grandfather, Martin Peterson, who came from somewhere in Norway. He immigrated to the U.S. in the 1890s. He moved into the Bismarck, ND, area from Minnesota around 1916 and died around 1950.

You know that, in order to research Norwegian records, you need the name of the area (parish) he came from and his "farm name" or "address name," usually indicating a farm in Norway where the person once lived (see Chapter 1 for information on patronymic naming customs).

First, analyze what records you already have on him, then determine what records you still need to gather that will provide you with needed clues.

Next, check for a precise death date. Armed with that, you can search for a death certificate (which usually provides the person's birth date and the name of his/her parents and cause of death—valuable for genetic medical information purposes). The computerized death index at the North Dakota State Archives and Historical Research Library in Bismarck can be checked also to determine Martin's death date. The death index can also be searched at secure.apps.state.nd.us/doh/certificates/deathCertSearch.htm.

An even more revealing record is an obituary. To locate Martin's obituary, you'll need to check the newspapers (they're on microfilm at the State Archives of both Dakotas; see Chapter 3 on research

sites, and the section on printed sources in Chapter 2, for more information) that were printed shortly after, in a newspaper covering the vicinity of his death. Ideally, the obituary should yield a birth date and place, parents' names, and a brief synopsis of Martin's life, including more clues—such as place of employment, where he lived during his lifetime, organizations to which he belonged, and whether he served in the military. This information can help point you to other records and add to your stack of clues.

From 1900 on, the censuses gave information on year of immigration and whether a person was naturalized. Check the 1900 Minnesota census Soundex to see if you can pick out your Martin Peterson and determine a locality. (Also check with relatives, the obituary, and other records to see if you can learn where Martin lived in Minnesota.)

When you establish Martin's pattern of migration and places he lived, check for county or area histories printed around the time his family was in that locality. Often, biographies of area pioneers were part of the contents. Refer to the obituary or check the churches in the area. The church records may reveal Martin's entry into the congregation and the name of his former parish (town) in Norway. ●

———

(Author's note: An early history of Mower County, MN, yielded the farm name and name of the region/ parish in Norway of my emigrant Norwegian ancestor, Ole Olson—a clue I had been seeking for years. The book also told when he had immigrated and his 1854 route via covered wagon from Dane County, WI, to a spot just south of present-day Racine, MN. The death/funeral information in the church records led me to a tombstone for my Ole Olson (there were three of them in that community!), which listed the death and birth date. Armed with the birth date and name of the parish, I was then able to "take the Genealogy Express" across the ocean to Etnedal, Norway—via the LDS Family History Center in Bismarck. There, through the Norwegian parish registers, I got to know my Ole, from his christening and confirmation, his marriage and the birth of his children, to his immigration and life in America.) —J.W.

parents or grandparents always used and then write it down using that pronunciation. Or try Anglicizing the name, as clerks and indexers and others, including your ancestors, might have done.

• Check all available records, even those you feel wouldn't have the informa-

tion you're seeking.

• Try "talking" to your ancestor. Tell him/her that you've run out of possibilities to search and that, if he/she wants to be known, he/she should speak to you now. A genealogist told us it worked for her, so it may just work for you, as well.

# How do I find my birth parents?

If you were adopted and have been searching for your birth parents for years without results, what else can you do?

For purposes of this dis-

## Exploring the possibilities

When researching your ancestors, try to put yourself in their shoes. It may help you to think of more sources for records. Here are some other ideas:

• Set research goals. Divide a standard-size sheet of paper into three vertical columns. On the left-hand side, write down "what you know" about your ancestor. In the center column, list things you don't know but would like to find out (your goals). On the right side of your sheet, list records that can help you answer the questions in the center column. Alongside the records, list the repository for the records (state archives, courthouse, LDS family history center and so on). Underline two or three items you'd like to investigate first.

• Use an outline map (there's one in the appendix of this book) of the U.S. to trace your ancestor's migration pattern across the country, from port to final place of residence. Use the census to track the family's whereabouts for each decade.

• Using the census for your statistics, fill out a separate family group sheet for a particular family for each census year. When you've completed about three decades, compare number of family members, ages, spelling variations, immigration date, etc., with the original group sheet you previously filled out for this family. •

cussion, let's assume you have already gone all of the initial routes—looking for the original birth certificate and contacting the adoption agency that placed you (assuming you know that). Let's go on from there:

• If you already know how old your birth mother was at the time you were born, consider researching high school yearbooks in the area where you were born. Granted, your mother may have gone to another town to give birth, but it is still a place to start.

Keeping in mind that physical traits, such as facial features, size and coloring tend to run in families, watch for pictures of students (both male and female, because your birth father could very well have been in the same school) with features, coloring, and

size similar to yours. Jot down all the likely candidates and research those names. It's a leap, but you never know where the mystery will be solved.

• If you know the hospital where you were born, research hospital records for all women who gave birth on the same day you were born. In addition to names, note where they were from.

• If you happen to know what occupation either of your birth parents worked in, try some routes like union rolls, pension records, teacher certifications, and other records.

• If you believe you know the area your birth mother lived (or lives) in, try placing a classified ad in that town's newspaper near the time of your birthday. The ad could go something like this: "Adopted son/daughter seeking birth

mother. Thinking of you on my birthday (list birth date)." Then add some data about yourself and a contact number. Who knows, if all else has failed, this may bring results.

• If all other research methods have failed, why not think "outside the box" and hire a psychic. You never know what leads you may get from such a session—leads that may prove fruitful down the road, if not immediately.

## What about Orphan Train children?

What if your ancestor came to the Dakotas on an Orphan Train?

• If you have such an ancestor, contact the Orphan Train Heritage Society of America, organized by Mary Ellen Johnson to locate and preserve

## What about Holocaust victims?

What if the ancestor you are searching for was sent to a Nazi concentration camp during World War II?

• Talk with other family members from that era and, if nothing else, get the name of the concentration camp the person was sent to.

• Check with the American Red Cross Holocaust and War Victims Tracing and Information Center in Baltimore, MD. You can get more information for the center from your local Red Cross Chapter or by visiting this Website: www.redcross.org •

# Researcher suggests, 'Talk to the moon!'

**B**ismarck genealogist and researcher Orlin Jacobson has a paper pedigree printout that's many times taller than he is. His roots stretch even farther, back to the Vikings and the European kings of the Middle Ages. Orlin, retired, has been a presenter at numerous family history workshops and served as a volunteer at the LDS Family History Center in Bismarck for a number of years. For many of those years, he shared his love for genealogy with his wife, Shirley (now deceased), also a skilled researcher. We asked Orlin if he'd share some problem-solving research ideas for this book. Here are his suggestions:

• Talk to the moon. That's right...on nights when you can't sleep, get up, look out the window at the moon and start brainstorming: "What things might my ancestor have signed his name to? What places did he move to? What records are unique to the areas he lived in?" Such self-grilling sessions, Orlin says, can be the ladder that helps you climb your family tree.

• Don't believe everything you read on a tombstone—including the name! For example, when a wife died, a husband may have bought a marker that included his name, assuming he'd be buried beside his wife upon his death. Instead, he may have remarried or moved away and actually be buried in some other locality.

• Don't trust the dates, either. Sometimes the burial date is listed, rather than the death date. If the inscription is weathered, try taking a "rubbing." Place a lightweight paper over the inscription, then rub the paper with a lead pencil or crayon. This method can sometimes pick up hard-to-read letters.

• The obituary, Orlin says, is "the first thing to look at. It's one of the most golden sources for information." It gives a history of the deceased and helps you establish family connections.

• Sometimes it's best to visit the area of your ancestors (rather than relying on letters to order records). Go to the local library and ask, "Are there any local histories or church histories?" Go to the courthouse in person to look through the records. That way, you might be able to spot associated names. "You can pick it up, where someone else wouldn't catch it," Orlin says.

• Make plans to visit the state law libraries, which have a collection of early Supreme Court cases for (then) 48 states. "Some of these cases could contain your relatives," Orlin says. The records are filed by state, in chronological order. One plus: They're indexed.

• Also check the local courts. "These are one of the most missed resources when we do our research," he says. The civil dockets and criminal dockets are both filed chronologically.

• Orlin says birth and death information was also recorded in the township records. These ledger-style records included, among other things, line entries denoting births and deaths of local (especially rural) citizens. When you've checked at the state and county level and haven't located a record of a person's birth or death, locate the township clerk to see whether she/he may have recorded the event in the township books. Many

## Find local historian

• Ask around to determine whether there's a local historian in the community you're researching. One such woman from Griggs County in east-central North Dakota compiled extensive scrapbooks on community members—a boon to anyone tracing roots in the area. For more information, contact the Institute for Regional Studies, NDSU, Fargo. •

the history of the orphan trains.

During its 75 years of operation, some 150,000 homeless children from the streets of New York and other East Coast cities were transported to the West and South by the New York Children's Aid Society and by Catholic Church organizations.

The Heritage Society address is 4912 Trout Farm Rd., Springdale, AR 72762; 479-756-2780. Or visit www.orphantrainriders.com.

(For more on adoption, turn to Chapter 2.)

## What if you reach a dead end?

When you've checked every resource you can think of and still can't find your ancestor's information, try a brainstorming session. Ask yourself (or even a relative) what resources are out there that you may not have checked as yet.

• Sometimes it helps to set your research material aside for a while—perhaps six months or more. When you pick it up again, you'll be looking at it from a fresh vantage point.

During the interim, try exploring other lines or perhaps collateral lines that might lead to or beyond the relative you're seeking. (This "time-out" period is a neat creativity trick to try when you're suffering from "ancestor burnout.")

• Try checking your old records and information again. You may have missed something the first time that could lead you to your missing ancestor.

If someone tells you, for

times these records are kept in the home of the clerk. These records vary in their completeness, but many continued into the 1940s and 1950s and beyond.

- If you had a relative who was in a state mental hospital, check to see if you might be able to secure the social history that would have been taken as part of his/her medical records. State penitentiary records (assuming your relative was a resident there) can also yield genealogical clues.

- Be aware that ministers may have kept a day book or other record of their parishioners and the services they performed, ranging from christenings to funerals. This is an alternative if the church records are missing or have been destroyed.

- Check photographer notations on frames holding old photographs. Often, the town where the studio was located was embossed on the photos or otherwise labeled on the elaborate cardboard frames. Don't discard the frames, as this town name may give clues as to where the people were living when they had their photograph taken.

- You may find clues in the most unexpected places! When you pull into a strange town, for example, don't think, "I won't find any information here." Instead, spend some time at the town's library. Browse through the reference section for indexes to nursing homes. Look around the library to see what histories and genealogies it might contain. These side-trips can lead to some mega-genealogy finds. (Orlin's wife, Shirley, found information on an ancestor from Iowa in an index she discovered while browsing through the Aberdeen, SD, library.)

- If your relatives struck oil on their land, they may also have hit a gusher when it comes to genealogy. Orlin says maps of oil country are extremely detailed, as are abstracts for lands affected by oil leases, wells, etc. The abstracts contain the chronological ownership history of the land. An abstract in his family "was the size of a Sears catalog," he says.

- Bring the death certificate of your ancestor to the Social Security office and ask for Form SSA-L997. This form, mailed along with a copy of the death certificate, will bring you a copy of your deceased ancestor's Social Security application. This can be a valuable genealogy-information generator.

- Visit with residents at the nursing home in the town where your ancestor used to live. Ask them whether they knew your family. You may pick up some family history this way.

- Take advantage of interlibrary loan. "You can do so much from your own home," says Orlin. "It's like having a library roll up to your front door."

- And finally, Orlin suggests you do something selfless for the cause of genealogy. Each year, he places a grave marker on a relative's unmarked grave, "to leave a trail for future genealogy researchers," he says. Such acts, he says "pay big dividends." •

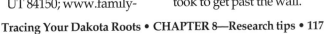

example, that the records for your family were destroyed in a church or courthouse fire, be aware that, in some cases, alternate records may exist—a minister's day book, for example, or duplicate church records books.

## Should I hire a professional researcher?

In some cases, finding a long-lost ancestor might require the services of a professional consultant or genealogist.

- One source for professional consulting is Heritage Consulting in Salt Lake City, UT; call 801-596-1028 or e-mail: inquiry@ heritageconsulting.com.
- The Directory of Professional Genealogists, which may be found at your local library, can provide you with researchers' names and addresses.
- Another source for a list of accredited genealogists is the Family History Library, 35 North West Temple St., Salt Lake City, UT 84150; www.family-search.org.
- Networking with other researchers can also be a key to your research success.

## Never give up hope!

As the above suggestions have shown, not many brick walls are truly impassable, impenetrable or invincible.

It may take removing one brick at a time, but the end results are what's important—not how long it took to get past the wall.

# Genetic genealogy

## What's in your genes?

- Each of us carries a unique biological record within the chromosomes of our cells: DNA (or "deosyribonucleic acid"). Our DNA holds our genetic code, unique to each of us (except in the case of identical twins). This genetic information is passed down to us from our ancestors. Genetic genealogy involves accessing that record to determine family relationships and verify genealogies.

- All males who share a common lineage will have the same or similar genetic code in their Y-chromosome. Through genetic testing of a man's Y-chromosome, a DNA lab can determine his Y-DNA markers, specific to his ancestry. The man can then enter these markers into a database to try to solve questions about his ancestry.

- To learn what firms offer DNA testing, do an Internet search. Here are a few: www.dnaancestryproject.com; www.tracegenetics.com; www.familytreedna.com. •

Pick up any genealogy magazine these days and you'll find ads promoting DNA testing. It's called "genealogy by genetics," and it's becoming the hottest and fastest growing branch of genealogy.

Indeed, there are many instances where a DNA analysis may help genealogy researchers to:
- Determine whether two people are related and whether they descend from a common ancestor
- Find out whether two people with the same surname might be related to each other
- Discover ethnic origins
- Confirm pedigrees

## Tests reveal ancestral trails

Genetic genealogy is an emerging science, with the potential to become even more valuable to genealogy researchers of the future.

Some companies are collecting DNA samples now as part of a study on such things as migration patterns of ancient peoples. One such study is the Genographic Project, sponsored by a partnership consisting of The National Geographic Society, IBM, and the Waitt Family Foundation.

Participants in this real-time research project will learn which of the migration paths out of Africa their ancestors followed, and the present-day countries along the trail.

They won't learn about their genetic background by race, ethnic, or geographic origin. Instead, they'll learn the fascinating anthropological story of their direct paternal or maternal ancestors—where they lived, and their migration path out of Africa thousands of years ago.

For information on this study, visit this Website: www3.nationalgeographic.com/genographic.

## SMGF builds DNA database

The Sorenson Molecular Genealogy Foundation (SMGF) is busy building the foremost collection of genetic genealogy data in the world.

The Sorenson database currently contains more than 60,000 DNA samples and family trees from men and women around the globe. The database consists of three DNA areas:
- Y-chromosome—for men only, as only males have the Y-chromosome; this online database can determine whether another male is a descendant on their paternal line. Ideal for surname research.
- Mitochondrial—currently being developed; due for release later in 2006. Can determine descent through female lines.
- Autosomal—inherited from all ancestors; a potential gold mine for genealogists of the future.

You, too, can be part of this project. For more information, visit this Website: www.smgf.org.

## Family Tree DNA

Family Tree DNA, which does testing for the Genographic Project, offers a variety of tests, including some that can pinpoint Native American, African, and Jewish ancestry. The firm's SuperDNA test provides data on maternal and paternal lines, as well as deep ancestry.

Such tests are expensive. For example, to be included in the Genographic Project, you pay $100. A full mtDNA sequence test by Family Tree DNA costs around $1,000. However, the cost may be well worth it, depending on what you learn.

## Relative Genetics

The firm that conducts testing for SMGF, Relative Genetics (Website: www.relativegenetics.com) claims its DNA tests can, among other things:
- Verify relationships
- Confirm relatedness of those with the same surname
- Prove or disprove genealogical paper research
- Solve family mysteries (such as parentage)
- Extend genealogies

This is a great site to visit for an in-depth explanation of DNA genealogy. Click on a family portrait on the right-hand side and you'll view a mini-movie of one man who found his family through DNA research. •

# Genealogy dos 'n' don'ts ...........•

## DO...

I'm Tweedle-Do!

I'm Tweedle-Don't!

• Start collecting family history information TODAY! Don't wait until it's too late to interview Grandma Anna or Uncle Allen. Get their history and their memories now, while there's still time.

• Double-check dates you collect to make sure they make sense. For example, if you find an 1849 birth date for someone whose marriage certificate is dated in 1857, you probably are barking up the wrong family tree (unless the person got married at the age of 8!).

• Double-check names, as well. Verify names with other records. In cases of common names, it's often necessary to check multiple records to make sure you're claiming the right ancestor. Keep a list of name variations for each ancestor. Be sure to keep track of all names used by the person—maiden names, nicknames, middle names, name changes, etc.

• Whenever possible, make photocopies of original documents containing family history information. When you must write notes instead, be sure to write legibly and to avoid using shorthand versions for such things as dates (for example, instead of writing them as 10/3/89, record them as 3 Oct. 1889. That way, no one will be confused as to the year, or whether you mean Oct. 3 or March 10. By the time you return to your notes, you may have forgotten the precise date. It will also be easier to decipher for your children or others who may inherit your family history research project someday.

• When sharing your pedigree charts and family group sheets with others, be sure you have noted those items that haven't been proven yet (perhaps by putting a question mark beside items you are checking on but haven't yet verified). Note this on your computer printouts of genealogy charts and group sheets also. By doing so, you'll be helping to prevent misleading information from being passed along.

• Be sure to list the sources of your information. The handy research log in the appendix of this book will help you do that. This is important because it provides the proof needed to verify information you have on your pedigree charts and family group sheets. It also helps you know where NOT to look again, thus saving you from doubling up on your research time.

• Remember that your search can be almost as exciting as the rewards of finding an elusive ancestor. So record some of the more humorous or frustrating aspects of your research. And especially remember to record the miracles: the time you found Great-great-grandpa Ole Olson in a musty old Minnesota history book, thus learning where he came from in Norway; or the letter you sent to a stranger bearing your surname, listed in an Amsterdam phone book, and the trip to Holland that developed out of that.

## DON'T...

• Don't say, "I don't have to do my family history. Uncle George has done an extensive history of all the family, so all the work is done." In order to "own" that family history and claim it as your own, you need to do some research on your own roots. (After all, they're not just Uncle George's roots; they're yours, too!) It will help you absorb the history and the story of your ancestors and help you get to know them as real human beings. Don't discard Uncle George's research, but check out his facts, verify material he's included in the book, and add some of your own. You also have family branches that you don't share with Uncle George, so get busy !

• Don't trust everything you read, or everything Grandma may tell you about the past. Verify, verify, verify—even if Grandma's word is as good as gospel. It's not uncommon for the older generations to not know, for example, their own birth date. It seems our ancestors weren't that hung up on precise dates.

• Don't trust pedigrees done by others. Always check them out to make sure they are accurate before accepting them as fact.

• Don't cut articles out of the newspaper without making sure the date is attached to the clipping. It's so frustrating to read, "Gerard Mason's funeral will be held Wednesday at 10 a.m. at the church..." without having the foggiest idea when "Wednesday" was—and whether it was in 1954, 1984 or 2004. At the very least, write the date on the clipping right after you've cut it out, so you don't have to add it later, when you're more apt to jot down the wrong date.

• Don't ignore hunches you may have about your family history. Sometimes hunches pay off! Check them out and you may be pleasantly surprised.

• Don't forget to share what you know—to give back what you receive. Write a family history book, volunteer to help at places that store and share genealogy information (it's a learning experience that will surely benefit you), keep the torch lit, carry on the good work. •

# ARE YOU STUMPED?

## THE FOLLOWING GUIDE CAN HELP YOU DETERMINE WHICH RECORDS TO SEARCH

| IF YOU NEED... | LOOK HERE FIRST... | THEN TRY... |
|---|---|---|
| Age | Census, vital records, cemeteries | Military records, taxation, SSA |
| Birth date | Vital records, church records, Bible | Cemeteries, obituaries, census |
| Birth place | Vital records, church records, census | Newspapers, obituaries |
| City/parish of foreign birth | Church records, genealogy, biography, naturalization, citizenship | Vital records, obituaries, history, emigration/immigration |
| Country of foreign birth | Emigration/immigration, naturalization and citizenship, census, church records | Military records, vital records, newspapers, obituaries |
| County origins and boundaries | History, maps | Gazetteers |
| Death | Vital records, cemeteries, probate records, church records, obituaries | Newspapers, Bible, military records |
| Divorce | Court records, vital records | Newspapers |
| Ethnic background | Ethnic organizations, societies, specialized research sites | Church records, emigration/ immigration, naturalization and citizenship |
| Historical background | History, periodicals | Minorities |
| Immigration date | Emigration/immigration, naturalization and citizenship, genealogy | Census, newspapers, biography |
| Living relatives (and adoptions) | Genealogy, directories, court records, obituaries | Census, biography, societies, church records, probate records |
| Maiden name | Vital records, church records, newspapers, Bible records | Cemeteries, military records, probate records, obituaries |
| Marriage | Vital records, church records, census, Bible records, newspapers, obituary | Cemeteries, military records, probate records, naturalization and citizenship, land and property |
| Occupation | Census, city directories, emigration/ immigration | Newspapers, court records |
| Parents, children and other family members | Vital records, church records, census, probate records, obituaries | Bible records, newspaper, emigration/immigration |
| Physical description | Military records, biography | Naturalization, citizenship, vital records, emigration/immigration, genealogy, passport, driver's lic. |
| Place (location/land) | Gazetteers, maps | History, periodicals |
| Place (town) when only state is known | Census (indexed), genealogy, military records, vital records, other indexed records | Biography, probate records, history |
| Places family lived | Census, land and property, history | Military records, taxation, obituaries |
| Previous research (compiled genealogy) | Genealogy, periodicals, societies | History, biography |
| Record-finding aids | Archives and libraries, genealogical and ethnic societies | Periodicals |
| Religion | Church records, history, biography | Bible, cemeteries, genealogy |
| Social activities | Biography, history, newspapers, societies | Town records, court records, cemeteries, directories, obituaries |

Editor's note: The sources listed here correspond to the subject categories of the LDS Family History Library Catalog. The information is adapted from information in the Zion Genealogical Society newsletter, Vol. 13, 1997, No. 4; reprinted in the Bismarck-Mandan Historical and Genealogical Society newsletter, "Dakota Homestead."

**122 • Genealogy management:
Filing your family history**

- **Where to start?**
- **Track, sort family events**
- **Build library of reference material**
- **Develop family group sheets**
- **Other recordkeeping systems**
- **Talk to the moon!**
- **Take care of artifacts**
- **Numbering systems aid research**

## System depends on your lifestyle!

Each genealogist has his or her favorite filing method. Which one you choose is less important than that it works for you. You can easily be overwhelmed by all the papers you accumulate when you collect data on your family. Organizing it is vitally important.

- Many genealogists use file folders to organize their data, color-keying them to each branch of the family. When they travel to an archive or courthouse, they load the files into a plastic file container or cardboard box and take it along for easy reference.

- Three-ring binders with acid-free, plastic sheet protectors are the favorite storage method for other family history buffs. Depending on the volume of your material, you can use a separate book for each branch of your family. A tip: If you're like us, you'll soon accumulate lots of these binders. Make sure you have space to store them. You may also want to color-coordinate these according to family groups.

- A legal-sized "Book of Memories" (especially geared for Mormons who are researching their roots) holds family group sheets and pedigree charts. •

# Genealogy management:

Let's say you've begun collecting information on your family history. Already, you may be surprised at how much material you have gathered.

Back when you first started, there may have been little reason to develop an extensive filing or recordkeeping system. But now the story is probably much different. By now, you can see tremendous progress in your research efforts, and the time has undoubtedly come to decide on a system to organize and track all the wonderful information you have gathered about your ancestors.

## Decision time is here!

Deciding on a system for organizing your research material is important to the success of your project. Perhaps you are a "filing" sort of person and can already see some logical divisions for your materials.

If so, you are very fortunate. But if you are the opposite—a person who hates filing or has no feel for it—this process could be much more difficult.

The really important thing, however, is that you go through the process. You'll be glad you did, and your future research will be much easier. Organizing your information will help you see what you have and what you still need. It will provide you with information on what

records you have already researched and what ones are left to review.

## Where to start?

Though there are many recordkeeping methods to choose from, much of the information for this chapter comes from William Dollarhide's "Managing a Genealogical Project—a Complete Manual for the Management and Organization of Genealogical Materials."

Even before you've decided on a specific system for recordkeeping, however, you can sort your materials into three piles. One pile will be for documents, notes, photocopies, and actual records about people—like certificates, deeds, and wills. This will likely be your largest pile once you've finished the sorting step and perhaps the most difficult one to organize later.

Dollarhide suggests keeping all references to a person, no matter how trivial they may seem right now. The information may prove valuable later.

## Track family events

The documents in the first pile will show various events in the lives of your ancestors, such as birth, marriage, death, and residence events.

Birth events or records might include:
- Birth certificates
- Hospital records

- Baptismal records
Marriage events documentation would include:
- Marriage licenses
- Newspaper announcements
- Wedding photographs
Residence events or records would be any documents that show where someone lived but do not show birth, marriage, or death events. Residence records might include:
- Military records
- Land records
- Censuses
- Wills
- Tax lists
Death events may involve:
- Cemetery records
- Funeral programs
- Obituaries
- Death certificates
General family events might be shown on a family group sheet received from someone or compiled yourself, family photographs, or reunion information.

Some documents may fall under more than one of the events. But for now, just decide on which one you want to file it under.

## Sort away!

A second pile will be for information that has been compiled on various forms, such as family group sheets, pedigree charts, surname lists, descendancies, and other forms. These forms might have been compiled for you by someone else or come from information in the notes and documents you

# Filing your family history

sorted into the first pile.

This will probably be the easiest of the three piles to sort and organize. For now, simply further sort the pile into each type of form—family group sheets into one, pedigree charts into another, etc.

## Build library of reference material

The third breakout of information is research aids. This category includes how-to information, lists of research facilities and libraries, assorted maps, lists of genealogical societies, your personal library of genealogical books and publications, and other types of general reference material.

This pile should be simple to sort and organize. For example, you might sort by place or geographic location (i.e., all informa-tion for North Dakota in one pile and all informa-tion for South Dakota in another). Or you might sort by types of informa-tion—books, maps, lists of resources, etc.

Dollarhide suggests leaving the first pile—notes and documents—until last, since it will likely be the largest and most dif-ficult one to organize. Of course, that's unless you are the type of person who wants to do the most diffi-cult job first. Then you may want to tackle the largest pile.

No matter, the end re-sult will be that your ma-terial is more retrievable.

Now we will discuss how to further break down the three piles into more divisions.

## Sort by surname

Dollarhide suggests get-ting the idea of sorting by family groups out of your head and concentrating on sorting by surnames instead. One of the reasons for this is that, when first starting a genealogical project, you don't know family groups.

For sorting the first pile, it is more likely that you know only a few surnames at this point. Therefore, try developing a surname-oriented filing system, which should work well for organizing and pre-serving your notes and documents.

Sort all of the material in the first pile by sur-name. You'll sort it further later, but for now, concen-trate only on surnames.

The materials will be for three types of people:

- **Ancestors.** These are people in your direct bloodline, and you want to save every bit of infor-mation you have gath-ered about them.
- **Collaterals.** These are the brothers and sisters and descendants of your

## The system you choose should be easy to use!

Here are some suggestions regarding management and numbering systems:

- Choose a filing system that others will be able to follow as well. If someone takes over your genealogy material someday, your system of filing should be easy for them to understand and enable them to locate items quickly.

- Use a simple ancestor/descendant numbering system—one that enables you to add names and other data as your search continues.

- Use a numbering system that conforms to those used by other genealogists rather than inventing your own. This is especially important if you plan to publish your genealogy charts, family history, etc., in the future.

- It's a good idea to jot down details on how your numbering system works, so if a novice should "inherit" your genealogy someday, he/she will know how to decipher and to continue with the same system. •

# Ancestor numbering systems aid in research, recordkeeping

A numbering system is an important part of your recordkeeping system. Let's review some of the possibilities.

• **The Ahnentafel ancestor numbering system** is similar to that used on a standard pedigree chart: The person whose chart it is would be No. 1, his/her father No. 2, his/her mother No. 3, No. 2's parents Nos. 4 and 5, No. 3's parents Nos. 6 and 7, etc. The males receive an even number, females an odd number. When a pedigree chart continues onto a second page, the numbers keep going from the first page. Any person on the first page can be the first person on the sec-

ond page and will retain the same number as on the first page. By doubling a person's number, you can know his/her father's number; doubled plus one gives the mother's number. While there are advantages to this method, most printed pedigree charts do not work without some modifications.

• **The Henry system,** devised by William Dollarhide, assigns ID numbers to bloodline descendants, with numbers indicating birth order, and number of generations removed from person No. 1. The progenitor is No. 1 (or other number), his oldest child 11, next child 12, etc. The oldest child of 11 is 111 and so on. When there are more than nine children, X = 10, A = 11, B = 12, etc.

Example:
1. JOHN JONES
     m. Mary Smith
11  John Jr.
     12  Mary

13  Henry
       m. Lorna Mack
131  Mary
132  Allen
14  James
15  Anne (s. Henry Mann)
151  John

• **The combined Henry-Ahnentafel system** involves numbering children of ancestors by dividing the father's number by two and adding the birth order number following a decimal point. This system can be easily adapted to computer use.

Example:
Family No. 16/17
16  JOHN JONES
17  Mary Smith
8.1    John Jr.
8.2    Mary
8.3    Henry
8.4    James
8.5    Anne
8.5s  Henry Mann (spouse)

• **The Register descendant numbering system** is formal, rigid, and time-honored. While highly acceptible to genealogists, it doesn't allow for additions. Each child is numbered with lower-case Roman numerals; those whose lines carry on are also given an Ara-

bic number. Example:
1. JOHN JONES
     (m. Mary Smith)
     Children:
        i   John Jr.
       ii   Mary
2.  iii   Henry
       iv   James
3.   v   Anne
             (m. Henry Mann)

• **The Record system,** also called the modified register system, gives every descendant of person No. 1 a number (spouses do not get a number, as they're not related by blood). Like the register system, it is not flexible when it comes to adding names or making changes.
     Example:
1. JOHN JONES
     (m. Mary Smith)
     2.i.    John Jr.
     3.ii.   Mary
   + 4.iii.  Henry
     5.iv.   James
   + 6.v.   Anne (m. Henry Mann)

For more on numbering systems, read William Dollarhide's book, "Managing a Genealogical Project." Or go online to view Richard Pence's article on ancestor numbering: saintclair.mikestclair.org/numbers/numreg.html •

---

ancestors.

• **Suspicious.** Someone who is very likely your ancestor or someone related to you, but you don't have the necessary evidence yet to prove it. Remember that, in this

part of the sorting process, you probably have not created a family group sheet yet. Therefore, concentrate on creating a database of information that is not limited to familial relationships.

In addition to surname, further sort the data by place. Ultimately, this breakdown will probably lead to logical family groupings for the family group sheets, making that effort much easier.

## Work toward uniformity

In sorting your notes and documents, try to do the following:
- Control sheet size.
- Separate sheets by surname.
- Separate surname sheets by place.
- Give each sheet a page number.

Making sheets a uniform size gives you a neater notebook, filing drawer or box in the end. If you have small notes or slips of paper, simply tape them onto the full-size sheets of paper. They will be much easier to handle and keep track of that way. And, as mentioned, the result will be a neater filing system.

Larger size documents can be photocopied and reduced to the size you have decided on, or they can be folded and stored in plastic sheet protectors.

Next, sort by surname and write the surname in a consistent place on each sheet of paper (for ease of use, the top, right-hand corner may be best). If a note or document includes more than one surname, make copies so that you can file the document under each of the surnames. Or make a note under the one surname that there is a document in the other surname section that also applies to this surname.

This method of sorting information by surnames solves another problem—what to do with non-relatives. At this point in

# KEYS
## to organizing your records

Try these suggestions for your recordkeeping system:
- Purchase three-ring binders, the quantity and size depending on how you plan to break out your information, such as by surnames and how much material you have gathered for each division. Other options might be file boxes or file folders.
- Use divider or index sheets to mark separations.
- Keep important documents, photographs, etc., in sheet protectors. Look for the word(s) "polypropylene," "polyethylene," "polyester," "poly-vu," "triacetate," "no PVCs" or "acid-free" on the product package.
- Use pedigree charts and family group sheets to separate family groups within a binder or file.
- Use research logs, journals, and other tools to keep track of your research—where you've been, what you've found, and other information.
- Try to find, at a minimum, the following records for each family section:

  –Naturalization records and passenger lists
  –Birth certificates and newspaper announcements of births
  –Census records
  –Land and homestead records

  –Death certificates and obituaries
  –Photographs
  –Family histories compiled by others
  –Research and correspondence logs
  –Court records
  –Church and cemetery records

With your materials organized, it will be much easier to find information for each person and to determine what more you want to know about that person. •

---

your research, you may not be sure if someone is related to you or not. But for now, you can file the information under that surname and not worry about it until later. Eventually, if you discover there is no relationship, you can then discard the information.

Within the surname system, sort material by place or origin of the record being filed. Of the three vital pieces of information you need to be concerned with—name, date, and place—place is the most likely to lead you to further information, making it very important. Therefore, there is justification for sorting by place, and this job is easy because virtually every note or doc-

ument will have a place associated with it. Information could be further divided by sections of a county, if necessary.

Write the place in the spot you have decided on for each sheet and below or beside the surname already written on the sheet. Consider using the standard U.S. postal code abbreviations for states.

Now you are ready to start a numbering system. The simplest method is to just make the top page number one and so on through each surname section, writing the page number on each sheet of paper.

Since you will be collecting records in random order anyway, it is not nec-

## Electronic filing aids genealogy research

- Let's look at other recordkeeping systems. An obvious example is computerized genealogy recordkeeping.

- Software programs allow you to create pedigree charts, family group sheets, and graphic images.

- Computers allow for passing information back and forth and for researching over the Internet. (Much of this was discussed in Chapter 6—check it out!) •

## Label those photos!

When you think "records management," don't just think of your papers. Also think of organizing your photographs and providing a description of each. Pictures should be identified with the following information:

- Identity of the person (or people) in the picture.
- Date (or time frame) the photo was taken (if precise date is unknown, write "circa" and the estimated date).
- Family connections of people in the photo (Jean Allison and Mary Meade, cousins, daughters of ———)
- Setting of the photo (Aunt Anna Meade's farm near Lemmon, SD).
- Reason photo was taken (family reunion, vacation, etc.).
- Any interesting or inside information surrounding the photo (for example: "Taken just two weeks before Grandma Mary Meade died"). •

essary to further sort by date or anything else. This method also makes it easy to return sheets to their proper place or to add documents as your research continues by using the next available page number under that surname.

Preprinted forms could have spaces designated for surname, place, and page, providing a reminder to note that information for filing convenience later.

Here is an example to consider:

- Sort documents by the surname. Let's just use Hanson for this example.
- Further sort documents by place (i.e., all of the Hansons who were in Minnesota).
- Then number each sheet in the pile of Hansons in Minnesota (i.e., MN-1, MN-2, MN-3, etc.).

Once you have all of your information sorted and filed, you are ready for some serious work on creating family group sheets and pedigree charts.

## Fill out charts

Carefully transferring information from various sources to the family group sheets is important. Take the necessary time now to do the job correctly, avoiding errors that will cause a great deal of confusion later in your research.

It is also important at this point to note the source for each piece of information transferred to the family group sheet or Compiled Family Data Sheet (CFDS) —i.e., the surname book, the place, and the page number. This could be done in narrative form or in an itemized listing.

The back side of the CFDS can be used to list every resource, reference, and Reference Family Data Sheet (RFDS) used for information.

It's important to note the surname, place, and page number of where the information came from for future reference.

Another method is to make a sheet for each pedigree ancestor—called a Master Data Sheet. This sheet would include all of the information you know about that one person and where the information came from. The references or sources could be listed on the back—called a Research Log, thus forming a complete listing of information sources and RFDS's for that person.

This work can be done by hand, typewriter, or computer. Regardless of what system you choose, a well-organized record-keeping system for your genealogical materials allows you to more easily analyze what information you have and what you still need to research. •

# Preserving artifacts

Once you start contacting relatives for genealogical information and have thereby announced yourself as the keeper of the family history, you may find you are suddenly in possession of many precious family heirlooms.

Whether it's Great-grandma Jensen's quilt made 150 years ago, a favorite crystal vase from Aunt Mabel, the cream separator and oxen yokes from Uncle John's farm, precious photographs or

documents, such as land deeds, naturalization papers, and the family Bible, you may feel responsible for the preservation and care of these items. But you don't have a clue what to do to save them for future generations. Here's a list that can help:

• The primary lesson to be learned from this list is to store your precious artifacts in safe, dark, dry, and cool places. An unheated garage or shed will not meet the temperature requirement (55 to 70 de-

grees Fahrenheit). Your basement may or may not work, depending on how damp it is, and the attic will very likely be too hot. The closets inside your home would work great for most items, assuming there is sufficient space.

• If you want to display some of the items, like the family Bible, wedding dress, or photographs, keep them out of direct sunlight and encased to keep dust, insects, and other potential damage from them. In some cases, you

# Dating your daguerreotype!

Dating old photographs can be a challenge. Here's a little help:

- **Calotype:** The first type of image produced, it was developed in 1837 by Fox Talbot.
- **Daguerreotype:** 1839-60. The oldest of the commercially made photographs having a shiny mirrorlike appearance—a fragile silver surface on a copper plate. Originally enclosed in a case and still needs that protection.
- **Ambrotype:** 1854-63. A negative image on glass that appears positive because it will have a coating of red or black lacquer applied to the back or enclosed in a case with black paper or cloth behind it.
- **Tintype:** 1855-1915. Can range in size. Not on glass, but an image on thin metal. If encased or pasted into paper frames, likely earlier; if slipped into a paper frame,

likely later. Often taken at fairs and amusement parks. Study clothes to determine date. Popular during Civil War. They could be touched up with color.

- **Albumen print:** Brown-toned prints made on paper coated with egg albumen.
- **Carte de Viste:** 1860-1920. First of paper photographs. The thinnest are earliest. If shiny, from the latter part of the period. Discontinued in the U.S. around 1890.
- **Cabinet:** 1875-1920. Found in albums, on wall, or in cabinet frames. Look closely at the clothes to determine date. If oval and pasted on the card or if surrounded by dark or black pasted on a card, likely after 1900.
- **Cyanotype:** Bright blue print on very thin paper. Print made by amateurs.

- **Postcard photos:** 1905-30. Lots of them made and sometimes mailed.
- **Revenue stamp:** Used only from 1866-68. •

*—From Marin Kin Tracer, Vol. 19, No. 4, 1996*

---

may want to make copies of photographs and display the copies, rather than the originals.

- Provide good ventilation to control humidity, but not so much that it blows the dust and other things around. The dust can be controlled somewhat by sealing windows and keeping outside doors and windows closed.

- Be extremely careful in cleaning dust from books. Use a soft cloth or brush for dusting individual books. Do not use a cloth treated with furniture spray, oils or other chemicals. It is best to use straight water or water mixed with disinfectant for cleaning the book shelves.

- Do not use a vacuum cleaner to clean books,

although it can be used to clean the book shelves or the general area around the shelves. The best vacuum cleaners for the job are those with HEPA (high-efficiency particulate air) filters, which screen out much of the things stirred up by the vacuuming process.

- Various fungi, like mold and mildew, can be hazardous to the health of your artifacts. They attack paper and books and can cause serious damage, basically eating the cellulose and starches. They will stain textiles and weaken the fabric. The only way to prevent mold and mildew is to control the temperature, keeping it within 55 to 70 degrees Fahrenheit and the relative humidity within the 45- to

65-degree range.

- There are many indoor pollutants that can damage your artifacts, also. Just a few of them are tobacco smoke; carpentry shop fumes; paint; products containing oils, ammonia, sulfur, and formaldehyde; glues; and pesticides.

Many of these can be harmful to people, as well as to artifacts, so use them carefully or not at all.

ART & ARTIFACTS

## Marking, storing photos and negs

- Use an archivally safe pen or a graphite or No. 2 lead pencil to write on the back of the photos. Do not press so hard that your writing creates a raised impression on the face of the picture.

- Do not use felt-tip markers of any kind, or any pens with ink that might transfer to the front of a photograph (or to a stack of photos laid on top of each other).

- Store your photographs with preservation in mind. Use archival-quality photograph albums.

- Place the photo in an acid-free, plastic sheet protector, then add a photo description on a separate sheet of acid-free paper and store that in the sheet protector along with the photograph.

- Check your local photography shop for acid-free products (sleeves, files, envelopes, etc.) for protecting and storing your negatives. Keep them separate from the photographs, but labeled and keyed to the photos for ease in locating them, should you wish to reprint a picture. •

Some signs of indoor-generated pollutants are yellow-brown stains on textiles and paper, unusually fast tarnishing of silver, and excessive corrosion.

• Use only sheet protectors, document holders, storage boxes, and tissue paper that are archivally safe. Basically, this means acid-free or with a neutral pH level of 7. Though products may be labeled "archivally safe," check for more specific information about the acidity or alkalinity (pH) levels. On a scale of 1 to 14, 7 is neutral or acid-free. Acidic solutions have a lower pH number, and alkaline solutions have a higher number.

Keep in mind that the artifacts themselves have acid and alkaline, as well as lignins, tannins, and resins (in wood-based products such as paper) in them.

Though there are methods to reduce the destructive elements in an artifact, it may be difficult to find a professional to do it, and the process could be very expensive. At least, what you store your artifacts in can be safe for them, such as products that are made of polyester, polypropylene, triacetate or polyethylene, or labeled "no PVCs" or "acid-free."

• Don't use paper clips or rubber bands on paper documents or in books. The paper clips can rust, and the rubber bands may melt and leave stains.

• Do not write directly on paper documents. Label the sheet protector instead.

• Use special archivally

safe pens or graphite or No. 2 lead pencils to label photographs.

• Do not store newspaper clippings near photographs or paper documents. Newsprint is very high in acid content and other chemicals.

## The acid test

Deacidify your newspaper clippings, if possible, with Wei T'o No. 10 and then encapsulate them in Mylar for preservation. Another method is to dissolve 1 tablespoon (or one tablet) of milk of magnesia in one quart of club soda. Mix the two fluids together and store overnight in the refrigerator.

Next day, pour the solution into a glass cake pan and gently lay the clipping into the solution for two hours, being careful not to tear the paper. Take the clipping out of the solution and place it between two pieces of white paper towels. Then place it between two pages of white blotter paper with books set on top to keep it flat. Store overnight. (Note: This method is not meant for use on manuscripts or letters, as the ink will run.)

## Dating photos

You may have boxes full of old photographs of what may or may not be family members—you don't know because none of them are labeled. The process of organizing and identifying them could be an exciting part of your research project.

If you don't know who is in the photographs and you have no one to ask, dating the photographs is a way to determine who is in them. If you can somehow decide the time frame during which the photograph was taken—from the clothes or the location or whatever, you may then be able to decide who is in the photograph.

Other artifacts can also be identified by markings, the manufacturer or other details in the style or color.

There may be professionals available in your community who can help. If not, you may be able to do library research and make other contacts to figure it all out.

A lot can be told by textiles and garments—from the style, the trim and buttons, the fabric blend and other details.

## If it's broke...

If an item has severe damage, you may need to turn to a professional to repair it. There are businesses that specialize in restoring photographs or repairing glass, ceramic and wood. If the item is truly a precious heirloom, it will likely be worth the cost to have it restored. •

# History book: Recipe for

So you've collected umpteen boxes of family history material and now you'd like to organize it, duplicate it, and distribute it to other relatives who have expressed an interest.

Or, you have a compelling urge to write about life in the Great Depression and World War II days so you can hand those memories on to your grandchildren.

Your next logical step is to organize it—and turn it into a book!

"But, hey, I'm not a writer!" you say. Not to worry! This chapter contains tips that can help guide you in producing a book of which you can be proud —one that will preserve your memories and mementos for future generations of your family or your community, state, and world.

WON'T YOU HAVE A BITE OF FAMILY HISTORY?

## Why a book?

There are lots of reasons to write a book about yourself or your family. As we already mentioned, one is to preserve family memories for the next generations. Here are a few more:

• Your own unique family stories will be lost if not recorded.

• A book is a compact way to store information. The fact that you can have multiple copies printed (or photocopied) means you can share it with others at the same time that you're preserving the records.

• Writing a book is therapeutic. It gives you a deep appreciation for your ancestors and helps you to better understand their lives and times.

• A book is a tangible product, one you can hold in your hand later and say, "I did this!" It will earn you prestige and recognition as

the "family historian."

• Perhaps best of all, it promotes family togetherness. And isn't that what being a family is all about?

A family history book can be a rewarding family project, involving young and old. It connects the generations and promotes communication—both before printing (when you're collecting information and gathering family stories) and after (when the book is distributed to grandparents, uncles and aunts, nieces and nephews).

## Consider your 'diners'

Just as a good cook checks to see who'll be partaking of the feast before deciding what or how much to serve, you must consider your audience before you begin a book project.

---

## Sifting out the lumps

Deciding what NOT to put in your book can also be important to the book's outcome: facts that might embarrass your readers, observations that aren't proven or accurate, or things that may have been "plagarized" from other publications (copyrighted items used without the author's or publisher's permission).

Too often we writers are inclined to add a dash of imagination or a pinch of conclusion-jumping to our recipes. This can result in a book that misrepresents the truth—yet is being presented as an honest representation. As one writer warns, "Be careful not to weave fiction into reality, based on imagination rather than fact."

What about family legends that haven't been

proven by press time? You can add a statement such as: "Although this legend has yet to be proven, we are printing it in hopes a reader or family member might delve into researching it at a future date."

What about the fact that Uncle Harry spent time in the state pen? Or Great-grandma had an illegitimate child? Do you spill everything—warts and all?

One way to handle this is to talk to members of Uncle Harry's immediate family to learn their feelings. You may find they have accepted Harry's indiscretion and won't mind if the truth is printed in the family record. If Harry's family feels strongly that his prison record should not be published in your book, you may have to balance your quest for the truth with their request for

# family togetherness

Ask yourself: "Who is this book for? Will the book be a memoir that only I will see? Will it be a history of my immediate family? Or do I want to publish a book that appeals to many generations of my family? Perhaps my community—or even a wider audience?"

Then let your intended audience guide you in deciding your goal for the book—what to put in, as well as what to leave out.

Knowing your audience will influence the goals you set, the approach you take, how personal you will make your book, and your writing style.

One of your goals should be to attract your readers and hold their interest. You might also set goals to make your book reliable and trustworthy, entertaining, educational, a resource for genealogists, and a keepsake for your family.

## Choosing your recipe

Now that you're leaning toward writing a book, how do you know what to focus on (when you have overwhelming amounts of material and limited space and time)? Do you start now or do you wait till you have filled in all the gaps?

Again, know your audience—and the goals you've set for your book. If this is a book about your personal life, for example, or about a hobby you enjoy, weed out anything that doesn't fit that theme and concentrate on the things that do.

Creating a family history book, however, requires a broader focus. Yet the focus must not be so broad as to overwhelm both you and your audience. You will need to decide how much (or how little) of your family history to cover.

If you have a lot to cover, consider printing several volumes, one representing each branch of your family or a certain era or generation.

You might also narrow the focus of your book to:
- Grandparents down to present generation
- First immigrant ancestors to present
- Your father or mother's family branches only
- Immediate family
- Your personal biography

Select a format for your book that provides a smooth, logical flow for the material you plan to present.

Here are some ideas for arranging your book:

## Theme schemes

Build your book around a theme, to give it a flavor that sets it apart from the books of others. Here are a few ideas:

- Lots of musicians in the family? Jazz up your book with songs popular during different eras—using several stanzas of a hit song, for example, to introduce each chronological section and following with memories from that era.

- Do a pictorial history of your family (using descriptive captions to provide photo details).

- Create a cookbook using traditional family recipes from different branches, surrounded by history information about the family. •

---

silence. Get their input and try to come up with an acceptable compromise.

As to Great-grandma's illegitimate child? Again, talk it over with family, and they may agree that it's a crucial part of Great-grandma's history and that her story should be told honestly but tastefully.

What if Aunt Margaret recalls a different version of a family event than Aunt Sarah does? Which account do you print? Give the most weight to the account backed by evidence. Or print both accounts, with a statement such as, "There are two versions of this story in our family—one recalled by Uncle David and one by Aunt Margaret. We are printing them both. Documentation, which includes [list sources] seems to point to the first account as being the more likely."

Unless you are writing your personal memoirs or targeting your immediate family only, check with oth-er family members to get different angles and viewpoints on the same ancestors and events. This can lead to a more balanced presentation.

As you know, no two siblings in one family view their parents the same way, each having their own unique vantage point and perspective, depending on their position in the family, sex, age, personality, etc. Interviewing each for their specific memories can lead to a more well-rounded description of family members.

How much liberty can you take at guessing at the choices an ancestor made—or judging his or her actions? Or must you stick to the facts? Our advice: If you deviate from the facts to make an assumption, tell your readers that it's an assumption.

This will add credibility to your book. Readers will know what's fact and what's assumption. You'll gain their trust. •

# Beware of book schemes 'n' scams

**"I have exciting news for you and all the Knudsons! Now, an astounding new book, 'THE WORLDWIDE BOOK OF KNUDSONS,' is about to be published for you..."**

- When you get a pronouncement like this in the mail, think twice—maybe even thrice—before ordering the book. The information it contains is almost certainly generic—not specific to your surname, not even to your family's country of origin.

- Don't waste your time or money on information that misleads and interferes with (rather than aids) your quest.

- "Instant" might be fine for mashed potatoes or oatmeal. But don't rely on the instant genealogy claims made by such a book. •

INSTANT FAMILY HISTORY

---

- Use chronological order (from earliest history to present).
- Start with your parents' history, then separate the book into chapters featuring each child.
- Start with a milestone event, then work your way backward and forward from that event.
- Start with yourself and your family, then work backward in time.
- Write your book as a letter to someone—your grandchildren, perhaps.

Should you wait until you have all the gaps filled in on Great-grandpa Jones's life story? Or should you "go for it" now?

The danger with waiting is that you probably will never publish a book. That's because there will always be some missing puzzle pieces lurking out there somewhere. Finding family history is a never-ending project. You must decide when you have sufficient material to publish.

## Picking your ingredients

What "ingredients" should you add to the family book you're cooking up?

Our advice to you is to go to your local library and browse through their genealogy book section. There you'll find examples of family history books others have produced. Write down things you like, things you don't, and ideas you'd like to include in your book. Observe how other books are arranged and their basic "ingredients."

Here are our suggestions for items to include in your book:

- **Cover/spine:** The cover is the gateway to your book, the invitation for readers to "come on in." Make it as inviting as possible, with type that's easy to read and not lost in the illustration.

The title should be creative and catchy, yet provide clear information on what the book is about.

The "spine" (the portion of your book that you view when the book is closed and on the shelf) should also include your title, written from top to bottom. If you decide to use a spiral binding, use one on which you can imprint the title, so it can readily be viewed on a library or bookstore shelf.

- **Title page:** List the title, subtitle, name of author or compiler (your name and that of any co-authors), your address, etc. You may also want to add a Library of Congress Catalog Card Number and copyright information.

- **Foreword/prologue/ dedication/acknowledgment:** Use these pages to explain your purpose in writing the book, dedicate the book to an ancestor or thank those who helped or set the stage for your book.

- **Table of contents:** Include a complete table of contents, listing page numbers for each category.

- **Chapter divider pages:** Separate topics by means of divider pages. These pages can contain drawings or illustrations, a headline explaining what the upcoming chapter contains and other details. This will add visual interest to your book and help to break the book into organized sections.

- **History:** Provide information on the history, as well as the customs and lifestyles, of the periods in which the ancestors you're writing about were living.

- **Charts:** Include multi-generation pedigree charts, and family group sheets filled with information about family members you're featuring in the book. Add documentation for items on the charts.

- **Biographies:** Feature biographical vignettes of people on the group sheets.

- **Details:** Add items such as physical description, church affiliation, occupation, medical history, education, military service, talents, and traditions.

- **Special memories and anecdotes:** List family members' recollections of events or amusing or dramatic incidents that happened in your family. These items will add some flavor to your otherwise dry stew of family names, dates, and places.

- **Keepsakes and family collectibles:** Items such as newspaper clippings, funeral cards, birth and marriage announcements, wedding certificates, old letters, etc., can be featured here to add an interesting design element, as well as family information.

These materials can be scanned into a computer or photocopied for inclusion in your book.

- **Maps:** Include maps of places your ancestors lived—and a map or two tracing their migration across the country or across the ocean.

# Adding meat to your ancestral stew

Names, dates, and places written on a pedigree chart or family group sheet are the framework of a person's life.

Once the framework is constructed, you can "flesh out" the person with details of his or her life, embellish it with historical events that took place during their lifetimes, add human interest with family stories about the person. This will put meat on the bones of your ancestors.

"Close your eyes and try to think about your ancestors' lives," writes Patricia Law Hatcher in "Turning Paper Into People" (excerpted from "Producing a Quality Family History").

To bring the details into sharp focus, Hatcher suggests you use your "mind-camera" to picture your ancestor standing in his or her own kitchen—zooming in on the clothing, the utensils, the setting, the person's activities.

If you're getting a fuzzy picture, research can help you to get a sharper focus.

Hatcher recommends you place your ancestors in the following contexts:

• **Times and lifestyle**— homes or farms they lived in, transportation, clothing, foods they ate, neighborhood, town, school, diseases, treatment.

• **Work**— farmer, blue collar worker, professional; implements used; duties performed.

• **Environment**— geography or topography of land, soil type, trees, birds, and wildlife, weather conditions and climate, major environmental events, such as blizzards or prairie fires.

• **Military duties**— branch of service, uniform worn, weapons used, campaigns, battles.

• **Religion**— denomination, parish, name of minister, religious beliefs and customs, ceremonies.

• **Family**— size, spacing between children, age at marriage, child mortality, first or second marriage, story behind names.

• **History and politics**— history and politics that affected your ancestor and his family significantly or distantly; political affiliation.

• **Community**— settled community or frontier? Nearest town?

• **Ethnic group**— how did ethnic background affect your ancestor's life?

• **Society**— social structure: view of children, courtship customs; whether slave/slave owner or indentured servant.

• **Law**— what happened when someone died without a will? Who inherited the land/property? Did widow have dower rights? What was required to get a divorce? Could your ancestor vote?

• **Records**— documents he/she is listed in: contracts, papers, registrations, directories, etc. Did ancestor's church keep records? Is he/she listed in a city or business directory?

Think, think, think! •

---

• **Photographs:** Add photos of ancestors and their homes or farms, family groupings, etc. (Be sure to include captions with names, dates, places, and relationships under any photos you reproduce.) Use a computer to scan photos. You can also photocopy them, but scanning will give better quality. Some computer programs let you touch up or enhance your photos as necessary.

You may also be able to secure historical photos from state archives libraries or to pick them up via the Internet. (Note: Before you print photos, check copyright restrictions, get permission, and give proper credit.)

If you don't have art for your book, consider using appropriate "clip art," available on computer disk or in book form.

• **Epilogue, appendix, bibliography, index:** If applicable, add an epilogue, appendix, and/or bibliography. Make sure your book has a thorough index. An index is an absolute must.

Your index can be alphabetical, surname, location, or all three. An index will aid your readers—as well as researchers and librarians—in finding names and/or topics of interest.

• **Names and addresses:** Include names and addresses of families listed in your book, as well as your name and address so people interested in buying or commenting on your book can contact you.

## 'Cooking' your book

Let's say you decide to have a book printed. How do you go about lining up a printer, and preparing your material for printing? What decisions must be made?

• **To print or to photo-**

## History mystery?

• Still have pieces of your genealogical puzzle missing? Don't wait until all your gaps are filled in to publish your family history book. Instead, include a section at the back of your book labeled "Wanted: Detectives to help solve family history mystery." Then list unsolved research problems. This may prompt some of your readers to tackle the problem as a research project in the future. •

# What if you're not a good 'cook'?

Here are some tips to help you cook up a good story even though you might not consider yourself a writer:

• Keep a personal journal or notebook to get in the habit of writing. Practice, practice, practice. Jot down ideas, observations, reflections, memories.

• Use description to bring your settings and characters to life. According to the book "Writing A to Z," "description . . . is the art of showing the reader how a person, place or thing looks, tastes, feels, sounds, smells, or acts. . . . it is bringing something to life by carefully choosing and arranging words and phrases to produce the desired effect."

• Use your common sense—and your five senses—when you write. Describe sights (Aunt Emma's bridal gown), tastes (Grandma's tangy spaghetti sauce), sounds (meadowlark's trill), smells ( lilacs in spring), and touch (Grandpa's whisker rubs).

• Use dialogue. Let your readers "hear" your characters speak. Add quotes to your book.

• Write concisely. Long pages of description with little or no dialogue turns readers off.

• Avoid $10 words when a nickel word will do. As the saying goes, "Write to express, not to impress."

• Employ clear writing, with proper grammar, punctuation, and spelling.

• Give your readers short, entertaining accounts spiced with plenty of anecdotes to make the story more palatable. Study the styles of other writers to learn how they handle anecdotes. Especially check out *Readers Digest*, which specializes in short stories with a catchy lead, entertaining body, and satisfying closing. •

## 'Tense' sense

• What tone do you want your book to convey: formal or friendly, personal or impersonal? Do you want it in anecdotal (story) form, or in narrative style, where the author writes in the third person, past tense, about an event (as in "they marched, he proceeded on")?

First person is appropriate for memoirs, or for books such as "Grandmother Remembers." For example, "I went to the 1939 World's Fair. . ."

Most family history writers use the third-person, narrative form, as it allows them the most flexibility for telling their story. •

copy? That is the question! There are other ways to reproduce your book besides standard printing methods—such as photocopying pages and firing them off to family members.

Photocopying can be the answer when only a small quantity of books will be distributed. Provide a packet of photocopied pages and urge those receiving the packets to invest in a three-ring binder (with a clear window in front and spine to slip in a printed sheet indicating the name of the book), plus clear plastic, acid-free sheet protectors for three-ring binders. Pages from the packet can be slipped into these protectors and filed in page order in the binder.

If photocopying, check with a copy center, such as Mail Boxes Etc. or Kinkos, or a quick-print shop, to see what discounts they might offer for multiple copies.

If quality and quantity aren't major issues, then photocopying or a quick-print shop might be your choice. If you want a more professional job with multiple copies, the print shop route may be best for you.

Here are some production suggestions:

## Planning

• Decide the scope of your book (how many books you plan to reproduce and roughly how many pages to make it), method of printing (photocopying versus quick-print versus full-scale printing), and production method (do-it-yourself desktop design, on disk and/or pdf files, versus having the printer do it all). That will determine how you craft your pages for best reproduction.

• Create a rough "dummy" of how you want your book arranged. We'd suggest using a three-ring binder and plastic sheet protectors to "build" the framework of your book. Roughly label each blank sheet of paper with the item that will appear on that page and insert it, back to back, into the sheet protectors in the order in which they will appear in the finished book.

• Outline the main categories you plan to cover in the book; these can be your chapter intro pages and your table of contents.

• Create file folders for each chapter; group items pertaining to each category into the appropriate folder.

## Production

• Use a computer with a good word-processing or desktop publishing program to set up your pages.

Use a genealogy program for group sheets, pedigree charts, and other forms. (Note: You can use a typewriter, but it is a lot less forgiving!)

If you don't have access to or know how to use a computer, consider hiring someone who does to prepare your manuscript for publication.

• Develop a design format for each related group of pages (i.e., chapter divider pages, biographies, genealogy forms, etc.) and keep them consistent throughout.

• Leave spaces on your pages for pasting in halftones (photos screened for publication) later, or use a scanner and insert the scanned photos onto your page yourself.

• Place special emphasis on consistency. This will give your book unity. Make your larger heads the same typeface and size; make subheads consistent, as well. Apply the same spacing throughout your book; use the same body type.

• Allow an adequate margin of white space around your page edges and

between columns of type, with enough space in the gutter (inside center) to allow you to open the book wide. Place page numbers in a consistent location on each page. Page 1 should begin on a right-hand page (odd numbers go on the right, even on the left.) Use Roman numerals for intro pages before Chapter 1.

• For variety, you can use another style (or bolder type of the same style) for related text blocks, such as photo captions or items in boxes. Vary the length of your headlines; stack some of them in a two-line format, rather than straight across.

Use a different column width for boxed items, sprinkle appropriate line art throughout, use different-sized photos and place them in different positions on your pages.

You can also use boxes or set some things in reverse (white) type on a black background. When you do, make sure that the text is bold enough to prevent the serifs (fine lines at top and bottom

that give type its character) from getting lost.

• For better readability, divide your pages into two or three vertical columns, rather than having your type run all the way across the page horizontally.

• Use type that's easy to read (serif type is usually considered most readable), large enough to read (10 point at the least) and with adequate "leading" (spacing between rows of type).

• Avoid unsightly gaps between words in your body type. (Setting material flush left, with a ragged right margin, is one way to avoid this problem.)

• Think "alignment." Align your lines of body type across the page, top and bottom. Make sure picture edges are straight before affixing them to your page. Align box and picture edges with columns of type.

• Graphic devices, such as large initial caps at paragraph beginnings, bullets (dots) to denote items in lists, etc., can help add visual punch to your book. Boxes can be used to draw attention to special items, or separate them from the main story.

• Clip art can be used to spice up your pages. If you have access to a computer, you can buy clip art on disc or CD-ROM, then extract it and place it into your page layout via computer. Or you can scan in illustrations. (Note: Copyright laws apply to art, as well as to printed material.)

• If you're an artist, you might try inking

# Print shop scenarios

• You furnish a manuscript, rough layout, and unprocessed photos (identified and labeled as to placement in book). The professional staff at the print shop then handles the design and layout details, producing your book from scratch.

• You do (or you hire someone to do) a camera-ready "paste-up," with pages looking just as they will appear in printed form (complete with type, headlines, halftoned photos, page numbers, etc.). The printer will shoot negatives directly from your pages.

• You use a computer word-processing program or desktop publishing program, prepare pages, then scan photos and clip art into place. When done, pages will be disk-ready. Many printers will request pages in the form of "pdf's" (portable document files). Check with your printer to make sure programs, type faces, disks you're using, formats, etc., are compatible with his/her equipment. Most graphic designers and printers, for example, use Macintosh hardware. •

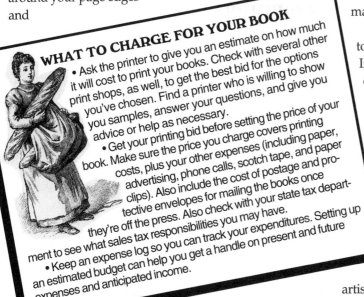

WHAT TO CHARGE FOR YOUR BOOK

• Ask the printer to give you an estimate on how much it will cost to print your books. Check with several other print shops, as well, to get the best bid for the options you've chosen. Find a printer who is willing to show you samples, answer your questions, and give you advice or help as necessary.

• Get your printing bid before setting the price of your book. Make sure the price you charge covers printing costs, plus your other expenses (including paper, advertising, phone calls, scotch tape, and paper clips). Also include the cost of postage and protective envelopes for mailing the books once they're off the press. Also check with your state tax department to see what sales tax responsibilities you may have.

• Keep an expense log so you can track your expenditures. Setting up an estimated budget can help you get a handle on present and future expenses and anticipated income.

# Collecting family 'recipes'

When producing your family history book, chances are you will, in many cases, be as much a compiler of other people's information as you will be a writer.

You will be collecting data from families who will be featured in your book. Here's how to proceed:

• Contact relatives by letter to involve them in your plans and get their support. Send them blank family group sheets and pedigree charts, along with instructions on how to fill out the charts. Include a self-addressed, stamped envelope. Ask them to return the sheets to you, along with a brief history of their family—interesting family stories, childhood memories, etc. Give them a deadline.

Rather than sending letters to every relative, send to family heads and have them pass the informa-tion to others in their family. Janet Gallagher of Audu-bon, MN, author of a family history entitled "The Book I Wish Grandmother Bacon Had Written: An Ingredient Called Kate," sent a letter, pedi-gree chart, and family group sheets to each family. "The family was responsible for duplicating the form for their children and grand-children," she says.

Gallagher especially stresses get-ting stories of living relatives. "Sometimes I think we dwell too much on our ancestors and forget to obtain the stories of our own generation," she writes in her book.

• Have relatives send photos (reprints preferred, in case of loss) of family members—a family por-trait, individual photos, group pic-tures with extended family. Cap-tions should be included. Rather than writing IDs on the backs of pictures, encourage senders to write descriptive information on a separate note and key it to the pic-ture. Ask, too, for copies of interest-ing family documents. Return materials when done.

If you don't receive material by deadline, call or write relatives urg-ing them to send their material or risk being left out of the book. "I begged my relatives with letters and telephone calls when they didn't respond," says Gallagher.

• Organize material as soon as you receive it. Gallagher used 9-by-13 envelopes and a numerical filing system. "The envelopes keep pre-cious pieces from getting lost," she says. As each relative writes, Gal-lagher suggests putting their infor-mation in an envelope labeled with their name, address, and phone number.

• Enter your data into a genealo-gy or word-processing program. You may also have to edit some of the material you receive. Send out proofs of the material you've typed up so relatives can check it for possi-ble errors and return it to you with corrections or an "O.K." •

## Orts

• Proof "bluelines" furnished by your printer prior to printing. This is your final chance to catch and correct errors.

• When you get the call from the print shop that your book is done, check quality and quantity before accepting the order. Make sure you got what you paid for!

• When sending out book orders to rela-tives featured in your book, return photos and/or documents in the same envelope. •

your own illustrations onto your pages. (Note that pencil illustrations need to be halftoned or screened, just like a photograph, painting, or anything else containing shades of gray or color.)

• Don't place non-text elements in a spot where they might interfere with the flow of the text.

• Set deadlines. Allow adequate time for compil-ing, writing, typing, proof-ing, editing, correcting, and laying out the book.

• Before you send your book to the printer, go over it thoroughly, line by line, word by word, to make sure it is error-free.

Better yet, get a fresh pair of eyes to scan it for errors. It's often easier for someone else to spot mis-takes than it is for the per-son who wrote the material. We writers often are too "close" to the mat-erial to view it objectively.

Have this "second par-ty" review it for spelling, sense, and grammar, as well as consistency (to see, for example, that all the heads and captions are sim-ilar in style to other items of their kind and that names are consistent throughout).

Also have them check to make sure pictures are placed with the correct cap-tions.

Your "second party" should also double-check index page numbers to make sure items listed in your table of contents or index can actually be found on the pages indicated.

Now you're ready for a trip to the print shop.

## Printing options

Here are decisions you'll need to make regarding printing of your book:

• **Number of pages**
• **Paper size and weight**
• **Paper color**
• **Binding style**
• **Hard or soft cover**
• **One color or more**

Ask the advice of your printer or of someone who has recently had a book printed. Ask to see samples before you make your decision. Also check out your local library or book store to see how you want your book to "fit" on the shelf.

Prepare an outline and "dummy" of your book to help you determine number of pages.

Examine paper and cover stock options and pick the stock that suits your needs and price range. You can also use colored paper, rather than white. If you opt for this method, be sure the color doesn't detract from photos (for example, portraits on green or blue paper) and that it allows for good readability.

Paper comes in different weights, ranging from standard page weights and degrees of opacity, to thicker, heavier stocks used for covers. Select a durable stock for your cover and paper opaque enough to prevent bleed-through of material printed on the reverse side.

You'll need to choose a binding—such as a spiral, plastic-comb, or perfect binding—and whether you want your book in hard or soft cover. Some people choose both!

Do you want the book in color or black-and-white (black ink on white paper)? Remember, the more colors you choose, the steeper the printing bill.

Whatever you decide, the rewards of having a printed book that preserves your family history will be worth the effort. •

## More orts

- When you finish your book, distribute it to your state's archives library, to your community library and to your state's genealogy repositories. This way, others will be able to benefit from your work and contact you if they tie in to your lines. •

# Marketing your family history book

How do you finance that book you're cooking up? Do you tackle it alone? Or do you collaborate with someone else, such as another relative?

- **Form a family organization,** in which family members band together and cooperate to publish a book on their mutual families. Getting people together can be a help when it comes to financing your project or rounding up material for a book. Some groups publish a periodical newsletter going to reader-subscribers with family connections. Or they may combine forces to stage family reunions. Many multi-member groups elect officers, collect dues, and operate as businesses.

- **Write down potential markets** for your book. Query relatives whose histories are listed in the book and encourage them to make a commitment, before the book is printed, on the number of books they will buy. That will help you estimate how many books you'll need to print. If you plan to sell to a much broader market, you'll need to have more books produced. Let prospective buyers know that only a limited number of books will be available, and that they'll have to order while supplies last—or go without.

- **Offer discounts.** Offer discounts on pre-publication sales; if applicable, price your book high enough to cover sales through retail book outlets.

- **Consider community, commercial markets.** If the book has information about your community or county, your local library or historical society can be viewed as a potential customer. A well-researched, high-quality book with broad appeal has the potential of being picked up by specialty book stores, genealogy and history outlets, or other commercial markets.

- **Try flyers.** Use your computer to print up simple flyers with information on your book. You can also have extra copies of your cover printed for display and promotional purposes.

- **Check with a genealogy group.** Check to see whether you can set your flyers or book covers out at your local historical or genealogy society meetings (where you're a member, of course!), the library, or other appropriate places. If genealogy-related groups you belong to have a newsletter, see if you can run a small ad or possibly get some free publicity.

- **Plan a family reunion.** Then have the books prominently displayed on your genealogy table, ready for purchase by family and friends who view your exhibit and fall in love with your book. Organize a team of family members to help peddle the book.

- **Print contact information.** As mentioned earlier, your name and address should be prominently positioned in your book so that a potential purchaser will know how to contact you to order the book. You can also include a mail-in ad in your book that can be copied and sent in, along with a check.

- **Give gift of family heritage.** Don't forget yourself as a buyer! You'll want extra copies for gifts, to enter in contests (yes, there are competitions that cater strictly to family histories!) and to give to members of your family. There's no greater gift than family heritage. •

## Don't forget the kiddies!

- The main reason for holding a reunion is family connections that span the generations. Therefore, it's important that your gathering appeal to kids, as well as older folks. After all, the kids are the ones who will be planning the family reunion 30 years from now! So get them involved—have plenty of fun things for them to do at the reunion.

- Assign teens to organize kids' activities, such as talent contests, scavenger hunts, and games.

- Have the youngsters put on costumes and perform a skit based on family history. Give plenty of fun prizes.

- Make your reunion a fun time for the kids—you'll be reinforcing future family ties. •

# Planning and staging a

So you've gathered several binders full of genealogy information, you've finally discovered where your great-great-grandfather was born, and you've even located the only living descendent of your great-great Aunt Julia. Now what?

Perhaps it's time for a family reunion—a chance to connect all those branches of the family tree that have sprouted over the past several years! Perhaps it's time to make all those relatives you know only by name on a family group sheet come alive.

A family reunion would also be an opportunity for them to get to know each other—or to become re-acquainted if it's been a while since they saw each other.

## Where to start—it's up to you!

Yes, you can do it. You can plan your family's get-together for next summer or the year after.

This section will help you do that—it will provide you with ideas on suitable reunion locations; how to find addresses for all the relatives in that family line; planning activities that attendees will enjoy, and raising the funds necessary to finance a gathering of several hundred family members.

The best way to start is by getting organized and developing a plan—sort of a "who-what-when-where-why" list.

If your family has never had a reunion before or if it has been a number of years since the last one, surveying key family members might be a good idea. Ask those people to contact others you may not know or may not have addresses for. From this, compile a list of names, addresses, and phone numbers which will continue to grow throughout the planning process and beyond.

Consider including an information form for each person to complete and return. These forms provide lots of interesting tidbits about family members, useful for planning awards and activities at the reunion and for future reference, as well.

You can find samples of good information forms in a number of resources, including "Reunions for Fun Loving Families" by Nancy Funk Bagley (see bibliography, Appendix).

Results of the survey could give you some great ideas on the best time and place for the reunion and how to reach other people who might be interested.

Respondents may be able to tell you about previous family reunions and how successful—or unsuccessful—they were and how to make this one even better.

It might be fun to have a "theme" reunion—how about "100 years in Dakota" if your ancestors arrived in the area a century ago, or stealing from John Denver's "Take me

**GET THE REUNION BALL ROLLING!**

"Keep the Ball a-rolling on a-rolling on!" Exceedingly polite attention given to Fancy Balls and Dress Balls.

**Start out by getting as many family members involved as you can. Make them feel they're part of the reunion planning—and give them credit when it succeeds.**

Set up committees of family members for such items as planning, facility arrangements, entertainment, activities, food—and finances. Don't forget to choose someone with a love of family history to be in charge of collecting items for a special genealogy display. •

# successful family reunion

home, country road" or "It's family round-up time" with a western flavor.

Regardless of the theme, it could add to the reunion fun, with special dress, food and decorations.

Ideas for reunion locations are endless—the beach, a dude ranch, a Bahamas cruise, the local college dorm and cafeteria, or the hometown park.

Better yet, if you can afford to, hire a professional reunion destination planner to take care of the site details. The important thing is getting together, regardless of where that might be. Choose a location best suited to the types of people attending—considering ages, physical limitations, lifestyles, financial resources and other issues.

## Share the work and the glory

If you want to live through all of the planning and the reunion itself, you might consider setting up committees to involve as many relatives as possible.

Ask several family members to serve on the planning committee. Or assign people to various committees in the first or second reunion contact letter. The decision to use that method depends on your family and if members have been involved in reunions before. It might be safer to ask, rather than

to arbitrarily assign.

Either way, you don't have to take care of all the details yourself, nor do you have to be totally responsible for how the event goes. Share the responsibility, the work and the initial expense.

## Allow plenty of lead time

Your plan needs to include a month-by-month timetable, starting about 18 to 24 months before the reunion date, working up to the day of the reunion and then beyond for paperwork, clean-up and other recap activities.

Committee assignments would work best if everyone on a particular committee lives in the same geographic area, whether it be the same town, state or even region. It saves on travel and long-distance calling expenses during the planning process.

Obviously, facility and food arrangements committees need to be near the reunion site to look over the facilities and taste-test the food. Other committees, like registration, finances, decorating and entertainment/activities, may not need to be near the reunion site.

## Budget for expenses

Once you have a plan— whether it be a draft one or a firm one—you can develop a budget for the re-

union. The budget should include all of the costs you expect to incur in planning the reunion, big dollar items and small expenses alike. The specific budget line items will depend upon the size and location of the reunion.

Regardless of where you and your committee decide to hold the reunion, don't forget about the art of negotiating. Negotiate the prices for everything— rooms (both meeting and sleeping), meals, transportation for local tours, even the rental fee for audiovisual and other equipment.

Look for weekend or off-season package specials. The number of rooms you're reserving may make a difference in the cost of the meeting room. Obviously, the bigger the reunion, the more negotiating clout you will have.

## Plan timely contacts with family

If this is the first-ever or the first in many years for your family's reunion, you may want to survey people about possible times, themes, budget numbers, activities and other details. That way, family members will have more say in the reunion, making them more interested in attending and more willing to participate while there.

After the initial contact, plan on sending two or three additional letters,

## Out of reunion ideas? Go online!

The Internet is the place to go for reunion ideas, how-to books, and gimmicks and gifts with a reunion tie-in. Here are our favorites:

- Bookmark www. reuniontips.com as a "favorite" site. Besides suggestions for your reunion, you'll find a highly recommended how-to book on holding a family gathering: "Family Reunion Handbook" by Tom Ninkovich. To order, visit the Website above or call 800-289-0963.

- Another great site is that of The Family Reunion Institute. Visit www.temple. edu/fri/familyreunion/ organize.html for practical tips on everything from forming a family association to creating a heritage quilt.

- For a free booklet called "The Family Reunion Planning Guide," check out www.reunionwear. com/php/guide.php and fill out the online registration. Also check out their t-shirts and over 70 family reunion logos.

- www.family-reunion. com bills itself as "the Web's most popular family reunion planning site." On it you can order "Family Reunion Organizer," a software program that covers nearly everything pertaining to family reunions. •

## Use reunion to display, take photos

Family reunions are great places to display old family photos—and to snap new ones! They're also an ideal time to get those old "Mr. and Mrs. I. Dunno" photos identified by other family members. Rather than have the pictures lying loose, arrange them in acid-free plastic photo protectors that fit into three-ring binders and set them on a display table. Instead of bringing the originals of your antique photos, reproduce them (by using your digital camera, perhaps) before displaying them at the reunion. Invite reunion attendees to bring their photos, as well. Be ready to take orders for reprints of some especially treasured photos of a common ancestor. •

## Reunions can be genealogy generators

• One of your primary goals at your reunion should be to display items you've already gleaned about your joint family history—and to collect new information.

• Have a booth or table containing the following: a family tree or wall chart (including all known branches of those attending your reunion), old family photographs, and filled-out pedigree charts and family group sheets.

• Have blank family group sheets and pedigree charts on hand so that those who have not as yet filled one out can do so at the reunion—and turn them over to you for inclusion in a forthcoming family history book.

• Collect memories from old-timers at your reunion. You may wish to have them deliver a talk about the "good old days." Or invite them to write down their memories for distribution at the reunion. •

depending on the planning timetable you're working under. These letters will serve to build enthusiasm for the reunion.

An option to the letters would be setting up a reunion e-mail address and Web page. This will work only if a large number of family members are computer-literate and have access to the Internet.

After the initial survey, your next letter must include dates, times and location to give people plenty of time to plan their vacation from work and to save money for the reunion and the travel involved.

You also need to provide hotel, campground, and travel options in this contact. Try to find group travel discounts for more than one person traveling from the same area at the same time.

If not in the first letter, the second letter must include the registration cost and deadline dates for early and late registration. Keep in mind that advance registrations will help finance the mailings and other up-front expenses for the reunion. However, the cost difference must be sig-

nificant enough to influence people to register early.

At this point in the planning process, it would be good to provide the tourism department in the state where the reunion will be held with the names and addresses of reunion attendees. This office can then mail state tourist and events information directly to the individuals.

The second letter should also include at least a preliminary schedule for reunion activities. It might offer attendees a choice of tours and other activities to satisfy many interests, ages and lifestyles.

Suggested activities might be icebreakers, a Family Olympics, whether it be sports-related or intellectual, or more structured sessions and demonstrations on computer genealogy, genealogical research ideas or sharing family health history.

Sitting around and listening to the elders' stories can be a wonderful addition to any reunion. Videotaping and/or audiotaping these sessions gives others a chance to hear the stories.

However, resist the temptation to fill every minute of the reunion with activities—let people just sit around and visit and catch up with one another. Depending upon where people are coming from, some may even need to catch up from jet lag.

If you plan to sell reunion souvenirs, that order information could be included in the first or second letter. Souvenirs might include mugs,

t-shirts, key rings or other items with the reunion name, date and place on them. Or sell videos of previous reunions.

Hold an auction where family members contribute white-elephant and other items. Compiling a cookbook of favorite family recipes contributed at previous reunions can be a profitable fundraiser. You can use all of these sales to help cover the reunion planning expenses.

A third letter would include all of the final details for the reunion—including dates, location, schedule for entertainment and activities, total cost, and what to bring (food, genealogy information, photos, games, etc.).

With this contact, food assignments (if meals will not be served by the reunion facility or otherwise catered) can be made using a system similar to the following: main entrees—last names beginning with A-E; vegetables/side dishes—F-J; breads/rolls—K-L; salads—M-Q; desserts—R-V, and beverages—W-Z.

The breakdown will depend on the number of different surnames in your family group. The decision to make food assignments will also depend on how far people are traveling, whether the reunion is being held in a city where supermarkets and delis are available, or if there are cooking equipment and utensils at the reunion site.

This last contact could also invite last-minute registrations, but at a higher fee than earlier ones.

# Finally, it's reunion time

After all that planning, the day is finally here. Now what? Organization is the key for a successful event—whether it be registration, activities or meals. You already know who's coming to the reunion, so ask some of them to help with the various duties during the reunion.

You could set up shifts at the registration table and at the souvenir booth. Ask someone who's a good joke or story-teller or public speaker to emcee the program.

Line up the best photographer and videographer in the family to take photos and videos to record the event for posterity. After all, that's what a reunion is about, isn't it? The photos and videos will become precious family mementos.

Most importantly, don't try to do it all yourself!

People want to help—they just need to be asked.

And remember those binders full of genealogy information we talked about at the beginning of this section? Don't forget to take them to the reunion—they'll be a hit on the display table!

In fact, print out extra copies of the pedigree charts and other items for people to take home with them. They will appreciate it beyond measure. •

# Share your ethnic story

• One of your reunion goals should be to tell your family's unique heritage story. You can build your theme around your ethnic roots. Try featuring ethnic decorations, flags, music and foods, maps of the Old Country pinpointing your family's origins, plus family memorabilia that ties in with your heritage. •

# SAMPLE REUNION TIME-TABLE

• **18 to 24 months before:** Send survey to determine interest; talk to past reunion organizers; attend reunion organizing workshop if necessary; develop reunion checklist; prepare mailing list; form committee; consider hiring reunion planner; develop recordkeeping system and budget; visit possible locations and facilities; set date(s) and choose location and theme if any; reserve reunion facility; send first letter with date(s), location and preliminary cost.

• **12 months before:** Arrange for entertainment, caterer, photographer and videographer; decide on souvenirs; finalize menu choices; send second letter with registration form, cost, registration deadlines, preliminary activity schedule, souvenir order form and list of missing persons; reserve block of rooms at hotel; review reunion checklist.

• **6 to 9 months before:** Send reunion announcement to appropriate media; schedule awards, activities and tours; prepare preliminary list of attendees; finalize menu choices; adjust numbers for block of rooms if necessary; review reunion checklist.

• **5 months before:** Confirm with facility, entertainment, caterer, photographer and videographer; send letter to newly located people; send third letter to others with final details, what to bring and food assignments if necessary; update list of attendees; review reunion checklist.

• **2 to 4 months before:** Meet with hotel staff; select decorations, signs, banners and other printed items; reserve rental equipment; update attendee list; review checklist.

• **6 weeks before:** Update attendee list; make duty assignments for volunteers; send last letter with final details; update attendee list; review checklist.

• **2 weeks before:** Complete registration list and program and deliver to printer; purchase decorations and other supplies (name tags, pens, tape, scissors, etc.); reconfirm accommodations; review reunion checklist.

• **1 week before:** Determine facility staff contacts for reunion day(s); review final details with committee; assemble registration packets; review reunion checklist.

• **Day of reunion:** Set up registration tables, rental equipment, souvenir booth, displays, etc.; decorate; enjoy!

• **After reunion:** Reflect and evaluate; complete bookkeeping and settle accounts; write thank you notes to volunteers, facility staff, etc.; make changes in reunion checklist if necessary; start planning next reunion. •

UNITY AND FREEDOM

# Our ancestors wore coats— of armor!

## Heraldry helpers

- Read books on heraldry to learn more about this fascinating subject! You can also check out heraldry sites on the Internet. •

Ever wondered whether an ancestor of yours may have sported a coat of arms? Heraldry was big business in the days of our forefathers and mothers. And it still is!

Today, heraldry is a worldwide phenomenon— with heraldic emblems used on everything from family crests and company logos to flags of nations.

Heraldry is the science of armory, or the systematic arrangement of devices on a shield. Heraldic shields are commonly referred to as "family crests," "family shields," or "coats of arms." The shield is the basic element of the armorial bearing.

What sets heraldic shields apart from shields of ancient warriors is that they were hereditary, handed down from father to son (or sometimes daughter). Heraldry thus has ties to genealogy and, in some cases, can yield genealogical information.

## History of heraldry

Experts are divided on the origins of heraldry. The most commonly touted theory is that emblems on shields were used to help identify medieval battle participants. Others argue that such devices would have been hard to spot in the thick of battle, and, instead, may have been decorations or individual identification symbols.

No matter heraldry's origins, it took root during the period of enlightenment known as the 12th century renaissance—about the time medieval knights began vying in tournaments. These early jousting bouts served as military training for knights, as well as for their horses. Later, the tournaments became glorified spectator sports, full of pomp and pageantry, with strict rules governing the design and display of arms, as well as the competitions themselves.

Once the heraldic flame was lit, it quickly spread over Europe and the British

## Don't fall for 'heraldry hype'

If you receive a letter inviting you to purchase your family's "authentic" coat of arms, beware! You could be the target of a heraldry scam. Some firms, passing themselves off as reputable, send direct-mail solicitations claiming they can furnish your coat of arms—for a price.

Rather than doing the intensive research required to determine whether your ancestor was the bearer of arms, such firms may supply you with a generic shield—one they concoct themselves. The literature they include with the trumped-up shield is generic, as well.

Or they may provide you with a copy of a shield that was granted to someone with your surname—but one that has no connection to your family. Not every family had a shield. And, in cases involving a commonly used surname, there may be a number of shields for that name.

Keep in mind that coats of arms were not granted to families or names, but to individuals. Therefore, there's no such thing as a coat of arms belonging to a certain surname—contrary to what these "pretender" firms would have you believe.

Coats of arms were generally handed down from father to eldest son, in a continuous line. If you are a descendant of a second or third son, or of a daughter, you may not be able to legally claim that particular shield.

Even if you're not officially "entitled" to a coat of arms, it's still fun to discover a shield bearing your surname. And, if you explore its history, you may find it was once borne by an ancestor. So keep looking for the family connection. •

# Tournament garb served as model for coats of arms

**P**erhaps the simplest way to make sense of armorial bearings is to imagine a knight, dressed in armor, going forth to compete in a tournament.

Here's what your typical well-dressed knight wore to the tournaments: From head to toe, he was dressed in armor. Wrapped around the armor was a fabric coat—called his coat of arms—to protect his suit of mail from cold, heat and rain. This coat was decorated with a design uniquely his. You might say this was his "logo." Even the knight's horse wore a fabric garment bearing his master's logo.

The knight's shield was painted

with the same design as on the coat covering his armor. A helmet covered his head and face. On top of his helmet was a crest (or a crown). This crest was a three-dimensional object, a figure or a distinctive shape, made of a light-weight material. The crest was strapped onto the helmet. A rope-like wreath of twisted silk attached to the top of the helmet and the base of the crest.

Knights also wore a "mantle" to protect their helmets in hot and cold weather. This cloth cascaded down the back and sides of the helmet. You might also imagine two squires, or supporters, one on each side, carrying the knight's weaponry.

Based on these tournament trappings, a drawing of the knight's family arms includes the **shield,** topped by the **helmet,** on which sits the **wreath**, and a **crest or crown.** The shield usually adds a **mantle** draped from the crest and flowing down the sides of the shield. Fanciful **supporters** (ranging from monsters and humans to composite creatures) at either side appear to "support" the shield.

Together, the elements of a complete coat of arms—crest, crown, mantling, shield, supporters, and motto (used in some instances)—are called an **achievement.** •

---

Isles. The Crusades further enhanced its influence.

Heraldry fulfilled three purposes: to identify the bearer (and his or her family connections), to serve as a mark of ownership (like a brand or a logo), and to act as a decorative motif.

The emblem used on shields soon spread to other objects—such as flags, jewelry, clothing, furnishings, china, and silverware. After a man died, his coat of arms outlived him—appearing on his tombstone or in a stained glass cathedral window as a memorial.

By the 13th century, heraldry had acquired rules and its own language. Men called "heralds" were appointed to identify heraldic devices and to make

sure no two men bore the same shield. By 1300, heraldic books such as "De Heraudie" contained descriptions of arms. Over the centuries, many such books recorded the armorial bearings of families of Europe and Great Britain.

In the 15th century in France and England, heraldic colleges were formed, with permanent headquarters and libraries. Officers of arms kept heraldic records and issued new grants for arms. Rules of heraldry became formalized and regulated.

When medieval warfare ceased in the late 15th century, heraldry continued to flourish. Regional differences emerged as strong monarchies formed their

own colleges of arms.

In the late 1600s, a conservative movement all but snuffed out the heraldic flame. But it was rekindled in the 1700s following a revival of interest in the Middle Ages.

During the late 1700s, heraldry was abolished in France when the shield, considered a symbol of the aristocracy, was targeted by French Revolutionaries. Heraldry was re-established in France in 1814, with the French again free to adopt the arms of their choice.

In the New World, many colonists used whatever arms they pleased. Later, American Revolutionary War Patriots—considered traitors by the

## Heraldry helpers

• Beware of companies claiming to issue authentic coats of arms by mail. The arms they send you are almost always improvised or generic, with no connection to your family. •

**DID YOU KNOW...**
The first known genealogy-heraldry connection is recorded in 1170 . A book dating from that time describes King Henry I as giving his son-in-law, Geoffrey Plantagenet, in 1127, a blue shield with three gold lions. Geoffrey's tomb plate shows this same shield. Geoffrey's grandson, William Longespee, Earl of Salisbury, died in 1226. His tomb is decked with an identical shield design. •

## Pun intended!

- Design your own coat of arms! Decorate your shield with charges representing a family legend, or a sport your family enjoys. If you have a surname such as Wolf or Horne, use "canting arms," featuring designs representing your name. Have pun—er, fun!!! •

English—were denied rights to heraldic shields.

To this day, the U.S. government does not recognize or issue coats of arms. The authenticity of an armorial bearing is determined by laws prevailing in the country in which it was granted.

Heraldic authorities no longer govern the arms of Europe. The English Kings of Arms, however, still follow strict heraldic rules and continue to grant new armorial bearings.

## Crest quest

There are lots of great books on heraldry. If you're interested in the subject, head for the library or check the Internet. Even if you don't find your own family crest, you'll learn something about the lore, the language, and the laws of heraldry and its links with genealogy.

A good place to start is the "Armorial General," a multi-volume set of books, published in 1696, containing thousands of family crests. The books contain illustrations and heraldic descriptions of shields used by the families of Europe, many dating back to the Crusades.

If you have located a registered English coat of arms that you feel you're entitled to claim, you can apply to the College of Arms in England. To qualify for existing arms, you must prove your direct descent through male lines from the original bearer of those arms.

You can also design your very own coat of arms, perhaps based on your own family's history, your occupation, or a pun on your surname. To register it, you can apply to an armorial college—or have it copyrighted to protect your design.

An excellent book to help you design your own family crest is Rosemary A. Chorzempa's "Design Your Own Coat of Arms: An Introduction to Heraldry." This book also serves as a primer on heraldic terms and rules. •

## The language and laws of heraldry

The language of heraldry is Old Norman French, used by scholars when heraldry began. Each coat of arms is described in technical terms called **blazoning.** Strict rules determined elements placed on a shield. Most important was that each shield differed from others.

In English heraldry, each legitimate son received a specific mark of **differencing (or cadency)** to place over a replica of his father's coat of arms, according to his birth order. The oldest sported a label (usually, a horizontal bar with three legs), which was removed when the father died and the son inherited his father's arms. The second son had a crescent, the third a star, and so on. Illegitimate sons had a special mark, such as a diagonal line, across their shield.

By courtesy, daughters were allowed to use their father's arms, but on a diamond-shaped shield called a **lozenge.** When they married, they were allowed to place their coat of arms beside their husband's, **impaled** on his shield.

Daughters could inherit coats of arms if there were no sons. When their father died, they became heraldic heiresses and could place their family shield in the middle of their husband's shield—a practice called **escutcheon of pretence.**

There are three basic **tinctures** found in heraldry: metals (gold and silver), colors (red, blue, sable, green, and purple), and fur.

Some shields were plain, but usually a **charge,** or ornamental device, was placed on the shield. Certain principal charges were called **ordinaries.** These included bold linear shapes such as crosses, stripes, and diagonal bars. Lesser charges were called **subordinaries.** Charges called **augmentations** were added to symbolize a brave feat or a family legend. Flora and fauna—in stylized, fantasy or composite form—were among the more ornamental devices used on shields.

Many shields contained puns of the owners' names. These were called **canting arms.** Examples from history include the spear on the Shakespeare arms, and the dolphin on the shield of the dauphin (future king) of France. •

**LOOKING
FOR
ANCESTORS**

# Charts map your family's history

- Pedigree charts map out the skeleton of a genealogy. They come in many different formats.

- Family group sheets provide the details of the pedigree chart. When completed, these sheets can be a valuable tool for writing your family history.

- Both forms let you see where you're going and what you need to search for next. Photocopies of your charts can also easily be exchanged with others who are tracing the same families. •

# HOW TO USE THE PEDIGREE CHART & FAMILY GROUP SHEETS

## PEDIGREE CHART

The pedigree chart on the next page will help you chart your progress and help you visualize what data you still need to collect. Use it as a master copy; have multiple photocopies made, then record your information on one of the copies. Use your copies as working documents, adding to them and making changes as needed.

Take them with you when you visit a Family History Center, archives, library, or courthouse. This will enable anyone looking at the chart to see what information you need to look up to fill in the blanks.

When you've filled your chart(s) in completely, you can then make separate, permanent pedigree charts. The following information will guide you in filling them out:

- Begin with yourself, putting your name (or your spouse's name, if you're doing his/her pedigree chart) in Blank No. 1.

- Record the male (paternal) names at the top of each group of lines; the females (maternal) on the lines beneath the male names. Enter names in this order: given name, middle name, last name (surname).

- Enter the date in day/month/year order. Write the year as four digits; spell the month out completely, or use standard abbreviation (don't record months as numbers).

- When you get to the end of one of your lines on your first sheet, begin a second sheet, numbering that one Chart No. 2. Continue with as many charts as you need to complete your pedigree.

- Note that the father's number will always be double that of the child. For example: The father of person No. 7 on your pedigree chart would be No. 14; the father of person No. 124 would be No. 248. The mother's number is her husband's number plus 1. (Thus the wife of person No. 248 would be No. 249.)

- Our sample sheet is numbered from 1 to 15; ancestors listed on successive sheets will have new, higher, numbers.

- Keep in mind that genealogy pedigree charts come in many forms. If you'd rather "start big," you can order 12- and 15-generation pedigree charts from genealogy supply houses (see address section of the appendix).

Pedigree charts and family group sheets are living documents that change as people marry and start new families, as divorces occur, as family members die, as you uncover a new ancestor, etc. That means they'll need updating. •

## FAMILY GROUP SHEET

Begin by making front-and-back copies of the two-sided master family group sheets on the following pages. Fill out one of the copies for your own immediate family. Fill out a second one for your parents and their children; another for your brothers' or sisters' families, aunts' or uncles' families, etc. Fill them out as completely as you can, using the following tips to guide you:

- Record names in full. If you run out of room for recording one family, continue on another sheet.

- Record maiden names of all females.

- Record dates in the order of day, month and year. Don't use numbers for months; use four digits for year, as in: 28 Jan. 1837.

- Record places from smallest to largest, as in: Bismarck, Burleigh Co., North Dakota, USA.

- Record the sources of the data you enter. For example: A birth date may have come from a birth certificate; marriage statistics from an LDS Family History Center microfilm; a death date from a tombstone in a particular cemetery. List these sources (plus film number if applicable ) on your chart.

- Never record data on more than one family on a single group sheet; use additional group sheets.

- If a person was married more than once, use a separate group sheet for recording the families of each marriage. •.

# PEDIGREE CHART

- B. = birth
- M. = marriage
- D. = death
- Pl. = place

CHART # _____

Date compiled: _____

Name of compiler: _____

Address: _____

City: _____

State, zip: _____

Phone: _____

E-mail: _____

## PERSON 1

(SAME PERSON AS # _____ ON CHART # _____)

Name: _____

B.date: _____

Pl: _____

M.date: _____

Pl: _____

D.date: _____

Pl: _____

## SPOUSE

Name: _____

B.date: _____

Pl: _____

D.date: _____

Pl: _____

## 2—FATHER

Name: _____

B.date: _____

Pl: _____

M.date: _____

Pl: _____

D.date: _____

Pl: _____

## 3—MOTHER

Name: _____

B.date: _____

Pl: _____

D.date: _____

Pl: _____

## 4—PATERNAL GRANDFATHER

Name: _____

B.date: _____

Pl: _____

M.date: _____

Pl: _____

D.date: _____

Pl: _____

## 5—PATERNAL GRANDMOTHER

Name: _____

B.date: _____

Pl: _____

D.date: _____

Pl: _____

## 6—MATERNAL GRANDFATHER

Name: _____

B.date: _____

Pl: _____

M.date: _____

Pl: _____

D.date: _____

Pl: _____

## 7—MATERNAL GRANDMOTHER

Name: _____

B.date: _____

Pl: _____

D.date: _____

Pl: _____

## 8—GREAT-GRANDFATHER

Name: _____

B.date: _____ Pl: _____

M.date: _____ Pl: _____

D.date: _____ Pl: _____

## 9—GREAT-GRANDMOTHER

Name: _____

B.date: _____ Pl: _____

D.date: _____ Pl: _____

## 10—GREAT-GRANDFATHER

Name: _____

B.date: _____ Pl: _____

M.date: _____ Pl: _____

D.date: _____ Pl: _____

## 11—GREAT-GRANDMOTHER

Name: _____

B.date: _____ Pl: _____

D.date: _____ Pl: _____

## 12—GREAT-GRANDFATHER

Name: _____

B.date: _____ Pl: _____

M.date: _____ Pl: _____

D.date: _____ Pl: _____

## 13—GREAT-GRANDMOTHER

Name: _____

B.date: _____ Pl: _____

D.date: _____ Pl: _____

## 14—GREAT-GRANDFATHER

Name: _____

B.date: _____ Pl: _____

M.date: _____ Pl: _____

D.date: _____ Pl: _____

## 15—GREAT-GRANDMOTHER

Name: _____

B.date: _____ Pl: _____

D.date: _____ Pl: _____

# FAMILY GROUP SHEET—Side 1

## HUSBAND

Birth date _____ Place _____
Marriage date _____ Place _____
Death date _____ Place _____
Burial date _____ Place _____
Other spouse(s) _____

**FATHER**
Name _____
B. _____ Place _____
M. _____ Place _____
D. _____ Place _____

**GRANDFATHER**
Name: _____

**GRANDMOTHER**
Name: _____

**MOTHER**
Name _____
B. _____ Place _____
D. _____ Place _____

**GRANDFATHER**
Name: _____

**GRANDMOTHER**
Name: _____

COMMENTS: _____

## WIFE

Birth date _____ Place _____
Death date _____ Place _____
Burial date _____ Place _____
Other spouse(s) _____

**FATHER**
Name _____
B. _____ Place _____
M. _____ Place _____
D. _____ Place _____

**GRANDFATHER**
Name: _____

**GRANDMOTHER**
Name: _____

**MOTHER**
Name _____
B. _____ Place _____
D. _____ Place _____

**GRANDFATHER**
Name: _____

**GRANDMOTHER**
Name: _____

| | Sex | Child's given name | Surname | Dates | Town/county/state/country | First spouse |
|---|---|---|---|---|---|---|
| 1 | | | | B. ___ M. ___ D. ___ | | B. ___ D. ___ |
| 2 | | | | B. ___ M. ___ D. ___ | | B. ___ D. ___ |
| 3 | | | | B. ___ M. ___ D. ___ | | B. ___ D. ___ |
| 4 | | | | B. ___ M. ___ D. ___ | | B. ___ D. ___ |
| 5 | | | | B. ___ M. ___ D. ___ | | B. ___ D. ___ |
| 6 | | | | B. ___ M. ___ D. ___ | | B. ___ D. ___ |
| 7 | | | | B. ___ M. ___ D. ___ | | B. ___ D. ___ |

# FAMILY GROUP SHEET—Side 2

(Continued from Sheet 1)

HUSBAND _____

WIFE _____

| Sex | Child's given name | Surname | Dates | Town/county/state/country | First spouse |
|---|---|---|---|---|---|
| 8 | | | B.___ M.___ D.___ | | B.___ D.___ |
| 9 | | | B.___ M.___ D.___ | | B.___ D.___ |
| 10 | | | B.___ M.___ D.___ | | B.___ D.___ |
| 11 | | | B.___ M.___ D.___ | | B.___ D.___ |
| 12 | | | B.___ M.___ D.___ | | B.___ D.___ |
| 13 | | | B.___ M.___ D.___ | | B.___ D.___ |
| 14 | | | B.___ M.___ D.___ | | B.___ D.___ |
| 15 | | | B.___ M.___ D.___ | | B.___ D.___ |
| 16 | | | B.___ M.___ D.___ | | B.___ D.___ |

NOTES: _____

Date: _____

Sheet compiled by: _____

Address: _____

SOURCES: _____

Tracing Your Dakota Roots • APPENDIX A—Forms • 149

# RESEARCH LOG

ANCESTOR'S NAME _____

| Date of search | Collection/call no. (microfilm no., etc.) | Source description (country, book, film, title, type of document, etc.) | Results of search |
|---|---|---|---|
| | | | |
| | | | |
| | | | |
| | | | |
| | | | |
| | | | |
| | | | |
| | | | |
| | | | |
| | | | |
| | | | |
| | | | |
| | | | |
| | | | |
| | | | |
| | | | |
| | | | |
| | | | |
| | | | |

# CORRESPONDENCE LOG

| Date of letter | Money/ check no. | Sent to: (name, address) | Reason for letter (subject) | Results/reply (date of reply) |
|---|---|---|---|---|
| | | | | |
| | | | | |
| | | | | |
| | | | | |
| | | | | |
| | | | | |
| | | | | |
| | | | | |
| | | | | |
| | | | | |
| | | | | |
| | | | | |
| | | | | |
| | | | | |
| | | | | |
| | | | | |
| | | | | |
| | | | | |
| | | | | |
| | | | | |

# REQUEST FOR COPY OF BIRTH CERTIFICATE
## NORTH DAKOTA DEPARTMENT OF HEALTH
## DIVISION OF VITAL RECORDS
SFN 8140 (Rev. 03-98)

**PLEASE PRINT - ALL ITEMS MUST BE COMPLETED FOR US TO LOCATE AND IDENTIFY THE RECORD**

| 1. Full Name at Birth | 2. Sex |
|---|---|
| | ☐ Male ☐ Female |

| 3. Date of Birth (Month, Day, Year) | 4. Place of Birth (City or Township) | County |
|---|---|---|

| 5. Residence of Parents at Time of this Birth (City & State) | 6. Order of Birth (1st Child, 2nd, etc.) |
|---|---|

7. Full Name of Father (First, Middle, Last)

8. Full Name of Mother (First, Middle, Maiden)

| 9. Certificate for An Adopted Child ☐ Yes ☐ No | 10. Purpose of Requested Copy |
|---|---|

11. Type of Copy Desired
☐ Paper Copy ☐ Plastic Birth Card - (Birth card **may not** be acceptable for travel outside the U.S.)

| 12. Your Relationship to Person on Line 1 * | 13. Fee Enclosed (see schedule) $ | No. of Copies |
|---|---|---|

* Birth certificates relating to an out of wedlock birth can be furnished only to the parent of the child, the child's guardian, to the person to whom the record relates if that person is at least 18 years old, or upon order of a court of competent jurisdiction.

## This Section Is To Be Completed By Person Making Request

Signature

| Printed Name | Daytime Telephone Number ( ) |
|---|---|

| Address | Apartment No. | City | State | Zip Code |
|---|---|---|---|---|

## If Copy Is To Be Mailed Elsewhere

Name

| Address | Apartment No. | City | State | Zip Code |
|---|---|---|---|---|

### FEE SCHEDULE

The fee for a search of the files is $7.00; one search fee pays for one certified copy. Additional copies of the same certificate issued at the same time are $4.00 each. (Two dollars of this fee is used to support the Children's Trust Fund, a state fund for aiding in the prevention of child abuse and neglect.)

NOTE: Make all checks or money orders payable to "NORTH DAKOTA DEPARTMENT OF HEALTH". Cash is sent at your own risk!

Mail Request with fee to:
**NORTH DAKOTA DEPARTMENT OF HEALTH
VITAL RECORDS
STATE CAPITOL
600 E BOULEVARD AVE DEPT 301
BISMARCK ND 58505-0200**

**WARNING:** ND Century Code Chapter 23-02.1.32. Penalties. (c) Any person who willfully and knowingly uses or attempts to use or to furnish to another for use, for any purpose of deception, any certificate, record, report, or certified copy thereof so made, altered, amended, or mutilated shall be guilty of a class A misdemeanor.

## THIS PORTION FOR VITAL RECORDS OFFICE USE ONLY

## REQUEST FOR COPY OF MARRIAGE RECORD
NORTH DAKOTA DEPARTMENT OF HEALTH
DIVISION OF VITAL RECORDS
SFN 8141 (12-97)

**PLEASE PRINT - ALL ITEMS MUST BE COMPLETED FOR US TO LOCATE AND IDENTIFY THE RECORD**

| Full Name of Groom | Full Maiden Name of Bride | | |
|---|---|---|---|
| Residence of Groom At Marriage (City & State) | Residence of Bride At Marriage (City & State) | | |
| Date of Marriage (Mo/Day/Year) | County Where License Issued | City Where Married | County Where Married |
| For What Purpose is Copy Needed | | | Fee Enclosed (see schedule) $ |
| Your Relationship to Groom/Bride (e.g., self, parent, attorney-specify) | | | Number of Copies |

**This Section Is To Be Completed By Person Making Request**

| Signature | | | | |
|---|---|---|---|---|
| Printed Name | | | Daytime Telephone Number ( ) | |
| Address | Apt. No. | City | State | Zip Code |

**THIS PORTION FOR VITAL RECORDS OFFICE USE ONLY**

Original Licenses and Certificates of Marriage are filed in the office of the **Clerk of District Court** of the **COUNTY WHERE LICENSE WAS ISSUED**. It is recommended that requests for certified copies be directed to the custodian of the underlined original record.

The fee for the county offices is $10 for one copy and $5 for each additional copy issued of the same certificate at the same time.

See reverse side of this form for a list of the North Dakota counties, respective county seats, addresses, and zip codes.

• • • • • • • • • • • • • • • • • • • • • • • • •

Since July 1, 1925, copies of Licenses and Certificates of Marriage have been forwarded to the State Registrar for statistical purposes and for maintaining a state-wide index. The state office is also authorized to issue certified copies. For marriages which have occurred since July 1, 1925, you may secure copies from the County Office (as noted above) or from address listed below.

The fee at the State Vital Records Office is $5 for one copy and $2 for each additional copy issued of the same certificate at the same time.

Mail request with fee to:

NORTH DAKOTA DEPARTMENT OF HEALTH
DIVISION OF VITAL RECORDS
STATE CAPITOL, 600 EAST BOULEVARD AVENUE
BISMARCK, NORTH DAKOTA 58505-0200

**REQUEST FOR COPY OF DEATH CERTIFICATE**
NORTH DAKOTA DEPARTMENT OF HEALTH
DIVISION OF VITAL RECORDS
SFN 5531 (6-95)

**PLEASE PRINT - ALL ITEMS MUST BE COMPLETED FOR US TO LOCATE AND IDENTIFY THE RECORD**

| Full Name of Deceased | Sex ☐ Male ☐ Female |
|---|---|
| Date of Death (Month, Day, Year) | Name of Spouse | |

| Place of Death (Name of Hospital) | City | County |
|---|---|---|

| Your Relationship to the Deceased* | Name of Funeral Home |
|---|---|

\* The <u>cause of death</u> on death certificates is by law confidential and copies showing the cause of death are to be furnished only to a relative or personal representative of the deceased, to the attorney or the agent of a relative or personal representative of the deceased or upon order of a court of competent jurisdiction.

| For what purpose is this copy requested? | Amount Enclosed (see fee schduled below) $ | No. of Certified Copies |
|---|---|---|

**This Section Is To Be Completed By Person Making Request**

| Signature | |
|---|---|
| Printed Name | Telephone Number ( ) |

| Address | City | State | Zip Code |
|---|---|---|---|

**If Copy Is To Be Mailed Elsewhere**

| Name | | | |
|---|---|---|---|
| Address | City | State | Zip Code |

**THIS PORTION FOR VITAL RECORD'S OFFICE USE ONLY**

<u>The fee for a search of the files is $5</u>; one search fee pays for one certified copy. Additional copies of the same certificate issued at the same time are $2 each.

NOTE:  Make all checks or money orders payable to the "NORTH DAKOTA DEPARTMENT OF HEALTH" Cash is sent at your own risk!

Mail request with fee to:

NORTH DAKOTA DEPARTMENT OF HEALTH
DIVISION OF VITAL RECORDS
STATE CAPITOL, 600 EAST BOULEVARD AVENUE
BISMARCK, NORTH DAKOTA 58505-0200

**VITAL RECORDS**
**South Dakota Department of Health**
**600 E. Capitol Ave.**
**Pierre, SD 57501-2536**
**(605) 773-4961**
**www.state.sd.us/doh/VitalRec/Vital.htm**

| | |
|---|---|
| **BIRTH** | FULL NAME AT BIRTH OR ADOPTIVE NAME _____<br><br>DATE OF BIRTH (Month, Day & Year) _____<br><br>PLACE OF BIRTH (City & County) _____<br><br>FATHER'S FULL NAME _____<br><br>MOTHER'S FULL MAIDEN NAME _____<br><br>_____<br>(Signature of person requesting record) |
| **DEATH** | FULL NAME AT TIME OF DEATH _____<br><br>DATE OF DEATH (Month, Day & Year) _____<br><br>PLACE OF DEATH  (City & County) _____ |
| **MARRIAGE** | FULL NAME OF GROOM _____<br><br>FULL NAME OF BRIDE _____<br><br>DATE OF MARRIAGE (Month, Day & Year) _____<br><br>WHERE LICENSE WAS OBTAINED _____ |
| **DIVORCE** | FULL NAME OF HUSBAND _____<br><br>FULL NAME OF WIFE _____<br><br>DATE OF DIVORCE (Month, Day & Year) _____<br><br>PLACE OF DIVORCE _____ |

<u>PRINT OR TYPE</u> NAME AND ADDRESS OF PERSON TO WHOM CERTIFICATE IS TO BE SENT

_____
(Name)

_____
(Street or Box)

_____
(City, State and Zip+)

HAS-0252   REV. 8/97

**SEE REVERSE SIDE FOR FEE SCHEDULE**

**NOTE:**
**See information on reverse side of this page.**

LEAHM.VIRECORD.VIT

# —FEE SCHEDULE—
# SOUTH DAKOTA VITAL STATISTICS

**VITAL RECORDS • South Dakota Department of Health**
600 E. Capitol Ave. • Pierre, SD 57501-2536 • (605) 773-4961
www.state.sd.us/doh/VitalRec/Vital.htm

By state law, vital records filed in the state of South Dakota are not open for public inspection. The State Vital Records Office in the Department of Health can issue either an informational or a certified copy of a vital record. Applicants must meet eligibility requirements to obtain certified copies.

## Informational copies

Anyone who submits an application and the applicable fee can obtain an informational copy of a vital record. Informational copies are issued on plain paper and contain the statement "For Informational Purposes only. Not for legal proof of identification." Informational copies do not contain a raised seal or the signature of the issuing agent. When possible, all informational copies are issued from the computer unless a photocopy of the original is specifically requested. ARSD 44:09:06

## Certified copies

Eligible individuals who submit an application and the applicable fee can obtain a certified copy of a vital record. When possible, the record will be computer generated and issued on security paper with a raised seal and the signature of the issuing agent. Applicants can request a photo copy of the original when the computer generated copy does not contain the needed information.

## Requesting records

The information requested for each type of record is essential for searching our files and locating the record you are requesting. For birth records, we need the exact date of birth; for death, marriage, and divorce records, we need the approximate date. Please be as specific as possible.

If you are ordering a record for genealogy purposes, please place your order directly through the mail. The mail order process is designed to allow flexibility with possible different spellings or dates and will ensure a more accurate search with a greater chance of the record being found. You will be required to complete and sign an application for the appropriate vital records (birth, death, marriage), submit the appropriate fee and provide proof of identity. Per ARSD 44:09:06:02, vital records are released only as certified or informational copies. Fees payable to South Dakota Department of Health.

## How to access records

• By mail to any Register of Deeds or to the State Office. Mail requests require a completed application for the appropriate vital records (birth, death, mar-riage), signed in front of a notary OR a clear copy of a photo ID, along with the appropriate fee.

• In person or by mail at the State Office, 600 E. Capitol Avenue, Pierre, SD 57501-2536. The state office is open from 8 a.m. to 5 p.m., Monday-Friday.

• By phone using a credit card by calling (605) 773-4961. There is an additional expedite fee.

• Online using a credit card at www.vitalchek.com. There is an additional expedite fee.

## Fees

Certified or informational copy of birth, death, marriage or divorce record, verification or notification of record searched (we do not have death, marriage, or divorce records filed before July of 1905) . . . . . . . . . . . . . . . . . . . . . . . . . . . . . $10.00

Expedite fee (only applies to phone and internet requests) includes shipping via regular mail, handling and electronic authentication. If Federal Express shipment is requested, customer will pay the additional shipping costs . . . . . . . . . . . . . . $11.50

Preparation and filing of a delayed birth, death or marriage certificate (fee does not include a certified or informational copy). . . . . . . . . . . . $15.00

Amending a birth, death or marriage record after 1 year after the event (fee does not include a certified or informational copy). Certified or informational copies already purchased can be exchanged at no cost. (Requires a birth, death or marriage amendment) . . . . . . . . . . . . . . . . . . $8.00

Preparation of new birth certificate with paternity (fee does not include a certified or informational copy). . . . . . . . . . . . . . . . . . . . . . . $5.00

Preparation of a new birth certificate following adoption (fee does not include a certified or informational copy) . . . . . . . . . . . . . . . . . . . . . . $10.00

*Fee waivers for Military – Head Start, school enrollment, baseball*

## Additional information

If this form and the balance of the required fee are not returned to this office within 30 days, your partial fee will be transmitted to the State General Fund. A refund cannot be made by the Health Department after it has been transferred to the General Fund. •

# —U.S. CENSUS FORMS—

The following pages contain forms for each of the U.S. censuses used between the years 1860 and 1930 (the last census to which the public has access). The census is a superior tool for finding family groups and their migration patterns.

Every 10 years, the U.S. government collects data for its "decennial census." The first U.S. census was taken in 1790 to determine representation. The first census to actually record the names and ages of members of households was in 1850, 11 years before Dakota Territory was officially formed. Succeeding censuses elicited increasingly more detailed information.

We did not include the 1890 census form on these pages, since most of the records for that census were destroyed by water used to fight a January 1921 fire that swept through the Commerce Department building in Washington, D.C., where the 1890 census records were housed. The only Dakota census data to survive the fire was that of Jefferson Township, Union County, SD. Neighboring Minnesota's Rockford Township in Wright County also came through relatively unscathed. Some records from eight other states and the

District of Columbia also survived—part of the 6,000 legible entries out of nearly 63 million enumerated. Also surviving the fire were some records on Civil War Union veterans and their widows (including those for the Dakotas).

The 1900 and 1910 censuses asked people if they were naturalized (whether they had taken out naturalization papers to become citizens), and how many years they had resided in the U.S.

The 1880, 1900, and 1920 censuses are "Soundexed," a phonetic filing system that enables seekers to find their ancestors' data even though the name may have been spelled incorrectly, and without knowing the location—county, township, etc. Less than half of the states included in the 1910 census have been Soundexed; North and South Dakota 1910 censuses are not Soundexed.

The 1930 census is the most recent census to be released as of this writing (privacy protects the records for 72 years). The 1940 census will be available in 2012. (You can, however, request information on your family from the Bureau of the Census for more recent years.) ●

## 1860 CENSUS

Post Office or
Local Community _____ County _____ State _____

Enumerator _____ Date Census Taken _____ Enumerator District # _____

Supervisor District # _____

| Written Page No. | Printed Page No. | Dwelling Number | Family Number | Name of every person whose usual place of abode on 1 June 1860 was with this family | Description | | | Profession, Occupation, or Trade of each person over 15 | Value of Real Estate Owned | Value of Personal Estate Owned | Place of Birth naming state, territory or country | Married within the year | In school within the year | Persons over 20 unable to read & write | Deaf & dumb, blind, insane, idiotic, pauper, or convict |
|---|---|---|---|---|---|---|---|---|---|---|---|---|---|---|---|
| | | | | | Age | Sex | Color | | | | | | | | |
| | | 1 | 2 | 3 | 4 | 5 | 6 | 7 | 8 | 9 | 10 | 11 | 12 | 13 | 14 |
| | | | | | | | | | | | | | | | |
| | | | | | | | | | | | | | | | |
| | | | | | | | | | | | | | | | |
| | | | | | | | | | | | | | | | |
| | | | | | | | | | | | | | | | |
| | | | | | | | | | | | | | | | |
| | | | | | | | | | | | | | | | |
| | | | | | | | | | | | | | | | |
| | | | | | | | | | | | | | | | |
| | | | | | | | | | | | | | | | |
| | | | | | | | | | | | | | | | |
| | | | | | | | | | | | | | | | |
| | | | | | | | | | | | | | | | |

*Appendix F: Form #8. 1860 Census*

# 1870 CENSUS OF THE UNITED STATES

Date of Search_____

Legibility of Record: ☐ ☐
Good Poor

Original Copy ☐
Extract Copy ☐
Microfilm Copy ☐
Printed Copy ☐

(For those who use the Calendar Method of keeping research notes)

Search No._____

Enclosure No._____

Call No._____

Notes:_____

Place of Enumeration:_____

| Page | Dwelling No. | Family No. | Names | Age | Sex | Color | Occupation, etc. | Value–Real Estate | Value–Personal Property | Birthplace | Father foreign bn. | Mother foreign bn. | Month born in year | Month married in year | School in year | Can't read or write | Eligible to vote | Date of Enumeration | Remarks |
|---|---|---|---|---|---|---|---|---|---|---|---|---|---|---|---|---|---|---|---|
| | | | | | | | | | | | | | | | | | | | |
| | | | | | | | | | | | | | | | | | | | |
| | | | | | | | | | | | | | | | | | | | |
| | | | | | | | | | | | | | | | | | | | |

# 1880 CENSUS

Local Community _____ County _____ State _____

Enumerator _____ Date Census Taken _____ Supervisor District # _____

Enumerator District # _____

| Written Page No. | Printed Page No. | Street Name | House Number | Dwelling Number | Family Number | Name of every person whose place of abode on 1 June 1880 was in this family | Description | | | Month born if during census year | Relationship to head of this household | Single | Married | Widowed/Divorced | Married during year | Profession, Occupation or Trade | Months unemployed this year | Health | | | | | | School this year | Cannot read | Cannot write | Birthplace | Birthplace of Father | Birthplace of Mother |
|---|---|---|---|---|---|---|---|---|---|---|---|---|---|---|---|---|---|---|---|---|---|---|---|---|---|---|---|---|---|
| | | | | | | | Color | Sex | Age | | | | | | | | | Currently ill? If so, specify. | Blind | Deaf & dumb | Idiotic | Insane | Disabled | | | | | | |
| | | | | 1 | 2 | 3 | 4 | 5 | 6 | 7 | 8 | 9 | 10 | 11 | 12 | 13 | 14 | 15 | 16 | 17 | 18 | 19 | 20 | 21 | 22 | 23 | 24 | 25 | 26 |
| | | | | | | | | | | | | | | | | | | | | | | | | | | | | | |
| | | | | | | | | | | | | | | | | | | | | | | | | | | | | | |
| | | | | | | | | | | | | | | | | | | | | | | | | | | | | | |

# 1900 CENSUS

Local Community _____ County _____ State _____

Ward _____                                    Supervisor District # _____

Enumerator _____ Date Census Taken _____ Enumeration District # _____

| Written Page No. | Printed Page No. | Street | House Number | Dwelling Number | Family Number | Name of every person whose place of abode on 1 June 1900 was in this family | Relationship to head of family | Color | Sex | Birth Date | | Age | Marital status | # Years married | Mother of how many children? | # of these children living | Birthplace of | | | Year of Immigration | # Years in U.S. | Naturalized Citizen | Occupation of every person 10 & older | # months not employed | Education | | | | Owned or rented | Owned free of mortgage | Farm or house | No. of farm schedule |
|---|---|---|---|---|---|---|---|---|---|---|---|---|---|---|---|---|---|---|---|---|---|---|---|---|---|---|---|---|---|---|---|---|
| | | | | | | | | | | Month | Year | | | | | | This Person | This Person's Father | This Person's Mother | | | | | | # months in school | Can read | Can write | Speaks English | | | | |
| | | 7 | 1 | 2 | | 3 | 4 | 5 | 6 | 7 | | 8 | 9 | 10 | 11 | 12 | 13 | 14 | 15 | 16 | 17 | 18 | 19 | 20 | 21 | 22 | 23 | 24 | 25 | 26 | 27 | 28 |

# 1910 CENSUS

Local Community _____ County _____ State _____

Ward _____                                    Supervisor's District No. _____

Enumerator _____ Date Census Taken _____ Enumeration District No. _____

| Page No. | Street | House No. | Dwelling No. | Family No. | Name of each person whose place of abode on 15 April 1910 was in this family | Relationship | Sex | Color | Age | Marital Status | # Years — Present Marriage | Mother of how many children? | # living children | Birthplace of | | | Year of Immigration | Naturalized or alien? | Speaks English? If not, give name of language | Profession or Occupation & nature of business | Employer or Wage Earner or Working on Own Account | Out of work 15 April 1910? | # weeks out of work in 1909 | Can read | Can write | School since 1 September 1909 | Owned /rented | Owned free of mortgage | Farm or house | No. on farm schedule | Civil War Veteran | Blind | Deaf & dumb |
|---|---|---|---|---|---|---|---|---|---|---|---|---|---|---|---|---|---|---|---|---|---|---|---|---|---|---|---|---|---|---|---|---|---|
| | | | | | | | | | | | | | | This Person | Father | Mother | | | | | | | | | | | | | | | | | |
| | | | 1 | 2 | 3 | 4 | 5 | 6 | 7 | 8 | 9 | 10 | 11 | 12 | 13 | 14 | 15 | 16 | 17 | 18 | 19 | 20 | 21 | 22 | 23 | 24 | 25 | 26 | 27 | 28 | 29 | 30 | 31 | 32 |

# 1920 CENSUS—SIDE 1

**Department of Commerce — Bureau of the Census**    Sheet # _____ Roll # _____

## FOURTEENTH CENSUS OF THE UNITED STATES: 1920 - POPULATION

State _____ Supervisor's District _____ Enumerator District _____
County _____ Township or other division of county _____
Name of Incorporated Place _____ Ward of City _____
Name of Institution _____
Enumerated on the _____ day of _____ 1920 - Enumerator _____

| Place of abode | | | | NAME | Rel./tenure | | | Personal Desc. | | | | Citizenship | | | Education | | |
|---|---|---|---|---|---|---|---|---|---|---|---|---|---|---|---|---|---|
| Street, Avenue, Road, etc. | House number of farm | Number of dwelling house in order of visitation | Number of family in order of visitation | of each person whose place of abode on January 1, 1920, was in this family. Enter surname first, then the given name and middle initial, if any. Include every living person on January 1, 1920. Omit children born since January 1, 1920. | To head of household | Home owned or rented | If owned, free or mortgaged | Sex | Color of race | Age at last birthday | Single/married/widowed/divorced | Year immigrated to U.S. | If naturalized, year of naturalization | Naturalized or alien | Attended school any time since Sept. 1, 1919? | Able to read? | Able to write? |
| | | | | 1 | | | | | | | | | | | | | |
| | | | | 2 | | | | | | | | | | | | | |
| | | | | 3 | | | | | | | | | | | | | |
| | | | | 4 | | | | | | | | | | | | | |

# 1920 CENSUS—SIDE 2

**Department of Commerce — Bureau of the Census**    Sheet # _____ Roll # _____

## FOURTEENTH CENSUS OF THE UNITED STATES: 1920 - POPULATION

State _____ Supervisor's District _____ Enumerator District _____
County _____ Township or other division of county _____
Name of Incorporated Place _____ Ward of City _____
Name of Institution _____
Enumerated on the _____ day of _____ 1920 - Enumerator _____

| NATIVITY AND MOTHER TONGUE | | | | | | | OCCUPATION | | | |
|---|---|---|---|---|---|---|---|---|---|---|
| Place of birth of each person and parents of each enumerated. If born in the United States, give the state or territory. If of foreign birth, give the place of birth and, in addition, the mother tongue. | | | | | | Able to speak English? | Trade, profession, or particular kind of work done, as spinner, salesman, laborer, etc. | Industry, business, or establishment in which at work, as cotton mill, dry goods store, farm, etc. | Employer, salary, or wage worker, or working as own acct | Number of farm schedule |
| PERSON | | FATHER | | MOTHER | | | | | | |
| Place of Birth | Mother Tongue | Place of Birth | Mother Tongue | Place of Birth | Mother Tongue | | | | | |
| 1 | | | | | | | | | | |
| 2 | | | | | | | | | | |
| 3 | | | | | | | | | | |
| 4 | | | | | | | | | | |

# 1930 Federal Census

Extracted from the original text of the 1930 Census Schedules

State:

County

Township, Town, Precinct, etc.:

Researcher:

Date:

Incorporated place:

Ward of city:

Unincorporated place:

Institution:

NARA Microfilm Series:

Roll no.:

Sheet no.:

Enumeration district no.:

Supervisor's district no:

Block no.:

Enumeration date:

| Place of Abode | | | | Name | Relationship to head of house | Home data | | | | Personal description | | | | | Education | | Place of birth of each person enumerated and of his or her parents. | | | Language spoken in home before coming to the U.S. | Year of immigration to the U.S. | Naturalization to U.S. | Speaks English? | Trade or profession or kind of work | Occupation and industry | | | | | Veteran? | What war? | Farm? |
|---|---|---|---|---|---|---|---|---|---|---|---|---|---|---|---|---|---|---|---|---|---|---|---|---|---|---|---|---|---|---|---|
| Street, ave., road, etc. | House no. (in cities) | No. of dwelling house in order of enumeration | Family no. | Name of Person — Each person whose place of abode on April 1, 1930, was in this family. | | Home owned or rented | Value of home or monthly payment | Radio set | Live on farm? | Sex | Color or race | Age, last birthday | Marital condition | Age, 1st marriage | Attended school? | Can read & write? | Person | Father | Mother | | | | | | Industry or business | Census office code | Class of work | At work yesterday? | Unemployment Sched. no. | | | |
| 1 | 2 | 3 | 4 | 5 | 6 | 7 | 8 | 9 | 10 | 11 | 12 | 13 | 14 | 15 | 16 | 17 | 18 | 19 | 20 | 21 ABC | 22 | 23 | 24 | 25 | 26 | D | 27 | 28 | 29 | 30 | 31 | 32 |

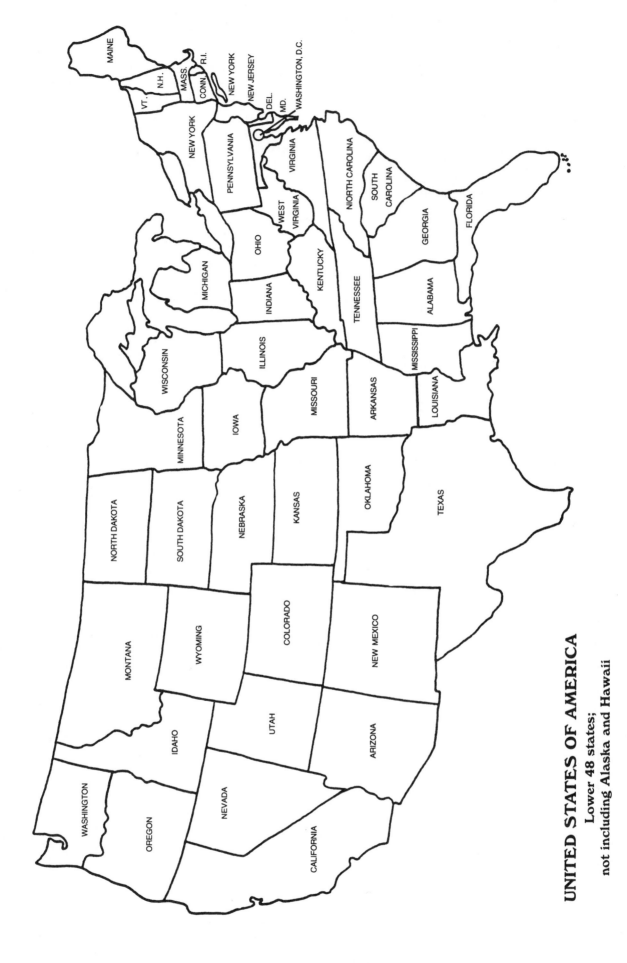

## UNITED STATES OF AMERICA
### Lower 48 states;
### not including Alaska and Hawaii

## DAKOTA TERRITORY—CIRCA 1884
From State Historical Society of North Dakota collections,
File No. 978.3:1884.0722: Colton Dakota map

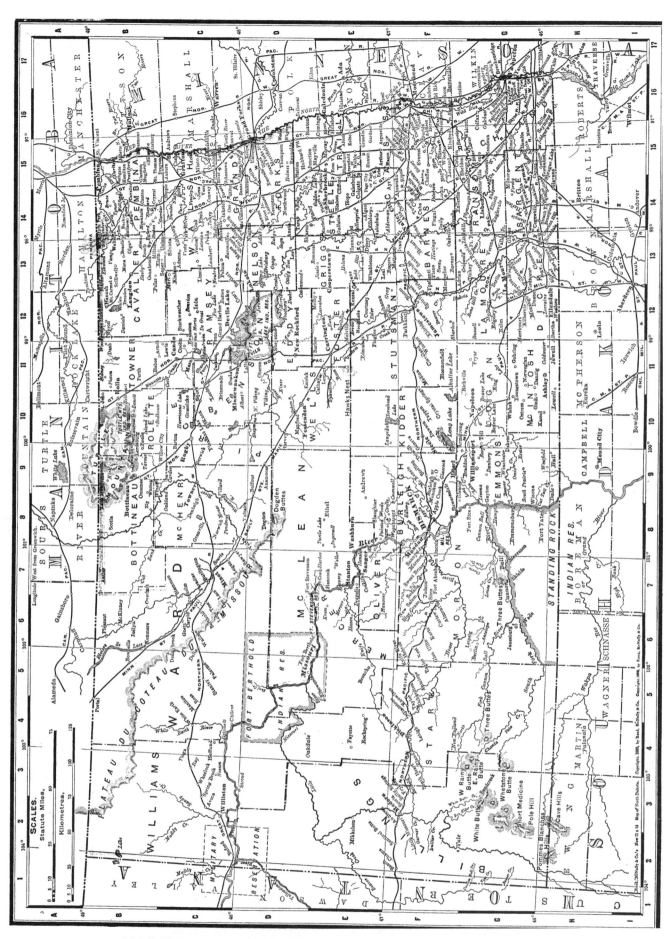

**NORTH DAKOTA MAP FROM ATLAS—CIRCA 1890**

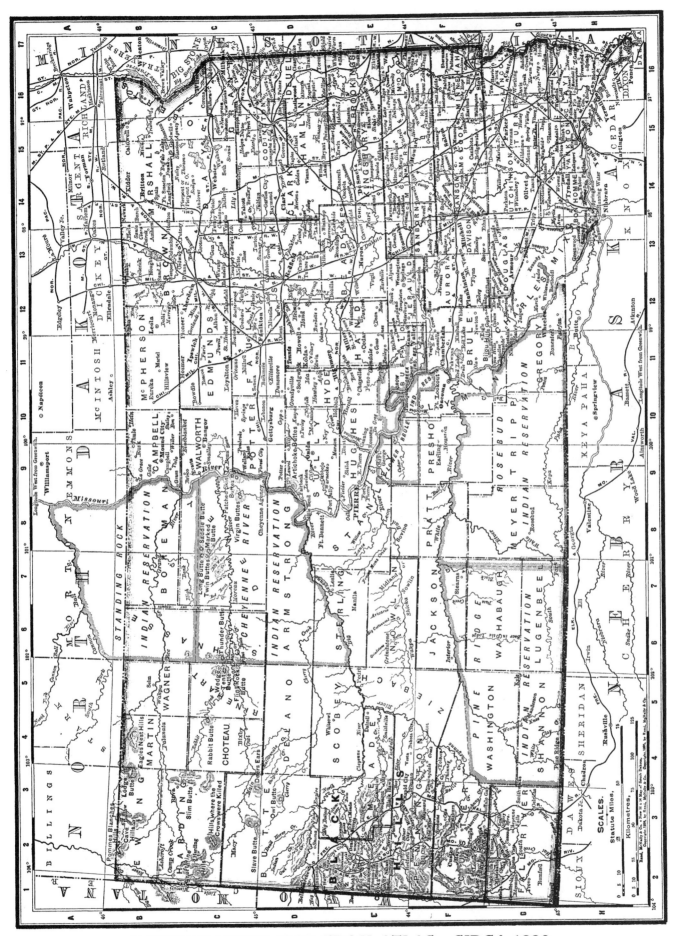

# SOUTH DAKOTA MAP FROM ATLAS—CIRCA 1890

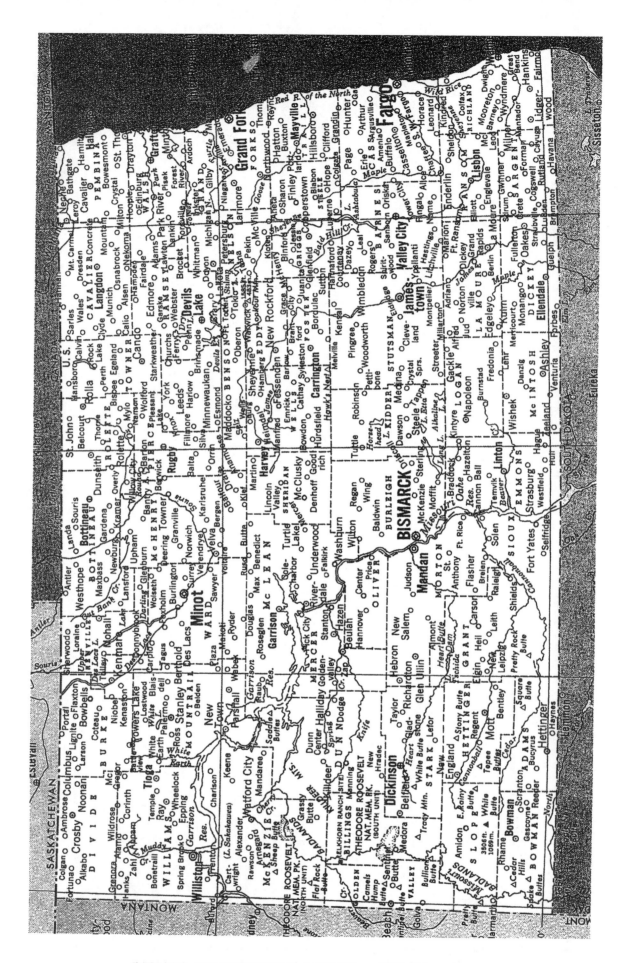

**STATE OF NORTH DAKOTA—CIRCA 1970**

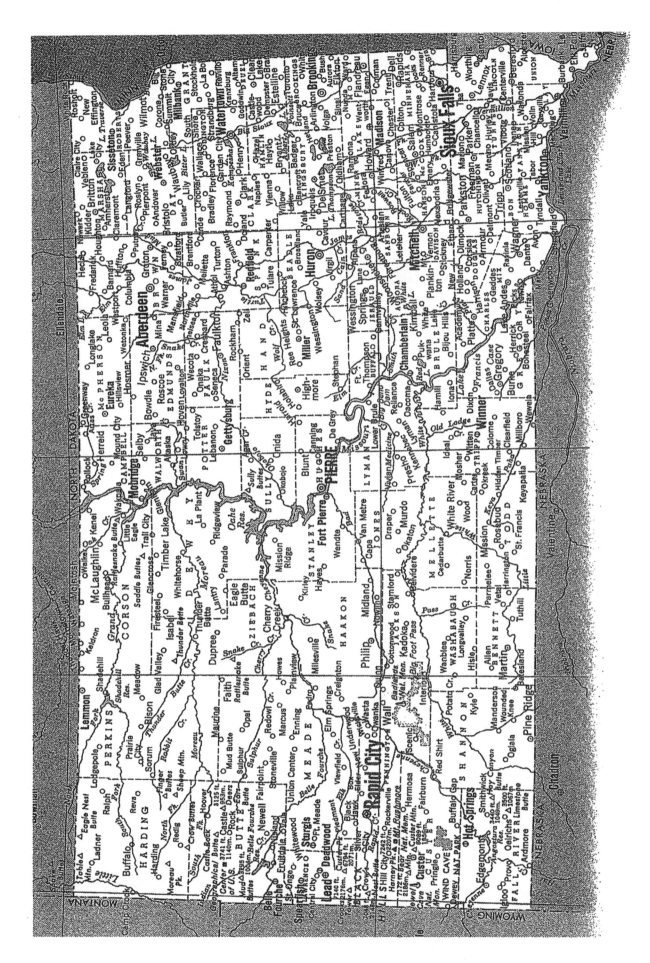

**STATE OF SOUTH DAKOTA—CIRCA 1970**

# Helpful addresses ....................

### U.S. GOVERNMENT

Library of Congress and Annex, 1st-2nd Sts. S.E., Washington, DC 20504; 202-426-5000
www.lcweb.loc.gov/rr/genealogy

National Archives and Records Administration (NARA), 700 Pennsylvania Ave. N.W., Washington, DC 20408
archives.gov/genealogy

NARA—Central Plains Region, 2312 East Bannister Road, Kansas City, MO 64131; 816-926-6272

NARA—Rocky Mountain Region, Denver Branch, Building 48, P.O. Box 25307, Denver Federal Center, Denver, CO 80225; 303-236-0817

Social Security Administration, 6401 Security Blvd., Baltimore, MD 21235
www.ssa.gov

Superintendent of Documents, R.W., CIC-9C, P.O. Box 100, Pueblo, CO 81002
www. pueblo. gsa.gov

U.S. vital records:
www.vitalrec.com

### ASSOCIATIONS, GENEALOGY SOCIETIES

Association of Professional Genealogists, P.O. Box 40393, Denver, CO 80204-0393 E-mail: apg-admin@genealogy.org
www.apgen.org

Board for Certification of Genealogists, P.O. Box 14291, Washington, DC 20004-4291
www.bcgcertification.org

Brigham Young University, 206 HCEB, Provo, UT 84602
www.byu.edu
Library: www.lib.byu.edu

Federation of Genealogical Societies, P.O. Box 830220, Richardson, TX 75083-0220; 800-888-FGS-1500 or 972-907-9727
www/fgs/org

Genealogical Institute of Mid-America Continuing Education, Sangamon State University, Springfield, IL 62794-9243
www.rootdig.com

Hereditary Register of the United States of America, Heritage Consulting and Services, P.O. Box 4152, Salt Lake City, UT 84110; 1-801-565-8046

Institute of Genealogical Studies, P.O. Box 12648, Dallas, TX 75225-0648
www.progenealogists.com

Institute of Genealogy and Historical Research, Samford University, 800 Lakeshore Drive, Birmingham, AL 35229
www.samford.edu/schools/ ighr/ighr. html

National Genealogical Society, 3108 Columbia Pike, Suite 300, Arlington, VA 22204-4304 ; 800-473-0060
www.ngsgenealogy.org

National Institute on Genealogical Research, P.O. Box 14274, Washington, DC 20044-4274
www.rootsweb.com/~nigraa

New England Historic Genealogical Society, 101 Newberry St., Boston, MA 02116; 617-536-5740
www.newenglandancestors.org

Salt Lake Institute of Genealogy, P.O. Box 1144, Salt Lake City, UT 84110
www.infouga.org

## MAJOR REPOSITORIES

Allen County Public Library, 900 Webster St., Fort Wayne, IN 46802; 219-421-1200
www.acpl.lib.in.us

American Association for State and Local History, c/o National Archives and Records Administration (NARA), 700 Pennsylvania Ave. N.W., Washington, DC 20408
www.aaslh.org

American Antiquarian Society Library, 185 Salisbury St., Worcester, MA 01609
www.americanantiquarian.org

American Family Immigration History Center, Ellis Island Immigration Museum, Dept. W, 52 Vanderbilt Ave., New York, NY 10017-3898; 212-883-1986
www.ellisisland.org

American Genealogical Lending Library (AGLL), P.O. Box 244, Bountiful, UT 84011-0244
www.agll.com

Genealogical Library of the Church of Jesus Christ of Latter-Day Saints, 50 E. N. Temple St., Salt Lake City, UT 84150; 801-531-2331
www.lds.org

LDS Family History Library, 35 North West Temple St., Salt Lake City, UT 84150
www.familysearch. org

National Genealogical Society Library, 4527 17th St. N., Arlington, VA 22207-2399; 703-525-0050 or 800-473-0060.
www.ngsgenealogy.org/ bookloan.cfm

National Society of the Daughters of the American Revolution (DAR), 1776 D Street N.W., Washington, DC 20006; 202-628-1776
www.dar.org

Newberry Library, 60 W. Walton St., Chicago, IL 60610-3305; 312-255-3512
www.newberry.org/genealogy

University of Michigan Library, 837 Greene St., Ann Arbor, MI 48104; 313-763-6980
www.umich.edu/libraries

# STATE & LOCAL

Web addresses for state information:
North Dakota:
   www.state.nd.us/host
South Dakota:
   www.state.sd.us/host
Other states:
   www.state.[*insert state
   abbreviation here*].us/host

USGENWEB Dakota sites:
North Dakota:
   www.rootsweb.com/~ndgenweb
South Dakota:
   www.rootsweb.com/~sdgenweb

## STATE ARCHIVES

### North Dakota

North Dakota State Archives and
Historical Research Library, North
Dakota Heritage Center, 612 E.
Boulevard Ave., Bismarck, ND 58505-
0830; 701-328-2091
   www.state.nd.us/hist/sal.htm

### South Dakota

South Dakota State Archives, Cultural
Heritage Center, 900 Governors Drive,
Pierre, S.D. 57501- 2217; 605-773-3804,
   www.sdhistory.org

## STATE GENEALOGICAL SOCIETIES

### North Dakota

North Dakota State Genealogical Society
Inc., P.O. Box 485, Bismarck, ND 58502-
0485

### South Dakota

South Dakota Genealogical Society, P.O.
Box 1101, Pierre, SD 57501-1101
   www.rootsweb.com/~sdgenweb/
   gensoc/sdgensoc.html

## LOCAL GENEALOGICAL SOCIETIES

### North Dakota

Bismarck-Mandan Historical and
Genealogical Society, P.O. Box 485, Bismarck, ND 58502-0485
   www.rootsweb.com/~ndbmhgs

Bowman County Genealogical Society
P.O. Box 78, Bowman, ND 58623-0078

James River Genealogy Club, 651 Fourth
St., Carrington, ND 58421
   www.rootsweb.com/~ndjrgc/
   index.htm

McLean County Genealogical Society
P.O. Box 84, Garrison, ND 58540

Minnkota Genealogical Society
P.O. Box 12744, Grand Forks, ND 58208-
2744

Mouse River Loop Genealogical Society,
P.O. Box 1391, Minot, ND 58702-1391;
701-852-1045
   ww.mrlgs-nd.org

Red River Valley Genealogical Society,
112 N. University Drive, Suite L-116
(P.O. Box 9284 mailing address), Fargo,
ND 58106-9284; 701-239-4129
   fargocity.com/~rrvgs

South Western North Dakota Genealogical Society, HCR 01, Box 32A , Regent
ND 58650
   www.rootsweb.com/~ndstark/
   hartsearch

Wilkin County, MN, and Richland
County, ND, Genealogy Guild of
Leach Public Library, 417 Second Ave.
N, Wahpeton, ND 58075

Williams County Genealogical Society,
Williston, ND 58801

### South Dakota

Aberdeen Area Genealogical Society,
P.O. Box 493, Aberdeen, SD 57402-0493

Bennett County Genealogical Society,
P.O. Box 483, Allen, SD 57714-0483

Brookings Area Genealogical Society,
524 4th St., Brookings, SD 57006

East River Genealogical Forum, Rt. 2,
Box 148, Wolsey, SD 57384

Family Tree Society, P.O. Box 202, Win-
ner, SD 57580-0202

Heritage Club-Platte, P.O. Box 144,
Platte, SD 57369-0144

Hyde County Historical and Genealogical Society, P.O. Box 392, Highmore, SD
57345-0392

Kingsbury Genealogical Society, P. O.
Box 5, DeSmet, SD 57249

Lake County Genealogical Society, c/o
Karl Mundt Library, Dakota State College, Madison, SD 57042

Lyman-Brule Genealogical Society, c/o
Marlys Swanson, P.O. Box 555, Cham-
berlain, SD 57325

Mitchell Area Genealogical Society, 620
N. Edmunds, Mitchell, SD 57301

Moody County Genealogical Society, 501
W. First Ave., Flandreau, SD 57028-1003

Murdo Genealogical Society, P.O. Box
441, Murdo, SD 57559-0441

Nordland Heritage Foundation, Augustana College, Sioux Falls, SD 57197

North Central South Dakota Genealogical Society, 178 Southshore Dr., Mina, SD
57462-3000

Pierre-Ft. Pierre Genealogical Society ,
P.O. Box 925, Pierre, SD 57501-0925

Rapid City Society for Genealogical
Research Inc., P.O. Box 1495, Rapid City,
SD 57709-1495

SDGOLD (SD Genealogical Organization of Lyman Descendents), P.O. Box
145, Oacoma, SD 57365-0145

Sioux Valley Genealogical Society, 200
West 6th St., Sioux Falls, SD 57104-6001

Tri-State Genealogical Society, c/o Public Library, 905 5th St., Belle Fourche, SD
57717-1705

Watertown Genealogical Society, 611
N.E. B Ave., Watertown, SD 57201

Yankton Genealogical Society,  1803
Douglas Ave., Yankton, SD 57078

## STATE HISTORICAL SOCIETIES

### North Dakota
State Historical Society of North Dakota, North Dakota Heritage Center, 612 E. Boulevard Ave., Bismarck, ND 58505-0830; 701-328-2666
www.state.nd.us/hist

### South Dakota
South Dakota State Historical Society, 900 Governors Drive, Pierre, SD 57501-2217
www.state.sd.us/state/capitol/cultural/cultural.html

### Minnesota
Minnesota Historical Society, 340 Kellogg Blvd. W., St. Paul, MN 55102-1906; 612-29602143
www.mnhs.org

### Montana
Montana Historical Society Archives, 225 N. Roberts, Helena, MT 59620; 406-44402694
www.his.state.mt.us/research

### Nebraska
Nebraska State Historical Society, P.O. Box 82554, 1500 R St., Lincoln, NE 68501
www.nebraskahistory.org

## STATE LIBRARIES

### North Dakota
North Dakota State Library, 604 E. Boulevard Ave-Dept. 250, Bismarck, ND 58505-0800; 701-328-4657, Fax 701-328-2040
ndsl.lib.state.nd.us

### South Dakota
South Dakota State Library, 800 Governors Drive, Pierre, SD 57501-2294; 605-773-3131
www.sdstatelibrary.com

## STATE VITAL RECORDS

### North Dakota
North Dakota Department of Health-Division of Vital Records, 600 E. Boulevard Ave., Bismarck, ND 58505-0200; 701-328-2360, Fax 701-328-1850

### South Dakota
South Dakota Department of Health-Data, Statistics and Vital Records, 600 E. Capitol, Pierre, SD 57501-2536; 605-773-4961 or 800-738-2301, Fax 605-773-5683
South Dakota births prior to 1905: www.state.sd.us/doh/vitalrec/birthrecords/index.cfm

## SPECIAL COLLECTIONS

### North Dakota
Bonanzaville, U.S.A., 1351 W. Main Ave., Interstate 94, Exit 343, West Fargo, ND 58078; 701-282-2822
www.museumsusa.org/museums/info/1163814

Elwyn B. Robinson Department of Special Collections, P.O. Box 9000-UND, Grand Forks, ND 58202-9000; 701-777-4627
www.und.nodak.edu/dept/library/Collections/Robinson/og198.html

Fargo Moorhead St. Andrew's Society, 73 Prairiewood Crossing S.W., Fargo, ND 58103-4667; 701-293-7374 or 701-235-6687; 218-293-7374
st-andrews-society.tripod.com

Fargo Public Library, 102 N. 3rd St., Fargo, ND 58102; 701-241-1492
www.cityoffargo.com/library

North Dakota Institute for Regional Studies, Germans from Russia Heritage Collection, North Dakota State University Libraries, P.O. Box 5599, Fargo, ND 58105-5599; 701-237-8416
www.lib.ndsu.nodak.edu/grhc

Sons of Norway Library, 509 14th Ave. N., Fargo, ND 58102; 701-232-6331

West Fargo Historical Center, 401 7th St. E., West Fargo, ND 58078; 701-282-0415

### South Dakota
Berry, E.Y., Library Special Collections, Black Hills State University Archives, 1200 University St., Unit 9548, Spearfish, SD 57799-9548; 605-642-6361
iis.bhsu.edu/lis/specialcollections/index.cfm

I.D. Weeks Library, University of South Dakota, 414 E. Clark St., Vermillion, SD 57069; 605-677-5371
www.usd.edu/library

Institute of American Indian Studies, University of South Dakota, 414 E. Clark St., Vermillion, SD 57069; 605-677-5209
www.usd.edu/iais

Mikkelsen Library, Augustana College, P.O. Box 727, Sioux Falls, SD 57197-0727; 605-336-4007 or 800-727-2844
www.augie.edu/library

South Dakota National Guard Museum, 301 E. Dakota Ave., Pierre, SD 57501-3225; 605-224-9991
mva.sd.gov/?navid=23

### Minnesota
Moorhead State University Library, 1104 7th Ave. S., Moorhead, MN 56563; 218-236-2922
www.mnstate.edu/library

Ylvisaker, Carl B., Library, Concordia College, 920 S. 8th St., Moorhead, MN 56562; 218-299-4640
www4.cord.edu/library

## LOCAL LDS FAMILY HISTORY CENTERS

### North Dakota
Bismarck LDS Family History Center, 1500 Country West Road, Bismarck, ND 58501; 701-223-6384

Dickinson LDS Family History Center, LDS Church, 1200 N. Alder Road, Dickinson, ND 58601; 701-227-0267

Fargo LDS Family History Center, 2501 17th Ave. S.W., Fargo, ND 58102; 701-232-4003

Grand Forks LDS Family History Center, 2814 Cherry St., Grand Forks, ND 58201; 701-746-6126

Jamestown LDS Family History Center, 2237 S.E. 2nd St., Jamestown, ND 58401; 701-237-9505

Minot LDS Family History Center, 2025 9th St. N.W., Minot, ND 58701; 701-838-4486

Wahpeton LDS Family History Center, 505 Richland St. W., Wahpeton, ND 58075; 701-572-3502

Williston LDS Family History Center, LDS Church, 1805 26th St. W., Williston, ND 58801; 701-572-3502

## South Dakota
Aberdeen LDS Family History Center, 1115 24th Ave. N.E., Aberdeen, SD 57401; 605-225-0601

Belle Fourche LDS Family History Center, 1105 Todd St., Belle Fourche, SD 57717; 605-892-3700

Brookings LDS Family History Center, 200 22nd Ave., Brookings, SD 57006; 605-692-9350

Gettysburg LDS Family History Center, 530 S. Mannston St., Gettysburg, SD 57442; 605-765-9270

Hot Springs LDS Family History Center, 2133 Albany St., Hot Springs, SD 57747; 605-745-6119

Huron LDS Family History Center, 1450 Frank St. S.E., Huron, SD 57350; 605-352-6849

Madison LDS Family History Center, 927 N. Lee Ave., Madison, SD 57042; 605-256-6335

Pierre LDS Family History Center, 506 N. Jefferson, Pierre, SD 57501; 605-224-9117

Rapid City LDS Family History Center, 2822 Canyon Lake Drive, Rapid City, SD 57701; 605-343-8656

Rosebud LDS Family History Center, Highway 7, West St., Rosebud, SD 57570; 605-747-2128

Sioux Falls LDS Family History Center, 3900 S. Fairhall Ave., Sioux Falls, SD 57101; 605-361-1070

Vermillion LDS Family History Center, 20 Michelsen Ave., Vermillon, SD 57069; 605-624-7139

Watertown LDS Family History Center, 1200 19th St. N.E., Watertown, SD 57201; 605-882-2299

Yankton LDS Family History Center, 23rd and Douglas, Yankton, SD 57078; 605-665-5307; 605-665-0901

## Nebraska
*(affiliated with South Dakota centers)*
Chadron LDS Family History Center, W. 10th St., Chadron, NE 69337; 308-432-5657

Gordon LDS Family History Center, 800 N. Ash, Gordon, NE 69343; 308-282-0635

# CHURCH

## CATHOLIC

Assumption Abbey, Richardton
www.assumptionabbey.com

Blue Cloud Abbey, Marvin, SD
www.bluecloud. org

Diocese of Bismarck, 420 Raymond St. P.O. Box 1575, Bismarck, ND 58502-1575; 701-223-1347

Diocese of Fargo, 1310 Broadway, Box 1750, Fargo, ND 58107, 701-235-6429
www.fargodiocese. org

Diocese of Sioux Falls, 523 N. Dulute Ave., Sioux Falls, SD 57104, 605-334-9861
www.Diocese- of-Sioux-Falls.org

Mother of God Monastery, Watertown, SD
www.dailypost.com/~monastery

## EPISCOPAL, EVANGELICAL REFORMED, UNITED CHURCH OF CHRIST

Mikkelsen Library/Center for Western Studies, Augustana College, Sioux Falls, SD
www.inst.augie.edu/library/services/services.html

## LUTHERAN

Aid Association for Lutherans: Lutherans Online genealogy exchange
www.aal.org/LutheransOnline/Gen_Ex

Archives of the Evangelical Lutheran Church in America, 321 Bonnie Lane, Elk Grove Village, IL 60007; 800-638-3522, ext. 2818
www.elca.org

Augustana Lutheran
(See Church, Swedish)
Gustavus Adolphus College, St. Peter, MN 56082

Lutheran Church-Missouri Synod, Concordia Historical Institute, 1333 S. Kirkwood Road, St. Louis, MO 63122; 314-965-9000
www.lcms.org

Swenson Swedish Immigration Research Center, Augustana College, 639 38th St., Rock Island, IL 61201-2296; 309-794-7204 (Augustana Lutheran, Mission, Covenant, Evangelical Free, Swedish Methodist, Swedish Baptist church records)
www.augustana.edu/administration/swenson

## MENNONITE
(See also Germans from Russia)

Archives of the Mennonite Church, 1700 S. Main St., Goshen, IN 46526

Mennonite Genealogy Inc., Box 393, Winnipeg, Manitoba, Canada R3C 2H6; 204-772-0747 or 204-669-6200

Mennonite Heritage Center, 600 Shaftesbury Blvd., Winnipeg, Manitoba, Canada R3P 0M4; 204-888-6781

Mennonite Library and Archives, Bethel College, 300 E. 27th N., Newton, KS 67117

## METHODIST

Dakotas Conference Office, Methodist Church, Mitchell, SD
www.umc/org/churchlibrary

## SEVENTH-DAY ADVENTIST

Seventh-Day Adventist Church, 1220 E. Robinson Ave., Pierre, SD 57501-2643; 605-224-7153 (regional headquarters for the Dakotas)

# ETHNIC ROOTS

## BOHEMIAN/CZECH

Czech Heritage Preservation Society, P.O. Box 3, Tabor, SD 57063

CzechoSlovak GenealogicalSociety, P.O. Box 16225, St. Paul, MN 55116-0225
www.cgsi.org

Newberry Library, 60 W. Walton St., Chicago, IL 60610-3305; 312-255-3512. (Bohemian-Czech genealogy records)
www.newberry.org

## BRITISH ISLES (including IRELAND and SCOTLAND)

Elwyn B. Robinson Department of Special Collections at the Chester Fritz Library, University of North Dakota, Grand Forks, ND 58201 (Canadian, English-Scotch-Irish settlements)

General Register Office, St. Catherine's House, 10 Kings- way, London, WC2B 6JP, England

Irish Genealogical Society International, P.O. Box 16585, St. Paul, MN 55116 -6585
www.rootsweb.com/~irish
www. rootsweb.com/~fianna

Newberry Library, 60 W. Walton St., Chicago, IL 60610-3305; 312-255-3512 (extensive collections, English genealogy)
www.newberry.org

## CANADIAN

### National archives
Library and Archives Canada, 395 Wellington St., Ottawa, Ontario, Canada K1A 0N4; 866-578-7777 toll-free
www.collectionscanada.ca

### Provincial/territorial archives
Archives nationales du Quebec, 1012, avenue du Séminaire, C.P. 10450, Sainte-Foy, Quebec, Canada G1V 4N1; 418-643-8904
www.anq. gouv.qc.ca

Archives of Northwest Territories, c/o Prince of Wales Northern Heritage Centre, Yellowknife, Northwest Territories, Canada X1A 2L9; 403-873-7698
pwnhc.learnnet. nt.ca/programs/archive.htm

Archives of Ontario, 77 Grenville St. W., Toronto, Ontario, Canada M7A 2R9; 416-327-1600
www.gov.on.ca/MCZCR/archives/english/index.html

British Columbia Archives, 655 Belleville St., Victoria, British Columbia, Canada V8V 1X4; 250-387-1952
www.bcars.gs.gov.bc.ca/bcars. htm

Nova Scotia Archives and Records Management (Public Archives of Nova Scotia); 6016 University Ave., Halifax, Nova Scotia, Canada B3H 1W4; 902-424-6060
www.nsarm.ednet.ns.ca

Provincial Archives of Alberta, 12845-102 Ave., Edmonton, Alberta, Canada T5N 0M6; 403-427-1750
www.gov.ab.ca/~mcd/mhs/paa/paa.htm

Provincial Archives of Manitoba, 200 Vaughan St., Winnipeg, Manitoba, Canada R3C 1T5; 204-945-3971
www.gov.mb.ca/chc/archives

Provincial Archives of New Brunswick, P.O. Box 6000, Frederickton, New Brunswick, Canada E3B 5H1; 506-453-2122
www.gov.nb.ca/supply/archives

Provincial Archives of Newfoundland and Labrador, Colonial Building, Military Road, St. Johns, Newfoundland, Canada A1C 2C9; 709-729-3065
www.anla.nf.ca/provarch.htm

Public Archives and Records Office, Box 1000, Charlottetown, Prince Edward Island, Canada C1A 7M4; 902-368-4290.
www.gov. pe.ca/educ/ archives/archives_index.asp

Saskatchewan Archives Board, Murray Building, University of Saskatchewan, 3 Campus Drive, Saskatoon, Saskatchewan, Canada S7N 5A4; 306-933-5832
www.gov.sk.ca/govt/archives/progserv.htm

Saskatchewan Archives Board, Regina Office, University of Regina, Regina, Saskatchewan, Canada S4S 0A2; 306-787-4068
www.gov.sk.ca/govt/archives/progserv.htm

Yukon Archives, P.O. Box 2703, Whitehorse, Yukon Territory, Canada Y1A 2C6; 403-667-5321
www.yukoncollege. yk.ca/archives/yarch.html

### National genealogical societies
Canadian Genealogy Centre, inGeneas
www.ingeneas.com/ingeneas/index.html

American-Canadian Genealogical Society, P.O. Box 668, Manchester, NH 03105

### Provincial genealogical societies
Alberta Genealogical Society, P.O. Box 30270, Station B, Edmonton, Alberta, Canada T2M 4P1; 204-669-6575

Manitoba Genealogical Society, South West Branch, 885 Notre Dame Ave., 53 Almond Crescent, Winnipeg, Manitoba, Canada R3C 3R4

Manitoba Genealogical Society, 167 Lombard Ave., Room 420, Winnipeg, Manitoba, Canada R3B 0T6; 20;4-944-1153

Ontario Genealogical Society, 40 Orchard View Blvd., Suite 102, Toronto, Ontario, Canada M4R 1B9

Quebec Family History Society, P.O. Box 1026, Pointe Claire QUE H9S 4H9
E-mail: hopkde@cam.org

Saskatchewan Genealogical Society, 1870 Lorrie St., 2nd Floor, P.O. Box 1894, Regina, Saskatchewan, Canada G1V 4A8; 306-780-9207

### Special collections
French-Canadian collections
www.oz.net/~johnbang genealogy/queblib.txt

## DUTCH
### (Hollander/Netherlander)

Algemeen Rijksarchief (General State Archives), P.O. Box 90520, 2509 LM, The Hague

Centraal Bureau voor Genealogie (Central Bureau for Genealogy), P.O. Box 11755, 2502, The Hague

Herrick District Library, Holland, 300 River Ave., Holland, MI 49423
    www.herrickdl.org/genealogy

Joint Archives of Holland, Hope College, 265 College Ave., Holland, MI 49423

Koninklijk huisarchief (Royal Home Archives), P.O. Box 30412, 2500 GK, The Hague

National Dutch Archives
    www.archief.nl

Nederlandse genealogische vereniging (Dutch Genealogical Society), P.O. Box 976, 1000 AZ, Amsterdam

## FRENCH
### (See also Canadian, German)

Archives Nationale de France, 60 rue des Francs-Bourgeois, F-3000, Paris, France.

French Embassy Press and Information Service, 4101 Reservoir Road N.W., Washington, DC 20007

## GERMAN
### (See also Germans from Russia)

Eastern Europe: FEEFHS (Federation of East European Family History Societies)
    www.feefhs.org

German Emigration Museum, Inselstr 6D, 2850, Bremerhaven, Germany

German Genealogical Digest, P.O. Box 112054, Salt Lake City, UT 84147
    www.german-digest.com

German research: Heimatortskartei Fur, Ostumsiedler, Rosenbergstrasse, 507000 Stuttgart 1, Germany

Historic Emigration Office, c\o Tourist Information and Unten Bei den St. Pauli, Landungsbrocken 3, P.O. Box 102249, 2000 Hamburg 1

Institut für Auslandsbeziehungen, Charlottenplatz 17, 7000 Stuttgart 1, Germany

Landau, Germany, research: Ehmer Egon, Morlheimer Haupt 14, 6740 Landau, Germany

Society for Ancestral Research of Germans from Poland and Volhynia, 3492 W. 39th Ave., Vancouver, British Columbia, Canada V6N 3A2; 604-263-3458

Time Voyages Bookstore, German page (lists books for German research)
    pages. prodigy.com/
    time voyagers/german.htm

## GERMANS FROM RUSSIA
### (See also German, Polish, Russian, Ukrainian)

American Historical Society of Germans from Russia, 631 D St., Lincoln, NE 68502-1199; 402-474-3363
    www.ahsgr.org

Bessarabian research: Leipzig Stadt Archive, Georgi-Dimitroff Platz 1, 07010 Leipzig, Germany

Cyndi's List of German-Russian sources
    www.cyndislist.com/germruss.html

Elwyn B. Robinson Department of Special Collections, Chester Fritz Library, University of North Dakota, P.O. Box 9000, Grand Forks, ND 58202; 701-777-4625
    www.library.und.edu/collections/
    spk.html

Federation of East European Family History Societies, P.O. Box 510898, Salt Lake City, UT 84151-0898
    feefhs.org

Germans from Russia Heritage Collection, North Dakota State University Libraries, P.O. Box 5599, Fargo, ND 58105-5599; 701-231-8416 or 701-231-6596
    www.lib.ndsu.nodak.edu/grhc

Germans from Russia Heritage Society, 1125 W. Turnpike Ave., Bismarck, ND 58501-8115; 701-223-6167
    www.grhs.org

Institute for Regional Studies, North Dakota State University Libraries, P.O. Box 5599, Fargo, ND 58105-5599; 701-231-8914
    www.lib.ndsu.nodak.edu/ndirs

Landsmannschaft der Russlanddeutschen, Raitelsbergstrasse 49, 70188 Stuttgart, Germany; 011-49-711-116-590 (calling from U.S.)
    www.lmdr.de

Society for Ancestral Research of Germans from Poland and Wolhynia, 3492 W. 39th Ave., Vancouver, British Columbia, Canada V6N 3A2; 604-263-3458

Society for German Genealogy in Eastern Europe, P.O. Box 905, Station M, Calgary, AB, Canada T2P 2J6
    www.sggee.org

### Germans from Russia regional interest groups

Beresan District Odessa
    www.grhs.org/beresan

Bessarabia District Germans from Russia
    www.grhs.org/bessarabia/
    body_index.html

Crimea Germans from Russia
    www.grhs.org/crimea

Germans to Russia, Poland to Russia
    www.grhs.org/gp-pr

Glueckstal Colonies Research Association, 611 Esplande, Redondo Beach, CA 90277; 310-540-1872)
    www.glueckstal.org

Grossliebental District Odessa, Germans from Russia
    www.grhs.org/grossliebental

Heimatmuseum der Deutschen aus Bessarabien, Florianstrasse 17, 70188 Stuttgart, Germany; 011-49-711-262-8092
    www.bessarabien.de/bess/start.htm

Hoffnungstal, Odessa Parish
    www.grhs.org/hop/Home.htm

Kutschurgan
    www.kutschurgan.com

Odessa: A German-Russian Genealogical Library
    www.odessa3.org

**(Germans from Russia—regional interest groups, continued)**

Volga Germans
www.webbitt.com/volga/
homehtml

Germans from Russia Heritage Collection Website "Links" section for Germans from Russia family and villages, genealogy, family history, Hutterites, Volhynian genealogy, Mennonite genealogy, and many other sources
www.lib.ndsu.nodak.edu/grhc/
links/links.html

## HUNGARIAN

Hungary
http://www.xcelco.on.ca/
~genealog/hungary1.htm

Maps, Hungary
lazarus.elte.hu/gb/hunkarta/
kezdo.htm

## INDIANS, AMERICAN

American Indian Culture Research Center, Blue Cloud Abbey, P.O. Box 98, Marvin, SD 57251-0098; phone 605-398-9200
www.bluecloud.org/dakota. html

American Indians: A Select Catalog of NARA Microfilm Publications
archives.gov/publications/micro
film/amerindians/indians.html

Brenorsome Historical Society, c/o Louis Garcia, P.O. Box 232, Tokio, ND 58379-0232

Center for Western Studies, P.O. Box 727, Augustana College, Sioux Falls, SD 57197-0727; 800-727-2844
www.augie.edu/CWS

Fort Totten State Historic Site, P.O. Box 224, Fort Totten, ND 58335-0224; 701-766-4441
www.state.nd.us/hist/totten/
totten.htm

Fort Union Trading Post National Historic Site, RR 3, Box 71, Williston, ND 58801; 701-572-9083
www.nps.gov/fous

Indian Museum of North America, c/o Crazy Horse Memorial, Avenue of the Chiefs, Crazy Horse, SD 57730-9506; 605-673-4681
www.crazyhorse.org

Institute of American Indian Studies, University of South Dakota, 414 E. Clark St., Vermillion, SD 57069; 605-677-5209, Fax 605-677-6525
www.usd.edu/iais

Knife River Indian Villages National Historic Site, P.O. Box 9, Stanton, ND 58571-0009; 701-745-3309
www.nps.gov/knri

Lakota genealogy, the Sisseton-Wahpeton Sioux tribe home page
hometown.aol.com/bbbenge/
front.html

Lewis and Clark Interpretive Center, Junction Hwy. 83 and 200A, Washburn, ND 58577
www.fortmandan.com/
planningyourvisit/
interpretivecenter.asp

Métis Genealogical Society, East 1658 Central, Spokane, WA 99208
www.saskgenealogy.com/special/
sgs_special_metis.htm

Mikkelsen Library, P.O. Box 727, Augustana College, Sioux Falls, SD 57197-0727; 605-336-4007 or 800-727-2844
www.augie.edu/library

Pembina State Museum, Exit 215 off Interstate 29, 805 Highway 59, P.O. Box 456, Pembina, ND, 58271-0456; 701-825-6840
www.state.nd.us/hist/mus/
pembmus. htm

Rosebud Sioux Indian Reservation
tradecorridor.com/rosebud

Three Affiliated Tribes Museum, c/o Marilyn Hudson, P.O. Box 147, New Town, ND 58763; 701-627-4477
lewisandclarktrail.com/section2/
ndcities/newtown/museum.htm

Turtle Mountain Chippewa Heritage Center, P. O. Box 257, Belcourt, ND 58316-0257; 701-477-6451
chippewa.utma.com/index2.html

Yankton Sioux Tribe, P.O. Box 248, Marty, SD 57361-0248; 605-384-3804 or 605-384-3641
lewisandclarktrail.com/sponsors/
yanktonsioux/sect2.htm

Other links:
www.genealogypages.com/Ethnic
_Groups/Native_ American
www- personal.umich.
edu/~cgaunt/amind.html

### Indian colleges, North Dakota
Fort Berthold Community College, P.O. Box 490, New Town, ND 58763-0490; 701-627-3665
www.fbcc.bia.edu

Little Hoop Community College, P.O. Box 269, Fort Totten, ND 58335-0269; 701-766-4415
www.skc.edu/student_congress/
littlehoop.html

Sitting Bull University, P.O. Box 100, Fort Yates, ND 58538-0100; 701-854-3861
www.sittingbull.edu

Turtle Mountain Community College, P.O. Box 340, Belcourt, ND 58316-0340; 701-477-5605
www.turtle-mountain.cc.nd.us

United Tribes Technical College, 3315 University Dr, Bismarck, ND 58501; 701-255-3285
www.uttc.edu

### Indian colleges, South Dakota
Cheyenne River Community College, P.O. Box 220, Eagle Butte, SD 57625-0220
www.state.sd.us/oia/chysioux.asp

Oglala Lakota College, P.O. Box 490, Kyle, SD 57752-0490; 605-455-2321
www.olc.edu

Sinte Gleska University, P.O. Box 490, Rosebud, SD 57570-0490; 605-747-2263
www.sinte.edu

Sisseton Wahpeton Community College, Old Agency, P.O. Box 689, Sisseton, SD 57262-0689; 605-698-3966
www.swc.tc

### IRISH
(See British Isles)

## ITALIAN

Italian resources
    members.aol.com/geneaita/
    indexen.html

## JEWISH

American Jewish Archives, 3101 Clifton
Ave., Cincinnati, OH 45220
    www.americanjewisharchives.org

Jewish Genealogical Society, P.O. Box
286398, New York, NY 10128-0004
    www.jgsny.org

Jewish Genealogical Society of Canada,
P.O. Box 446 Station A, Willowdale,
Ontario, Canada M2N 5TI
    www.jgstoronto.ca

## POLISH
(See also German, Germans from
Russia, Ukrainian)

FEEFHS (Federation of East European
Family History Societies) , P.O. Box
21346, Salt Lake City, UT 81421-0346
    www.feefhs.org

Newberry Library, 60 W. Walton St.,
Chicago, IL 60610-3305; 312-255-3512.
    www.newberry.org

Polish Genealogical Society of America
(PGSA), c/o Polish Museum of America,
984 Milwaukee Ave., Chicago, IL 60622-
4199
    www.pgsa.org

Society for Ancestral Research of Germans
from Poland and Volhynia, 3492 W. 39th
Ave., Vancouver, British Columbia, Canada V6N 3A2; 604-263-3458
    www.sggee.org/pipermail/
    ger-poland-volhynia

## RUSSIAN
(See also Germans from Russia,
Ukrainian)

Embassy of the U.S. in Moscow, c/o
Department of State, Washington, DC
20521

FEEFHS (Federation of East European
Family History Societies) , P.O. Box
21346, Salt Lake City, UT 81421-0346
    www.feeths.org/fri/ru/
    rusgens.html

## SCANDINAVIAN
(See also Danish, Finnish, Icelandic,
Norwegian, Swedish)

Dalesburg Scandinavian Association,
30595 University Road, Vermillion SD
57069-6507
    www.angelfire.com/sd/dalesburg99

North American Heritage Press, c/o
Creative Printing, 1831 Burdick Expy.
W., Minot, ND 58701-5667; 701-852-5552
    www.northamericanheritagepress.
    com

Norsk Høstfest Association, P.O. Box
1347, Minot, ND 58702-1347; 701-652-
2368
    www.hostfest.com

Scandinavian Heritage Association/
Scandinavian Heritage Park, 24 1st St.
N.E. (P.O. Box 862), Minot, ND 58702-
0862; 701-852-9161
    scandinavianheritage.org

### Danish
(See also Scandinavian)

Danish Emigration Archives, Arkiv-
straede 1, P.O. Box 1731, /dJ-9100 Aalborg, Denmark; +45 98 12 57-93
    www.feefhs.org/dk/frg-deaa. html

Danish Immigrant Archives, Grand
View College Library, 1351 Grandview
Ave., Des Moines, IA 50316
    www.ancestry.co.uk/learn/library

Danish Immigrant Museum, 4210 Main
St., Elk Horn, Iowa 51531-0249; 712-764-
7008
    www.danishmuseum.org/
    DanishCulture/DanishCulture101.
    html

Red River Danes, P.O. Box 1162,
Fargo ND 58107

Souris Valley Danish Society, c/o Scandinavian Heritage Association, 24 1st St.
N.E. (P.O. Box 862), Minot, ND 58702-
0862; 701-852-9161
    scandinavianheritage.org

## Finnish
(See also Scandinavian)

Dakota Finnish Society, c/o Scandinavian Heritage Association, 24 1st St. N.E.
(P.O. Box 862), Minot, ND 58702-0862;
701-852-9161
    scandinavianheritage.org

Family History Finland (part of the
WorldGenWeb project)
    www.open.org/~rumcd/genweb/
    finn.html

Family Sleuths (Finnish, Scandinavian
and U.S. Research), P.O. Box 526163, Salt
Lake City, UT 84152-6163; 801-467-4201
    www.feefhs.org/fi/frg-fs.html

Finnish-American Historical Society of
North Dakota, 108 W. 4th St., Lakota, ND
58344

Finnish Genealogy Group, 4444 Lyndale
Ave. S., Minneapolis, MN 55409-1855;
612-822-0743; library located at the Minnesota Genealogical Society, 1650 Carroll
Ave., St. Paul, MN

Genealogical Society of Finland,
Liisankatu 16 A, FIN-00170 Helsinki,
Finland
    www.genealogia. fi/indexe.htm

History of the Finns in Minnesota online
at this Website
    www.genealogia.fi/emi/art/
    410index.htm

Minnesota Finnish-American Historical
Society, Rt. 2, Box 16, Osage, MN 56570;
218-573-3641
    special.lib.umn.edu/findaid/xml/
    ihrctorma.xml

Online beginner's guide to Finnish family history research
    members.aol.com/dssaari/
    guide.htm

Towner County Historical Society, Rolla,
ND ( Finnish records and settlement
information)

## Icelandic
(See also Scandinavian)
Fargo-Moorhead Icelandic Klub, 744
48th St. S.W., Fargo, ND 58103; 701-281-
8824

Icelandic emigration to North America
    www.halfdan. is/vestur/vestur.htm

Icelandic Heritage Society, c/o Scandinavian Heritage Association, 24 1st St. N.E. (P.O. Box 862), Minot, ND 58702-0862; 701-852-9161
scandinavianheritage.org

Pembina County Icelandic resources, including maps, land patents, naturalization and census data
www.halfdan.is/vestur/pembina.htm

Pioneer Heritage Center, Icelandic State Park, Hwy. 5, Cavalier, ND 58220 (701-265-4561) (holdings include information on the area's settlement period of 1880-1930)
www.ndtourism.com

## Norwegian
(See also Scandinavian)
Astri My Astri Publishing, c/o Deb Nelson Gourley, 602 3rd Ave. S.W., Waukon, IA 52172; 563-568-6229 (specializing in Norwegian, Norse-English bilingual, and genealogy-related publications)
www.astrimyastri.com

Cyndi's List for Norwegian resources
www.cyndislist.com/norway. htm

Digitalarkivet, Regional State Archives, Bergen, Norway (see online guide called "How to Trace Your Ancestors in Norway"on this site)
digitalarkivet.uib.no/sab/howto.html

Elwyn B. Robinson Department of Special Collections, Chester Fritz Library, University of North Dakota, Grand Forks, ND 58202; 701-777-4625
www.library.und.edu/Collections/Robinson/home.html

Emigrant records
www.hist.uib.no/arkivverket

Medieval Scandinavian information and genealogy
the-orb.net/essays/text02.html

Norwegian-American Bygdelagenes Fellesraad, c/o Marilyn D. Somdahl, 10129 Goodrich Circle, Minneapolis, MN 55437; 952-831-4409
www.fellesraad.com

Norwegian-American Historical Association (NAHA), St. Olaf College, Northfield, MN 55057
www.naha.stolaf.edu/genealogy

Norwegian American homepage
www. lawzone.com/half-nor/nor-am.htm

Norwegian Emigrant Museum
museum.snett.no/emigrantmuseum/gensocie.htm

Norwegian Emigration Center, Strandkaien 31, 4005 Stavanger, Norway; +47 51 53 88 60
www.emigrationcenter.com

Norwegian Information Service, 2720 34th St. N.W., Washington, DC 20008
www.norway.org

Sons of Norway, 1455 W. Lake St., Minneapolis, MN 55408; 800-945-8851 or 612-827-3611
www.sofn.com

Sons of Norway Library, 509 14th Ave. N., Fargo, ND 58102; 701-232-6331

Vesterheim Genealogical Center and Naeseth Library, 415 W. Main St., Madison, WI 53703; 608-255-2224
www.vesterheim.org/genealogy

## Swedish
(See also Scandinavian)
American Swedish Institute (ASI); book entitled "Tracing Your Swedish Ancestry" is available from the institute's "Bokhandel" bookstore, 2600 Park Ave., Minneapolis, MN 55407; 612-871-4907
www.americanswedishinst.org
View book online at
genealogy.about.com/library/authors/ucolsson1c.htm

American West: European emigration Website (excellent depiction of Swedish emigration)
www.americanwest. com/swedemigr/pages/emigra.htm

Anderson Butik, 127 N. Main, Lindsborg, KS 67456(785) 227-2356 or 800-782-4132 (maps, books on Sweden)
www.andersonbutik.com

Federation of Swedish Genealogical Societies
www.genealogi.se/roots

## BOOKS

Park Genealogical Books, Dept. WWW, P.O. Box 130968, Roseville, MN 55113-0968
www. parkbooks.com
Riksarchivet (Swedish Archives, or SVAR), P.O. Box 125 41, SE-102 29 Stockholm, Sweden 4687376474
www.ra.se
www.svar.ra.se

Swedish Council of America, 2600 Park Ave., Minneapolis, MN 55407; 612-871-0593
www.swedishcouncil.org

Swedish Cultural Heritage Society, 3107 S. Rivershore Drive, Moorhead, MN 56560-4963; 218-233-8484

Swedish Genealogy Group (of the Minnesota Genealogy Society)
www.mtn.org/mgs/branches/swedish.html

Swedish Heritage Society, c/o Scandinavian Heritage Association, 24 1st St. N.E. (P.O. Box 862), Minot, ND 58702-0862; 701-852-9161
scandinavianheritage.org

Swenson Swedish Immigration Center
www. augustana.edu/swenson

## SCOTTISH
(See British Isles)

## UKRAINIAN
(See also Russian, Germans from Russia)

### General
InfoUkes Inc., Suite 185, 3044 Bloor St. W., Etobicoke, Ontario, Canada M8X 2Y8; 416-236-4865
www.infoukes.com

Ukrainian Cultural Institute, 1221 Villard St. W., Dickinson, ND 58601
www.ukrainianculturalinstitute.org

Ukrainian Genealogical and Historical Society of Canada, R.R.2, Cochrane, AB, TOL 0W0, Canada
www.feefhs.org/CA/frgughsc.html

### Eastern Ukraine

Ukraine Main Archives, Ukraina, 252601, Kiev-110, MSP, vul. Solomianska, 24, Holovne Arkhivne Upravlinnia Ukrainy, Attn: Georgiy Papakin, International Dept. Central State Historical Archives in Kiev, Ukraine, Ukraina, 252601 Kiev—110, vul. Solomianska, 24, Tsentrainyiderzhavny istorichyni arkhiv Ukraony, Kiev (TsDIA-K)

### Western Ukraine

Central State Historical Archives in Lviv, Ukraine: Ukraina 290008, Lviv-8, pl. Soborna, 3-a, Tsentrainyl derzhavnyi istorychnyi arkhiv Ukraony, Lviv (TsDIA-L). Director: Orest Iaroslavoych Matsiuk. Deputy director: Diana Pelc.

## MISCELLANEOUS

### ADOPTION

ADOPT Assistance Information Support
www.adopting. org/serch.html

Adoption Policy Resource Center
www.fpsol.com/adoption/links.html

Adoption search
www.cyfc.umn.edu/
Adoptinfo/howtosearch.html

ALMA (Adoptee Liberty Movement Association), P.O. Box 727, Radio City Station, New York, NY 10101-0727; 212-581-1568
www.almasociety.org

Assistance Information Support
www.adopting.org/ serch.html

National Adoption Information Clearinghouse (NAIC)
www.calib.com/naic/publications/
search.html

North Dakota Department of Human Services, Post Adoption Unit, State Capitol, Dept. 325, Bismarck, ND 58505-0250; 701-328-4805
www.ndgov/humanservices/
services/childfamily.adoption

Orphan Train Heritage Society of America, 4912 Trout Farm Rd., Springdale, AR 72762; 479-756-2780
www.orphantrainriders.com

South Dakota Department of Social Service, Post Adoption Unit, 700 Governor's Drive, Pierre, SD 57501; 605-773-3227
www.dss.sd.gov

## CENSUS & NATURALIZATION

Census forms pdf (including 1930 census) at
heritagequestonline.com/prod/
genealogy/images/censusbook/
Section5.pdf

Census online
www.archives.gov/genealogy
www.census-online.com/links/
index.html
www.genealogysitefinder.com
www.glorecords.blm.gov

Geographic Names Information System
www.geonames.usgs.gov

U.S. Census Bureau gazetteer
www.census.gov/cgi-bin/gazetteer

## GENETIC (DNA) GENEALOGY

Family Tree DNA
www.familytreedna.com

Genographic Project (partnership among the National Geographic Society, IBM and the Waitt Family Foundation)
www3.nationalgeographic.com/
genographic

Relative Genetics
www.relativegenetics.com

Sorenson Molecular Genealogy Foundation
www.smgf.org

Others
www.dnaancestryproject.com
www.tracegenetics.com

## IMMIGRATION

American Genealogical Lending Library, P.O. Box 244, Bountiful, UT 84011-0244
www.agll.com

Library and Archives Canada, 395 Wellington St., Ottawa, Ontario, Canada K1A0N3 (Canadian port records)
www.collectionscanada.ca

Merseyside Maritime Museum, Albert Dock, Liverpool, England L3 4AA
www.liverpoolmuseums.org.uk/
maritime

National Archives Trust Fund, Dept. 510, P.O. Box 100793, Atlanta, GA 30384: (Immigration/Passenger Arrivals: Select Catalog, National Archives Microfilms)
www.libs.uga.edu/researchcentral/
subjectguides/genealogy.html
www.heritagelib.org/HowTo/
Passenger_Immigration.htm

Peabody & Essex Museum, East India Square, Salem, MA 01970
www.pem.org

Steamship Historical Society, Langsdale Library, University of Baltimore, 1420 Maryland Ave., Baltimore, MD 21201-5779
www.sshsa.net

## MAPS

Anderson Butik, 127 N. Main, Lindsborg, KS 67456; 785-227-2356 or 800-782-4132 (maps, books on Sweden)
www.andersonbutik.com

Germans from Russia Heritage Collection, NDSU Library, P.O. Box 5599, Fargo, ND 58105-5599
www.lib.ndsu.nodak.edu/grhc/
order/maps.html

Gold Bug, The, P.O. Box 588, Alamo, CA 94507-0588
www.goldbug.com

Map Store (includes North Dakota and South Dakota atlases and gazetteers)
mapstore.delorme.com

Map Store, The (Maps.com), 120 Cremona Dr., Suite H, Santa Barbara, CA 93117; 800-430-7532
www. maps. com

Rand McNally Map Store, 50 S. Wacker Dr., Chicago, IL; 312-332-2009
www.randmcnallystore.com/
find.asp

Sons of Norway, 1455 W. Lake St., Minneapolis, MN 55408; 800-945-8851 or 612-827-3611 (maps, booklet on genealogy)
www.sofn.com

### (Miscellaneous—maps, continued)

Travel Genie Maps, 3815 Calhoun Ave., Ames, IA 50010; 515-232-1070
showcase.netins.net/web/travelgenie/norway.htm

U.S. Geological Survey: Nationwide map products, including nearly 70,000 topographic maps, available in a variety of scales; 888-ASK-USGS
store.usgs.go

Vesterheim Genealogical Center and Naeseth Library, 415 W. Main St., Madison, WI 53703; 608-255-2224 (closeup maps of Norway)
www.vesterheim.org/genealogy

## MILITARY

C & D Jarnagin Company (Revolutionary War information and other colonial links)
www.jarnaginco.com/revlinks.html

Cemetery Service, National Cemetery System, Dept. of Veterans Affairs, 810 Vermont Ave., Washington, DC 20422 (veteran burial information)
www.cem.va.go

"Civil War Soldiers and Sailors Project," Federation of Genealogical Societies Business Office, Civil War Project, P.O. Box 830220, Richardson, TX 75083-0220
www.fgs.org
www.civilwardata.com

"GI Tracks" pamphlets: Heritage Consulting, P.O. Box 4152, Salt Lake City, UT 84110
expertgenealogy.com

National Archives and Records Administration (NARA), 700 Pennsylvania Ave. N.W., Washington, DC 20408
archives. gov/genealogy

National Personnel Records Center (NPRC), General Services Administration, 9700 Page Blvd., St. Louis, MO 63132
archives.gov/research_room/obtain_copies/veterans_service_records.html

Superintendent of Documents, R.W., CIC-9C, P.O. Box 100, Pueblo, CO 81002.
origin.www.gpo.gov/pueblo

Treasurer General, National Society of the DAR, 1776 D Street N.W., Washington, DC 20006
www.dar.org/natsociety

Wars:
www.rootsweb.com/~varockbr/wars.htm

## ...AND MORE MISCELLANEOUS!

Bible archives (names collected from old Bibles)
www.geocities.com/Heartland/Fields/2403

Blank family tree (pedigree chart)
users/erols.com/emcrcc/Family_Record.htm

Blogging
search.blogger.com
www.blogger.com
www.brandi.org/geneablogy

Family history book notification (posting spot for notifying others you are preparing or have published a family history book)
www.gen-gateway.com/listings.html

Family Tree Maker
www.familtreemaker.com

Heraldry
www.geocities.com/Athens/Academy/4574/heraldry_hst.html

International Black Sheep Society of Genealogists (IBSSG)
www.homepages.rootsweb.com/~blksheep

Mailing lists
members.aol.com/johnf14246/gen_mail.html

MSNBC
www.msnbc.com/news/254376.asp#general

Numbering systems
www.genealogy.com/links/c/c-numbering-systems.html

Psychic roots (Henry Z. Jones site)
www.hankjones.com/psychic.htm

Rootsweb:Kids (for younger generation):
www.rootsweb.com/~usgwkidz

Serendipity site (stories of amazing coincidences in family research)
genealogytoday.com/family/stories/serendipity.html

Video production: Edgewater Productions, St. Paul, MN; 612-633-2296
www.edgewaterproductions.com

Video, instructional; "Gift of Heritage": Mary Lou Productions, 800-224-8511
www.giftofheritage.com

## PRESERVATION & RESTORATION

Conservation Resources International, 800 Forbes Place, Springfield, VA 22151-2204; 800-634-6932
www.conservationresources.com

Gaylord Bros., P.O. Box 4901, Syracuse, NY 13221-4901; 1-800-448-6160
www.gaylord.com

North Dakota State Historical Records Advisory Board, 612 E. Boulevard Ave., Bismarck, ND 58505-0830; 701-328-2668
www.state.nd.us/hist/shrab.htm

Northeast Document Conservation Center, 100 Brickstone Square, Andover, MA 01810-1494; 978-470-1010
www.nedcc.org

Photographs, care of:
palimpsest.stanford.edu/byauth/nyberg/spore.html

Restoration Source, P.O. Box 9384, Salt Lake City, UT 84109-9384; 801-278-7880
www.colorado.gov/dpa/doit/archives/cpa/coservices.htm

University of Minnesota Extension Service Distribution Center, 1420 Eckles Ave., St. Paul, MN 55108-6069
order@extension.umn.edu

University Products Inc., P.O. Box 101, Holyoke, MA 01041-0101; 1-800-628-1912
web.uflib.ufl.edu/preserve/conserve/ univpro.htm

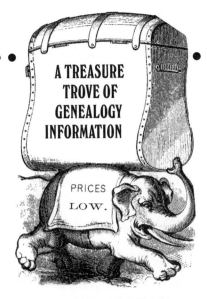

# A TREASURE TROVE OF GENEALOGY INFORMATION

PRICES LOW.

## PUBLISHERS & PUBLICATIONS

Ancestry Daily News
www.ancestry.com

Astri My Astri Publishing, c/o Deb Nelson Gourley, 602 3rd Ave. S.W., Waukon, IA 52172; 563-568-6229 (specializing in Norwegian, Norse-English bilingual, and genealogy-related publications)
www.astrimyastri.com

Betterway Books, 1507 Dana Ave., Cincinnati, OH 45207; 1-800-289-0963
www.familytreemagazine.com/store

Brighton Publications Inc., P.O. Box 120706, St. Paul, MN 55112, 1-800-536-2665
www.partybooks.com

Dear Myrtle's online newsletter, a daily collection of tips, online courses, etc.
members.aol.com/dearmyrtle

Everton Publishers Inc., P.O. Box 368, Logan, UT 84323-0368; 801-752-6022 www.everton.com

Family History Publishers Inc., 845 S. Main St., Bountiful, UT 84010; 801-295-7490
www.familyhistorypublisher.com

Genealogical Periodical Annual Index:
www.amazon.com

"Genealogy Bulletin," Heritage Quest, P.O. Box 329, Bountiful, UT 84011-0329; 1-801-298-5446, Fax 1-801-298-5468:
www.heritagequest.com

"Genealogy Today" online newsletter
www.enoch.com/genealogy/
newslet.htm

G&R Publishing Co., 507 Industrial St., Waverly, IA 50677; 800-383-1679
www.cookbookprinting.com

Genealogical Publishing Co., 1001 N. Calvert St., Baltimore, MD 21202
www.genealogical.com

Goodman Lauren Publishing, 11661 San Vincente Blvd., Ste. 505, Los Angeles, CA 90049; 310-820-5554
www.publisher-services.com

Heritage Quest, P.O. Box 329, Bountiful, UT 84011-0329; 800-760-2455, Fax 801-298-5468
www.heritagequest.com

"History News: The Magazine of the American Association for State and Local History" by American Association for State and Local History, National Archives and Records Administration (NARA), 700 Pennsylvania Ave. N.W., Washington, DC 20408
archives.gov/genealogy

Lineages Inc., P.O. Box 417, Salt Lake City, UT 84110; 800-643-4303
www.lineages.com

"NGS Quarterly" and "NGS Newsletter," National Genealogical Society, 4527 17th St. N.W., Arlington, VA 22207-23991-800-473-0060
www.ngsgenealogy.org

North American Heritage Press, c/o Creative Printing, 1831 Burdick Expy. W., Minot, ND 58701-5667; 701-852-5552
www.northamericanheritagepress.com

"North Dakota History: Journal of the Northern Plains" by State Historical Society of North Dakota, North Dakota Heritage Center, 612 E. Boulevard Ave., Bismarck, ND 58505-0830; 701-328-2091
www.state.nd.us/hist

"Prologue: Quarterly of the National Archives and Records Administration" by National Archives Trust Fund Board, National Archives and Records Administration (NARA), 700 Pennsylvania Ave. N.W., Washington, DC 20408
archives.gov/genealogy

Reunions Magazine, P.O. Box 11727, Milwaukee, WI 53211-1727; 414-263-4567
www.reunionsmag.com

Rootsweb electronic magazine, for genealogy news and information
ezine.rootsweb.com

Warren Research and Publishing, c/o Paula Stuart Warren and James W. Warren, 1869 Laurel Ave., St. Paul, MN 55104-5938; 612-644-6581

## RESEARCH SITES & REGISTRIES

Ancestor name registry
www.gensource.com/common

Ancestry sites
www.ancestry.com/articles/
interview.htm
MyFamily.com
shop.ancestry.com
Yourfamily.com

"Cousins" records/research sites
Cousinconnect.com
DistantCousin.com

Cyndi Howell's Website/research tool
www.cyndislist.com

FamilySearch Internet Genealogy Service, other family search sites
www.online-genealogy.com
www.genconnect.com
www.the-seeker.com

Genealogy.about.com; 10-step guideline for Internet research
genealogy.about.com/od/basics/
a/internet.htm

Genealogy links for beginners
biz.ipa.net/arkresearch/
guide.html
msnbc.com/news/254376.asp
#general
heritagequest.com/gen101
www.firstct.com
www.rootsweb.com/~newbie

Genealogy links: Links to 4,300 resources ranging from passenger lists to census records
www.genealogylinks.net

## (Miscellaneous—research sites & registries, continued)

Genealogy Portal (enables full-text search of Federation of Family History Societies [ffhs.org.uk] and Federation of Genealogical Societies [fgs.org])
www.genealogyportal.com

Genealogy queries
www.lineages.com/queries
www. genealogy.com
genealogicalstudies.com
genealogytoolbox.com
ngsgenealogy.org

Genealogy's Most Wanted
www.citynet.net/mostwanted

Geocities.com
www.geocities.com

Heritage Consulting and Services
www.heritageconsulting.com

Heritage Quest
www.heritagequest.com

Institute of Genealogy and Historical Research, Samford University, 800 Lakeshore Drive, Birmingham, AL 35229
www.samford.edu/schools/igh

Internet Family Finder from Genealogy.com (search engine of 325-million name index from 3.,000,000 Websites)
www.genealogy.com/genealogy/ifftop.html

Irene's Genealogy Post Forum (surname posting place)
www.thecore.com/~hand/genealogy/post

Kindred Konnections
www.kindredkonnections.com

LDS online:
www.familysearch.org

National Institute for Genealogical Studies
globalgenealogy.com

National Institute on Genealogical Research, P.O. Box 14274, Washington, DC 20044-4274
www.rootsweb.com/~natgenin

Newspaper indexes
www.historicnewspaper.com
www.historybuff.com
www.ida.net/users/dhanco/news.htm
www.lcweb.loc.gov/rr/news
www.vfamily.com/news.htm

Olive Tree genealogy site
olivetreegenealogy.com

Professional genealogy researchers
www.bcgcertification.org
www.genealogyPro.com

RootsWeb
www.rootsweb.com
RootsWeb, North Dakota
www.rootsweb.com/roots-1/USA/nd.html

RootsWeb, South Dakota
www.rootsweb.com/roots-1/USA/sd.html

RootsWeb searches
searches.rootsweb.com

RootsWeb surname list:
rsl.rootsweb.com/cgi-bin/rslsql.cgi

Salt Lake Institute of Genealogy, P.O. Box 1144, Salt Lake City, UT 84110
www.infouga.org
www.progenealogists.com/ugainstitute.htm

Surname sites
gentree.com
surnames.com
www.citynet.net/mostwanted
www.familyhistory.com
www.familytreemaker.com
www.genconnect.com
www.genealogytoolbox.com
www.GenExchange.com
www.genforum.genealogy.com
www.gengateway.com
www.gensource.com
www.hamrick.com
www.isleuth.com
www.lineages.com
www.one-name.org
www.online-genealogy.com
www.rootsweb.com
www.rsl.rootsweb.com
www.soc.genealogy.surnames
www.ssa.gov
www.thecore.com

Time-Passages.com: North Dakota-based research firm; site provides educational information about records online
www.time-passages.com

USGENWEB Project (broken down into individual state and county projects; set up under RootsWeb.com domain name)
www.usgenweb.org

USGENWEB Dakota sites:
North Dakota:
www.rootsweb.com/~ndgenweb
South Dakota:
www.rootsweb.com/~sdgenweb
Web addresses for state information:
North Dakota:
www.state.nd.us/host
South Dakota:
www.state.sd.us/host
Other states:
www.state.[insert state abbreviation here].us/host

## REUNIONS

Budget reunion accommodations guide: Budget/Campus Lodging Guides by B&J Publications, P.O. Box 5486, Fullerton, CA 92838-5486; 800-525-6633
www.campus-lodging.com

Family Tree Maker's Reunion Kit:
www.familytreemaker. com

Family Reunion Institute
www.temple.edu/fri/familyreunion/organize.html

Family Reunion Planning Guide
www.reunionwear.com/php/guide.php

Family Reunion Planning Site (Family Reunion Organizer software)
www.family-reunion.com

"Fun and Games for Family Gatherings: With a Focus on Reunions," Reunion Research, 40609 Auberry Road, Auberry, CA 93602; 209-855-2101
www.reuniontips.com

"Generations, The Game of Family Knowledge"; 918-495-1000
www.generationsgame.com
www.genealogy4fun.com

Military reunion: CYBERCON,
573 Pine St. #50, Neptune Beach, FL 32266
web.cybercon.com

Party books
www.partybooks.com

Reunion information
www.gemneye.com/
reunions/reunions.html

Reunion planner
www.reunionplanner.com

Reunions Magazine
www.reunionsmag.com

## SEARCH ENGINES

altavista.com
askjeeves.com
dogpile.com
excite.com
google.com
hotbot.com
infoseek.com
metacrawler.com
vivisimo.com
yahoo.com

## SOFTWARE, GENEALOGY

Ancestral Quest, Version 11
www.ancquest.com

Brother's Keeper, Version 6.2
www.bkwin.org

Cumberland Family Tree, Version 3.1
www.cf-software.com

DoroTree, Version 2.1
www.dorotree.com

Family Historian, Version 3
www.family-historian.co.uk

Family Tree Legends, Version 5.0
www.familytreelegends.com
Family Tree Maker, Version 11
www.genealogy.com/soft_ftm.html

Famtree, Version 4.42
members.aol.com/famtree

GEDitCOM, Version 3.72 (Macintosh)
www.geditcom.com

Genbox Family History, Version 5
www.genbox.com

Heredis, Version 7.2
www.heredis.com

Legacy Family Tree, 6.0
www.legacyfamilytree.com

LifeLines, Version 3.0.50
lifelines.sourceforge.net

Master Genealogist (Wholly Genes)
www.whollygenes.com

Personal Ancestral File (PAF), Version 5.2
genealogy.about.com/library/
blpaf.htm

Reunion, Version 8 (Macintosh)
www.leisterpro.com

RootsMagic, Version 3
www.rootsmagic.com

WinFamily, Version 6.02
www.winfamily.com

Miscellaneous software
filemine.com
itprodownloads.com

Software, online directories
dmoz.org/Society/Genealogy/
Software
www.genealogytoday.com/
roots/xweb.mv

## VENDORS

AGLL Genealogical Services, P.O. Box
329, Bountiful, UT 84011-0329; 800-760-
AGLL

Ancestry, 266 W. Center St., Orem, UT
84057
www.ancestry.com

Anderson Butik, 127 N. Main, Lindsborg,
KS 67456; 785-227-2356 or 800-782-4132
(maps, books on Sweden, etc.)
www.andersonbutik.com
Bokhandel, 2600 Park Ave., Minneapolis,
MN 55407; 612-871-4907 or 1-800-579-3336
www.americanswedishinst.org

Everton Publishers Inc.
www.everton.com

Genealogy Mall on the Internet:
www.genmall.com

Light Impressions, 439 Monroe Ave.
(P.O. Box 940), Rochester, NY 14603-0940;
716-271-8960
www.lightimpressionsdirect.com

Lineages Inc., P.O. Box 417, Salt Lake
City, UT 84110; 800-643-4303
www.lineages.com

Park Genealogical Books, Dept. WWW,
P.O. Box 130968, Roseville, MN 55113-0968
www.parkbooks.com

Publication Sales Branch, General Services Administration, Washington, D.C.
20408

Sons of Norway, 1455 W. Lake St., Minneapolis, MN 55408; 800-945-8851 or 612-
827-3611 (maps, books, "Viking"
magazine, booklets on Norwegian
genealogy)
www.sofn.com/norwegianculture/
viking

Stevenson's Genealogy Center, 230 W.
1230 North, Provo, UT 84604; 801-374-
9600; Fax: 801-374-9622
www.sgenealogy.com

Storbeck's Genealogy, P.O. Box 510062,
New Berlin, WI 53151-0062; 1-800-360-
3555 (books, CDs, supplies)
www.storbecks.com

Thomsen's Genealogical Center, P.O.
Box 588, Bountiful UT 84011;
801-294-5105

Time Voyagers Bookstore
www.timevoyagers.com

Travel Genie Maps, 1113 Kennedy St.,
Ames, IA 50010; 515-232-1070
showcase.netins.net/web/
travelgenie

Vesterheim Genealogical Center, Norwegian American Museum, 502 W. Water St.,
Decorah, IA 62101 (closeup maps of Norway)
www.vesterheim.org/genealogy

Ye Olde Genealogie Shoppe, P.O. Box
39128, Indianapolis, IN 46239
www.yogs.com •

# Bibliography ........

## A prayer for a genealogist

Lord, help me dig
    into the past
And sift the sands of time,
That I might find
    the roots that made
This family tree of mine.

Lord, help me trace
    the ancient roads
On which my fathers trod,
And led them through
    so many lands
To find their present sod.

Lord, help me find
    an ancient book
Or dusty manuscript
That's safely hidden
    now away
In some forgotten crypt.

Lord, let it bridge
    the gap that haunts
My soul when I can't find
The missing link
    between some name
That ends
    the same as mine!
—Curtis Woods

*(Reprinted from Bismarck-Mandan Historical and Genealogical Society publication)*

On these pages we have listed some of the resources we used in this book. Please check our helpful addresses section for contact information on the following:

- **National, regional and state record repositories, archives and libraries**
- **National and state genealogical societies**
- **LDS family history centers**
- **Ethnic roots addresses**
- **Records and resources**

. . . . . . . . . . . . .

### AUTHORS' NOTE:
**The following publications were used throughout the book, so reference will be omitted from the rest of the bibliography to save space**

"Archives, The: A Guide to the National Archives Field Branches" by Loretto Dennis Szucs and Sandra Hargreaves Luebking; Ancestry Inc., 1988

"Complete Idiot's Guide to Genealogy, The," by Christine Rose and Kay Germain Ingalls; Alpha Books, 1997

"Dakota Panorama,"edited by J. Leonard Jennewein and Jane Boorman; Dakota Territory Centennial Commission, 1961, 1962, 1973

"Discover Your Roots: How to Trace Your Family Tree" by Bill R. Linder; New York, 1978

"Ethnic Heritage in North Dakota," edited by Francie Berg, Flying Diamond Books, Hettinger, ND; by Attiyeh Foundation, 1983

"Everything Family Tree Book, The: Finding, Charting and Preserving Your Family History," by William G. Hartley; Adams Media Corp., 1998

"Handy Book for Genealogists,10th Edition, The," edited by George B. Everton Sr.; published by Everton Publishers, Logan, UT, 2002

"History of North Dakota," by Elwyn B. Robinson; University of Nebraska Press, Lincoln, NE, 1966

"History of South Dakota," by Herbert S. Schell; University of Nebraska Press, Lincoln, NE, 1961

"How to Climb Your Family Tree: Genealogy for Beginners" by Harriet Stryker-Rodda

"Plains Folk: North Dakota's Ethnic History," by William C. Sherman, Playford V. Thorson, Warren A. Henke, Timothy J. Kloberdanz, Theodore B. Pedeliski and Robert P. Wilkins; North Dakota Institute for Regional Studies at North Dakota State University, Fargo (in cooperation with North Dakota Humanities Council and University of North Dakota), 1988

"Redbook: American State, County and Town Sources," edited by Alice Eichholz, Ph.D., C.G.; Ancestry Inc., 2004

"Shaking Your Family Tree: A Basic Guide to Tracing Your Family's Genealogy," by Ralph Crandall; Yankee Publishing Inc., Dublin, NH

"Source, The: A Guidebook of American Genealogy," edited by Arlene Eakle and Johni Cerni; Ancestry Publishing Co., Salt Lake City, UT, 1996

"Story of North Dakota, The" by Erling Nicolai Rolfsrud; Lantern Books, Alexandria, MN, 4th printing, 1972

"Tracing Your Ancestry: A Step-by-step Guide to Researching Your Family History" and accompanying "Tracing your Ancestry Logbook," by F. Wilbur Helmbold

"Tracing Your Roots in North Dakota" by Jo Ann Winistorfer; North Dakota REC/RTC Magazine, North Dakota Association of Rural Electric Cooperatives, 1989

"Unpuzzling Your Past: A Basic Guide to Genealogy" by Emily Anne Croom; Betterway Books, Cincinnati, OH, 1995

## INTRODUCTION

### HISTORY
(See books listed above)

## CHAPTER 1

### GENEALOGY BASICS

"Ancestry Newsletter," Vol. V, No. 6, Nov.-Dec. 1987 (article on patronymic names), by Freeman E. Morgan Jr., Maryland Enterprises

"Beginner's Guide to Family History Research" by Desmond Walls Allen, 1997

"Beginning Genealogy and A Guide to Continuing Research" by Marilyn Lind, 1984

"Climb It Right: A High-Tech Genealogy Primer," by John and Carolyn Cosgriff

"Do's and Don't's for Ancestor Hunters" by Angus Baxter, 1989

"Finding Your Roots" by Jeane Eddy Westin, Ballantine Books, New York, 1977

"Genealogical Handbook for New England Research" by Marcia Wiswall Lindberg, 1993

"Genealogical Register of the First Settlers of New England" by John Farmer, 1989

"Genealogical Research: Methods and Sources" by The American Society of Genealogists, Milton Rubincam and Kenn Stryker-Rodda, editors; Polyanthos, New Orleans, LA, 1980-83

"Genealogies in the Library of Congress: A Bibliography" by Marion J. Kaminkow, Magna Carta Book Co., Baltimore, MD, 1974

"Genealogist's Bibliography, A" by Cecil R. Humphrey-Smith; Baltimore, MD, 1985

"Genealogist's Companion and Sourcebook, The" by Emily Anne Croom

"Genealogist's Guide to Discovering Your Female Ancestors" by Sharon DeBartolo Carmack, Betterway Books, Cincinnati, OH, 1998

"Genealogist's Handbook: Modern Methods for Researching Family History" by Raymond S. Wright III, 1995

"Genealogy: A Selected Bibliography" by Milton Rubincam; Banner Press, Birmingham, AL, 1983

"Genealogy as Pastime and Profession" by Donald Lines Jacobus; Baltimore, MD, 1991

"North Dakota Place Names" by Douglas A. Wick; Hedemarken Collectibles, 1988

"Pitfalls in Genealogical Research" by Milton Rubincam

"Recording Your Family History" by William Fletcher, 1989

"Researcher's Guide to American Genealogy" by Val D. Greenwood, GPC; Baltimore, MD, 1990

"Roots for Kids, a Genealogical Guide for Young People" by Susan Provost Beller, 1989

"Searching for Your Ancestors: The How and Why of Genealogy" by Gilbert H. Doane and James B. Bell , University of Minnesota, Minneapolis, MN, 1992

"Simplified Genealogy for Americans" by E. Kay Kirkham, Salt Lake City, UT, 1977

# CHAPTER 2

## THE RECORDS

### ADOPTION

"Adoption Agencies, Orphanages and Maternity Homes: A Historical Directory" by Reg. Niles; Phileas Deigh Corp., 1981

"Adoption Searchbook: Techniques for Tracing People, The," by Mary Jo Rillera; ca. 1991

ALMA (Adoptee Liberty Movement Association), New York, NY

"Birthright, the Guide to Search and Reunion for Adoptees, Birthparents and Adoptive Parents" by Jean Strauss; 1994

"Finding Lost and Missing Persons" by Marilyn S. Chang; Denver Public Library, Denver, CO

"How to Find Almost Anyone, Anywhere" by Norma Mott Tillman; Rutledge Hill Press, Nashville, TN, 1994

KinQuest BBS, 505-268-0321

"Lifeline: The Action Guide to Adoption Search" by Virgil L. Klunder; Caradium Publishing, 1991

"Search: A Handbook for Adoptees and Birthparents," by Jayne Askin; 1992

### CEMETERY RECORDS

"Burleigh County Book of Remembrances, The," compiled by Beth Bauman, Gail Gorden and Dorothy Jackman; Bismarck-Mandan Historical and Genealogical Society, 1994

"National Yellow Book of Funeral Directors and Supplies, The," published by Nomis Publications Inc., Youngstown, OH

### CENSUS

Family History Library Catalog (FHLC)

"Map Guide to the U.S. Federal Censuses, 1790-1920" by William Thorndale and William Dollarhide; Genealogical Publishing Co., Inc., Baltimore, MD, 1987

"State Census Records" by Ann S. Lainhard

"U.S. and Special Census Catalog," Ancestry Inc.

### CHURCH RECORDS

"Encyclopedia of American Religions, 2nd edition, The," by J. Gordon Melton; Gale Research Co., Detroit, 1987

"Genealogy Bulletin" No.45, (re Bible records)

(See address section for church archives addresses)

### IMMIGRATION AND NATURALIZATION

"American Passenger Arrival Records" by Michael Tepper; Genealogical Publishing Co., 1988

"Genealogy Bulletin," No. 45 "Guide to Naturalization Records of the United States" by Christina K. Schaefer; 1997

"Immigration and Passenger Arrivals: A Select Catalog of National Archives Microfilms" (1820 -1954); National Archives Trust Fund, Dept. 510, P.O. Box 100793, Atlanta, GA 30384

"Passenger and Immigration Lists Index: Between the 16th and Mid-20th Centuries," edited by P. William Filby and Paula K. Byers; 1995

"They Came in Ships,"second edition, by John P. Colleta; Ancestry Inc., 1993

"Württemberg Emigration Index" (five volumes; includes Germans leaving Russia )

### LAND RECORDS

Denver Branch of the National Archives: Denver Branch Building 48, Denver Federal Center, Denver, CO 80225; 303-236-0817

"Land Laws," State Archives and Historical Research Library; State Historical Society of North Dakota,1998

North Dakota State Genealogical Society Newsletter, May 1999

"Records of Land Ownership and Settlement," State Archives and Historical Research Library; State Historical Society of North Dakota,1998

### MAPS

Glass Box Gift Shop, North Dakota Heritage Center, State Capitol Grounds, Bismarck, ND

Magellan Geographix Inc.'s "The Map Store," Santa Barbara, CA

North and South Dakota "Atlas & Gazetteer" (separate books), available via DeLorme's "The Map Store"

Rand McNally Map Store, Chicago, IL

"Where to Write for County Maps" by Desmond Walls Allen

(For maps of foreign countries, see related ethnic section)

### MILITARY RECORDS

"Ancestry Daily News," 25 May 1999 and 26 May 1999; www.ancestry.com

Bureau Co. Genealogical Society Newsletter, Vol. III, No. 3, May 1992

Cemetery Service, National Cemetery System, Dept. of Veterans Affairs, Washington, DC

"Civil War at a Glance" (134F), a map illlustrating and describing major Civil War battle campaigns. Superintendent of Documents, Pueblo, CO

"Civil War Soldiers and Sailors Project," Federation of Genealogical Societies Business Office, Civil War Project, Richardson, TX

Consumer Information Catalog, Summer 1999; Superintendent of Documents, Pueblo, CO

"Genealogy Bulletin," No. 43 and 44; "Genealogy, Etc." column; January/February 1998, March/ April 1998

"GI Tracks" pamphlets: "Understanding U.S. Military Records" and "Revolutionary War Records"; Heritage Consulting, Salt Lake City, UT

"How to Locate Anyone Who Is or Has Been in the Military," 7th edition, by Richard S. Johnson; Military Enterprises, 1996

"Military Service Records in the National Archives of the United States, Leaflet No. 7." Publication Sales Branch, General Services Administration, Washington, DV

North Dakota State Genealogical Society Newsletter, May 1999

Research Outline: U.S. Military Records; Family History Library, Salt Lake City, UT

"Standard Form 180—Request Pertaining to Military Personnel Records," National Personnel Records Center (NPRC), General Services Administration, St. Louis, MO

"U.S. Military Records: A Guide to Federal and State Sources, Colonial America to the Present," by James C. Neagles

## MISCELLANEOUS RECORDS
"Social Security Applications: A Genealogical Resource" by Desmond Walls Allen and Carolyn Earle Billingsley

### PRINTED SOURCES
"American Newspapers, 1821-1936: A Union List of Files Available in the United States and Canada," edited by Gregory Winifred, reprinted in 1967

"Burleigh County Book of Remembrances, The," compiled by Beth Bauman, Gail Gorden and Dorothy Jackman; Bismarck-Mandan Historical and Genealogical Society, 1994

"Gale Directory of Publications and Broadcast Media" (formerly Ayer Directory of Publications), edited by Julie Winklepleck. Printed annually since 1869. Gale Research Inc., Detroit, MI

"Handy Book for Genealogists, The," edited by George B. Everton Sr.,; Everton Publishers Inc., Logan, UT

"Obituaries: A Guide to Sources" by Betty M. Jarboe; Boston, 1989

"Union Lists of North Dakota Newspapers, 1864-1976," by Carol Koehmstedt Kolar; North Dakota Institute for Regional Studies (NDSU, Fargo), 1981

### VITAL RECORDS
Consumer Information Catalog, Summer 1999; Superintendent of Documents, Pueblo, CO

"Where to Write for Birth and Death Records" and "Where to Write for Marriage Records," Superintendent of Documents, U.S. Government Printing Office, Washington, DC

"Where to Write for Vital Records," U.S. Department of Health and Human Services Publication No. 82-1184; U.S. Government Printing Office, Washington, DC

## CHAPTER 3

## RESEARCH SITES

"Access to Ancestry: A Genealogical Resources Manual for Canadians Tracing Their Heritage" by Elizabeth Briggs

American Library Directory, by R.R. Bowker Co., New York

America's "Best Genealogy Resource Centers" by William Dollarhide and Ronald Bremer

"Ayer Directory of Publications," Ayer Press, Philadelphia, PA (See "Gale Directory of Publications" imder RECORDS, Printed Sources)

"Cemeteries of Cass County, ND" by Fargo Genealogical Society

"Cemeteries of North Dakota, Fargo City Cemeteries: North of Highway I-94" by Shirley Simmons, ed.

"Concise Genealogical Dictionary" by Maurine and Glen Harris

"County Courthouse Book" by Elizabeth Bentley

"Directory, Historical Societies and Agencies in the United States and Canada" by American Assn. for State and Local History, Nashville, TN

"Directory of American Libraries with Genealogy Collections" by P. William Filby; Wilmington, DE, 1988

"Directory of Genealogical Researchers in North America: Volume III the Midwestern States" by Rogan Hart Moore, ed.

"Directory of Genealogical Societies in the U.S.A. and Canada" by Mary Keysor Meyer, ed.; Libra Publications, Lithicum, MD

"Directory of Special Libraries and Information Centers" by Gale Research Company, Detroit, MI

"Earliest Records of Riverside Cemetery, 1877-1911" by Red River Valley Genealogical Society

"Find Public Records Fast: The Complete State, County and Courthouse Locator," Genealogical Periodical Annual Index (GPAI), Heritage Books, Bowie, MD, 1977 "Genealogical Records in the National Archives" by NARA

"Genealogical Research and Resources: A Guide for Library Use" by Lois C. Gilmer

"Genealogical Research: Methods and Sources" by American Society of Genealogists

"Genealogical Research: Volumes I and II" by American Society of Genealogists

"Genealogical Resources of the Minnesota Historical Society"

Genealogist's "Address Book" by Elizabeth P. Bentley

Genealogist's "Companion and Source Book" by Emily Anne Croom

"Getting Started: Beginning your Genealogical Research in the National Archives" by NARA

"Getting the Most Mileage from Genealogical Research Trips" by James W. Warren and Paul Stuart Warren

"Going to Salt Lake to Do Family History Research" by J. Carlyle Parker

"Guide to Genealogical/Family History Resources" by Chester Fritz Library-University of North Dakota

"Guide to Genealogical Research in the National Archives" by U.S. National Archives and Records Administration; Washington, DC, 1982

"Guide to Genealogical Resources in Fargo-Moorhead" by Moorhead State University Heritage Education Commission, 1982

"Guide to Local and Family History at the Newberry Library" by Peggy Tuck Sinko

"Guide to Naturalization Records of the United States" by Christina Schaefer

"Guide to Research: Case Studies in American Genealogy," by Johni Cerni and Arlene Eakle; Ancestry Inc.

"Guide to the Holdings of the Archives of Ontario"

"Guide to the Small Collection Manuscripts of the North Dakota Institute for Regional Studies" by John E. Bye, 1977

"History News: The Magazine of the American Association for State and Local History" by American Association for State and Local History

"Information Outlook" by Special Libraries Association

"Lest We Forget: A Guide to Genealogical Research in the Nation's Capital," Annandale, VA, Stake of the Church of Jesus Christ of Latter-Day Saints

"Librarian's Guide to Public Records, The"

"Library of Congress, The: A Guide to Genealogical and Historical Research" by James C. Neagles, assisted by Mark C. Neagles

"Library, The: A Guide to the LDS Family History Library," edited by Johni Cerny and Wendy Elliott

"Making the Most of Your Research Trip to Salt Lake City" by Paul Stuart Warren and James W. Warren

"Military Service Records in the National Archives of the United States"

"National Director of Weekly Newspapers," National Newspaper Association and Publisher's Auxiliary annual

"North Dakota History: Journal of the Northern Plains" by State Historical Society of North Dakota

"North Dakota Place Names" by Douglas Wick, Hedemarken Collectibles, Bismarck, ND, 1988

"Origin of Certain Place Names in the United States, The" by Henry Gannett

"Periodical Source Index (PERSI)," Allen County Public Library, Fort Wayne, IN

"Pitfalls in Genealogical Research" by Milton Rubincam

"Prologue: Quarterly of the National Archives and Records Administration" by National Archives Trust Fund Board

"Record: News from the National Archives and Records Administration, The" by NARA

"Researcher's Guide to American Genealogy" by Val D. Greenwood

"Scandinavian Genealogical Research Manual" by Finn A. Thomsen

"Searching for your Ancestors: The How and Why of Genealogy" by Harry Gilbert Doane and James B. Bell

"Sourcebook of State Public Records, The"

"South Dakota History" by South Dakota State Historical Society

"U.S. Military Records: A Guide to Federal and State Sources Colonial America to the Present" by James C. Neagles

"U.S. Research Outline: Family History Library"

"Vital Records Handbook" by Thomas Jay Kemp

**CHAPTER 4**

## ETHNIC GROUPS

### GENERAL

(See also listings at beginning of bibliography; Helpful Addresses section of Appendix)

"Experiment Station Bulletin No. 313: Immigrant Settlements and Social Organization in South Dakota" by John P. Johansen: settlement pattern of various religious groups (including German-Russians)

"Prairie Mosaic" by William C. Sherman; North Dakota Institute for Regional Studies, North Dakota State University, Fargo, 1983

### BANAT GERMAN-HUNGARIAN
(See also Hungarian)
"Banat German Hungarians Who Came to Southwestern North Dakota: Wiver Sach (Women's Stuff)," compiled by Theresa K. Bogner Montee-Nelson; Dickinson, ND, 1999

"Family History Research for North Dakota Pioneers from the Banat" by David Dreyer; San Francisco, 1999

### BELGIAN
"Ancestral Research in Belgium" by Erica Hartman Nederhand; Salt Lake City, 1973

### BOHEMIAN/CZECH
"Czech Immigration Passenger Lists" by Leonard Baca. Old Homestead, 1983. Vol. 1: Misc. lists. Vol. 2: Galveston 1896-1906; New Orleans 1879-1899. Vol. 3: Galveston 1907-1914. Vol. 4: New York 1847-1869. Vol. 5: New York 1870-1880

"Czechoslovakia: A Handbook of Czechoslovak Genealogical Research" by Daniel M. Schlyter; Genun, 1985

"Genealogical Research for Czech and Slovak Americans" by Olga K. Miller; Gale, 1978

### BRITISH ISLES/ SCOTLAND/IRELAND
"Alphabetical Index to the Townlands and Towns of Ireland, The" by Alexander Thom, 1877

"Bibliography of Irish Family History and Genealogy" by Brian deBreffny; Golden Eagle Books, 1974

"Genealogical Gazetteer of England, The" by Frank Smith; Genealogical Publishing Co., 1968

"Genealogist's Guide, The" by Geoffrey B. Barrow; A.L.A., 1977 (English genealogy)

"Guide to Irish Parish Registers, A" Genealogical Publishing Co., 1988

"In Search of Scottish Ancestry" by Gerald Hamilton-Edwards; Phillimore and Company, London, 1972

"In Search of Your British and Irish Roots" by Angus Baxter; 3rd edition, Genealogical Publishing Co., 1991

"Irish and Scotch-Irish Ancestral Research: A Guide to the Genealogical Records, Methods and Sources in Ireland" by Margaret Dickson Falley; Falley, 1962

"Irish Families, Their Names, Arms and Origins" by Edward MacLysaght; Irish Academic Press, Dublin, 1991

"Irish Genealogy: a Record Finder" by Donald F. Begley; Heraldic Artists, 1981

"Irish Passenger Lists, 1847-1871: Lists of passengers sailing from Londonderry to America on ships of the J. & J. Cooke Line and the McCorkell Line" by Brian Mitchell. Genealogical Publishing Co., 1988

"Irish Records: Sources for Family and Local History" by James G. Ryan; Ancestry, 1997

"Major Genealogical Record Sources in Scotland," LDS Family History Library

Ordnance Townland Survey of Ireland, Dublin, 1831-42. (Detailed set of Irish maps; available on microfiche at Newberry Library, Chicago)

"Parliamentary Gazetteer of England and Wales, The," 4 volumes, London, 1843

"Surnames of Scotland, The" by George F. Black

"Tracing Your British Ancestors" by Colin R. Chapman, Genealogical Publishing Co., 1993

## CANADIAN
"Access to Ancestry: A Genealogical Resources Manual for Canadians Tracing Their Heritage" by Elizabeth Briggs

## DUTCH (HOLLANDER/ NETHERLANDER)
"Dutch Households in U.S. population censuses 1850, 1860, 1870. An alphabetical listing by family heads," by R.P. Swieringa; 3 volumes, Scholarly Resources Inc., 1985-87

## FRENCH
(See also Canadian)
"French and French-Canadian Family Research," revised edition, by J. Konrad; Summit Publications, 1993 (available through Ye Olde Genealogie Shoppe; see address section)

"History of the Huguenot Emigration to America" by Charles W. Baird; Genealogical Publishing Co.

## GERMAN
(See also Russian, Germans from Russia)
"Finding Your German Ancestors" by Dr. Ronald M. Smelser

Gazetteer: "Meyers Orts und Verkehrs-Lexikon des Deutschen Reichs," Bibliographisches Institut, Leipzig; 1912-13

"In Search of Your German Roots: A Complete Guide to Tracing Your Ancestors in the German Areas of Europe" by Angus Baxter

Institut für Auslandsbeziehungen, Charlottenplatz 17, 7000 Stuttgart 1, Germany; 011-49-711-221766 (calling from U.S.).

## GERMANS FROM RUSSIA
(See also Russian, German, Ukrainian)
"Emigration from Germany to Russia in the Years 1763-1862, The" by Dr. Karl Stumpp
"German Colonies in South Russia, The," Volumes I & II, by Rev. P. Conrad Keller, S.J.; published in Odessa, Russia, 1904 (translated and published in English by Dr. Anthony Becker)

"Extended Relationships of the Kulm, Leipzig and Tarutini Communities in Bessarabia, Russia" by Arthur E. Flegel; 2005

"Fond 53: Grossliebental, Odessa State Archives," guide

"Fond 252: Odessa Office of Foreign Settlers in Southern Russia (1806, 1814-1834, 1843, 1850)," guide

"Germans from Russia, The: Children of the Steppes, Children of the Prairies," video documentary co-produced by Prairie Public Television and North Dakota Institute for Regional Studies, North Dakota State University Libraries, Fargo; 1998

"Glueckstal Colonies Births and Marriages: 1833-1900," compiled by Harold M. Ehrman; Germans from Russia Heritage Collection, NDSU Libraries, 1999

"Glueckstal Colonies Deaths: 1833-1900," compiled by Harold M. Ehrman; Germans from Russia Heritage Collection, NDSU Libraries, 1999

"Glueckstalers of New Russia and North America, The: A Bicentennial Collection of History, Genealogy and Folklore," book and two CDs; published by the Glueckstal Colonies Research Association, Redondo Beach, CA, 2004

"Handbook for Researching Family Roots," compiled and written by Diane J. Wandler; published by the Bismarck Prairie Heritage Chapter, Germans from Russia Heritage Society, 1992

"Heaven Is Our Homeland: The Glueckstalers of New Russia and North America," award-winning documentary; published by the Glueckstal Colonies Research Association, Redondo Beach, CA, 2004

"Homeland Book of the Bessarabian Germans" by Pastor Albert Kern

"Pietism and the Russian Germans in the United States" by George J. Eisenach

"Prairie Churches of Bon Homme County, Dakota Territory" by Maxine Schuurmans Kinsley

"Prairie Crosses, Prairie Voices: Iron Crosses of the Great Plains," video documentary co-produced by Prairie Public Television and North Dakota Institute for Regional Studies, North Dakota State University Libraries, Fargo; 1998

"Researcher's Guide to McPherson County, SD, Cemeteries" by Selma Job Lapp and Keenan L. Stoecker, edited by Duane E. Stabler; 2005

"Researching the Germans from Russia, an Annotated Bibliography," compiled by Michael M. Miller, Bibliographer, Germans from Russia Heritage Collection, North Dakota Institute for Regional Studies, North Dakota State University Libraries, Fargo; 1987

## HUNGARIAN
(See also Banat German Hungarian)
Atlas: "Magyarorszag Autoatlasza"; printed by Cartographia in Hungary

Gazetteer: "Magyarorszag Helysegnevtara Ket Kotethen" by Janos Dvorzsak

"Handy Guide to Hungarian Genealogical Records" by Jared H. Suess

"Magyar-Angol Keziszotar" by Laszlo Orszagh; Hungarian-English dictionary

## INDIANS, AMERICAN
"American Indians: A Select Catalog of National Archives Microfilm Publications," NARA

"Collections of the State Historical Society," Volume 5, edited by O.G. Libby; collection housed in the North Dakota State Archives and Historical Research Library, Bismarck

"Guide to Records in the National Archives of the United States Relating to American Indians ," by Edward E. Hill; Washington, DC

"Indian Tribes of North America, The," by John R. Swanson; published by the Smithsonian Institution Press

"Native American Genealogical Sourcebook," from Gale Research Inc., Detroit

"North Dakota's Indian Heritage," by Mary Jane Schneider; University of North Dakota Press, Grand Forks, ND 1990

"Our Native Americans and Their Records of Genealogical Value," by E. Kay Kirkham; Everton Publishers, 1984

"Student's Guide to Native American Genealogy, A," by E. Barrie Kavasch; Oryx American Family Tree Series

## JEWISH
(See Germans from Russia, Russian, Ukrainian)

## RUSSIAN
(See Germans from Russia, Ukrainian)

## SCANDINAVIAN

### Danish
"History of the Danish Settlement in Hill Township, Cass County, ND" by Waldemar C. Westergaard, 1906

### Finnish
"History of Rolla, North Dakota Finnish Settlement, Towner County and Surrounding Area, Rolla, North Dakota," compiled and edited by Waino E. Kontio, Rolla Historical Society, 1962

"History of the Finnish Settlement in Brown and Dickey Counties of South and North Dakota, A, 1881-1955," 2nd edition, Northwestern Publishing Company, New York Mills, MN, 1956

### Icelandic
"Gimli Saga: A History of Gimli, Manitoba," Gimli Women's Institute, Altona, Manitoba, 1974

"History of Pembina County, A," Pembina Centennial Committee, 1967

"Icelandic People in Manitoba"; Winnipeg, 1965

" Icelandic Settlement of Pembina County, The," Vol. 1 (Bismarck, 1906; collections of the State Historical Society of North Dakota)

"Modern Sagas: The Story of the Icelanders in North America" by Thorstina Jackson Walters; North Dakota Institute for Regional Studies, Fargo, 1953

"Pembina Settlement Heritage: A History of the Pembina, North Dakota, Area," Pembina Settlement Heritage Book Committee and the Red River Valley Historical Society, 1976

"Walsh Heritage: A Story of Walsh County and Its Pioneers," Vol. 1; Walsh County Historical Society, 1976

"80th Anniversary 1897-1997 Melankton Lutheran Church, Upham, ND"; 1997

### Norwegian
"Genealogical Guidebook and Atlas of Norway" by Finn Thomsen and Frank Smith; Everton Publishers

"History of the Norwegian Settlements: A Translated and Expanded Version of the 1908 De Norske Settlementers Historie and the 1930 Den Siste Folkevandring Sagastubber fra Nybyggerlivet i Amerika" by Hjalmar Rued Holand; Astri My Astri Publishing, Waukon, IA, 2006

"How to Trace Your Ancestors in Norway," Norwegian Information Service, Washington, DC

"Tracing Your Norwegian Roots" by Maralyn A. Wellauer, Milwaukee, WI

### Swedish
"Beginner's Guide to Swedish Genealogical Research" by Finn A. Thomsen. Thomsen's Genealogical Center, Bountiful, UT, 1984

"Cradled in Sweden [a practical help to genealogical research in Swedish records]" by Carl-Erik Johansson; Everton Publishers, Logan, UT, 1977

"Finding Your Forefathers: Some hints for Americans of Swedish origin," published by Royal Ministry for Foreign Affairs, Stockholm, 1957

"Genealogical Guidebook & Atlas of Sweden" by Finn Thomsen

"Of Swedish Ways" by Lilly Lorenzen

"Swedes in America" by Benson and Hedin

"Swedish Exodus" by Lars Ljungmark

"Tracing Your Swedish Ancestry," Bokhandel, Minneapolis, MN

"Vägatlas över Sverige" (Lantmäteriet ), the largest scale map book available for Sweden

Vilhelm Moberg's series of four books on Swedish emigration: "The Emigrants," "Unto a Good Land," "The Settlers" and "Last Letter Home."

## SYRIAN-LEBANESE
"Lebanese and Syrians in America, The" by Edward Wakin; Claretian, Chicago, 1971

"Prairie Peddlers: The Syrian-Lebanese in North Dakota," by William C. Sherman, Paul L. Whitney and John Guerrero; University of Mary Press, 2002

"Syrians in America" by Philip K. Hitti; George H. Doran Co., New York, 1924

"Syrian Lebanese in America, The" by Joseph Kayal; Twayne, Boston, 1975

## UKRAINIAN
(See Russian, Germans from Russia)

## CHAPTER 5

# ORAL INTERVIEWS

"Awakening the Hidden Storyteller: How to Build a Storytelling Tradition inYour Family," by Robin Moore; Shambhala Publications

"Craft of Interviewing, The," by John Brady; Writer's Digest Books

"Creative Interviewing—The Writer's Guide to Gathering Information by Asking Questions," by Ken Metzler; Prentice-Hall

"Family Reunion Handbook," by Barbara Brown and Tom Ninkovich; Reunion Research, Auberry, CA

"Family Tales, Family Wisdom: How to Gather the Stories of a Lifetime and Share Them with Your Family," by Robert U. Akeret, with Daniel Klein; William Morrow and Company

"From Memories to Manuscript, the Five-step Method of Writing Your Life Story," by Joan R. Neubauer; Ancestry, Orem, UT

"Gift of Heritage—An Instructional Video," by Mary Lou Productions

"Instant Oral Biographies: How to Tape Record, Video or Film Your Life Stories," by William Zimmerman; Guarionex Press

" Keeping Family Stories Alive," by Vera Rosenbluth; Hartley and Marks Publishing

" Like It Was: A Complete Guide to Writing Oral History," by Cynthia Stokes Brown

"Once Upon a Memory: Your Family Tales and Treasures" by Jean Alessi and Jan Miller; Betterway Publications, White Hall, VA, 1987

"Recording Your Family History: A Guide to Preserving Oral History and Using Audio and Video Tape" by William Fletcher; Berkeley, CA, 1990

"Tape-recorded Interview, The: A Manual for Field Workers in Folklore and Oral History" by Edward D. Ives; University of Tennessee Press, Knoxville, 1980

"Third Degree, The: Tips for a Successful Interview," by George Thurston, Ancestry Magazine Article, Jan/Feb 1998, Vol. 16, No. 1

"Video Family History" by Duane and Pat Sturm

"Your Life and Times: How to Put a Life Story on Tape: An Oral History Handbook" by Stephen Arthur and Julia Arthur; Baltimore, MD, 1987

## CHAPTER 6

### HIGH-TECH GENEALOGY

"Computer Genealogy: A Guide to Research Through High Technology" by Paul A. Andereck and Richard A. Pence; Salt Lake City, UT, 1991

"Guide to Genealogy Software" by Donna Przecha and Joan Lowrey; 1993

"More Psychic Roots: Further Adventures in Serendipity and Intuition in Genealogy" by Henry Z. Jones Jr.; 1999

"Netting Your Ancestors: Genealogical Research on the Internet" by Cyndi Howells; 1997

"Psychic Roots: Serendipity and Intuition in Genealogy" by Henry Z. Jones Jr.; 1996

"Virtual Roots: A Guide to Genealogy and Local History on the World Wide Web" by Thomas Jay Kemp; 1997

**GENEALOGY SOFTWARE**
(See Helpful Addresses section)

## CHAPTER 7

### NETWORKING

"Becoming an Accredited Genealogist—Plus 100 Tips to Ensure Your Success," by Karen CliffordÃavailable through: shop.Ancestry.com

"Genealogical Helper," Everton Publishers Inc.,Logan, UT

"Genealogical Periodical Annual Index" by Laird C. Towle, Bowie, MD, 1962

"Genealogy Bulletin," Heritage Quest, Bountiful, UT

"Index to NGS & FGS Conference Syllabi," National Genealogical Society,Arlington, VA

"NGS Quarterly" and "NGS Newsletter," National Genealogical Society, Arlington, VA

"Survey of American Genealogical Periodicals and Periodical Indexes, A" by Kip Sperry; Detroit, MI, 1978

## CHAPTER 8

### RESEARCH TIPS

"Ancestry's Guide to Research: Case Studies in American Genealogy" by Johni Cerny and Arlene Eakle; Ancestry, Salt Lake City, UT, 1985

"BCG Genealogical Standards Manual, The" by the Board for Certification of Genealogists, 2000

"Evidence! Citation & Analysis for the Family Historian" by Elizabeth Shown Mills; 1997

## CHAPTER 9

### MANAGEMENT

"Care of Antiques and Historical Collections, The," by Per E. Guldbeck; American Assn. for State and Local History, Nashville, TN

"Care of Fine Books, The," by Jane Greenfield; available through AGLL

"Caring for Your Collections: Preserving and Protecting Your Art and Other Collectibles," edited by NCSACC; available through AGLL

"Cite Your Sources: A Manual for Documenting Family Histories and Genealogical Records" by Richard S. Lackey; Oracle Press Ltd., New Orleans, LA, 1985

"Conceptual Approach to Genealogy, The," by David C. Chamberlin; available at Park Genealogical Books
"Conservation Treatment Procedures," by C. Clark Morrow and C. Dyal; available through AGLL

"Curatorial Care of Works of Art on Paper," by Anne. F. Clapp; available through AGLL

"Fading Memories: Albums Damage Photos," by Glenn Collins, The New York Times, Oct. 3, 1987

"Fundamentals of Genealogical Research," by Laureen R. Jaussi and Gloria D. Chaston; Deseret Book Company, Salt Lake City, UT

"Genealogical Documentation Checklist," available at Park Genealogical Books

"Genealogical Evidence: A Guide to the Standard of Proof Relating to Pedigrees, Ancestry, Heirship and Family History," by Noel Stevenson; available through Park Genealogical Books

"Genealogical Research and Organization," by John W. Heisey; available through Park Genealogical Books and AGLL

"Managing a Genealogical Project" by William Dollarhide, 1988

"Managing a Stacks Cleaning Project," by Shannon Zachary; University of Michigan Library, Ann Arbor, MI

"Numbering Your Genealogy: Sound and Simple Systems" by Joan Ferris Curran; National Genealogical Society Quarterly, 79, No. 3 (September 1991): 183-93

"Numbering Your Genealogy—Special Cases: Surname Changes, Step Relationships and Adoptions" by Madilyn Coen Crane, National Genealogical Society Quarterly 83, No. 2; June 1995: 84-95

"Organizing Your Family History Search," by Sharon DeBartolo Carmack; available at Park Genealogical Books
"Ounce of Preservation: A Guide to the Care of Paper and Photographs, An," by Craig A. Tuttle; available through AGLL

"Preservation Guide, A: Saving the Past and the Present for the Future," by Barbara Sagraves; Ancestry.com

"Preserving Family Keepsakes: Do's and Don'ts," by Ilene C. Miller; available through AGLL

"Restoring Photos Rebuilds Memories," by Bob. D Gibson, The Elks Magazine, February 1991

"Searching for Your Ancestors: The How and Why of Genealogy," by Gilbert H. Doane, FASG; Bantam Book-Whittlesey House

"Who Gets Grandma's Yellow Pie Plate?", University of MN Extension Service Distribution Center, St. Paul, MN

## CHAPTER 10

# CELEBRATING FAMILY

(See also Oral Interviews section)

### FAMILY HISTORY BOOK

"Complete Guide to Self-Publishing, The," by Tom and Marilyn Ross; Writer's Digest Books, Cincinnati, OH, 1994

"Family Tales, Family Wisdom: How to Gather the Stories of a Lifetime and Share Them with Your Family" by Robert U. Akeret, with Daniel Klein; 1991

"How to Publish and Market Your Family History" by Carl Boyer; 1985

"Indexing Family Histories" by Patricia Law Hatcher

"Legacy: A Step-by-step Guide to Writing Personal History" by Linda Spence; Swallow Press/Ohio University Press, Athens, OH, 1997

"Life Writing: A Guide to Family Journal and Personal Memoirs" by William T. Hofman; St. Martin's Press, New York, 1982

"Printing and Publishing Your Family History" by Marilyn Lind; 1986

"Producing a Quality Family History: by Patricia Law Hatcher; Ancestry Publishing, Salt Lake City, UT, 1996

"Write It Right: A Manual for Writing Family Histories and Genealogies" by Richard S. Lackey and Donald R. Barnes; Lyon Press, Ocala, FL, 1988

"Writing Family Histories and Memoirs" by Kirk Polking; Betterway Books, Cincinnati, 1995

"Writing the Family Narrative" by Lawrence P. Gouldrup; Ancestry Publishing, Salt Lake City, UT, 1987

### FAMILY REUNIONS

"Budget Lodging Guide" by B&J Publications, Fullerton, CA

"Campus Lodging Guide" by B&J Publications, Fullerton, CA

"Celebrating the Family: Steps to Planning a Family Reunion" by Vandella Brown; Ancestry, Salt Lake City, UT

"Consolidators: Air Travel's Bargain Basement" by Kelly Monaghan; 212-569-1081

"Family Reunion" by Jennifer Chrichton; Workman Publishing, New York, NY

"Family Reunion Handbook: A Guide for Reunion Planning" by Barbara E. Brown, 1992

"Family Reunion Organizer" by Emma J. Wisdom; Post Oak Publications, Nashville

"Family Reunion Potluck" by Carol McGarvey; Wooden Spoon Cook Book Series STA-Kris

"Family Reunions and Clan Gatherings: How to Assemble a Memorable Event" by Shari L. Fiock; Coyote Publications, 1991

"Family Reunions: How to Plan Yours" by Harry McKinzie, McKinzie Publishing Company, Los Angeles, CA

"FamilyTies" by Obasi Haki Akan and Lynn Harvey-Akan, 24th Century Solutions, Cleveland, OH

"Find Anyone Fast" by R. Johnson

"Fun and Games for Family Gatherings: With a Focus on Reunions" by Adrienne Anderson; Reunion Research, Auberry, CA

"Heart of a Family, The," by Meg Cox; Random House Inc., New York, NY

"Hotel Secrets on Booking your Military Reunion," CYBERCON, Neptune Beach, FL

"How to Have a Successful Family Reunion" by Elsie G. Holloman; B&E Enterprise, Washington, DC

"How to Plan Your Affordable Family Reunion" by James Reynolds and James Slaughter; Portunity Publications, Los Angeles, CA

"Make a Family Video Album," a videotape by Edgewater Productions

"Practical Guide to Planning a Family Reunion, A," by Emma J. Wisdom; Post Oak Publications, Nashville, TN

"Reunion Planner, The," by Linda Hoffman; Goodman Lauren Publishing, Los Angeles, CA

Reunions Workbook (8th edition) from Reunions Magazine, Milwaukee, WI

"Reunions for Fun Loving Families," by Nancy Funk Bagley; Brighton Publications Inc., St. Paul, MN

"So You're Going to Plan a Family Reunion" by Frances M. Keitt; FMK Publishing, Philadelphia, PA

### HERALDRY

"Art of Heraldry: Origins, Symbols and Designs, The," by Peter Gwynn-Jones, Garter King of Arms (1998, Barnes & Noble Inc., by arrangement with Parkgate Books Ltd.)

"Brief History of Heraldry, A," by Joseph C. Wolf

"Complete Book of Heraldry, The: An international history of heraldry and its contemporary uses" by Stephen Slater; Anness Publishing Ltd.; 2003

"Complete Guide to Heraldry, A," by Arthur C. Fox-Davies; J.P. Brooke-Little, New York, 1969

"Design Your Own Coat of Arms: An Introduction to Heraldry" by Rosemary A. Chorzempa; Dover Publications Inc., 1987

"Heraldry: An Introduction to a Noble Tradition" by Michel Pastoureau

"Manual of Heraldry, The," by Francis J. Grant; Edinburgh

"Oxford Guide to Heraldry, The," by Thomas Woodcock, Somerset Herald, and John Martin Robinson, Maltravers Herald Extraordinary; Oxford, 1988

"Simple Heraldry" by Sir Iain Moncreiffe and Don Pottinger; Mayflower Books •

## Climbing your family tree

The search for hidden ancestry is an alluring quest

Which never gives its devotees a single moment's rest.

To all whose minds are in a groove, or prone to slothful ease,

We recommend the exercise of climbing family trees!

*—Minerva Isabel Freeman*

## Identity crisis

I started out calmly
Tracing my tree,
to see if I could find
the makings of me.

And all that I had was my
great-grandpa's name,
not knowing his wife
or from whence he came.

I chased him across
a long line of states,
and came up with pages
and pages of dates.

When all put together,
it made me forlorn—
it proved poor
Great-grandpa
had never been born!

One day I was sure
the truth I had found.
Determined to turn this
whole thing upside down,

I looked up the records
of one Uncle John,
and found the old man to
be younger than his son!

Then when my hopes
were fast growing dim,
I came across records
that must have been him.

The facts I collected then
made me quite sad:
Dear old Great-granddad
was never a dad!

I think maybe someone
is pulling my leg.
I'm not at all sure I wasn't
hatched from an egg.

After hundreds of dollars
I've spent on my tree,
I can't help but wonder
if I'm really me!

—*Author unknown*

# Glossary ················

**· A ·**

**Accelerated Indexing System (AIS)** refers to an index of names from the U.S. censuses. It is available on microfiche at the LDS family history centers.

**Acid-free (or archivally safe)** means products that do not contain acid or that have neutral pH (7), such as those made of polyester, polypropylene, triacetate or polyethylene or products labeled "no PVCs."

**Achievement,** in heraldry, refers to all the elements of a coat of arms—crest, crown, mantling, shield, supporters and motto.

**Ahnentafel** (literally, "ancestor table" in German) is a pedigree numbering system in which the father's number is always double the number assigned to the child; the mother is the father's number plus 1.

**Albumen print** is a paper developed by L.D. Blanquart-Evard. It was extremely thin and glossy, with a sepia-brown color, and used in photography from 1851 to 1895.

**Ambrotype** (developed in 1854-63) is a process of creating photographs in which the image is displayed on glass backed with black material.

**Ancestor** is a person from whom one is descended.

**Ancestry** is the line or lineage of ancestors for a person, beginning with his/ her parents and going back in time.

**Archives** is a collection of records for a governmental entity, an organization, or an institution. It can also refer to the place where these records are held.

**· B ·**

**Blogging** for genealogists involves "blogging" (logging on your Website) your ongoing family history research, so others who access the site can learn from your personal experiences (also called "geneablogy"). TheseWeb loggers are called "bloggers."

**Bounty land** is the first distribution of public domain lands and used as a reward for military service. The land could be assigned (sold) to another person.

**· C ·**

**Calotype** is a process of creating photographs by using negatives to make positive printed on paper. It was first produced in 1837.

**Canting arms** are coats of arms that portrayed a pun of the name of the bearer. For example, someone named Carpenter might have a hammer and nail on his shield. The dauphin (future king) of France bore a dolphin on his shield.

**Censuses** are enumerations that count the number of people in a given area and are records containing very valuable genealogical information, especially those censuses since 1880. A census is taken every 10 years at the beginning of each decade by the U.S. government and are closed for 72 years except to immediate family members and legal heirs.

**Certified American Indian Lineage Specialist (CAILS)** conducts research on descendancy from historical Indian tribes indigenous to North America.

**Certified Genealogist (CG)** is certified by the Board for Certification of Genealogists (BCG) as proficient in research ing genealogical records and lineages. A GC is qualified to do broadly based genealogical projects, find evidence, assemble proof, and compile an account of the history and relationships of descendants.

**Certified Genealogical Lecturer (CGL)** has been certified by the BCG as qualified to deliver presentations on genealogical subjects.

**Certified Genealogical Instructure (CGI)** has been certified by the BCG as qualified to present classes in genealogy studies.

**Church of Jesus Christ of Latter-day Saints (LDS or Mormons)** was organized in 1830 in New York. The Mormons believe in family life after death, and they perform the saving ordinances for their dead, resulting in the creation of huge amounts of genealogical resources.

**Clip art** is art work placed on pages of a publication. Usually this art is electronic (stored on computer disks).

**Codicil** is an addition to a will.

**Common ancestor** is an ancestor that two or more people have in common.

**Confidential intermediary a** is a person who is authorized to serve as a communications link between adoptees and birth parents, when one of the parties desires to know the whereabouts of the other.

**Cyanotype** is the use of blueprint paper for developing photographs. It was developed between 1855 and 1910.

**· D ·**

**Daguerreotype** is a photography process introduced by J.J.M. Daguerre in which pictures were reproduced on silver plates by sensitizing them with iodine and developing that with mercury.

**Declaration of intention (first papers)** is an immigrant's statement that he/she wants to be an American citizen.

**Descendancy** is those who are descendants or offspring of a certain ancestor.

**Desktop publishing** refers to computer-based page layout and word-processing used to produce a publication.

**Dummy** is a rough layout created as a guide when producing a family history book or any other publication that will be printed. The dummy ranges from sketches on scraps of paper to electronic pages.

### • E •

**Emigration** is the process of departing from one's country and moving to another.

### • F •

**Family association** is an organization of family members who correspond and share ancestral information.

**Family group sheet** contains information about a specific family group (parents and children).

**Family history** is a gathering of information about one's ancestors (usually into book form), then publishing and distributing it to others.

**Family history center** is just one of thousands of research sites located around the country and supported and maintained by the LDS church.

**Ferrotype** is a photography process using Ambrotype (thin metal). Developed in 1855 to 1900, it involves creating positive images on pieces of iron.

**Fiduciary** is an individual like a guardian, executor, agent, administrator, attorney, conservator or trustee who acts for the benefit of another.

### • G •

**Genealogy** is the process of researching and developing a family history and pedigree of one's ancestors.

**Genetics** is the latest buzzword in genealogy. Based on careful DNA testing, our "genetic code," handed down to us from our ancestors, can connect us with others who carry a similar code, or point out which migratory path our deep ancestors took eons ago as they spread out around the world. This fastest-growing branch of genealogy is called "genealogy by genetics."

**Government records** might include military discharge papers and awards, citizenship or naturalization papers, passports, licenses, Social Security cards, and income tax forms.

**Gregorian calendar** was a calendar adopted by the English in 1752 which eliminated 11 days that had been added to the Julian calendar over the years. It was named after Pope Gregory and is sometimes referred to as the "New Style" calendar.

### • H •

**Halftone** is any art with shades of gray or color that has been converted by a printer or through special computer programs into a series of small dots to render it printable.

**Health records** might include vaccination records and hospital, insurance, and doctor bills.

**Henry system** is a system of identification numbers assigned to persons on a pedigree. The first number(s) indicates the generation, the following number(s) the birth order. Example: 25 indicatesa fifth child, two generations removed from person number 1 on the chart. An "s" at the end indicates a spouse.

**Heraldry** is the science of armory, the systematic arrangement of devices on a shield. It is also the art, practice or science of recording genealogies on arms or other items.

**Heralds** were men whose job it was to track the coats of arms of families in their country, and to ensure that no two persons bore the same shield.

**Hereditary** means those things passed on through blood lines or heredity.

**Historical records survey** was performed in 1936-43. A project through the Works Progress Administration, it resulted in an inventory of public records throughout the U.S.

**Homestead** was the house and adjoining land where a family lived and which passed on to the widow and was exempt from the claims of creditors.

**Homestead Act of 1862** offered American citizens or those who were intending to become citizens 160 acres of land from the federal government for only a small filing fee. Before receiving title to the land, the person had to complete the naturalization process, live on the land for at least five years and improve it somehow during that time.

### • I •

**Immigration** is the process of moving into a foreign country from another one, with plans to live there indefinitely.

**Indentured apprentice** is one who was "bound out" to a master who, under the terms of indenture, had to provide the apprentice training in his craft or trade and give him board, lodging, and clothes and perhaps a certain sum of money at the end of the apprenticeship. An apprenticeship was usually seven years or until a boy came of age.

**Indentured servant** is one way an immigrant came to the U.S., with his/her passage paid by someone who then received the immigrant's services for an agreed-upon period of time.

**Internet** is a system of computer networks joined together by high-speed data lines called "backbones." Basically, it is the telephone cables used to transmit information on the Web.

**Intestate** means a person had no will when he/she died.

### • J •

**Julian calendar** was established by Julius Caesar in 46 B.C. and began each new year on March 25. For many years, a system of "double dating" was practiced where both the Julian and Gregorian calendar dates were listed. (See also Gregorian calendar)

### • L •

**Labels,** three-legged bars placed over the shield decoration, were used to distinguish between a father's otherwise identical coat of arms and that of his eldest son. When the father died, the son removed the label from his shield, thus inheriting his father's arms.

**Land Grant Act** (or the Morrill Act) granted public land to the states for agricultural colleges.

**Land patent (or first deed)** is a transfer of land from government ownership into the hands of an individual.

**LDS** is a shortened name for the Church of Jesus Christ of Latter-Day Saints.

**Legal description of land** means the section, township, and range numbers used to identify property.

**Legal papers** might include contracts, tax bills, wills, deeds, and mortgages.

**Lineage** is ancestry or descent from a specific ancestor.

• **M** •

**Maternal** is relationship through the mother.

**Matronymics** is a system in which surnames are derived from the mother's side.

**Muster roll** is a list of troops present on parade or otherwise accounted for at the daily muster or review of troops under arms.

**Mutual consent registry** is a registry signed by those seeking birth parents or birth children. This registry can be checked by either party to see whether the other wishes to be contacted. (Both North and South Dakota have a mutual consent registry system.)

• **N** •

**National archives** is the central depository for U.S. government records.

**Non-identifying background information** is the limited information on the birth parents provided to adoptive parents and the adoptee by the social services or adoption agency.

• **O** •

**Oral history** is the recording (by handwriting, audiotaping or videotaping) of stories, experiences, and events as told by an individual (typically an elder family member).

• **P** •

**Paternal** is relationship through the father.

**Patronymics** is a naming system in which surnames

are derived from the father's first name (as in "Anfinson," meaning "son of Anfin").

**Pedigree** is ancestry or lineage.

**Personal records** might include journals, diaries, letters, newspaper clippings, baby books, wedding albums, and employment papers.

**Petition for naturalization (or second papers)** is the court's review of an immigrant's desire to become an American citizen.

**Platbooks (atlases)** show visual representations of the land description from the tract book.

**Pre-emption Act,** passed in 1841, allowed anyone who was the head of a family or over 21 and a U.S. citizen, or who had declared intention to become one, to stake a claim on tracts of land up to 160 acres and then buy it from the government for $1.25 per acre.

**Primary records** are principally any documents or registers recorded soon after an event (such as a birth, marriage, divorce, or death) took place. Vital records are considered primary, since they were usually the first documents to record such events.

**Probate records** include wills, property inventories, letters of administration and guardianships that go into effect after a person's death.

**Public domain state** is one in which the land was once owned by the Federal government and then transferred from public to private land. There were 30 such states, mostly in the West and Midwest, including North and South Dakota.

**Public records** are those government records that are of interest to the public and to which the public has access.

• **R** •

**Record system** is a pedigree numbering system devised by the National Genealogical Society Quarterly. In this sytem, every bloodline descendant of person number 1 receives a number; spouses do not get a number, as they are not related by blood.

**Register system** is a formal, rigid system of numbering a pedigree.

**Religious records** might include marriage, baptismal, christening certificates; membership; and a family Bible.

**Rubbing** is a way to capture the information on a tombstone by laying a tissue over the inscription and rubbing with a soft-lead pencil or a crayon.

• **S** •

**School records** might include diplomas, yearbooks, awards, and alumni papers.

**Second papers** are the final petitions for naturalization.

**Secondary records** are secondhand sources of information, such as oral or written history, newspaper clippings, and family Bibles if the information was clearly recorded all at one time, rather than when an event took place.

**Section** of land amounts to 640 acres.

**Soundex system** is used to group similar names together, such as those that are close in sound or spelling or may be mistaken for each other.

**Surnames** are last names or family names (see also patronymic names).

• **T** •

**Talbotype** is a photography process similar to calotype. It was developed in 1839.

**Testate** means someone died and left a will expressing his/her wishes.

**Township** contains 36 sections or 36 square miles. It is divided into 36 sections of 640 acres each.

**Tract books** contain land descriptions, with each land entry arranged by township, range, and section numbers.

• **V** •

**Vital records** consist of birth, marriage, divorce and death records, which provide essential information to the genealogist.

**Vital statistics** are data derived from birth, marriage, divorce and death events.

• **W** •

**Waiver of confidentiality** is a legal paper signed by the adoptee and birth parent(s) requesting that the adoption agency, hospital or other institution involved with an adoption release information on the adoption.

**Website** is a place on the World Wide Web that discusses a particular topic or issue or advertises certain products or activities.

**Will** is a document showing how a person wants his/her property divided upon that person's death.

**Works Progress Administration (WPA)** projects were performed throughout the U.S. from 1936 through 1943. These projects included oral interviewing of pioneers and indexing of data.

**World Wide Web (or Web)** is a system for viewing and using multimedia documents over the Internet. •

# Index •••••••••••••••••••••

## Dear ancestor...

Your tombstone stands
among the rest,
Neglected and alone.

The name and date
are chiseled out
On polished, marbled
stone.

It reaches out
to all who care;
It is too late to mourn.

You did not know
that I exist. You died,
and I was born.

Yet each of us
are cells of you,
In flesh, in blood, in bone.

Our blood contracts
and beats a pulse
Entirely not our own.

Dear ancestor,
the place you filled
One hundred years ago

Spreads out among
the ones you left
Who would have
loved you so.

I wonder if
you lived and loved,
I wonder if you knew

That someday I would
find this spot
And come to visit you.

—Author unknown

# Parting words of wisdom...

We hope that we've
inspired you
to climb
your family tree.

There are mysteries
lurking there,
so climb it carefully.

The steps provided
in this book
will help you
on your way

Don't let it rest,
begin your quest
as early as today.

Perhaps you'll find
a king and queen,
perhaps you'll find
a knave,

But ere the sheep
be black or white,
accept it
and be brave.

We hope the seeds
we've planted here
will flourish and will fly,

Until you have
a pedigree that
stretches to the sky.

When you begin
your climb, my friend,
you'll find these words
quite true:

In searching
for your ancestors,
you'll discover...
YOU!

—Jo Ann and Cathy

# Take time for the journey

For those of you who start a book from the back, welcome to your very own personal Voyage of Discovery. For those of you who read a book the traditional way (from front to back), we will close by wishing you happy ancestor hunting. You'll find that digging for your roots teaches you a lot about yourself, as well as about your ancestors. Enjoy your journey.

We also want to express once more how compelled we both felt to write the initial version of this book (published in 1999), reprinted in 2001). And here it is, 2006, and time for an updated, expanded book! Putting this second edition together was almost as much of a challenge as the first. We left much of the book intact, making only minor changes, such as address updates and sprinkling in fresh information here and there.

Our biggest changes were to our High-Tech and Research Tips chapters. We added information on expanding technology, including innovative new Websites, computer genealogy programs, and such things as genealogy "blogging," cleverly called "gene-ablogy." We also added material on genetic genealogy—DNA research—as it applies to making family connections. This emerging field of family history research holds much promise for genealogists of the future.

We have done our best to give you a book that's user-friendly, error-free, and a fun reading experience—one that has some practical, as well as some "out-of-the- box," research tips. We also wanted to present the Dakota pioneer experience and relay to readers how it molded and shaped our ancestors and led to the decisions they made and the standards they lived by. Most of all, we wanted you to know there are lots of records out there and lots of resources to help.

We don't pretend to know all the answers. In fact, writing a book is a very humbling experience. You realize how human you are when a typo slips past you (funny how huge they look when they're printed!), or you left out something that should have been included, or perhaps you misunderstood or misinterpreted something that you thought you knew. Those frantic sleepless nights trying to whip the book together by deadline were only partly to blame.

We hope you will enjoy this book and advise us as to any errors or omissions you may spot along the way. With your help, this—our revised, updated version—will be as flawless as we can possibly make it. Of course, we hope you'll also let us know how the book has helped you, or if you're enjoying your own personal Voyage of Discovery. Keep in touch, fellow traveler.

This book is really a compilation. After all, anything that one writes is based on something from the past, gems someone else has penned or uttered, the thousands of mentors who have written books or shared insights over a cup of coffee—who flit through one's life and leave bright steppingstones along life's obscure path. Perhaps there's even some divine inspiration tossed in. And then there are the mentors who inspired us to seek our own family's roots. To all of them we owe an enormous debt.

• • • • • • • • • • • • • • • • • • • • • • • • • • • • • • • • • • • •

Keep the torch of curiosity about your family's history burning brightly for yourself and for future generations. The time to collect that history is now, while records are accessible, while you can, while there's time—while the older generations of your family, storehouses of history, are with you and able to pass down what they know, while they can, while there's time. Start your Voyage of Discovery today! •

—*Jo Ann and Cathy*

# —ORDER FORM—

## TRACING YOUR DAKOTA ROOTS
### A Guide to Genealogical Research in the Dakotas

*(2nd edition/update of award-winning book by same name)*
*by Jo Ann B. Winistorfer and Cathy A. Langemo*

## —FEATURES—

- 216-page, 8 1/2 x 11-inch soft-cover book with beautiful full-color cover
- Historical timeline of the Dakotas, along with early settlement history
- Resources for ethnic research ranging from American Indians to Germans from Russia, Scandinavia, and British Isles emigrants
- Easy and fun to read, appealing to all ages
- Spiced with illustrations, photos and genealogy tidbits
- A good Dakota history & genealogy guide for use in schools or workshops
- Sections include genealogy forms, census forms, early Dakota Territory and state maps, and more!
- Glossary, bibliography and thorough index
- Multi-page list of addresses of Web businesses, archives, libraries, genealogy and ethnic societies, publishers, vendors, etc.
- Original version received awards from AdFed, North Dakota Professional Communicators, and National Federation of Press Women; honored with the prestigious G.K. Haukebo Heritage Resource Award from the Family History Workshop in Moorhead, Minn.

• • • • • • • • • • • • • • • • • • • • • • • • • • • • • •

To order, send check or money order for $24.95 (U.S. money)
for each book ordered (North Dakota residents add 5% sales tax).
Add $4.00 (Canadian orders add $8.00 U.S. funds) for postage and handling
per book ordered. Make check payable to: DAKOTA ROOTS

**Mail to: DAKOTA ROOTS**
**c/o Jo Ann B. Winistorfer • 625 44th Ave. NW, Hazen, ND 58545**
701-487-3312 • genesis@westriv.com
*Call, write or e-mail for discount prices on multiple orders, other books available, etc.,*
*or if you need a speaker for a genealogy-related workshop, class, etc.*

NAME: _____

ADDRESS: _____

CITY/STATE/ZIP: _____

PHONE: _____   E-MAIL: _____

NO. OF BOOKS ORDERED: _____   AMOUNT ENCLOSED: _____

—PHOTOCOPY ORDER FORM—

—PHOTOCOPY ORDER FORM—